CROWTHER'S ENCYCLOPÆDIA OF PHRASES AND ORIGINS

The typography and binding of this book conform to the authorized economy standard

THIS BOOK IS WAR-TIME PRODUCTION.
It is easy to handle, completely legible, takes up less space on your bookshelf, is cheaper to post, and withal is full length and value.

Made and Printed in Great Britain by
JOHN CROWTHER & GOODSMAN (MARGATE) LTD. for
JOHN CROWTHER LTD., BOGNOR REGIS and
14, HENRIETTA PLACE, LONDON, W.1, ENGLAND

AGENTS : NEW YORK, MELBOURNE, BUENOS AIRES
BARCELONA AND AUCKLAND

CROWTHER'S ENCYCLOPÆDIA OF PHRASES *and* ORIGINS

by

EDWIN RADFORD

FIRST EDITION
1945

A
JOHN CROWTHER
PUBLICATION

*To all those fortunate people who,
like myself, find pleasure in sifting
among the curious things in life.*

PREFACE

FOR generations English-speaking people have been pulling to pieces the words of their language and refitting them into other words explanatory of some current event; displaying in so doing an impish wit, a clever cynicism, or a delightful turn of improvization. A generation passed away, but the new words remained. A new generation practiced their use in the circumstances for which they were designed, without appreciating the reason for the coining. In time the words, frequently corrupted in spelling as the result of phonetic handing-down, became part of the colloquial language.

Then, the inevitable happened. Inquiring minds began to wonder why their tongues used the phrases; they wondered why, as a matter of course, someone was "as mad as a hatter." Why should a good honest hatter be regarded as more prone to mental deficiency than, say, a tailor? Of recent years the demand for knowledge of the origin of the host of phrases which are now a part of the language, and of the many single words which seem *outré* in use, has grown enormously. For some years the author has edited that popular feature-column of the *Daily Mirror*, titled *Live Letters*. During that time thousands of letters demanding "origins" have been answered, and are still being answered daily The object of the present work is to make available to the bookshelves of people of ordinary means an arranged collection in a single volume of the principal proverbial "tags," phrases and words which have formed the subject of inquiries of the author over a space of years, together with their origins or derivations.

The explanations given have been penned only after the most complete research; a reference library of some two thousand volumes forming in itself a complete story of the customs, speech, life and anecdotal history of the English people over six centuries, has gone into the searching. No attempt has been made to include those numerous phrases and words in common usage which have merely grown into the language as slang, without any etymological foundation; explanations of such words and phrases already exist in the many good slang or colloquial dictionaries already on the market. Only those words associated with some definite custom, or arising out of corrupted words of a past age, which present light on customs and conditions, are included.

Students will find that quite a number differ from previously published "origins": the author would point out that many previous attempts to explain various phrases have been guess-work; others represent only a part of the antiquity; as regards the remainder, new facts continually appear which cast a fresh light on customs and habits and on the translation of idioms. Very careful examination of all the information available has been made before a decision has been arrived at; and the completed work is put forward in the author's belief that it represents absolute accuracy of origins, in so far as accuracy can be obtained from the welter of legend and ancient custom and habit.

In order to economize in paper in these rationed times, as little cross reference as possible has been carried out. A moment's reflection will enable the seeker to find the word wanted; if *Hobson's Choice* is missing from "Hobson," it will be found under "Choice."

The author acknowledges with grateful thanks assistance he has received from many sources; from the researches of Mrs. Esme Leonard, and from Mr. Gerald O'Driscoll for Naval terms on which he is so great an authority; from that great delver, "Jackdaw" of *John O'London's Weekly*; and to the works of that master of words, Professor Ernest Weekley.

E. R.

Embercourt Road,
Thames Ditton,
Surrey.

CROWTHER'S ENCYCLOPÆDIA OF PHRASES AND ORIGINS

A

A1. An expression meaning first-rate. In Lloyds Register of Shipping, letters denote the quality of the ship's hull, and fittings are denoted by figures. Thus, A1 means hull first-rate, and also all fittings, such as anchors, cables and stores. A2 signifies hull first-rate but the fittings only second-rate.

Aaron's Serpent. A force so powerful as to eliminate all minor powers. The allusion is to *Exodus* vii, 10-12.

A.B. Short for Able seaman, or able-bodied seaman. A skilled sailor. A ship's crew is divided into three classes: (1) Skilled seaman, called an A.B.; (2) Ordinary seaman; and (3) Boys, a term which covers not only youths but green-horns, or inexperienced men of any age or size.

Aberdeen Cutlet. An R.A.F. term since 1936 for an aeroplane crash, or a heavy fall. Also referred to as a "belly landing."

Above Board. The term originated in racing circles, where one of the course attractions was, at one time, spinning wheels. They were in the form of stands, covered down to the ground with gaily-coloured flouncings. The owners of the tables unsuspectingly regulated the issue of the spinning wheel on the board by working a hidden treadle. Thus, anything underhand came to be called "not above board." For obvious reasons "under-hand work" is associated, also, with this origin.

Absence makes the heart grow fonder. While opinions may differ as to the truth of the adage, there can be no doubt of it being one of the most used of cliches. It comes from the song, "Isle of Beauty," by Thomas Haynes Bayly (1797-1839).

Absquatulate. To run away, to leave, to abscond. An American word from the gold-diggings. The reverse to "squat," as when a "squatter" quitted after staking a claim which proved to be without gold.

Academy. The name comes from a garden founded in a suburb of Athens by Academus. It was at one time a pleasure resort, consecrated to the Goddess Athenes. In its grove Plato held his morning philosophical conferences, hence its application to learning. Plato's academy was divided into the *Old*, wherein was taught his own philosophic doctrine, and that of Xenocrates, Crates, and his followers; the *Middle*, a modified Platonism founded by Arcesilaus; and the *New*, of Carneades. English ROYAL ACADEMY OF ARTS was founded by George III in 1768 for the establishment of an art school and the holding of annual exhibitions of works by living artists.

According to Cocker. Meaning strictly correct. The word comes from Edward Cocker (1631-75), who published a popular arithmetic. It ran into sixty editions, and was accounted the acme of correctness. The phrase was first used, and popularized, in a farce, "The Apprentice," by Murphy, produced in London in 1756.

According to Gunter. The American equivalent to "Cocker." Edmund Gunter, celebrated mathematician, invented a chain and scale for measuring.

Acestes, "The Arrow of Acestes." A reference to Æneid, V. 525. Acestes, in a trial of skill, discharged his arrow with such force that it caught fire. The phrase is used to describe the arguments of an orator who makes his point with telling force by fiery vehemence.

Achilles, Heel of. A vulnerable spot. The metaphor comes from Mythology. When Thetis, mother of Achilles, dipped her son in the River Styx to make him invulnerable, she held him by one heel which, being untouched by the Stygian water, remained liable to attack. It was in this heel that Achilles did, in fact, receive his mortal wound at the Scaean gate, before Troy was taken, from an arrow.

Achilles of England. The name given to the Duke of Wellington (1769-1852).

Achilles Tendon. The sinew running along the heel to the calf of the leg.

Acme, the acme of. The highest pitch (of perfection), the limit. Early doctors divided a disease into four periods: the *arche*, beginning; *anotasis*, increase; the *acme*, state of its utmost violence; and the *paracme*, the decline.

Acre. A measured size of ground. But originally the word meant any field, whatever its size, being derived from the Anglo-Saxon word *aecer*, meaning land, or anything sown. Up to the thirteenth century an acre meant in England as much land as a yoke of oxen could plough in a day. It was not until the time of Edward I that the word became more definite; and by an act of George IV the varying measures of the acre then current in the kingdom were reduced to one uniform standard. But even now, the Scottish and Irish acres differ in size from the English.

Acrobat. Has nothing to do with acting, or with bats. It is from the Greek *akros*, the point or extremity, and *baino*, to go. It means a person who goes on his extremities, i.e., uses only his fingers or toes in moving about.

Adam. "When Adam delved and Eve span; Who was, then, the gentleman?" According to Thomas Walsingham's *Historia Anglicana*, the origin of this oft-quoted couplet was an address given to the rebels in Wat Tyler's insurrection at Blackheath (1381), the speaker John Ball. In point of fact, it was a misquotation, or adaptation, of lines written by Richard Rolle of Hampole, who died about 1349:—

"When Adam dalfe and Eve
 spanne
To spire of thou may spede,
Where was then the pride of
 man,
That now marres his meed?"

Adam's Apple. The protuberance in the forepart of the throat formed by the anterior part of the thyroid cartilage of the larynx, is so-called from the notion that a piece of the Forbidden Fruit stuck in Adam's throat.

Adam's Wine. Water, because Adam knew not the fermented juice of the grape.

Adding Insult to Injury. In this tag, to express a double injury we quote, unknowingly, the classics. The phrase is from a fable quoted by the Latin writer Phaedrus, who took it from the more ancient version of Æsop. It relates how a bald man who was bitten on his bald head by a fly, in trying to kill the insect, gave himself a hard smack. The fly said, jeeringly, "You wanted to kill me for a touch—what will you do to yourself now that you have added insult to injury?"

Adelphi. Once noted streets and a terrace on the south side of the Strand, London. Adelphi is a Greek word meaning brothers; the street and terrace were built by the famous Adams brothers.

Adieu. Used as "good-bye" to the party left, as farewell is to the party going. In the original French: "I commend you to God." *Dieu*, French, God.

Admiral. The author has been asked on several hundred occasions what relation to the command of a fleet the word Admiral possesses. The answer is, none. The word is derived from the Arabic *amir* or *emir*, ruler or commander. The "*al*" is the Arabic article *al* present in Arabian and Turkish titles containing the word, as *amir-al-umara*, ruler of rulers, *amir-el-bahr,* ruler of the sea. It is to *amir-el-bahr* that we owe our word admiral. The Arabic title was Latinised as *admiralius maris.* Edward III anglicised it as " amyrel of the se " ; and it was gradually corrupted to admiral.

Adulterous Bible. *See* " Bible."

Advowson. The gift of a living in the Church of England ; the right of appointing an incumbent to a church. The word comes from the Latin *advocatio,* a calling to, a summons. Originally, it meant the obligation to be the advocate of a benefice and to defend its rights.

Æneid. Virgil's epic poem in twelve books. From *Aenas* and the suffix *-is,* belonging to.

Æson's Bath. To take Æson's Bath to be renovated. Medea is said to have renovated Æson, father of Jason, with a concoction made from various juices.

Æsop's Fables, were not by any means the work of Æsop. Æsop was a deformed Phrygian slave, who lived in the sixth century B.C. Most of the fables have been discovered on Egyptian papyri of a thousand years earlier.

After Meat, Mustard, is an English tag adapted from the Latin *Post bellum, auxilium.* It means offering to do a service when there is no longer need of it. A rebuke to hypocracy.

After Me, the Deluge. Famous phrase of Madame de Pompadour (*Après moi, le déluge*). " I care not what happens after I am dead." Some twelve years afterwards Metternich, the Austrian statesman, used the same words, meaning that when he died the State which his guiding hand had brought to greatness would deteriorate, since there was none to take his place. Louis XV also used the phrase to express his indifference to the effect of his policy of selfish and reckless extravagance.

Ages. Lucretius held that there were three ages : The *age of stone,* when implements of stone were used ; the *age of bronze,* which followed, when stone implements gave way to that metal ; and the *age of iron,* when implements were made of iron.

Golden Age. Used to describe the period of prosperity of a nation, when it was at the height of its power. In England, the Golden Age is usually ascribed to the reign of Elizabeth (1558-1603).

Middle Ages. In England from the Heptarchy to the accession of Henry VII (1409-1461).

Dark Ages. In England, the earlier part of the Middle Ages (up to 1200). Viewed in history, the Dark Ages were, roughly, between the death of Charlemagne and the close of the Carlovingian Dynasty. They were so called because of the dearth of men of letters and science and intellect during the period. It was an age of intellectual darkness.

Ages of Animals. It is often said that for every year of a dog's age, man lives seven years. Dr. Brewer has translated an old Celtic rhyme into English as follows :—

" Thrice the age of a dog is that of a horse.
Thrice the age of a horse is that of a man.
Thrice the age of a man is that of a deer.
Thrice the age of a man is that of an eagle."

Age of Woman. *See* " Bible."

Aggie Westons, or Aggies. The Royal Sailors' Rest in any of the three famous Naval ports of Portsmouth, Devonport and Chatham. They were founded by the late Dame Agnes E. Weston.

Aghast. To be frightened. A number of authorities give the origin incorrectly, as connected with ghost. The word should properly be spelt " gast," without the " h." It is from the Anglo-Saxon *gaestan,* to frighten, whereas ghost is derived from the Anglo-Saxon *gast,* soul, spirit.

Agnes, Saint. Commemorated on 21st January. The patron saint of virgins. She was martyred in 303, at the age of thirteen. Ordered to be burned at the stake, the fire went out, and Aspasius, who had been ordered to watch the martyrdom, drew his sword and cut off her head. The legend of St. Agnes' Eve is that the virgin who takes a row of pins, pulls them out one by one and, saying a paternoster, sticks a pin in her sleeve, will dream of him she is to marry.

Agnostic. A curious thing about this word is the common idea that it is age-old. In point of fact, it was coined by Professor Huxley, in 1869, to define one who disclaims any knowledge beyond that which can be proved to him by fact, or experience. Huxley took the word from St. Paul's mention of the altar to the Unknown God. It is made up from the Greek *a,* without, and *gnomi,* to know.

Agog. " He's all agog." The phrase is connected with the old French phrase, *en gogues,* in mirth.

Agur's Wish. " Give me neither poverty nor riches." From *Prov.* xxx, 8.

Ahoy. " Ahoy, there." To call attention. The word comes from the old battle-cry of the Norsemen—*Aoi*—as they ran their galleys upon the enemy ships.

Aigrette. A diamond ornament which a lady wears on the crown of her head when in full evening dress. But its origin is the tall white plume of a heron. The diamond aigrette is, of course, a copy of the heron's plume.

Aisle (of a church). A much misused word. It should not be used to describe the central nave of a church—" the bridal couple walked down the aisle." It applies rightly only to the wings or wing of the church, *aile* being French for wing, through the Latin *ala,* a wing.

Alabama. The place to which all the song-writers declare they want to " go back to." And no wonder, for Alabama is an Indian (American Red Indians) word for " here we rest."

Alarm. Is certainly not a corruption of the Norman-French *larum,* a thief. It comes from the Italian *all'arme,* to the arms, through the Latin, *ad arma.*

Albert Chain. A watch-chain (usually on the heavy side). The Prince Consort of Queen Victoria when he visited Birmingham, in 1849, was presented by the jewellers of the city with a chain of this type. He set the fashion for Alberts. Usually, an Albert runs from one pocket to a button of the waistcoat.

Album. Originally had nothing whatever to do with autographs or pictures. In Roman times an album was a white-topped table (whitened with gypsum—sulphate of lime) on which the names of public officers and records of public transactions were made. It was kept in a public place. In the Middle Ages in Britain it was the name for a register or list. But the derivation in this case was *albus* (white), board.

Alderman. A city or town " elder " ; councillor. Hargrave states that the accepted signification is " elder-man." Dean Hoare rejected this, interpreting the term as meaning " of all men, chief," first in rank or council. In fact, the Anglo-Saxon *ealdormen* meant chieftain or lord. The office was both civil and military, and was tending to become a great hereditary benefice when it was replaced by Canute with the Earldom Afterwards, the name was applied to any headman of a Guild, thus the alderman of the town guilds of to-day—the town council.

Alderman. A thieves' weapon for forcing safes ; a heavier weapon is known as a Lord Mayor.

Alderman. A half-crown (half a king), in reference to the old standing of an alderman referred to above.

Aldgate. In the vicinity of the present London thoroughfare stood the Auld Gate of Saxon London, the earliest of the City gates.

Aldwych, however, is merely a modern use of the Saxon word for old (Auld),for it was originally Wych Street, leading to the old village, whose parish church was that of St. Giles's in the Fields. There was never any witch!

Ale. *Yard of Ale.* This old-time measurement of beer was a glass which held half a pint. It was a glass shaped like a coaching-horn without the mouthpiece, wide at the bottom and narrowing to a neck. A number of them are still in existence, and one was, at least a year ago, hanging up in the bar of the White Horse at Corley, near Kettering, England.

Ale-Stake. The word is now forgotten, but it is worth noting because it was the immediate forerunner of the name signs which now adorn our public-houses. It was, originally, a pole set up in front of an ale-house. At first the pole was surmounted by a bush in imitation of a wine-bush. Later the bush gave place to a sign. Incidentally, the bush gave rise to the saying, "A good wine needs no bush." The bush was displayed outside the ale-shops to denote that they sold wine; but well-known wine-houses eschewed the habit. A good wine, they said, needed no bush.

All Beer and Skittles. An allusion to the days when most country inns had a skittle-alley attached, where the players while enjoying their game drank their beer. The phrase expresses the height, the perfection of enjoyment.

All bosh. Came into the language through the Oriental romances of James Morier, "The Adventures of Haiji Baba of Ispahan," and "Ayesha," where the word frequently appears. Bosh is Persian and Turkish, meaning rubbish, nonsense.

Allergic. A much misused word, an adjective, now in popular use. It is from the Greek word meaning "other reaction." Strictly a medical term, it has been in use since 1913. It is properly applied to the special sensitiveness of an individual to certain foods, pollens, or other products of plants, animal organizations, etc., so that conditions like hay-fever, nettle-rash or asthma are produced.

All-Hallows' Eve. 31st October. There is a tradition among the Scots that persons born on All-Hallows' Eve have the gift of double sight, and are able to command spirits. Scott, in "The Monastery," says: "Being born on All Hallows' Eve she (Mary Avenell) was supposed to be invested with power over the invisible world."

All is not Gold that Glitters. The origin is unknown; but it was old in Chaucer's day (1328-1400). In the "Chanones Yemannes Tale," he says:—

"All thing, which shineth as the gold,
Ne is no gold, as I have herd it told."

All men have their price. Attributed to Sir Robert Walpole (1674-1746). Bribery was at that time the universal weapon of the politician. A price was in fact, an accepted axiom of political life.

All Moonshine. Not the real thing. The light of the moon is reflected from the sun. So an incredible statement, received at second-hand, is said to be all moonshine.

"All My Eye and Betty Martin." The story goes that a British sailor looking into a church in an Italian port heard an ill-dressed man muttering, from his knees, "*Ah mihi, beate Martini*" (Ah, Grant me, Blessed Martin). Telling his shipmates of the scene afterwards, he said that it sounded to him like, "All my eye and Betty Martin." Brewer and other authorities dismiss the story as "absurd." We disagree. St. Martin, who was stated once to have split his coat to give a beggar half, is the patron saint of Italian beggars, and a book of old Italian cosmopolitan life in our possession mentions this prayer to St. Martin by beggars.

All Serene. Everything is all right. The word is Spanish, *serena*, a countersign used by sentries for all's well.

All Sir Garnet. A reference to the brilliant military successes of Sir Garnet Wolseley during the Egyptian campaign of the 'eighties. "How's the war? All Sir Garnet"—going well.

All the go. "It's all the go," was originally a draper's phrase meaning that a certain line of goods was going fast and would soon be gone.

All this for a Song. Said to have been Burleigh's angry retort when Queen Elizabeth ordered him to give £100 to Spencer, poet author of the "Faerie Queen," as a Royal gratuity.

Almighty Dollar. The phrase for the coinage unit of the United States of America was born after Washington Irving in a sketch, "The Creole Village" (1837) had written: "The Almighty Dollar, the great object of universal devotion throughout the land."

Alpaca. Is cloth made from the wool of the Peruvian sheep of the same name.

Alphabet. Is a word unique in the English language because it is purely Greek—a combination of the two Greek letters *alpha* (a) and *Beta* (b).

Alter ego. A Latin expression for "my other self," or "double."

Amazons. A reputed race of women warriors who dwelt on the coast of the Black Sea. Males were excluded from their state. If a boy was born to them it was either killed or sent to the father who lived in a neighbouring state. The Amazons devoted themselves to war and hunting. Amazon is a Greek word meaning "without breast," and in Greek legend the girls of the Amazons had their right breast burned off in order that it might not interfere with their use of the bow and javelin.

Ambition. "He has ambition." The word is derived from the Latin *ambitio*, to go around. It was used in Roman days of a candidate for election who went round on a house to house canvass for votes. He was described as "ambitious for office."

Ambrosia. "This drink is like ambrosia." The name given to the food of the Gods of Greek mythology, which made them immortal, now applied to anything delectable. Ambrosia is also the name given to an American weed, known here as ragweed.

Amen Corner. Name given to a corner of Paternoster Row in the City of London. According to Stow it derived its name from the stopping up of the lane in his time, so that people said "Amen" on finding that they had to retrace their steps. We should imagine they said something directly opposite to Amen! The more likely origin lies in the Corpus Christi Day procession to St. Paul's Cathedral. The monks used to finish the Lord's Prayer in Latin (started at Paternoster Row) at the corner, reaching the "Amen" as they turned. The procession is continued in the names of Ave Marie Lane, where they began chanting the "Hail Mary," and Creed Lane, where they began the chanting of the *Credo*.

Amende honorable. A gentlemanly apology. But in ancient French law a person making an amende honorable was taken through the streets bareheaded and barefoot with a rope round his neck to the seat of Justice, and there forced to ask pardon of the person he had wronged, and of God and the Court. The ritual was abolished in 1791, reintroduced in 1826, and finally abolished in 1830.

Amen-Ra. The supreme God of the ancient Egyptians.

America, after Amerigo Vespucci, Florentine adventurer. He embarked on a rival expedition to that of Columbus, and subsequently discovered the Bay of All Saints.

Amgot. The initials of "Allied Military Government of Occupied Territory." A committee formed of leaders in the Military and Economic fields to administer territory occupied from the enemy during the World War of 1939. It first came into active operation in Sicily, when the Allied

Forces captured and occupied that piece of Italy in July, 1943.

Amok. To run amok, comes from the Malay adjective *amoq*, meaning a furious combat while in a state of frenzy.

Among the Gods. A theatre term meaning up in the gallery. It arose from the fact that the ceiling of Drury Lane Theatre was embellished with Classical deities on a blue sky—and the gallery was nearest to the ceiling.

Amour propre. To wound one's amour propre; to hurt one's self esteem. The word means also self vanity. French from *amour*, love.

Amyris plays the fool. The phrase is now used to describe anyone who assumes a false character with an ulterior object. Amyris, a Sybarite, was sent to Delphi to consult the Oracle, who informed him that the nation would be destroyed. He fled from the country amid the jeers of his countrymen. He thereby saved his life.

Anathema. "It's anathema to me." The present meaning of evil, hateful, a curse, is a corruption. Far from being a curse originally it was an offering accepted by the Gods. The Greeks and Romans brought votive offerings to be set up in the Temple. The healed lame man, for instance, brought his crutch, the sailor returning from a voyage offered a model of his ship, as thank-offerings. Set up in the Temple they were *anathema* (*ana*, Greek "up," and *tithemi*, "to set"). An object refused by the priests was an an-anathema, and "an-anathema" is the word which should be used to-day in the sense of hateful.

Ancient Lights. The sign so often seen on buildings means that the occupier or occupiers of the buildings has enjoyed the light of a window on the premises for twenty years uninterruptedly and may, by displaying the notice, prevent in law the light from being intercepted by any other building.

Andrew Millar. The alpha and omega of the Royal Navy. Even in the 'Seventies this name was substituted for the Service. One often said, "When I joined the Andrew," meaning, of course, the Navy. When more edible rations, particularly soft bread, made their welcome appearance on board men-of-war, the firm of Andrew Millar had the biggest contract. Arthur Miller was the name of a notorious Press-gang leader of Nelson's day, but his activities have no connection (as some people have said) with the Service.

Anecdote. This word, meaning a story which is told to all and sundry, has come to a curious corruption. Strictly speaking, it should be something told in confidence, its origin being the Greek *a* (or *an*) not, and *ekdotos*, published, or given out—not to be published or given out.

Angels could do no more. "Who does the best his circumstance allows, does well, acts nobly; angels could do no more."—*Young*, 1684-1765.

Angostura Bitters. One of the ingredients of the modern cocktail. The interesting point about this is that its origin belongs to the Capuchin monks of the Venezuelan monastery city, Angostura, the name of which means a strait. The bitters are prepared from a medicinal bark discovered by the monks.

Animals in Heaven. Mohammedan legend gives the following ten animals as having been accorded a place in Paradise: (1) Jonah's whale; (2) the ant of Solomon; (3) the ram caught by Abraham and sacrificed on the mountain in place of his son, Isaac; (4) the lapwing of Balkis; (5) the prophet Saleh's camel; (6) Balaam's ass; (7) the ox of Moses; (8) the dog Kratim of the Seven Sleepers; (9) Mahomet's ass; and (10) Noah's dove from the Ark.

Annie Laurie. There really was an Annie Laurie. She was the eldest daughter of Sir Robert Laurie of Maxwellton. The famous song was written by William Douglas of Fingland, Kirkcumbright, but Annie married James Ferguson of Craigdarroch, and became the grandmother of Alexander Ferguson, hero of Burns's "The Whistler" song.

Anon. "*I'll see you Anon.*" The word is Old English "in one," meaning in one instant, at once. But by misuse the phrase has now come to signify the future, some indefinite time, but not far removed.

Another Lie nailed to the Counter. From America, where it was the custom in the country stores to nail counterfeit coins, or bad coins, to the counter of the stores. When he found such a counterfeit in his till, the shopkeeper "nailed another lie to the counter."

Anthem is not what the choir in a church sings, though we now call it so. It was originally a hymn sung by the entire congregation. A special hymn sung by the choir was called an Antiphone.

Antipodes is worth mentioning in any book of origins, because it shows the belief of Plato that the world was round, for he introduced the word to describe "the other side of the earth" in his teachings. It is composed of *anti*, opposite to, and *podes*, feet—people living on the opposite side of the world whose feet are opposite to ours.

Appetite. It has been computated that, taking the average span of life at seventy years, the food consumed by a single person during his, or her, life-time amounts to 8,000 lb. of meat, 44,000 pints of liquid, 265 cwt. of bread, 12,000 eggs, and 50 cwt. of vegetables.

A pigga back. Carried on the back or the shoulders as a pack is carried. The phrase for a ride for a child has been in use for nearly four hundred years, but its origin and the reason for the "pigga" or "pick-a-back" is unknown.

Apple of Discord. Something to quarrel about; a disputed subject. Attending unbidden at the wedding of Thetis and Peleus, in the gathering of the Gods, Discord threw a golden apple on the banqueting table "for the most beautiful." Juno, Minerva and Venus each laid claim to it. Paris, delivering judgment, gave the apple to Venus. It brought on his head the vengeance of Juno and Minerva. To their spite is attributed the fall of Troy.

Apple-pie Bed. A bed made up as a practical joke with the bottom sheet doubled upwards in the middle so that it prevents the user pushing his legs down. The "apple-pie" is a corruption of "*nap-pe-pli*," from the French *nappe plice*, a folded sheet.

Apple-pie Order. Denoting perfect order. The origin is doubtful but is probably from *cap-a-pie*, like a knight in complete armour.

April Fool. The custom of April Fool-ing originated in France, which country took the lead (in 1564) in shifting the New Year from what is now known as Lady Day (25th March) to 1st January. From the earliest periods of history people of all nations bestowed gifts upon their neighbours on New Year's Day. As the old New Year's Day (25th March) so often fell in Holy Week, the Church uniformly postponed the celebrations until the octave—1st April. When, therefore, New Year's Day was transferred to 1st January, people in France paid mock visits to their friends on 1st April, with the object of fooling them into the belief that that date was still New Year's Day.

Arena. Should not be applied strictly to any open space, playing area or meeting-place. *Arena* is Latin, "sand," from the days when the Coliseum in Rome was strewn with sand to absorb the blood spilt in combats between the gladiators, or the Christians and the lions.

Aristocracy. From the Greek *aristo-cratia*, "rule of the best born." It originally meant government of the state by its best citizens. This did not, however, mean the best in intellect and activities, because " best " in those times meant the best in birth.

Argus-eyed. In Greek mythology Argus, a fabulous creature, had a hundred eyes, and was set by Juno to watch the heifer Io. Mercury charmed Argus to sleep and slew him, whereupon Juno changed him into a peacock with his hundred eyes in that bird's tail feathers.

Aryan race. According to Adolf Hitler the German people. Actually, the parent stock of what is known as the Indo-European family of nations. The original home is lost in antiquity, but was most likely between the River Oxus and the Hindu-Kush Mountains. Hitler claims it as being in Central Europe.

As cross as two sticks. There is nothing more in this rebuke than the fact that two sticks crossed in the centre make a cross like the letter X.

Ash Wednesday. From the ancient Catholic custom of spreading on the heads of the people ashes from the palms of the previous year's Palm Sunday, which palms had at that time been blessed by the priests, who subsequently burned them to the ashes. Gregory the Great introduced the custom.

Aspen. " To shake like an aspen leaf." It is held that Christ's Cross was made from aspen wood, and the leaf is said to tremble from the shame of it. Actually, the shape of the aspen leaf renders it particularly prone to movement by even a breath of wind blowing against its long, flexible stalk.

As poor as a church mouse. Since there is no kitchen or larder, or food of any kind in a church, a mouse who lives there obviously has a poor time of it.

As rich as a Jew. From mediæval times in England Jews were the first money-lenders, bankers and bill brokers. They possessed practically all the ready money in the country, the wealth of the Nobles being vested in lands and stock.

Ashes, The. To win the ashes. When the English cricket team was beaten in 1882, a sporting paper printed a humorous epitaph which ended: " The body (English cricket) will be cremated and the ashes taken to Australia." The ashes are, of course, mythical.

Assassin. The name given to a murderer. The origins of the name were a sect of Oriental religious and military fanatics founded in Persia in 1090 by Hassan ben Sabbah. They were known as Hashshashins. For two hundred years the sect were the terror of the world. Their name was derived from *haschisch*, an intoxicating drink with which they drugged themselves before engaging in their massacres.

Ass's Shadow, To wrangle for. Demosthenes told how a traveller hired an ass to take him to Megara. At noon, the sun being very hot, he dismounted and sat himself in the shade of the ass. The owner disputed with him the right to sit in the shady spot, saying that he had let out the ass for hire, but there was no hire of the shadow of the ass. The two fell to blows over the dispute.

Assurance, life. So often confused with INsurance. Assurance is life assurance. Insurance covers burglary, damage, loss, fire, etc.

As thick as thieves. The phrase is incomplete from the original. The words " at a fair " should be added. Theodore Hook in " The Parson's Daughter " (1833) wrote " as thick as thieves." He seems to have copied the earlier French, *Ils s'entendent comme larrons en foire*, cutting out of his quotation the final words " at a fair," where pickpockets notoriously abound.

Atlantic Bridge. A popular catch question is whether there is, or is not, a bridge built over the Atlantic Ocean. Nine people out of every ten will answer, emphatically, " No." The answer is wrong. There IS such a bridge. Clachan Bridge, built by Telford in the early nineteenth century, connects the Isle of Seil to the mainland of Lorne, south of Oban, Argyllshire. By spanning the narrowest part of the straits it is the only bridge in the world that *spans the waters of the Atlantic Ocean.*

Atlantic Charter, The. The name given to an eight-point declaration by President Roosevelt, of the United States, and Mr. Churchill, after a four-day conference at sea, in August, 1941. This declaration of the British and American war and peace aims was:

(1) Britain and the United States to seek no aggrandizement.
(2) No territorial changes that do not accord with the freely expressed will of the peoples.
(3) Right of all peoples to choose their own form of government.
(4) Further trade and raw materials to all states needing them for economic prosperity.
(5) Fullest collaboration between all countries in the economic field.
(6) After the destruction of Nazi tyranny a peace to ensure to all nations the means of dwelling in safety.
(7) All men to traverse the high seas and oceans without hindrance.
(8) Pending the establishment of a wider and permanent system of social security, disarmament of warlike nations is essential.

Atlantis. Is a mythical island anciently supposed to have existed in the Atlantic Ocean. It was first mentioned by Plato. The belief is that the island was overwhelmed by an earthquake and sunk nine thousand years before the Christian Era.

At Sixes and Sevens. At cross purposes. The origin is obscure. " Notes and Queries " connect it with the unlucky number thirteen (*q.v.*); but it is more likely that it was derived from the old game of dicing. It is a pointer that the game of Baccarat depends on the number seven.

" At the Eleventh Hour." The phrase is derived from the Bible, " Parable of the Vineyard." You will remember the labourers who went in at the eleventh hour, and were rewarded with a penny exactly as those who had toiled all the day.

Augean stables. " To cleanse the Augean stables." Augeas was a mythical king of Elis. In the stables three thousand oxen were kept. The stables had not been cleaned for thirty years. One of the twelve labours given to Hercules, in order that he might attain immortality, was the cleansing of the Augean stables. He achieved it by causing two rivers to run through them. To " cleanse the Augean stables " in modern parlance means to clear away an accumulation of corruption in public life.

Augury. " A happy augury." Augury was the calling of an Augur, a functionary among the Romans whose duty was to foretell future events from omens derived from the Heavens, from the flight of birds, and the movements of animals.

Auld Reekie. Is the name given to the ancient part of the city of Edinburgh because of the cloud of " reek " (smoke) which usually hovers over it.

Aurora Borealis. Electrical lights seen in the northern parts of the sky.

Average. Is another word distorted in our language. It comes from the Latin *habere*, to have. The havings, or possessions, of a farmer were his cattle; and he was compelled, when called upon, to place the cattle at the disposal of his feudal lord's retainers for carrying their armour in times of strife. It was incumbent upon him to keep a stipulated number, say a hundred, " loads," and this was proclaimed as his " average." The *New Century Dictionary* regards this etymology as " doubtful "; but *aver*, mediæval Latin for average, appears in this connection in Domesday Book.

Axe to Grind, Another. Said of a man who propounds friendship, or proffers help, to anyone with an ulterior motive. It is said to have been first used by Benjamin Franklin. When he was a boy, a man who wanted to grind his axe persuaded young Franklin with flattery, to turn the heavy grindstone for him. When, an hour later, the axe was sharp, the man rudely told him to be off. The American philosopher states in his biography that whenever in after life he was flattered to his face, the memory of that boyhood experience always came to him, and made him speculate on whether his present flatterer had an axe to grind.

B

Bachelor. An unmarried man. Dr. Brewer says that the ultimate origin is unknown, and describes it as coming from the Old French *bachelor*, which is from a late Latin word, *baccalaris*; but the Latin *baccalaria* meant a herd of cows. Cows were attended by youths who were baccalarius. Old French corrupted this into bachelor, from which our word came. There is no doubt whatever of the origin of the word.

Bachelor of Arts (B.A.). The first and lowest degree conferred by a University.

Back Room Boys. The name given by Lord Beaverbrook, then Minister for Aircraft Production, to the Research Department of the Air Ministry. During the earlier, and later, stages of the World War the members of the department designed and worked out new aero engines, new bombs, and other methods of defence. In a broadcast on 24th March, 1941, Lord Beaverbrook, reviewing our air position, said that five new aero engines had been brought from experiment to manufacture in nine months; and, he added, " Who is responsible. To whom must praise be given? I will tell you. It is the boys in the back rooms. They do not sit in the limelight; but they are the men who do the work. Most of them are Civil Servants. There is Bulman and there is Farren. Air-Commander Huskinson is one of the leaders. He designs bombs—big bombs, fat bombs, thin bombs. Beautiful bombs." (While watching the effect of bursting bombs during a German air raid over London, Air-Commander Huskinson was blinded.)

Bacon, *To save one's.* The phrase has nothing whatever to do with bacon. The old Dutch word for bacon was *baec*; but then the earlier Anglo-Saxon word for back was also *baec*. Why any compiler of " origins " should go abroad for a word which already existed in our ancient language is difficult to understand. To save one's bacon is really to save one's baec (back) from a thrashing.

Bad Excuse is Better than None. First appeared in Udall's comedy, " Ralph Roister Doister " (about 1534). This was the first comedy of the English stage.

Bad Hat. Sir William Fraser's " Words on Wellington " suggest that the phrase was coined by the Duke in the 1830's. This is, however, purely hearsay. It was more like to have been Irish in origin, the worst Hibernian characters always wearing big high hats.

Bag and Baggage. " Bag " was the Celtic *bag*, a wallet or bundle, not the present English word bag, which was at that time a poke, pocket. Baggage came from the Old French *bagues*, goods, articles, belongings. To get rid of a person, " Bag and Baggage," was, therefore, to send him off with his bundle and goods.

Baggage. " She's a baggage." A worthless, saucy or flirtatious woman. It was first applied to the wives of soldiers, because when taken on foreign service with the regiment they invariably travelled with the stores and *baggage* of the regiment.

Bail. " *To stand bail*." The man who stands bail for an offender in the police court may be surprised to know that he has become a nurse. Yet, that is what he is. The word comes through the Low Latin *baila*, nurse, and the Latin, *bajulus*, the bearer of a burden.

Bailey. *Old Bailey*. Name of the Central Criminal Court in London. From Old French *bailler*, to enclose. It was the name given to the exterior wall of the mediæval castle, and also to the outer court of the castle between the inner and outer walls. The word subsequently came to include not only the court, but also the buildings surrounding it. When the court was abolished, the term was attached to the buildings of the castle itself, hence the Old Bailey.

Baker's Dozen. Thirteen instead of twelve. The extra one was the outcome of the imposition of a heavy penalty for underweight. To be on the safe side the baker gave the retailer an extra loaf to the dozen (called in-bread) to avoid all risk of incurring the fine.

Baldheaded. To go for someone baldheaded. To be impetuous or whole-hearted. Probably a perversion of the Dutch *bald dadig*, audacious.

Bale out, To. To leave an aeroplane by parachute. Contrary to popular belief, the parachute is by no means a modern invention. In, or about, the year 1660 Simonde La Loubere, in his " History of Siam," tells of a person in that country who made great leaps with what seemed to be two umbrellas attached to his belt. The earliest written records of a parachute dates from the fifteenth century. Leonardo da Vinci (1452-1519), however, may be said to have invented the parachute as we know it. It was not developed, however, to a practical extent until the invention of the balloon.

The first living thing in memory known to have come to earth by parachute was a dog. In August, 1785, Blanchard, the French balloonist, during a three hundred mile trip, threw out a parachute to which was attached a basket containing a dog. It descended, " according to plan," and the dog reached the ground unhurt. The first human descent by parachute, for which there is reliable authority, was Andre-Jacques Garnerin, on 22nd October, 1797.

Balk. *To balk him.* A " balk " is a piece of timber; and so is the verb " to balk." Both came from the Anglo-Saxon *balca*, a beam. For the log hut of those days was protected, not by lock and key or by bolts, but by a thick beam of wood which was thrown into sockets across the door to bar — or balk — an assailant's entry.

Ballad. Is now a sentimental song. But it was originally a song written for a dance. *See* " Ball," below.

Ball, dancing party. The word comes from the Latin *Bellare*, to dance. But our " ball " developed from the curious ancient ball-play in church by the Dean and choir-boys of Naples, Italy, during the Feast of Fools, at Easter time. The boys danced round the Dean, singing as they caught a ball thrown by him to them. Johnson records that at the earliest private dances in this country a ball was always thrown as the dancers whirled round in sets. Afterwards the ball was discarded, but the dance time received the name of ballad.

Balloon barrage. During the war of 1939-45, large cities and towns, vital works, and other vulnerable areas were protected by captive balloons, manned by Royal Air Force personnel. The object of the ring of balloons overhead was two-fold: to prevent enemy planes from flying directly over the buildings at a height which rendered bomb-aiming accurate, and to keep the enemy planes at sufficiently high an angle from the ground to enable anti-aircraft guns to engage them.

Balls, the Three Golden Balls. Sign in Britain of a pawnbroker's establishment. The Lombards of the Medici were the first money-lenders in this country, lending money to Henry III in return for certain privileges. They financed the Kings of England to the time of Edward III, having originally come to England as the financial agents of the Popes who had dues to collect. The three golden balls were the symbol which these merchants hung up in front of their houses. Dr. Brewer describes them as the arms of the Medici family representing three pills, in allusion to the Medici's old profession of medicine. This is really an extraordinary statement, since there is nothing to suggest that the Medici were anything other than scholars, bankers and merchants. They were famous in the fourteenth century, but the founder of the family's greatness was Giovanni de Medici, who amassed a huge fortune not by medicine but by banking and commerce. Dr. Brewer seems to have been misled by the fact that *medici*, Italian, was the original plural of *medico*, a physician.

Balmy. "He's balmy," meaning mentally deranged. The origin of this term for the meaning given is a complete mystery. Balmy is derived from balm (Latin *balsamum*), and balm is described as aromatic fragrance, sweet odour, or anything which heals or soothes pain. The dictionary definition of balmy is "having the qualities of balm; aromatic, fragrant. What relation this has to any lack of intelligence it is not easy to see.

There was, however, in Kent, in or about 1832, a house for the mad by name Barming Asylum, in which about that year John Nicholas Tom (or Thom) was confined after his notorious imposture as a Knight of Malta, and as a claimant to the Earldom of Devon. The institution was well-known (see the *Dictionary of National Biography*), and it is possible that the phrase "He's balmy" is a corruption of Barming, meaning that the person thus designated was fit only for Barming Asylum.

Bandy. To bandy words with. From the old game of *bandy*, in which a ball was struck, or bandied, from side to side by a stick shaped something like the present hockey-stick.

Bank, Banker. The first bankers of modern Europe were the money-changers of Venice, when that city was the resort of merchants from all over the world. They sat beneath awnings in the famous square of St. Mark's, with the money arranged in piles on benches in front of them. The bench gave us the name bankers and bank, for the Italian for bench is *banco*.

Bank Holidays. Until 1834 the banks made holiday on nearly every Saint's Day or Festival (they still do in France), amounting to thirty-three days in all. In 1834 the numbers were reduced to four—Good Friday, 1st May, 1st November, and Christmas Day. By an Act of Parliament in 1871 the days were again changed to their present order.

Banting. The name given to the method of reducing superfluous fat by dieting. In 1863, a London undertaker, William Banting, a man of great obesity, resorted to dieting. It evidently reduced his bulk, for he shortly afterwards recorded the operation in a letter on Corpulence. Since then, the diet method of reducing obesity has been called "banting."

Barbarians. Were by no means cruel, or uncivilized people. From the Greek *barbaros* (later, *barbarus*), it was the term used by the Greeks to describe any foreign people whose speech they could not understand and which sounded to them like "ba-ba."

Barber. The name for a hairdresser is not difficult to understand when it is remembered that the Latin for beard is *barba*. In those days hair was worn long, but beards were trimmed. So the trimmer of beards was a barba-r. When beards were no longer trimmed but shaved off, the shaver was still a barba-r or barber.

Barber's Pole. Is a relic of the days when barbers in England were also surgeons, and practised the popular blood-letting. The stripes on the pole, red and white, are symbolical of the winding of a bandage round the arm previous to the blood-letting. The red is the blood. The gilt knob at the top represents the brass basin used for catching the blood.

Bare Navy. A tragic memory of Edwardian times, when butter or even margarine was a luxury in the Navy. Living on bare Navy symbolized having to exist on the coarse fare supplied by the Service. It was experienced particularly on long cruises in pre-refrigerator days (up to 1907 in the Navy), when the ship's canteen ran out of the more edible viands. Hard biscuits and tinned beef were then the foremost delicacies.

Barmecide's Feast. An illusionary banquet. From the story in the "Arabian Nights." Barmecide invited a starving man to a feast, but gave him nothing to eat.

Bathchair. From that age-old resort of cripples for the waters—Bath—where it first made its appearance.

Battle Royal. A battle or fight of elimination, but first or generally applied to cock-fighting. A number of cocks, say sixteen, were pitted together in couples; then the four; then the two. The ultimate victor was the winner of the "battle royal."

Bawbee. A small Scottish coin. We doubt whether many Scotsmen know its origin. It commemorates the Scottish estate of Sillebawby, whose laird was a sixteenth century Mint-master.

Bayonet. After the name of the French city of Bayonne, where they are said first to have been made. There is, however, another story—that a Basque regiment at Bayonetta in 1647, surprised by Spaniards, stuck their knives into the muzzles of their muskets and, charging, drove off the enemy. It is a fanciful tale.

Bear, as an inn sign. Where this name is part of an old inn sign it denotes that the house had a bear-baiting garden attached to it. There is one exception—in the name, "The Bear and Ragged Staff"; this was the crest of the Earls of Warwick and of the Nevilles before them.

Beans. "He doesn't know his beans." The phrase originated in New England, especially in Boston, where the people regarded themselves as intelligent to the highest order. They also had a liking for beans baked in a pot with pork. From this grew up the contention in Boston that any unintelligent or ignorant person could not possibly have come from Boston, and not being a Bostonian could not "know his beans." It is a pretty story, worth the telling; but we take no responsibility for it.

Bedfellow, A Good. Men used formerly to sleep together, even those of rank, as Henry V and Lord Scroop. Charles VIII of France and the Duke of Orleans were also bedfellows.

Bedford Malt-horses. As Hampshire men were dubbed "hogs," in allusion to their breeding of pigs, so Bedford folk were nicknamed "malt-horses," because of the high quality of malt produced from the barley grown in the county.

Beefeater. Name given to the Yeoman of the Guard at the Tower of London. They were called Beefeaters because that is exactly what they were—eaters of beef. In mediæval England "Eater" was the synonym for a servant. "Loaf-eater" meant a menial servant, one who waited on the superior servants; the highest class of servant was the fighting-man, who ate beef—the Beef-Eater. In 1651, Cartwright wrote in "The Ordinary": "Those goodly juments of the Guard would fight (as they eat beef) after six stone a day." The story connecting Beefeaters with buffetiere, attendant at the Royal buffet or sideboard, is baseless.

Bee in his Bonnet. From the seemingly aimless buzzing of bees in the hive, a buzzing in the head; not able to think clearly. It is an exceedingly bad metaphor. There is nothing aimless or stupid about the buzzing of bees.

Beer. Who invented it nobody can now say; but as early as 1300 B.C. there was a report, on papyri, in the time of Pharoah Seti I of Egypt, of a citizen charged with being inebriated from an over-indulgence in beer.

Bees. *To tell it to the Bees.* A custom, many centuries old in country districts, is to tell the bees when a birth occurs in the family, and to hang a piece of black crêpe over the hive when a death occurs. The superstition attached to the custom is that unless the bees are told they will not stay. The superstition comes, probably, from the belief, as far back as the ancient Greeks, that there was some connection between bees and souls. Mohammed admits bees to Paradise. Porphyry, the Greek scholar, wrote, about A.D. 300: "Fountains are adapted to the nymphs or their souls, which the ancients called bees."

Behind the eight ball. An American expression for being in a fix, in a jam. The phrase means behind the baulk at the top of the table in a game of Pool.

Belcher Ring. Also Belcher handkerchief. Called after Jim Belcher, a famous pugilist (1781-1811), who dared to wear them. The ring was a massive gold one; and the handkerchief was blue with white spots.

Bell, Book and Candle. A form of solemn excommunication which was practised by the Roman Catholic Church. After the excommunication had been pronounced the book was closed, the candle thrown down and extinguished (symbolizing the spiritual darkness in which the person excommunicated must in future abide), and a bell was rung to signalize the disorder of his or her soul.

Belly-landing. *See* "Abdominal crash."

Best Man at a Wedding. He is a relic of a time when the bride was guarded by the groom's men against kidnapping by rivals. Weddings, for this reason, were most frequently held at night, and at the Swedish church of Husaby, long lances, which were fitted with sockets for torches, were kept. These were used by the groomsmen for possible defence and also to illuminate the night wedding ceremony. The groomsmen were the pick of the bridegroom's bravest and BEST friends who would volunteer for the task.

Beware the Ides of March. Take warning. Ides were (loosely) in the ancient Roman calendar, eight days in each month, ending on the 15th of March, May, July and October, and the 13th of other months. They followed the Nones. Reason everybody thinks of the Ides of March is, of course, Julius Cæsar.

Bible. The old description, "The Good Book," was nearer to the meaning of the Gospel than the word Bible, for Bible is from the Ecclesiastical Greek and Latin *biblia*, a diminutive of *biblos*, meaning the inner bark of the papyrus. Thus, a Bible originally meant any book made of papyrus paper. Here are some little-known facts about the Bible:

There are more acres in Yorkshire (3,723,724) than there are letters in the Bible (3,566,480). There are in the Authorized Version:

Chapters: 1,189.
Verses: 31,173.
Words: 774,746.
Shortest chapter: *Psalm CXVII.*
Longest chapter: *Psalm CXIX.*
The word "and" occurs 46,227 times.
The word "Jehovah" 6,855 times.
2 *Kings* xix and *Isaiah* xxxvii are exactly alike.
Ezra vii, 21, contains all the letters of the alphabet except "j."

Adulterous Bible. So-called because the word *not* was left out of the seventh commandment, making it read: "Thou shalt commit adultery."

The Breeches Bible, because in it, *Gen.* iii, 7, reads: "The eyes of them bothe were opened—and they sowed figge-tree leaves together and made themselves breeches." In the Authorized Version the word is, of course, aprons.

The Bug Bible, in which *Psalm XCI*, 5, is translated: "Thou shalt not nede to be afrayed for eny bugges by night." The word is "terror" in the Authorized and Revised Versions.

The Ear to Ears Bible. Matthew xiii, 43, reads: "Who hath ears to *ear* let him hear."

The Idle Bible. The translation of *Zech.* xi, 17, runs: "The idle shepherd," instead of "the idole shepherd." In the Revised Version, the word was changed to worthless.

The Murderers' Bible. The misprint *murderers* for murmurers makes of *Jude* 16: "These are murderers, complainers, walking after their own lusts."

The Standing Fishes Bible, because *Ezek.* xlvii, 10, reads: "And it shall come to pass that the fishes (instead of fishers) shall stand upon it. . . ."

The Treacle Bible. In it, *Jer.* viii, 22, reads: "Is there no tryacle in Gilead." The word should be "balm."

The Unrighteous Bible, because an error makes 1 *Cor.* vi, 9, read: "The unrighteous shall inherit the Kingdom of God." It should be, "The unrighteous shall *not* inherit," etc.

The Vinegar Bible. The chapter heading to *Luke*, xx, reads: "The parable of the Vinegar," instead of "Vineyard."

The Wicked Bible. Because the word *not* is omitted from the seventh commandment, making it read: "Thou shalt commit adultery."

The Wife-hater Bible. The word *life* in *Luke* xiv, 26, is printed as *wife.*

Bicycle. Latin *bis*, twice, and Greek *kyklos*, a circle. The first real bicycle in Britain was made by Fitzpatrick MacMillan, in Dumfries, 1840. He rode it, because he had been fined for furiously driving his horse and cart along the roads. But cycling did not become at all general until the penny-farthing was introduced in 1872. But perhaps the strangest thing about the bicycle is the fact of the newness of its invention. As early as 5000 B.C. the Assyrians had their chariots—two wheels with an axle joining them side by side—as a means of transport. The Egyptians, and later, the Romans, also had them; but though it must have been well-known that a wheel or any round, circular, object would balance itself in an upright position so long as it retained a rotary movement, not one person throughout the ages thought of applying that knowledge for the purpose of locomotion. It was left for the last part of the eighteenth century to invent.

The fastest speed ever reached on a bicycle is 108.92 miles per hour on a concrete highway by Alfred le Tourneur, in America. He was motor-paced.

Big Ben. Is not the name of the clock at Westminster, but of the bell which chimes the hour. It was named after Sir Benjamin Hall, who was First Commissioner of Works at the time it was cast. Incidentally, the first stroke of Big Ben, and not the last, is the exact hour.

Big-Wig. In the days when most men wore wigs judges, bishops and the nobility wore full-length wigs of the style which judges in the High Court still wear. To wear or be a big-wig meant that the wearer was someone of importance, and the meaning still rules to-day.

Bilker. To bilk someone is a corruption of Balker, one who balks or outwits another. It is related to balk, which see.

Billycock Hat. The origin that the term is a corruption of "bully-cocked" (cocked in the manner of a bully or "swell" of the dandy days) is not correct. Hatters of old-established London West End shops still refer to these hats as "Coke hats," following the introduction of the type by Mr. William Coke, familiarly known to Londoners as Billy Coke, at the shooting parties held at Holkham, round about the 1850's.

Blackfriars. A district in London and the name of a bridge over the Thames near Ludgate Circus. The area was originally the site of a Dominican Monastery which possessed the right of Sanctuary. The Dominicans' black cloaks earned for them the name of the black friars.

Blackguard. Has come to a queer corruption. There was nothing villainous about the original "black-guards." They were humble servants of the household who rode with the pots and pans, to guard them, during the passage of a wealthy household from country house to town house, or vice versa.

Blackleg. Was derived from the fact that sporting men of a low type invariably wore black leggings or top-boots.

Blackmail. This wicked tribute, one of the worst crimes in law, is of no modern usage, but is an old payment dating from the border warfare of England and Scotland. "Mail" in this sense is the old English and Scottish word meaning rent, or tax. In Scotland, for instance, rents of an estate, whether in cash or kind, were called *Mail.* Originally *black*mail was a tribute paid by Border farmers to free-booters in return for protection from molestation from either side of the Border. The modern signification will at once be seen.

Black Maria. The colloquial name for a prison van used to take away arrested men. The story goes that a huge and powerful negress named Maria Lee was the owner of a sailor's lodging house at Boston. On one occasion, seeing a policeman being overpowered, she went to his aid and rescued him, at the same time apprehending the attacker. Afterwards she assisted the police on a number of occasions, so much so that, recalling her strength, the police, when a refractory offender was troubling them, sent out the SOS, "Send for Black Maria."

Black Market. The term applied during the World War (1939-45) to describe the operations of dealers in foodstuffs, and other goods in rationed supply. By one means or other—by collusion with producers, or by actual theft—dealers managed to obtain stocks of the goods in question, and retail them at prices in excess of the maximum laid down by the authorities, to such of the public as were willing to pay to secure an unfair and illegal advantage over their fellow-beings. Drastic measures for Black Market offenders were announced on 12th March, 1942, by the then Home Secretary, Mr. Herbert Morrison. They included a maximum sentence of fourteen years penal servitude.

Black-out. The term applied to the complete darkness of streets and houses in Great Britain during the years of the World War, 1939-45, because of the danger of revealing positions to German aircraft for bombing. It was forbidden, under pain of heavy penalties, to show a light from any window, or from any street lamp, such restriction being in force until the late days of 1944, when the complete darkness was lessened to a "dim-out."

The term came, of course, from the stage term, "black-out," for the extinguishing of all lights on a stage during the changing of a scene in cases where the curtain could not be dropped, it being between acts.

Black-out Alphabet. There was, however, a much earlier mention of black-out. In the time of Napoleon, a French artillery officer seized upon the idea of embossing despatches, etc., on paper, so that they could be read by touch after dark, thus preventing a light that might give a position away to the enemy. Louis Braille, a blind boy, hearing of this, proceeded to draw up a system of dots representing the alphabet. This was at first called the black-out alphabet for the blind, but later it became known as Braille.

Blackthorn Winter. This is the name given to the cold spell which is often experienced at the end of April and the beginning of May, when the blackthorn is in blossom.

Blanket. The usual derivation tells how Mr. Thomas Blanket, of Bristol, first made them late in the fourteenth century. The writer has no doubt that Mr. Blanket did make blankets, but if he did, he adopted the name Blanket, for the word is a Norman French translation of the Anglo-Saxon *hwitel,* from *hwit,* white.

Blarney. Wheedling or flattering words to gain an object. In 1662, when besieged by the English at his castle at Blarney near Cork, Ireland, Cormach Macarthy asked for an armistice. Instead of surrendering at the time agreed upon he sent out evasive excuses, until the English commander realized that he had been duped. The incident gave rise to the expression, "None of your Blarneying."

Blarney stone. High up in the wall of Blarney Castle (*see* "Blarney," above) is a stone commemorating the event. The legend regarding the stone is that anybody who can reach and kiss the stone without assistance will be able to obtain anything he desires by wheedling.

Blighty. Soldiers' word for home, England. It comes from the Hindustani word *bilati,* "removed at some distance," and British troops in India first translated this into going back to England. The Egyptian *bilade* means "the village."

Blimp, Colonel. A character invented by the cartoonist, Low, in the London *Evening Standard.* The Colonel is a high falutin' pukha sahib, with a "By Gad, sir," accent and attitude.

Blind as a bat. A bat is not blind but, being a night hunter, can see better in the half-light than in full light of day.

Blind as a mole is nonsense. A mole is not blind, although like other underground creatures its eyes are very small.

Blind Man's Buff. The origin of this harmless, and amusing, children's game was a sinister one. It was the ritual for the selection of a victim for a Druidic sacrifice. The other children's game of "Tiggy" (q.v.) is probably from the same source.

Block Buster. British name for, firstly, a 4,000 lb. bomb, and later an 8,000 lb. bomb, designed for dropping on pin-pointed industrial targets in the World War. In March, 1944, they were augmented by the "Factory Buster," weighing five and a half tons. When first used, in April, 1944, they brought down the greater part of the large Gnome and Le Rhome Aero Engine Works at La Limoges. It was stated, and later proved, that no man-made structure could resist the factory buster. Only deep shelters, such as the deepest London Tube, offered any protection against them.

Blockhead. A stupid person, brainless. The expression is an allusion to the dummy head on which a wig-maker fits his wigs.

Blonde and Brunette. According to the statistics of Dr. John Beddoe, there are sixteen blondes in every hundred Scots and thirteen in every hundred English. There are few Irish or Welsh blondes.

Blood, toil, tears and sweat. The words were used by Mr. Winston Churchill, addressing the House of Commons for the first time after his election to the position of Prime Minister, on 13th May, 1940. The full text was: "I say to the House, as I said to the Ministers who have joined this Government, I have nothing to offer but blood, toil, tears and sweat."

Bloody. The origin of this word, now branded as a "swear-word," is "God's Blood." It once occupied a reverent place in the Church, and was so applied relative to the Blood of Christ, "The Bloody Sacrifice of the Mass."

Bloody Assizes. Those held by Judge Jeffreys ("The Hanging Judge") in 1685 for the punishment of those who had taken part in the Monmouth Rebellion. More than three hundred persons were executed and more than a thousand transported.

Bloody Butcher. The name given to the Duke of Cumberland, son of George II, because of his wholesale slaughter of the adherents of Prince Charles Stuart, the Young Pretender, after the Battle of Culloden.

Bloody Hand. Under the old Forest Law of Britain, a man whose hand was bloody was presumed to be a person guilty of killing the King's deer. In heraldry, the bloody hand is the badge of a baronet.

Bloomers. This now nearly extinct woman's garment was invented as a cycling suit by Mrs. Ann Bloomer of New York. The suit included a costume as well as the trousers.

Blue Blood. A term used to describe the Noble classes. "He has blue blood in his veins." The origin is Spain, and has reference to the fact that the veins showing through the skin of the pure-blooded Spanish aristocrat were more blue than those whose family tree showed a mixture of Moorish and other alien blood.

Blue Moon, Once in a. Very rare; seldom seen; almost impossible. Curiously enough, there WAS once a blue moon, caused by the dust from a volcanic upheaval in Java in 1883. The moon, shining through the dust blown up by the eruption, appeared as a bluish colour.

Blue Peter. The flag (blue ground with white square in centre) which is hoisted to signify that a ship is about to sail. "Peter" is a corruption of the French word "*partir*," to leave.

Blue Peter in Cards. Is a call to your partner at whist for trumps, by laying on your partner's card a higher card than is necessary.

Blue Peter in Navy. The Long Service and Good Conduct Silver Medal awarded to naval ratings after fifteen years' continuous good service. It carries with it the well-merited gratuity of twenty pounds. A facetious allusion to this award is that it is nobly earned for fifteen years' undiscovered crime.

Bluestocking. A derogative term for a studious woman, which came from a literary club formed by a Mrs. Montague in 1840. Benjamin Stillingfleet, who wore blue stockings, was a regular visitor, and blue stockings became the recognized emblem of membership. It was, however, a second-hand club, there having been a similar one four hundred years previously at Venice, called Dellas Calza from the colour of the stockings worn.

Blurb. A brief descriptive paragraph or note of the contents or character of a book, printed as a commendatory advertisement on the wrapper, or jacket, of a newly published work. The word was coined by Mr. Gilet Burgess, who thus becomes the rival of the late Mr. Arthur Roberts, the famous comedian, who coined the word "spoof." Blurb, originally American slang, came into the language, and the *Oxford English Dictionary*, in 1924.

Bob. Slang name for a shilling piece. It is suggested that the name came from Sir Robert (Bob) Walpole, who was Paymaster to the Army, then First Commissioner of the Treasury, and later Chancellor of the Exchequer. In the same way a "Joey," a fourpenny piece, was thus named after Joseph Hume, M.P., who during his Parliamentary career paid great attention to financial matters.

Bobby. Nickname for a policeman. A skit on the Christian name of Sir Robert Peel, to whom the introduction of the modern police system was due. Policemen were also nicknamed "peelers" for the same reason.

Bogey, Colonel. The name given in golf to an imaginary player whose score for each hole is settled by the club committee. It is presumed to be the lowest that any average good player can hole out in. Beating bogey is playing the whole in a fewer number of strokes.

Bogus. Lowell gives the derivation as a corruption of the French *bagasse*. But the *Boston Courier*, America, in 1857, gave the following authoritative origin: "The word bogus is a corruption of the name Borghese, a man who, twenty years ago, did a tremendous business in supplying the Great West of America with counterfeit bills and bills on fictitious banks. The western people came to shortening the name Borghese to bogus, and his bills were universally styled 'bogus currency'."

Bolshevik (not Bolshevist). Used properly, the term means a member of the Russian revolutionary party which, under Lenin, seized power in 1917 and declared war on capitalism and the capitalistic class of all nations. The policy has since, under Stalin, been considerably modified; and the word has now lost its meaning when applied to Soviet Russia.

Bolt. "*He's shot his bolt.*" Bolt, in this case, is the old Anglo-Saxon or Teutonic word meaning an arrow. The arrows used in the ancient cross-bow were called bolts. For a person to shoot his bolt means that he has expended his ammunition and has no further resources.

Bombs. The origin of bombs as a munition of war did not originate with the Germans or the British, neither in the first Great War or the present War (1939-45), in which they have played so havoc-making a part. The first aerial bombs were dropped by the Austrians on Venice, in the year 1849. In the Venetian revolt led by the patriot Danvil Manim, balloons bearing small bombs, fully equipped with fuses, were set adrift when the wind was in the correct direction. The fuses exploded the bombs shortly after they touched ground. The missiles now released from aeroplanes were originally cannon-balls fired from the earliest guns. The name is owed to the humming sound which the cannon-balls made as they sped on their way from the gun muzzle, *bombs* being a corruption of the Latin *bombus*, which meant the sound of a bee.

Bona fide. Latin, meaning good faith. To produce credentials to show that one will carry out one's bargains.

Bones. "*To make no bones about it*," was, in the fifteenth century, to find no bones in it (i.e., to swallow without difficulty). The word "to bone" (thieves' slang) is probably from a dog making off with a bone.

Bonfire. Is not derived from the French *bon*, good, nor from the Scandinavian *baun*, beacon, as is frequently stated. There is little doubt that it dates from Henry VIII and the burning of ecclesiastical relics, and was originally "bone-fire," a fire of bones.

Booking Office. In the olden days, when accommodation in the stage-coaches was limited, the would-be traveller entered his name in a book kept in the office of the coaching inn, and waited his turn to travel. The name persisted, and still persists to-day, even though no booking is now required.

Boot and Saddle. Has nothing to do with boots. It comes from the French *boute selle*, put on the saddle, and was an order to the cavalry to mount.

Born with a silver spoon in his mouth. The allusion is to the silver Apostle spoon formerly presented to an infant by its godfather at baptism. In the case of a child born to wealthy parents such a gift was anticipated at the moment of entering life.

Boudoir. From the French *bouder*, to sulk. Originally was a room in which the lady of the house went to sulk.

Bowdlerise, To. To expurgate a book, usually to an unnecessary degree. Thomas Bowdler in 1818 produced an expurgated edition of Shakespeare which could "with propriety be read aloud in the family." In other words, he had taken out all the "naughty" bits. Every expurgated book since has been alluded to as a "bowdlerised" edition.

Bowler hat. The origin is best described by quoting a paragraph from the London *Daily News* of 8th August, 1868: "Mr. Bowler, of 15 St. Swithin's Lane, has, by a very simple contrivance, invented a hat that is completely ventilated whilst, at the same time, the head is relieved of the pressure experienced in wearing hats of the ordinary description."

Bow. *Two strings to his bow.* An allusion to the custom of the archers of olden days in carrying a spare string in case of accident.

Boxing Day. In olden days charitable boxes placed in churches were opened on Christmas Day, and the contents were distributed among the poor next day—the "box day," or "Boxing Day." Later, apprentices used to carry boxes for contributions round to their master's customers, and the custom has now grown to every type of worker, who calls at customers' houses during the year, such as postmen, dustmen, shop deliverymen, and so on.

Box the Compass. A sea phrase. It means to be able to name the thirty-two points of the compass in their proper order. Now used also to express a person's change of political opinion, or *volte face*, in any opinion formerly held.

Boycott. To have no dealings with. In the Irish land troubles of 1881 a Captain Boycott, who was agent in Mayo for Lord Erne, declined to accept rents from tenants of the Erne Estate who had themselves reduced them. He demanded the full rents. Accordingly, he could obtain no labour to gather in his crops from the land.

Bramley Seedling (Apple). Called, most gardeners will be surprised to hear, from a Mr. Bramley, who far from being a fruit grower, was a butcher of Southwell, Notts.

Brand-new. The "brand," in this connection, is the Anglo-Saxon word which meant a torch, fire. And "brand-new" meant fire-new, or a metal article which had just come from the smith's fire after it had been forged into shape while white hot.

Bray, The Vicar of. Nothing is known historically of the Vicar of the song who changed his political views with every change of Government. But it might easily have been Simon Alleyn who, as the Vicar of Bray, was a Protestant in the reigns of Henry VIII and Edward VI, Catholic in Queen Mary's reign, and Protestant again under Elizabeth.

Simon Symonds, another Vicar of Bray, was Independent during the Protectorate, High Church in Charles II's regime, Papist under James II, and Moderate Protestant under William and Mary. The song may have been written as a combination of both the Vicars.

Breaking the Bank at Monte Carlo. There is a good deal of misapprehension about this "feat." Each table in the Casino at Monte Carlo has a till, into which a certain amount is placed before play opens. Should there be a run of winnings on the part of the players, there may not be enough money left in the till to pay all the winnings after a coup. In such case the bank is said to be broken. All that happens is that more money is brought to the table, and play is resumed. In the course of a season, the "bank" is thus "broken" many times.

Bridewell. The name stands in many parts of the country for a gaol. This is one instance of the difficulty with which the delver into the meanings of words has to contend. The connection between Bridewell and gaol, is that at St. Bridget's Well, London (Bridewell), there was at one time a royal dwelling which Edward VI converted into a hospital. Later it became a house of correction, but still kept its name of Bridewell. Hence provincial local rulers, having seen the Bridewell house of correction in London, promptly called their own gaols "bridewells."

Bridge-head. This word came into the English language during the Great War of 1939-45. It is a military term used to describe a penetration into the lines of the enemy. So soon as the penetration was established in sufficient strength to hold the penetration, and get reinforcements through, it was a *bridge-head.* The practice was to extend the bridge-head, first by widening it at the two extremes, and then by deepening the penetration at the apex. Once powerful armour had been landed on the bridge-head a major attack could be started.

Most famous bridge-heads of the War were those at which the Allied Armies landed in Normandy in 1944, when France was invaded; and the bridge-head across the Rhine at Remagen in February, 1945.

Bridge of Sighs. The bridge in Venice which crosses high over a narrow canal and joins the Palace of the Doges with the State prison. Over this bridge condemned prisoners were led from the Palace to their place of execution. In the centre of the bridge is a window; the guards would allow a prisoner to pause there and look for the last time at the light of day. Hence the bridge of sighs.

Britannia. The female figure of Britannia first appeared on a coin in the time of the Emperor Hadrian, A.D. 76-138. It reappeared on our copper coins in the reign of Charles II, 1665, when the model for Britannia was Miss Stewart, afterwards the Duchess of Richmond.

British Restaurants. Communal eating centres established during the World War to serve cheap and quick meals to workers, particularly in bombed areas. They were named "British Restaurants" in April, 1941, although they had been in existence some time before.

Brown. *John Brown's Body lies a'mouldering in the Grave.* John Brown was an American Abolitionist—that is, a supporter of the movement to abolish slavery in the cotton-fields. On 16th October, 1859, with his two sons, he seized the National Arsenal at Harper's Ferry, hoping to affect a general rising of the slaves to join his forces. The slaves, however, did not rise. Brown's two sons were killed and he himself was captured. He was tried for treason, condemned and hanged at Charleston on 2nd December, 1859. His soul did, indeed, go marching on, and slavery was at last abolished.

Broad Arrow. The mark placed on Government property. The sign of the Board of Ordnance. It was the crest of Viscount Sydney, Earl of Romney, Master-General of the Ordnance from 1693 to 1702. This is the most probable of a number of origins put forward; but there is a reference to "brode arrowes" in a grant of arms to John Cooke, on 20th February, 1551.

Browned Off. Nickname in the fighting services for being in a state of complete boredom. One origin is that it was first used by a man of the 1st Batt. Suffolk Regiment in Singapore, in 1927. The battalion was on a route march. They were sun-burnt, and when the company commander "looked black" at their performance, one of the men remarked, "He's blacked-off, and we're all browned-off." The Navy, however, claims to have used the phrase years before that. Probably the true origin lies in London. A "brown" in Cockney language was a penny. To be "browned-off" meant to be given a penny to go away and not be a nuisance.

Brummagem. This colloquial name for the city of Birmingham is not the slang nickname which it is so often represented to be. In another spelling it was the original name of the city. Originally, when the Midlands' capital was a small town of little importance, and even as late as the days of Charles I, the town was Bromicham. Clarendon, in "History of the Rebellion" (iii, p. 276), wrote: "At Bromicham, a town so generally wicked that it had risen upon small parties of the King's men and killed or taken them prisoner, and sent them to Coventry." Thus "Brummagem" is merely a return in modern pronunciation to the city's old name. (*See,* "Sent to Coventry.")

Brylcream Boys. Name given to the men of the Royal Air Force in 1939. It arose from the picture of an airman on recruiting posters, showing him with highly glossy black hair. (Brylcream is the trade name of a hair-cream.)

Bubble and Squeak. Is the name given to cold boiled potatoes and green vegetables fried together. They first bubbled in water when boiled, and afterwards squeaked together in the frying-pan.

Bucket. *To Kick the Bucket.* To die. We do not like the explanation usually given that the phrase evolved from the action of a suicide, who had stood on a bucket to fit the noose of a rope round his neck, and then kicked the bucket away, so that he hanged. A more likely derivation is that of the East Anglian *Bucket*—a frame in which a newly slaughtered pig is suspended by its heels. The heels might be said to be kicking the bucket; and the pig was dead.

Budget. Dr. Brewer puts forward the statement that the use of the term budget for the financial statement of the Chancellor of the Exchequer arose from the custom of bringing to the House of Commons the papers pertaining to these matters in a leather bag, or in the French, a *bugette.* The French word for bag is, in any case, *bouge.* The simple fact is that the Budget in these early days was literally a sack full of money, the various sums appropriated to special purposes being sorted into little pouches. And *bougette* is the diminutive of the French word *bouge,* and means a little bag, a pouch.

Bull and Gate, public-house or inn sign, is a corruption of Boulogne Gate, a compliment to Henry VIII, who captured Boulogne in 1544.

Bulldozer. Name given in America to a machine used for levelling ground, removing obstacles, and also for excavating at high speed. It was introduced into Britain by the American army for the levelling of ground at high speed for airfields, and encampments. In American dictionaries the word is described as (1) a means of intimidating, to coerce by violence; and (2) mach., an upsetting machine. The name had its origin in a southern word (Louisiana) meaning a whip or cowhide, or a species of "kurbatch" made from the *penis* of a bull. With these whips the negroes of Louisiana were flogged, or bull-dozed, into voting for the Democratic ticket. Thus, to be bull-dozed is to be intimidated by violence.

Bumper glass. The term is said to be a corruption of "*bon Pere,*" the Toast drunk to the Pope, the Good Father of the Faithful. It is more likely, however, that it is a corruption of Bombard, a drinking vessel, but originally signifying a cannon, the crew of which were, and still are, bombardiers.

Bunkum. It's all bunkum; all nonsense. The word is a corruption of Buncombe, in North Carolina. The representative of the town occupied the time of Congress so long with a meaningless speech that most of the members left the hall. Asked, later, his reason for such a display of words, he replied: "I was not speaking to the House, but to Buncombe."

Burke, To burke someone. William Burke and his confederate, Hare, were convicted, in 1829, of smothering people to death in order to sell their bodies to the anatomist Knox, in Edinburgh, for medical research. When Burke appeared on the public scaffold a large crowd exhorted the executioner with cries of "Burke him; Burke him," meaning, apparently, don't hang, but smother him to death. We still use the term "to burke" in the sense of stifling or shutting up something.

Burn one's boats. The Romans when they invaded a foreign country set fire to their boats, thus forcing their soldiers either to conquer or die. The phrase has thus come to mean to cut off all chance of retreat from any project embarked upon.

Bury the Hatchet, To. North American (Red) Indians, when they smoked the "pipe of peace," buried their hatchets, scalping-knives and clubs to ensure that there could be no chance of hostilities, and to show their good faith.

Busman's Holiday. We are indebted for the true origin of this popular phrase to Mr. G. Savidge, Munster Avenue, Hounslow, Middlesex. "Fifty years ago (he wrote us) I was a conductor on one of London's horse-buses. The driver and his horses were as one; there was a deep attachment between them. When my driver had a day off, knowing that his horses would miss him, he always came to the terminus to see them off on the journey. If he suspected the temporary driver of not treating them well, he would travel throughout the journey as a passenger. He was only one of many such drivers; and when we saw a driver riding on his bus during his day off we always said of him that he was "taking a busman's holiday."

Butler. Was originally, and still is, the man in charge of the wine. Note *Gen.* xi, 21: "He restored the chief butler unto his butlership again and he gave the cup into Pharoah's hand." The name is best described as "bottler."

Buttercup. The name was given to the little wild flower at a time when the view was held that cows eating them gave the yellow colour to the best butter. The truth is that the buttercup grows only on sound pasture, and is therefore always likely to improve butter by giving good feed to the cow.

By and Large. It seems to-day that hardly a speaker is there, in any address or lecture he may be called upon to give, but must include the term "by and large." Its origin, and its proper application, is nautical. It is a term used of sailing vessels. When a vessel was close-hauled, orders were given to sail "full and by"—that is, as close to the wind as possible; or "by and large"—that is, slightly off the wind. The latter is the easier and offers less chance of being "taken aback" to the inexperienced helmsman. Thus, to take a thing "by and large" implies a lack of meticulous accuracy, and has come to mean to speak about one's topic as an amateur rather than as a professional. In other words, one's statement is not guaranteed as entirely accurate.

By Hook or by Crook. It is rather a case of taking your choice here. One reputed origin is that more than a century ago the two leading K.C.'s were a Mr. Hook and a Mr. Crook, both very much sought after and both very successful. This gave rise to the saying: "I'll win by Hook or by Crook." Another version is that it referred to a tool carried by petty thieves. It had a hook to lift clothes off clothes-lines and a crook to gather articles from tables set near open windows. The third version is that the poor of a Manor were formerly allowed to go into forests to gather wood for the winter. The hook they carried raked the pieces together from the undergrowth; but they also had a crook which they attached to the staff to enable them to pull down dead branches from the trees. They intended to find wood by the usual hook—*or by crook.*

It should, however, be pointed out that in all probability neither is correct, for the terms hooke and crooke were pretty old in the time of Archbishop Cranmer (1489-1556), when he wrote to Bishop Gardiner: "For all your bragges, hookes and crookes, you have such a fall as you shall never be able to stand upright again."

By-law. NOT bye-law. The "by" comes from the Danish *by*, a town (Spilsby, for example), and a by-law is one enacted by a town or corporation. But a bye-election means an extra election.

By the Skin of my Teeth. It will probably surprise the users of this cliche to know that they are quoting the Scriptures. In *Job* xix, 20, there appears: ". . . I am escaped by the skin of my teeth."

C

Cab. Short for the French *cabriolet*, a one-horse cab. The French so-called it from the Italian *capri-ola*, which, in its turn, came from *capri*, a he-goat, after which the Isle of Capri is named. The lightness of the first cab, as compared to previous vehicles of transport, was thus likened to the lightness of the goats leaping along the rugged hills of Capri. The cab was introduced into London in 1823. It was recorded at the time that: "With great difficulty Messrs. Bradshaw and Rotch (the latter a Member of Parliament) obtained licenses for eight cabriolets and started them at fares one-third lower than those of hackney coaches. The new vehicles are hooded chaises drawn by one horse and carrying only one passenger, who sat in the cabriolet with his driver."

Cabal. The name given to a council of intriguers. A popular origin states that the name was formed out of the initials of the intriguing Ministry of 1670, thus: Clifford, Ashley, Buckingham, Arlington and Lauderdale. The "accident" may have popularized the word as a political reproach in England, but it existed in the French *cabale*, the German *cabala*, and the Hebrew *qabbalah* long before 1670. Of the British cabal named, Macaulay wrote: "These ministers were called the cabal . . . it has never since their time been used except as a term of reproach."

Cabinet. The executive council of a government The word is not derived, as is frequently stated, from the French *cabane*, a hut, but from the Italian *cabinetto*, a little room. The use of the word for purposes of State arose from the practice of Kings appointing their advisers, and taking them therefore into their private room—their cabinet.

Cable's length. Is a hundred fathoms, or one-tenth of a sea mile; 607.56 feet.

Caboodle. "The whole caboodle." The entire party. Probably a corruption of kit and boodle. The latter word is possibly a corruption of the Danish *boedel*, estate, possessions, inheritance, household goods. To take the kit and boedel (caboodle) is, therefore, to take the entire property, or party. The expression is a popular one with sailors on American coasting ships, and they use the word in that connection.

Ca' Canny. Scottish phrase meaning go slowly. Don't exert yourself. *Ca* is the *caw* to impel, or drive.

Caddy. When the housewife puts the tea in her tea-caddy, she is copying the Malay people. The word properly is the Malayan *kati*, a weight of one and one-third pound.

Cadge, To. Derived from the basket carried by itinerant peddlars in former days. The basket was called a *cadge*, and the peddlars *cadged* for a living.

Cakewalk. "It's a cakewalk." The description referred, originally, to a popular competition among the negroes of Southern America. Couples walked round a prize cake in pairs. The pair who the judges decided had walked most gracefully were awarded the cake.

To take the cake refers to the same competition. The winner took the cake.

Calabooze. A term revived recently in a music-hall song. It is a New Orleans name for a prison, from the Spanish *calabozo*, a dungeon.

Calculate, calculation. The word is worth recording because of the strangeness of its origin. It is from the Latin *calculus*, a small stone, a pebble. To calculate was to reckon by pebbles. The Greeks recorded their votes by dropping pebbles into an urn. It is therefore appropriate that integral calculus, invented by Newton, should have been called "the mathematician's pebble."

Calendar. Came to us from the Latin *calendarium* (in Classical Latin, *kalendarium*), which was an account book, or interest book, kept by money-lenders. It was so-called because interest became due on the *calends*, the first day of the month. Calends itself came from the Latin *calare*, to call, because the beginning of each month was proclaimed publicly.

The calendar of a year, months, weeks and days, was started by Romulus in Rome, in 738 B.C. His calendar consisted of ten months. Nama Pompilius added an extra two months, and Julius Cæsar fixed the year at three hundred and sixty-five days six hours. This proved to be eleven minutes too long, and the accumulated error had become ten days when, in 1582, Pope Gregory XIII put it right. (*See* "Year.")

Called over the Coals. Remonstrated with. The phrase was, originally, *hauled* over the coals, in reference to the treatment of heretics who were hauled over the coals of a slow fire. There is no evidence for the popularly circulated story that it comes from the mediæval torture of Jews in this country.

Caller. A word familiar to us through its frequent mention in Scottish songs and ballads, in "Caller Herring," for instance. Its meaning is cool, fresh; and its probable origin is the Icelandic *kaldr*.

Cambric. The fine cloth is so-called from Cambrai in France, where it was at one time the chief manufacture. The town in Flemish is spelt, and pronounced, Kameryk.

Camel. "*It is easier for a camel to go through the eye of a needle than for a rich man to enter the Kingdom of God.*" Despite suggestions to the contrary, it is unlikely that the word in the original text was camel. It was more probably *cable*. The housewife, even in Biblical days, knew the difficulty of threading a thick thread through the eye of a needle.

Camel Corps (Navy). Towards the close of the last century it was a common sight to see a young seaman or stoker struggling home beneath the weight of a great white bag of dirty clothes, hammocks, etc. The burden was his shipmates' washing, and he was taking it to his wife. There were no separation or children's allowances in those days, and the young married couple who faced life on 1s. 7d. to 2s. a day had to resort to the labour of the wash-tub in order to pay the rent for one room and make two ends meet.

Canary Islands. Not from the bird, canary, though these abound in the island; but from the multitude of large dogs which were found there in the days of the elder Pliny. The Latin name for a dog is *canis*.

Candidate. A person putting up for election to office. The origin is interesting. The Latin *candidus* means white, and *candere*, to shine. Romans who sought high office in the State vested themselves in white togas, emphasizing, apparently, their purity of character and intentions. The word candid, meaning open, above board, comes from the same derivation.

Candle. *The game is not worth the Candle.* This is an allusion to the days when in theatres, meetings and other places of public resort, illumination was provided by link-boys or link-men who held lighted candles. The game was not worth the (cost of the) candle when the performance was poor, or when the sport promised was small.

Candlemass. The Feast of the Purification of the Virgin Mary, held on 2nd February. The feast takes its name from the custom, as old as the seventh century, of carrying lighted candles in procession in memory of Simeon's words at the presentation of the Infant Christ: "To be a light to lighten the Gentiles, and the glory of thy people Israel."

On this day, also, Roman Catholics consecrate the candles to be used in their churches throughout the coming year.

Canoe. *Paddle your own canoe.* First recorded use of the phrase was by Captain Marryat, about 1843; but it was popularized in *Harper's Magazine*, in a poem by Sarah Bolton.

Canopy. Used to drape over personages, and "occasions." Comes from the Greek *konops*, a gnat, and it was a curtain net used by Nile boatmen to sleep under in peace from the attentions of gnats.

Cant. *Hypocracy.* It is not likely that the popular story of Alexander and Andrew Cant is the origin. This pair of bigoted Covenanters are said to have persecuted religious opponents with ferocity, and at the same time to have prayed for those who suffered on account of their religious opinions. Beaumont and Fletcher, the famous writers of comedies, used the word "cant" long before the brothers Cant, and the word is undoubtedly from the Latin *canto*, to sing, from which came the English *chant*, to whine.

Canteen. Is really a cellar. We hear a lot about canteens these war days as dining-rooms; but the word is derived from the Italian *cantina*, a wine cellar. Later it became a refreshment house in army barracks, and later still a vessel in which water or wine was carried by soldiers when on the march.

Canter. *To put one's horse to a canter.* Somewhat curiously, this word has nothing whatever to do with cant, see previous page. It was originally *Canterbury pace*, and was given by mockers to the ambling gait of horsed pilgrims on their way to the shrine of Thomas à Becket at Canterbury.

Canucks. Is the name given now to all Canadians, especially by Americans, but it should be confined to Canadians of French descent. It is believed to be a corruption of the French-Canadians' attempt to say Connaught, a term which they at one time applied to Irish emigrants.

Cap, considering. "*I must put on my considering cap.*" Judges in olden days used to put on an official cap before passing sentence. It is still preserved in the donning of the black cap before the passing of a death sentence. Curiously enough, the word considering dates back to the days when astrology was an accredited science. The word is derived from the Latin *considerare*, from *con*, together with, and *sideris*, a star.

Caper. To cut a caper. Another instance of a corrupted word. Cape should be *capra*, Italian for a goat; and it is an allusion to the friskiness of goats. To cut a *capra* is to "play the giddy goat."

Capful of wind. This phrase for a little wind, hardly sufficient to move a sailing ship, arises from the following legend: Eric, King of Sweden, was so familiar with evil spirits that, whichever way he turned his cap, the wind would blow. Hence his cap was said to be full of wind.

Carat. A weight measure for precious stones. It comes from the Arabic *qirat*, seed of the locust tree, the weight of which represented the *silequa* of the Romans and equalled one twenty-fourth part of the golden *solidus*. It is from this that gold takes its weight. Pure gold is twenty-four carats. Twenty-two carat gold is twenty-two parts pure gold and two parts alloy, and so on with other carat gold.

Care will kill a cat. First used by Ben Jonson (1573-1637) in "Every Man in his Humour," and repeated word for word by George Withers in "Poem on Christmas": "Hang sorrow. Care'll kill a cat."

Carpet Knight. In the Brave Days a man won his spurs of knighthood on the battlefield. When the honour of knighthood came to be conferred by the Sovereign on civilians, they usually received the accolade while kneeling on a strip of carpet.

Card. "*It's on the Cards.*" An allusion to the fortune which a fortune-teller sees in the cards spread in front of her.

A Sure Card. Dependable. An ace of the suit of cards is a certain card.

A Knowing Card. Allusion to a card-sharper.

A Queer Card. One whom it is difficult to sum up. It is probably derived, by card-players, from a "lead" given by a bad player at whist, one who has no knowledge of the conventions of the game. To lead a trump, for instance, is a sign to a partner that you want trumps led. To lead a King or a Jack would mean that you hold the Queen and want the Ace out of the way, but should, say, the nine of a suit be led, it would be a queer card for a partner to attempt to interpret.

A Leading Card. The best argument in a debate. In any card game a player leads from his strongest suit.

Cardinal virtues. They are justice, prudence, and fortitude. On these all the other virtues are considered to rest.

Carnival. This name, now applied to all kinds of merry-making at all times, belongs properly to the period preceding Lent. It ended on Shrove Tuesday. In the Roman Catholic countries carnival season was devoted to revelry and feasting, before the forty days' fasting began on Ash Wednesday, the first day of Lent. The word explains itself in the root—*caro*, *carnis*, Latin, flesh; and *levare*, to remove. There was an earlier, Italian word, *carnevale*, the vale being the Italian farewell—to meat.

Cartwheel Pennies. These were large copper twopenny and penny pieces struck by Matthew Bolton of Birmingham in 1797. The size of the coins earned for them the sobriquet of "cartwheels." It was about this time, or shortly afterwards, that 3s. pieces were issued for revenue-producing purposes. These weighed a considerable amount. The 3s.

pieces appear to have been discontinued about 1816, when so short was the Treasury of silver (*sic.*) that the Bank of England issued dollar tokens of 5s., 3s. and 1s. 6d. value. The circulation of these tokens was discontinued in 1818 after the Treasury had issued more silver coins.

Casement. Is not a window, but that small portion of the old-fashioned window which opens like a door, on a hinge.

Cash. Was originally the old French word *casse*, a case or box in which money was kept.

Cat. In Egypt the cat was held as sacred to the God Isis, and to the Moon. The Goddess Bast was portrayed with the head of a cat. To kill a cat in Egypt was punishable by death. In Rome of ancient times the cat was a symbol of liberty. In ancient England it was regarded as a "familiar" of witches.

Cat has nine lives. A reference to the care which a cat takes of itself. Its caution, its suspicious approach to anything unknown or unrecognized, its tenacity on life, its habit of always falling on its feet and thus escaping bodily injury, all serve to lengthen its spell of life. Hence the nine lives.

Cat may look at a King. Is best explained by the Scottish proverb: "A man's a man for 'a that." The phrase was popularized by a political pamphlet with that title in 1652.

Grin like a Cheshire Cat. The origin is believed to be from the custom of selling cheese in Cheshire in the form of a cat, made in a mould. The cat was invariably shown grinning.

Cat out of the bag, To let. At country fairs in olden England, sucking-pigs were sold. The habit developed of fastening the pig in a bag, or sack (poke), in order that the purchaser could take away his purchase in safety, but tricksters sprang up. They brought their bags tied up, with a cat inside in place of the expected sucking-pig. The unwary buyer went off with his "pig in a poke"; but the more wary insisted on opening the wrapping and inspecting his pig. He thus "let the cat out of the bag."

Cat and Fiddle. This popular name for a public-house is a corruption of *Caton le fidele*, a supposed reference to one Caton, an English Governor of Calais. But there is no trace of any such person.

Cat and Mouse Act. During the years round about 1913, when women were engaging in scenes of violence to gain the suffrage, a number of their leaders were imprisoned. They went on hunger strike, with the idea of so reducing themselves to a state of physical exhaustion that the authorities would be compelled to release them or let them die. The ruse succeeded; the women were released, but as soon as they had recovered in health they were re-arrested to undergo the remainder of the sentence. The act, which was not much of a success, was called the Cat and Mouse Act.

To fight like Kilkenny Cats. To fight with determination to the bitter end. The probable origin lies in the bitter struggle between the municipalities of Kilkenny and Irishtown over the question of their individual boundaries in the seventeenth century, which left both of them impoverished. There is, however, a story of the Rebellion of 1798, when soldiers garrisoned in Kilkenny tied two cats together by their tails and flung them across a line to fight each other for freedom. An officer was seen approaching, and one of the men released the cats by cutting through their tied tails. He explained the possession of the bleeding tails by "explaining" that two Kilkenny cats had fought and devoured each other, leaving only the remnants of their tails, which he produced.

Cat. "*Not enough room to swing a cat in.*" The reference may be to the old days of flogging in the Navy, when a man was taken on to the deck for the punishment, there being not room enough in the confined space below for the swing of the whip (cat o' nine tails), but we like better, and think more probable, the explanation that "cat" is a corruption of "cot." A sailor spending a night ashore was given a room in a boarding-house which was so small that, as he explained to his shipmates next day, there was not enough room to swing a cat in. The point of the story is that a sailor's hammock, which is swung, was called in those days his "cot."

Cat and Kittens. The origin of this public-house sign lies in the pots from which beer was drunk. There was a variety of sizes in pewter. The largest was referred to as the "cat," and the reducing pots as the "kittens."

Catchpenny. Something of little value except to secure a quick sale. The word is a corruption of "Catnach Penny." James Catnach did a thriving business selling "dying speeches" of famous and notorious men, and also printed reams of "topic-of-the-moment" songs at his printing works in Seven Dials, London. These were hawked round the streets at the price of one penny each. Usually the sellers of the catnach-pennies were called "chanter coves" because they sang, or chanted, the words in order to make their sales.

Caterpillar Club. A club, in name only, for airmen. The qualification is that a man must have made a parachute descent from a disabled machine. Practice jumps do not qualify. The badge of membership is a small golden caterpillar.

Catgut. Is not anything of the kind. Strings for musical instruments are made from the intestines of various animals (particularly sheep), but NEVER from cats. How the term catgut grew up is not known—unless it was in comment on the wails that come from the strings in the hands of any but an accomplished player.

Cat o' Nine Tails. It is said that the reason for the nine throngs is the belief that castigation by a trinity of trinities would be more sacred and efficacious than one with any other number. The "cat" origin is obvious; the marks made on the flesh by the thongs represent the scratches which a cat's claws might make. The "cat," however, has not always had nine tails. Lilburn, in 1637, says Dr. Brewer, was scourged with a whip having only three lashes. He received a lash every three paces between the Fleet and Old Palace Yard. Sixty thousand stripes are said to have been inflicted.

Cat's Paw. *To be made a cat's paw of.* To be the tool of a schemer. An allusion to the fable of the monkey who, wanting to get some roast chestnuts out of the fire, persuaded a cat to allow him to use her paw for the purpose.

Caucus. A meeting of politicians to debate on the claims of candidates for positions in the party leadership. The word came from America, and its origin is to be found in the native Indian *cau-cau-as-a*, meaning one who advises.

Cenotaph. The name is derived from the Greek *kenos*, empty, and *taphos*, a tomb, and means a monument of death in memory of a person buried in another place. The British Cenotaph in Whitehall, London, in memory of the fallen in the 1914-18 war, was dedicated on Armistice Day (11th November), 1920.

Centre of England. The reputed centre of England is Meridan Cross, between Birmingham and Coventry. It is roughtly eighty miles from the Wash, the Irish Sea, and the Bristol Channel.

Cess. "*Bad cess to him.*" The word cess means a tax; a contraction of assessment. It is also a contraction of success. Bad cess to him may mean either "bad success," i.e., ill-fortune;

or it may mean in a financial sense, bad assessment to him, i.e., may he have to pay more than he really owes.

C'est Magnifique, mais ce n'est pas la guerre. Criticism passed by the French General Bosquet to Mr. A. H. Layard on the charge of the Light Brigade, at Balaclava (25th October, 1854).

Chaff. Chaff is what is left from wheat after it has been thrashed. In the Midland counties of Leicestershire and Nottinghamshire it was the custom in country villages for neighbours to deposit a bagful of chaff outside the house of a man who ill-treated his wife. The insinuation was, of course, that thrashing was done inside. There is, however, another meaning of chaff; to irritate. This is derived from *chafe*, to chafe, to make it inflamed or hot with friction.

You can't catch an old bird with Chaff. An allusion to the practice of scattering chaff instead of seed as a trap to attract birds.

Chalk it up. The custom is still maintained in many country village public-houses of chalking up drinks supplied on credit on a slate kept in the bar.

Chalks. *To beat a person by long chalks.* An allusion to the old days when marks of merit were chalked up. The longer the chalk mark, the greater the merit.

Chancellor, The Lord. Meant, originally, a man at a lattice fence, from the Latin *Cancelli*, lattice-work, and *cancellus*, a grating. In the Roman Empire, a Chancellor was a low rank officer stationed at a fence of lattice-work in the courts to introduce such people as were entitled to pass inside. Later, in the Eastern Empire the Chancellor became a secretary who sat *inside* the lattice to write. It is interesting to note that the lattice bars persist in the courts to-day.

Chanter Cove. *See* "Catch-penny."

Chap. *A Good Chap.* Short for chap man, one who sold goods in a cheap market. *See* "Cheap."

Chapel. Printers may like to know the origin of this name for their meetings. The first printing press set up in England was that by Caxton *in a disused chapel of Westminster Abbey.*

Charity Begins at Home. There are few saws older than this one. Theocritus, the Greek pastoral poet (310-265 B.C.) used it.

Charlatan. Although it may not be the true origin, to the following story, told by Dr. Brewer on many occasions, is probably due the popularizing of the word for a quack: A. M. Latan, a famous quack dentist, used to tour Paris in a magnificent car, in which he had a travelling dispensary. A man blowing a horn went ahead to announce his approach. Sightseers used to cry out in delight, "*Voila, le char de Latan.*" Dr. Brewer describes how, on many occasions, he thus saw M. Latan, dressed in a long robe, with a variety of headgear, including a feathered hat and a brass helmet. The probability is, however, that M. Latan had assumed that name in a fit of mischievous humour to rhyme with his char (car), for the Italian word *ciarlatano* for a quack had long been in existence.

Charley More. The Navy's synonym for everything that is upright, honest and reasonable. As long ago as 1840 a Maltese publican of that name had a huge sign-board over his house of refreshment, on which was flamboyantly inscribed: "Charley More—the Fair Thing." It caught the eyes of Naval men, and the name was admitted into their vocabulary as the pinnacle of truth and integrity. "Come on, act Charley More," was an appeal to a man's sense of fair play.

Cheap. *To pay a low price.* The interest in this word lies in the large number of words and place-names associated with it. A chap-man was an itinerant seller who peddled a stock of cheap goods (and, incidentally, gave us the surname Chapman). "Chop and change" comes from the same source, meaning continually to reduce the first price demanded. Cheapside and Eastcheap in London reveal their origin in the word; and Chipping, as in Chipping Norton, and Chep-stow, are similarly derived. The word arose from the Sanscrit *kupa*, the beam of a balance.

Cheer-io. A popular parting greeting. One suggested origin is that it comes from the days of Sedan chairs, when a departing guest would call "chair-oh" in the same way that we now call taxi. But why the break of more than a hundred years in between? Its probable definition is the phrase "Good Cheer," meaning good health.

Cheese It! To tell someone jeeringly that what is being told is not true. This, again, is a corruption of the original remark, "Choose it better," or "You cannot expect us to believe that."

Chequers. Popular name for a public-house. Is not, as so often stated, derived from the presence in the house, in olden times, of boards for the playing of the game checkers. In early times payment of doles and other local taxes used to be made at certain stated public-houses, the landlord of which provided a chequer-board for the tallying. Such houses carried a sign of a chequer-board as an intimation that the dues could be paid there. Earlier, however, the name was given to houses in recognition that they were licensed to sell liquor, chequers being the arms of the Fitzwarren's who, in the days of the Henry's, was vested with the power of issuing licences to publicans.

Chess. The suggested origins of the game are legion. China, Persia and India have all been mentioned as the original home. The antiquity of the game has been put so far back as five thousand years. Dr. Brewer states that the word chess is the modern English representative of the Persian *shar* (King), and makes the call *check-mate* to be a translation of the Persian *shar mat*, "the King is dead." Perhaps the more reliable authority, however, is Van der Linde, whose book is regarded as the final word on the game. His opinion, after a lifetime spent in tracing the beginning of the game, is that it originated with the Buddhists in India not earlier than the third century A.D. He traces the word *Chess* to the Hindustani *chaturanga*, i.e., the four *angas*, or members, of an army—elephants, horses, chariots and foot soldiers. The name, he thinks, was corrupted by the Persians into *chatrang*, by the Arabs, subsequently, into *shatrang*, from which the French again corrupted it into *eschecs*. The English translated it to *checks*, and so it became chess. The names "rook" and "pawn" are both of Hindu origin, "rook" being the Hindu *rat'h*, an armed chariot, and "pawn" the Hindu *peon*, an attendant.

Chestnut. An old and often-told story. The tale goes that Edward Abbey, the painter, regularly told a story about a man who started a chestnut farm, but made no money out of it because he always gave the chestnuts away. Abbey invariably began the story differently on each occasion that he essayed to tell it, but his hearers (after some experience) invariably recognized it before he had gone far in the telling and interrupted the narration with a shout of "Chestnuts"!

Chicken. *Don't count your chickens before they are hatched.* The origin is one of Æsop's fables. A market woman was telling how she would get so much for her eggs. With the money she would buy a goose which, in turn, would provide her with enough money to get a cow, etc., etc. But in her excitement she dropped the basket of eggs and broke them.

Children. *Three hundred and sixty-five at a birth.* In an abbey near The Hague, Holland, is a plaque bearing the following inscription: "Margaret, daughter of the Illustrious Lord Florent,

Count of Holland, and of Mathilde, daughter of Henri, Duke of Brabant, sister of William, King of Germany, being 42 years of age, was delivered on the Friday before Easter, at nine o'clock in the morning, in the year 1276, of 365 babes, male and female which, in the presence of several Lords and Gentlemen were arranged in front of the font and were all baptised by a Bishop. The males were all called Jean and the females Elizabeth. All died soon after, as did the mother, and all were buried in the one sepulchre."

Doctor Brewer, referring to the births as a legend, tells the following story : "It is said that the Countess of Henneburg accused a beggar of adultery because she carried twins. Whereupon the beggar prayed that the Countess might carry as many children as there are days in the year."

The Babes in the Wood. The origin of this very popular pantomime story is said to be laid in Wayland, Norfolk. The Squire of Wayland died, leaving his little son and daughter in the care of their uncle, his wife's brother. If the children died first, the uncle was to inherit their fortune. The uncle hired two robbers to murder the children. One of the men, stricken by remorse at the sight of the children, killed his fellow, but left the children in the wood, where during the night they died, and a robin covered them over with leaves. After heavy misfortunes, the uncle died in prison. The story of the plot became known, it is stated, when the robber was apprehended for highway robbery and confessed to taking part in the plot against the children.

Chiltern Hundreds, The Steward of. A Member of Parliament cannot resign his seat. But he cannot hold an office of profit under the Crown, and still retain a seat in the House of Commons. The Chiltern Hundreds provides him with the way out.

The Chiltern Hundreds are a small range of beech-covered hill, in Buckinghamshire. (*Note.—See* "Hundred.") Named individually, they are the Hundred of Stoke, of Desborough, and of Burnham. Because they were the haunt of robbers in earlier times, a Steward was appointed by the Crown to patrol and guard the Hundreds. He became a paid servant of the Crown. The office to-day is a purely nominal one, carrying the salary of one guinea. But being an office of profit, under the Crown, it deprives any M.P. who applies for, and receives the Stewardship, from sitting any longer in the House. The procedure of applying for the Stewardship of the Chiltern Hundreds by M.P.'s anxious to vacate their constituency dates from 1740.

Chindits. During the early part of 1944, during the war against the Japanese in Burma, General Wingate raised and trained a corps of men in jungle fighting. The men were trained on Commando lines, with such variations as were needed for fighting in the jungle, and particularly the kind of fighting needed against the Japanese. These Commandos called themselves "Chindits," from the Burmese *Chindits*—statues, half lion and half griffin, which guard the Burmese temples and pagodas. The Burmese name for the mythical animal is Chinthey.

Chip of Bede's Chair in her Pouch. Apperson, in his "Proverbs," states that it has been a custom from time immemorable for the ladies, immediately after the conclusion of the marriage ceremony (before Hymen's altar in Jarrow Church), to proceed to the vestry and cut a chip off Bede's chair, to ensure their fruitfulness. The saying is generally applied to those females who show signs of fecundity rather early after entering into the state of matrimony.

Chip of the old Block. The phrase, meaning a worthy son of his father, was first used in this sense by Burke, in a reference in the House of Commons to Pitt, the Younger. It is, of course, associated with the "family tree."

Chivy. To chivy somebody. The word is merely a corruption of chase.

Choice. *To have Hobson's Choice.* The *Spectator* has given the authentic origin of this everyday cliche : "Tobias Hobson was an inn-keeper and carrier at Cambridge in the seventeenth century. He kept a stable of forty good horses always ready and fit for travelling ; but when a man came for a horse he was led to the stable where, although there was great choice, he was obliged to take that horse which stood nearest to the stable door, so that every customer was alike well served according to his chance and every horse ridden with the same justice." If the prospective hirer objected to the horse nearest the stable door, he was met with the uncompromising retort : "It's that or none."

Choke him off. Is a phrase which came from the recognized practice of gripping a dog by the throat in order to make him release his hold.

Christmas. We have on many occasions been asked why Christmas is regarded as a season for jollification and the giving of presents. That part of our celebration of Christmas has nothing whatever to do with the birth of Christ ; it is, in fact, a revival of the old Pagan feasts which were enacted many generations before Christianity. Most of the Feasts of the Church to-day came from these Pagan ages. For instance, Easter coincides with the Paschal Egg and the Mundane Egg of the Heathen days, celebration of the birth of new life in the earth. Now, in these old Pagan days feasts were part of the social life of the people, to which they looked forward with eagerness. When Christianity began to be preached as a doctrine, its teachers, wise in their generation, realized that they would have little chance of attracting the people to Christianity if they insisted that they must no longer observe the old Pagan Feasts. So they adapted the feasts to Christianity, at the same times of the year. The Pagans held the great feast of Saturn round about 25th December. It was one of the greatest events, when there was feasting, games and general enjoyment, called Saturnalia. The Christian leaders of those early days appropriated the feast for their converts, altered the worst features of it, and allowed their people to share in, but not of, the old custom. Actually, there is no absolute record of the date of the birth of Christ, though August is a generally accepted time ; but there are allusions by St. Chrysostom and St. Cyprian, and other early Christian writers, to the appropriateness of celebrating the birth of the Son of Righteousness at the time of the Solar, or Saturn festival, and thus adapting the Pagan feast to Christian usage.

Christmas Box. *See* "Boxing Day."

Christmas Card. The first Christmas Card is generally held to have been designed by J. C. Horsley, R.A., in the year 1843. It depicted, in colours, a party of grown-ups and children with glasses of wine raised in greeting, over the words, "A Merry Christmas and a Happy New Year to You." Still preserved, it bears the inscription : "James Peters, wife and family, from John Washbourn and his wife of 22, Theberton Street, Islington (London)." It is dated 23rd December.

Christmas Stockings. Hardly a house in Britain or America but puts up the children's stockings by the side of the chimney for Father Christmas, or Santa Claus, on Christmas Eve ; and generations of children have gone eagerly to them on Christmas morning to see what Santa Claus has deposited in them.

Yet the practice has nothing whatever to do with Christmas, or Christian festival. Its only connection is with Santa Claus, or, to give the name its correct appellation, Saint Nicholas. The saint, who liked to do good by stealth, heard that three lovely sisters, who lived in a poor cottage on the outskirts of a town, were so destitute that if they wanted to continue living at all, a life of shame was the only alternative. Accordingly, the good saint made his way to their home one night, and threw a gift of three gold pieces through the smoke-hole of the cottage. (There were, of course, no chimneys, as we know them, in those days. The smoke went out through a hole cut in the roof.)

Instead of the gold pieces falling on the hearth, as he had expected, they fell into the stockings of the girls, which had been hung up over the fire to dry, after washing. Hence, when the tale became known, the custom of hanging up stockings over the fire—in hopes; and Christmas Day was chosen for the doing, because it was Saint Nicholas's day.

Hence, also, the idea that Santa Claus comes down the chimney.

Christmas Trees came to us from Germany. They are probably related to the custom of the ancient Egyptians who, at the Winter Solstice, carried palm branches containing twelve leaves, symbol of the ending of the twelve months.

Christy Minstrels. Were so-called after Charles Christy, an American who introduced negro minstrel entertainment into England.

Church Ale. Specifically, the ale brewed by churchwardens for merry-making on the village green at Whitsuntide. Later, the assembly and merry-making itself came to be styled "The Church Ale."

Cider. It may come as a shock to teetotallers to learn that the word *cider* comes from the Hebrew *shekar*, through the Greek *sikera* and the Latin *sicera*, all signifying strong drink. It may not generally be known, either, that the name has appeared in one edition of the Bible. Wickliffe's Bible records *Luke* i, 15, in the following words: "He schal not drynke wyn and sydir." The Authorized rendering is: "He . . . shall drink neither wine nor strong drink."

Cigarette. The cigarette, as distinct from the cigar, is said to have been originated by artillerymen of Suleinan Bey in 1799 at the Siege of Acre. The big pipe which supplied the men with tobacco was destroyed by a shot. One of the men, famishing for a smoke, conceived the idea of rolling some tobacco in Indian paper which he was using for making gunpowder spills. The men liked the cigarette and continued with it after the siege. The first cigarette factory of any importance was established in St. Petersburg (now Leningrad) in 1850.

Cigar. Is derived from the Spanish *cigarro*, which was the original name of a brand of Cuban tobacco.

City. In Biblical days a city meant a town surrounded with a wall, having gates. Executions or burials were never allowed in the city precincts. Christ's Cross was erected, as the hymn says, "on a green hill *outside* ("without") the city wall." In Britain a city was originally a town having a cathedral, but of late years many towns have been created cities by reason of their commercial importance.

City of Magnificent Distances. Washington, U.S.A., because of its wide streets and avenues.

City of Palaces. Calcutta, India.

City of Saints. Montreal, Canada. All its streets are named after saints.

City of the Golden Gate. San Francisco.

City of the Seven Hills. Rome. Built on the seven hills of Aventine, Caelian, Capitoline, Esquiline, Palatine and Viminal.

City of the Tribes. Galway. It was the home of the thirteen tribes, or chief families, when they settled there with Richard de Burgh, in 1232.

City Golgotha. *Golgotha* is Hebrew for "the place of skulls." Because the heads of executed rebels were spiked on its top, Old Temple Bar, in the City of London, was called the City Golgotha.

Clam. *Close as a clam.* Anyone who has tried to open one of these bivalve molluscs will not need telling the meaning of this phrase.

Clap-trap. This word, in general use for an artifice to gain popularity or applause, has its origin in the theatre, where it was coined in description of the methods of Thomas Cobham, an actor. "Notes and Queries" quotes: "This actor . . . when approaching a *clap-trap*, gives such note of preparation that they must indeed be barren spectators who do not preceive that there is something coming." *See* "Claque," below.

Claque. Was the name given to a set of men, called *claquers*, distributed through a theatre audience and hired to applaud the piece or the actors, or any particular actor who had paid for their services. It first became a permanent system, openly organized in Paris in 1820, when M. Sauton established a business in the French capital to ensure the success of dramatic pieces. The manager of any theatre could order the number of claquers he required. They were duly coached in the play to be presented in order that the men might know at which of the jokes to laugh uproariously, and the women the sentimental parts at which to sob into their handkerchiefs. Although the British theatre has not adopted generally the claque system, there are in some instances, where a play is not doing too well, "friends of the house" who start applause at the end of a scene, or act.

Clark; Nobby Clarke. Every Clarke is nicknamed "Nobby." As in the case of "Nosey" Parker, there is no authentic origin. It is, however, definitely of Army beginning. Mr. C. O'Driscoll, an authority on Service slang, states: "Clarke was originally clerk. Clerks of the early part of last century were indigent and shabby genteel. They were expected to dress well on a starvation wage. They, however, tried to raise their social prestige by putting on airs; and to such an extent were they successful that they came to be regarded as 'nobs' (i.e., toffs) and were referred to as 'nobby clerks.' Again, 'nob' as a synonym for the 'upper ten' comes from University reference books, where graduates of high social rank have 'nob' (short for nobility) after their names to indicate that they are of noble blood."

Cleaned Out. To have one's pockets emptied of money. The allusion is to a saucepan, or other kitchen utensil, which is cleaned out of its contents after use.

Cleopatra's Needle. The obelisk on the Embankment, in London, which, though it is difficult to believe, is of *pink* stone. It has nothing whatever to do with Cleopatra. Hieroglyphics carved on it tell that it was erected by Thotmes III, a Pharoah of the eighteenth Dynasty, centuries before Cleopatra. It was reared in Heliopolis and moved thence to Alexandria round about the first decade B.C. The Needle was brought from Alexandria to London in 1878. Its fellow is in Central Park, New York.

Cleopatra's Nose. Blaise Pascall said: "If the nose of Cleopatra had been shorter the whole face of the earth would have been changed." The reference is to the beauty of Cleopatra which brought about the enslavement first of Cæsar and then Antony, with its subsequent effects on history.

Cleopatra's Pearl. The story goes that at a banquet given by Cleopatra to Antony, the latter expressed amazement at the costliness of the repast and surroundings. Cleopatra, taking a pearl eardrop, placed it in a glass of vinegar, and after it had dissolved drank to the health of her guest, with the words : " My draft to Antony shall far exceed it " (the costliness of the banquet). The story is a fable. Vinegar would not dissolve a pearl, and anything which would do so would also dissolve the throat of the person drinking it.

A similar story is told of Sir Thomas Gresham and Queen Elizabeth.

Clerkenwell. A London borough. When Clerkenwell was a small village, which sprang up round the Priory of St. John of Jerusalem round about 1100, it possessed a holy well. Later, round this well the parish clerks of London gathered on Church festival days to perform a Miracle Play. Hence, *Clerk*-en-*well*.

Client. Meaning a customer, has an interesting origin. In ancient Rome a *client* was a plebian under the patronage of a patrician. He performed certain services for his patron, who was thereby obliged to protect his life and interests.

Clock. The first clock, as we know clocks, is believed to have been invented by Pope Sylvester II in A.D. 996. Before then time was measured by water-clocks, sand-clocks, candles measured in lengths, and by hour glasses. Clock-making first took practical shape in Germany. About 1364 Charles V of France summoned Henry de Vick from Germany to make and fit up a turret clock at his palace in Paris.

Alarm Clock. The first alarm clock was invented by Plato (born 42 B.C.). He fitted a siphon to a water-clock. When the water was level with the top of the siphon it rushed down the tube so fast that the compressed air was pushed out with a loud whistle. And that was how Plato summoned his students to their studies at four o'clock in the morning.

" *Parliament Clocks.*" In 1797 a tax upon clocks of 5s. a year, and 7s. 6d. on watches, was imposed by Act of Parliament. So unpopular was it that it was short-lived, being repealed in 1798 after the demand for time-pieces had been reduced by more than half. In the meantime obliging tavern-keepers, anticipating the scarcity of timekeepers among their customers, put up cheaply-made clocks on the walls of their bars for the benefit of their customers. These were known as " Act of Parliament " clocks. They had usually a large dial of wood painted black, with gilt figures (says F. J. Britten in the " Watch and Clock-makers' Handbook "). The face was not glass-enclosed.

Clogs to Clogs. An old Lancashire saying runs, " Clogs to Clogs is only Three Generations," meaning that however rich a poor Lancashire man may become, his great-grandson will fall back into poverty and clogs.

Clothes-horse. In the course of the past three years the author has received no fewer than sixty requests to explain the meaning, and the origin, of this word. Why, it is asked, a " horse " ? This description of a very useful piece of kitchen furniture has nothing whatever to do with the now less common quadruped. The animal is not the only horse. One meaning of the word horse is " that by which something is supported. When a publican places his barrels of beer on a staging in his cellar for tapping, he " horses up the barrels." A horse, too, is the sloping table above a flat-bed printing machine, on which pressmen place their sheets of paper preparatory to printing. Again, " horse " is the name which, from early sailing days, has been given to the rope which supports sailors when they loosen reef or furl sails. Thus, the meaning of the term horse in clothes-horse is something by which clothes are supported, as a clothes-line is a line on which clothes are supported. In Yorkshire the clothes-horse goes by the name of " Winter-'edge," derived from the Yorkshire rural habit of laying clothes to dry on hedges in Summer. In Winter the hedge is brought inside, as it were, hence Winter-'edge.

Clover. To be in clover ; in luck. The allusion is to cattle feeding in a field of clover—the best pasturage known for cattle.

Club. The origin of the word is doubtful. It may be from the old German word *klimpfen*, to press together, or from another German word *gelubde*, a sacred vow. Both words, however, have a joint general meaning of " clump-ing " together.

One of the earliest London clubs was that established in the seventeenth century at the Mermaid Tavern, Friday Street, which included among its members Shakespeare, Sir Walter Raleigh, Beaumont and Fletcher.

Clue. In mediæval English *clewe* was a ball of thread. In Anglo-Saxon the word was *cleowen*. Bacon, in his " Politica Fables," wrote : " He (Theseus) formed the ingenious device of his clue which led directly through all the windings of the Labrynth." The only way of finding the way out of the Labrynth of Cretan was by following a skein of thread.

Coals, Called over. *See* " Called over the coals."

Coal-pits. The first recorded coal mine in Britain is lost in antiquity. The earliest records the Mining Association can trace is a licence granted by Henry III to the " good men " of Newcastle to dig coals in the Castlegarth. In 1291 there is mention of a coal mine at Pittencrief, Fifeshire. But there is little doubt that there were much earlier coal diggings than either of these.

Coast is Clear. The phrase comes from the olden smuggling days. Its meaning is thus obvious. The coast was clear of coastguards and the smugglers could land their brandy and rich silks in safety.

Coat Buttons. The origin of men's coats buttoning left over right, and a woman's right over left, goes back to the days when swords were commonly worn. A gentleman offered his left arm to a lady, thus leaving his right arm free to defend her in case of attack. She put her right arm through his left arm, and each placed the free arm into the openings of their coats for warmth. This, also, is the explanation of why a bridegroom leaves the church after his wedding with his bride on his left arm—again to defend her from attack by possible jealous rivals.

Coat of Arms. During the days of Chivalry when a Knight was encased in his armour the only means of identifying him was by the embroidered design of his armorial bearings on the sleeveless coat that he wore in the lists at tournaments. In warfare, however, the coat was not worn, but he was known to his comrades by a device on the *crest* of his helmet. Thus we get the coat of arms and the crest of noble families of the present day.

Cobweb. Is so-called to-day because a " cob " or " cop " is the old English word for a spider, dating back to the Anglo-Saxon *coppa*.

Cockade. From the party badge displayed on a cocked hat. *See* " Knocked into a Cocked Hat."

Cock-a-Hoop. Comes from the old custom of taking the *cock* (the spigot) out of the barrel and setting it on the *hoop* before commencing a drinking bout.

Cock a'Hoop, To set. The phrase seems to have arisen in a carousing connection. Cock on hoop, the cock, or spigot, being laid on the hoop, and the barrel of ale stunn'd—that is, drank out without intermission at the height of the carousal.

Cock-and-Bull-Story. After the old fables in which cocks, bulls and other animals were depicted as talking in the language of humans.

Cockney. The name given to a person born in London within the sound of Bow Bells. Johnson (not Dr. Johnson), has given a remarkable "origin" of the word which, he said, came from "cockayne," a fool's paradise where there is nothing but eating and drinking, described in a satire poem of the thirteenth century. He added: "The word had reference to London, where the conduits on occasion ran with wine, and good living fell to the lot of men." We cannot stomach this. Dr. Brewer asserts the origin as the mediæval *cokeney*, a cock's egg, i.e., a small egg with no yoke occasionally laid by hens as their first or last egg, and hence applied to a foolish child. From this the word came to signify among country people (then the majority of the population of the country) foolish people, and especially London people who were wholly ignorant of country life, animals, sports, and so on. We do not like this explanation much better than the first one; but there is no other extant.

Cock - of - the - North. Should properly be applied only in reference to George, Fifth Duke of Gordon, who raised the Gordon Highlanders in 1795.

Cock of the Walk. The leading spirit. The place where fowls are kept is called the walk. Should there be more than one cock in the confined space, they will fight for the supremacy of the domain.

Cocks, Fighting. *To live like fighting cocks.* To have the best of everything. In the days of the cock pits, the fighting-cock were highly fed to increase their fighting stamina and pugnacity.

Cockpit (of battle). Was derived from the hollowed pits in which game cocks were pitted against each other in the days when cock-fighting was a popular British sport.

Cocktail. A story was current in America (home of the cocktail) not long ago that an Aztec noble sent a drink made by him from the cactus plant to the Emperor by the hand of his daughter, Xochitl. The Emperor tried it, liked it, gulped it down—and married the maker's daughter. He named the drink Octel. This was, of course, a few generations before the dawn of the United States. When (the tale proceeds) soldiers of the American army invaded Mexico under General Scott, they tasted the drink, brought it back to America, and renamed Octel, cocktail. We fear the story is a pleasant invention.

Cocoa, Coco-nut. When used to denote the beverage *cocoa* is a corruption of *cacao*, adopted from the Mexican *cacautl*. In his "Conquest of Peru," Prescott states that as the followers of Pizarro sailed along the Pacific coast they saw the lower slopes of the hills covered with plantations of cacao. Referring to the use of chocolate in Mexico, he says that the Emperor Montezuma was so fond of it that fifty jars a day were prepared for his consumption. The botanical name of the plant is *Theobroma*, derived from the Greek, and meaning "god-plant."

The name for the coco-nut is a contraction of the Portuguese *macoco*, a kind of monkey, to the face of which the three marks at the end of the coco-nut bear some resemblance.

Coffee. The origin is the Arabic *gahwah*. In Turkish, it is pronounced *kahveh*. It is said by Arabic lexicographers to have meant, originally, a drink of wine, and to be a derivative of a verb-root, *gahiva*, meaning "to have no appetite." The origin widely given that the drink first came from Kaffa, in the South Abyssinia highlands, where the plant appears to be native, is not correct. That berry is called in Shoa, "bun."

Coffin. This is one of the most curious words in the language from an etymological point of view. Correctly speaking, it means a basket, from the Greek *kophinos*. It had nothing whatever to do with death or bodies. The Greeks used to cremate their dead, or bury them in a triangular urn of burnt clay which took the dead in a sitting-up position. There was, however, a Middle English word, *coffer*, which meant to deposit or lay up in a coffer, and in Piers' Plowman Crede there appears the sentence, "cefren it fast." It is likely that our coffin is a corruption of to coffer, i.e., lay up, a body.

Coger. We now refer to a person as "an old coger," meaning he is a nuisance, or curmudgeon. But the word comes from the Latin *cogito*, to think. There was for many years a celebrated Cogers Club in Salisbury Court, London, all the members being well-known literary or artistic men.

Cold as Charity. Theodore Hook used the expression a century ago. But *Matthew* xxiv, 12, in a translation of 1582, says "Notes and Queries," reads: "The charitie of many shall wax cold."

Cold Shoulder, To give the. When an unexpected visitor is a welcome one, the hostess puts herself to some trouble to prepare a dainty meal for the guest who has made a journey to visit her. But where the visitor is not particularly welcome and was not to be encouraged to pay similar visits in the future, cold meat, the remains of the shoulder which formed the last meal, is usually brought out. To be given the cold shoulder was a pretty plain hint that you were not encouraged by your hostess.

Coln. This suffix to many English place-names is a derivative of the Latin *colonia*, a colony. It is seen in Lincoln, Cologne, and Colne (Essex).

Come and take them. When you throw out this challenge you may not be aware that you are quoting the Classics. When Xerxes sent a message to Thermopylæ, "Go, tell these madmen to deliver up their arms," Leonidas, King of Sparta, replied, "Go tell Xerxes to come and take them."

Comedy. The origin of what we now call comedy is interesting. It was born in the village songs during merry-makings. The word is the Greek *kome-ode*. The Greeks held festal processions in honour of Dionysos in the suburbs of cities. These were called *komoi*, or village revels. An *ode* was generally sung. These odes gave birth to the Greek Drama.

Come Inside! Scornful remark made to a stupid person or one making an exaggerated statement. The reference is to a cartoon which appeared in *Punch*. A lunatic, looking over the asylum wall, had noted a fisherman sitting on the banks of a stream.

"Been there long?" he asked.
"All day."
"Caught anything?"
"No."
"Come inside!"

Come up to Scratch. In the old prize-fighting days a line was scratched out on the ground in the centre of the fighting ring, and the combatants had each to toe this with the left foot.

Common (people). There is nothing low or inferior about this phrase. The word is composed of the Latin *com*, together, and *munis*, serving.

Compass, The Mariner's. The compass, almost in the form in which it is to-day, was invented by the Chinese Emperor Ho-Ang-Ti, about 2634 B.C. It was, however, unknown in Europe until the twelfth century.

Compass, To box the. *See* "Box the Compass."

Con Amore. Italian words meaning for, or with, love. Used in England in the sense of "free." If you do something for someone "con amore," you do it without payment, "for love."

Concert pitch. In concert playing in England, the piano, as well as other instruments, is tuned slightly higher than the usual playing key. Thus, for a man to be at concert pitch means that he is tuned to perfection.

Conjuring cap. "I must put on my conjuring cap." The King of Sweden, in 1560-1577, was an addict of magic and sported an "enchanted cap" by which he pretended (says Brewer) to exercise power over the weather. His people used to say of storms: "The King has got on his conjuring cap."

Conk. The word conk, for nose, comes from the spouting fountain, the concha of the Romans.

Considering cap. "I must put on my considering cap" (or "thinking cap"). An allusion to the days when our judges donned a cap before passing sentence. It is now confined only to the black cap when passing sentence of death.

Constant Dropping wears away a Stone. The first mention of this phrase occurs in a fragment of Choerilus where it appears in the Greek.

Constitution Hill. A popular park thoroughfare leading to Buckingham Palace was so named because the great Duke of Buckingham, who built Buckingham House in 1703 and lived there, took his daily constitution along the road. (Buckingham Palace was built on the site of Buckingham House by George IV in 1825.)

Contemptibles, The Old. The original British Expeditionary Force of 160,000 men that left England for the Continent at the start of the 1914-18 War against Germany. In an Army Order given at Aix to his troops by Kaiser Wilhelm, the Emperor said: "It is my Royal and Imperial command that you . . . walk over General French's contemptible little army."

Coot. Bald as a coot. The coot's bill is straight and somewhat conical in shape. The base tends to push up the forehead and there dilates, forming a remarkable bare patch.

Copper - nosed Harry. When Henry VIII had spent his inheritance, he minted a very inferior silver coin. The copper alloy of the coin soon showed itself through the silver on the more prominent parts, particularly the nose of the face. It earned for Harry the nickname Copper-nose.

Copper. A policeman. One who cops. Is self-explanatory.

Cop, To. "*It's a fair cop.*" Cop, says Hotten, is derived from the Latin *capere*; but it is more likely to have come from the gypsy *kap* or *cop*, to take; or the Scottish *kep*, and Gaelic *clapan*.

"Corn in Egypt." A slang term for plenty. The allusion is to Egypt in the days of Genesis. Famine was haunting every country in proximity to Egypt; but Joseph, warned by God had, under Pharoah, stored vast supplies of corn in Egypt.

Corporation. Slang term for a man with a large paunch. Its origin is obscure; but it should be mentioned that the corporation of a town—the mayor, aldermen and councillors—were always supposed to be fat and prosperous from attending free banquets, and from "making a little" out of their inside knowledge as councillors.

Cosh. *To cosh him one.* A cosh was a stick, from the gypsy *kash*, wood in any form.

Cosmetics. Nobody can say when cosmetics as an aid to the beauty of women originated. They have been used in crude form from the very earliest of days. But it is probable that they had their origin in the East. Toilet articles have been found in the tombs of the ancient Pharoahs. In the British Museum are papyrii showing women having lumps of lard fixed to the tops of their heads. Their date is put at 1500 B.C. The ancient Egyptians were also the inventors of the artificial bath; their bathing was followed by the application of perfumed oils and unguents. Crude paints were also used by the Egyptian women; and this painting may be said to have reached its zenith in the days of Cleopatra, who was an adept at adding seduction to her beauty.

In 2 *Kings*, ix, 30, there is a reference to the make-up of Hebrew women: "When Jehu was come to Jezreel, Jezebel heard of it, and *she painted her face.*" In still later days Nero and his wife Poppæa, it is recorded, both used artificial aids to toilet—kohol for the eyelids, fucus (a kind of rouge), and barley-flour for the eradication of pimples.

In England, so great had become the use of cosmetics by women, that in 1770 a Bill was introduced into Parliament with the following drastic provision: "That all women of whatever age, rank, profession or degree, whether virgins, maids or widows, that shall from and after such Act, impose upon, seduce and betray into matrimony any of His Majesty's subjects by the scents, paints, cosmetic washes, artificial teeth, false hair, Spanish wool, iron stays, hoops, high-heeled shoes, bolstered hips, shall incur the penalty of the Law in force against Witchcraft and like misdemeanours, and that the marriage, upon conviction, shall stand null and void." It is not recorded whether any marriage was actually declared null and void by reason of any or all these "seductions."

Costermonger. Originally a seller of apples—from *costard*, a large, ribbed apple, and *monger* (Anglo-Saxon *mangian*) to trade.

Cotton. Was first brought to England from Cyprus and Smyrna in 1600, and made into fustians, dimities, etc. In 1697, two million pounds of cotton were imported for weft to work with linen warp as a domestic manufacture, the carding and spinning being done by children and women.

Court Cards. The word should be coat cards, from the heraldic devices shown on them.

Covent Garden. London's famous fruit and flower market, behind the Strand. The name is a corruption of Convent Garden. It was the garden and burial ground of, and attached to, Westminster Convent. It was turned into a market during the reign of Charles II. After the Dissolution, the area of Westminster Convent was given by the King to the Duke of Somerset. In 1552 it passed to the Earl of Bedford, and remained that family's property until, in 1914 the then Duke of Bedford sold it.

Coventrate, To. On the night of 14th-15th November, 1940, German bombers coming in wave after wave dropped thirty thousand incendiaries and many tons of high explosive on the Midlands' motor-manufacturing town. The famous cathedral, stores, cinemas and offices—in fact, the entire centre of the city, including almost the whole of the shopping centre—disappeared into a heap of debris. More than a thousand people lost their lives. Next day, the German radio put out a threat that they intended to "Coventrate" every industrial centre in Britain.

Coventry. *To be sent to Coventry.* To be banned, greeted with a chilly silence. The popular story is that the people of Coventry were at one time so hostile to soldiers that any woman seen talking to one was ostracized. Thus, any soldier unfortunate enough to be sent to Coventry was cut off from all friendly or social intercourse. But there is another, and perhaps more likely, version that Coventry was a Parliamentary stronghold in the Civil War, and troublesome Royalist prisoners were sent there for safe keeping.

Coventry, the name, is a corruption of Convent-town. The suffix *try* is Celtic for dwelling. Before the Reformation Coventry was far-famed for the number of its convents, or religious establishments.

Coventry, To. In 1670 ruffians waylaid Sir John Coventry, and his nose was slit as punishment for his criticism of the private life of Charles II. This led to an Act being passed against mutilation. The measure was called the Coventry Act.

Coward. Comes from the old French *couard*, through the Latin *cauda*, a tail. The phrase "to turn tail" is still used to express the action of a coward.

Coxcomb. A vain, empty-headed individual. The term comes from the cock's comb which was worn by the licensed Court jesters, because they were allowed to crow over their betters.

Crackers, Christmas, or Firework. The name is a corruption of *cracque*, the Norman description of "Greek Fire."

Cricket. Is first mentioned in England in the "Guild Merchant's Book of Guildford," dated 1598, where John Denwick is reported to have had a piece of land for fifty years where he and his "fellowes did play crickett." This would take the game back to the days of Henry VIII.

Cripplegate, the City district in London, gained its name from the large number of cripples who went there to beg—probably because it was one of the gates of the city.

Croesus, Rich as. Croesus was the King of Lydia (560-546 B.C.). So rich was he, and so powerful through his riches, that all the wise men of Ancient Greece came to his Court. His name, therefore, became proverbial for wealth.

Crop Clubs. When Mr. Pitt put a tax on hair powder, clubs were formed, called Crop Clubs, the object of which was to oblige every member to have his hair "cropped as close as the Duke of Bridgewater's old bay horses," thus evading the tax on the powder, since the powder was no longer needed.

Cross Keys. This name for a public-house is taken from the arms of the Archbishop of York.

Cross of Lorraine. Emblem of the Free, or Fighting, French during the second Great War. It was adopted by General de Gaulle, because the double cross was raised by Joan of Arc in her struggle to free France five centuries ago. It has been the historic symbol in France of resistance and fight for freedom.

Crow over him. A game fighting-cock always crowed over his vanquished rival in the cock-pit

Cubit. The old measure, so frequently mentioned in the Bible, comes from the Latin *cubitus*, a bend. The old cubit was the measure of the arm from the elbow to the tip of the second finger—from eighteen to twenty-two inches, according to the age of the individual.

Cup that cheers, but not inebriates. A transposition of lines first used by Cowper in "The Task," where he wrote :

"Let fall the curtains, wheel the sofa round,
And while the bubbling and loud hissing urn
Throws up a steamy column, and the cups
That cheer but not inebriate, wait on each.

Curry favour, To. To seek or gain favour by a display of kindliness or flattery. The term comes from the stable, and is a corruption of "to curry Favel." (*Curry*, mediæval English, to rub down.) Favel was the name of a horse in the French satire of the fourteenth century, "Roman de Fauvel," a kind of horse counterpart of Reynard the Fox.

Curse of Scotland. The card Nine of Diamonds is so-called because on the back of a card of this denomination the Duke of Cumberland (Bloody Duke) wrote the order for the massacre of Prince Charlie's men, wounded and prisoners, after the Battle of Culloden, in 1746. The phrase, however, was in use before that time in Scotland, it being recorded in Houston's *Memoirs* (1715-47) as applied to Lord Justice-Clerk Ormistone. He relates that when the card appeared from a pack it was referred to, also, as "The Justice Clerk."

Cut to the Quick. The quick of one's finger is the most sensitive to pain of any part of the body.

Cym. This Celtic word, frequently found at the end of place-names, means a cup-shaped depression in the hills. The English equivalent is *combe*, as Ilfracombe, Combe Martin.

D

Dab. "*He's a dab at it,*" meaning that he performs the job exceptionally well. The term is not slang, but a corruption of adept, from the Latin *adeptus*, past participle of *adipiscor—ad* to, *apiscor* attain.

But where the word dab is in the sense of dabbing a wound, the word is from Old Dutch *dabben* and Anglo-Saxon *dubben*, to strike. A man knighted by the application of a sword to his shoulders by the King is "dubbed a Knight."

Dachshund. The little dog so ungenerously maligned as a German dog, is so named because "badger-dog" in German is dachshund.

Daedalus. A Greek who built the Cretan Labyrnth. He is also said to have made himself wings which which he flew across the sea to Italy. What will probably interest more the ordinary citizen, however, is that he is said to have invented the saw, the auger, the gimlet and glue.

Daffodil. According to the legend, the daffodil was at first a white flower. Persephone, wearing a wreath of them in her hair while asleep, was captured by Pluto. At his touch the white flowers turned yellow. Since then the flowers have been planted as perpetual flowers for graves in Springtime.

Dagger. The dagger which appears in the Arms of the City of London commemorates the dagger with which Wat Tyler was slain by the then Lord Mayor of London, Sir William Walworth (1831).

Dagger in Parliament. During the French Revolution a dagger was thrown on the floor of the House of Commons by Edmund Burke, with reproachful and angry words against the French Jacobins. The effect was changed from the dramatic to the comic by E. Richard Sheridan, who exclaimed, quietly : "The gentleman has forgotten to bring the fork with him."

Dahlia. The popular garden flowering shrub was so named after Andrew Dahl, who introduced it into Europe from Mexico in 1784.

Dairy. Its use at the present time as a place in which milk is kept is not the original meaning. The word comes from the Anglo-Saxon *daege*, and the Middle English *dey*, meaning a maid-servant. The *-re* signifies the place where she carries out her work.

Daisy. "*Day's Eyes,*" from the fact that the flower folds up in the evening and re-opens at the dawn of day.

Dal. Appearing in place-names means a valley, or dale, from the Anglo-Saxon *del*. Arun-del and Lons-dale are examples.

Dalston. A London suburb. "Dales-town," which it was in the days when the North of London was pretty well wooded.

Dalton Bellropes, Like. It appears that after a series of vestry meetings by the good people of Dalton to consider the propriety of purchasing a new rope for the one and only bell of the parish, the churchwardens and ratepayers of the parish decided at last that the old one should be spliced.

Dam. "*Don't care a Damn.*" The phrase should be, "Don't care a Dam." A dam was an ancient Indian copper coin worth much less than half a farthing of English money. Not worth a dam, therefore, meant that it was of practically no value at all. Dr. Brewer, denying this origin, states that Goldsmith wrote that he did not care three damns ; and the Duke of Wellington commonly said that he did not care a twopenny damn. That may be so, but neither Goldsmith or the Duke were immune from misquoting.

Damask. That rich silk brocade comes to us, both in word and invention, from Damascus. There it was that damasks were made. They have become mostly, now, table linens with a woven design.

Damiens' Bed of Steel. For attempting the life of Louis XV, in 1757, Robert Damiens was chained to an iron bed that was heated, his right hand was burned in a slow fire, his flesh was torn with pincers, and molten lead and boiling oil poured into the wounds. Finally, he was pulled to pieces by wild horses.

Damn. Comes from the Latin *damnare*, to condemn. And damnare is derived from *damnum*, meaning a loss, a fine.

Damocles, The Sword of. Evil or misfortune hovering over one. Damocles was invited by Dionysius the Elder to test the felicity he (Damocles) so envied in his wealthy host. He was set down to a banquet of the richest viands. But over his head he saw a sword hanging by a single thread. Damocles, afraid to stir lest he should bring down the sword on top of him, found the banquet and the passing moments in luxury, a torture to him.

Dance. "*To dance attendance on.*" To be at someone's beck and call. The reference is to an old wedding custom where the bride, on her wedding night, had to dance with every guest, for fear of offending one of them. In the "State of Matrimony," 1543, appears the sentence: "Then must the poore bryde kepe foote with a dauncer, and refuse none, how scabbed, foule, droncken soever he be."

Dance, Vitus. *See* "Vitus, St."

Dandelion. It is not "dandy," but *dent-de-lion*, French for tooth of the lion, from the jagged, tooth-like edges of the leaves—like the teeth of a lion.

Dander. *To get one's dander up.* Various suggestions have been made as to the origin of the word, the most humorous being that it has something to do with dandruff. The most likely source is the *dander* of the West Indies, where dander was a ferment used in the preparation of molasses. If to get your dander up is not to be in a state of ferment, then we do not know the meaning of the word.

Dandy, for a fop, comes from the German *tandeln*, the same root as dandle, to play with, a toy. The use of the word for a fop dates from 1816.

Darbies. *To put the darbies on him.* Handcuffs. The word is derived from those two *inseparables*, Darby and Joan (q.v.).

Darby and Joan. The affectionate nickname given to old married couples in the evening of their life. The description first appeared in a ballad written by Henry Woodfall. In his younger days, Woodfall was apprenticed to a printer named John Darby, in Bartholomew Close, London. Darby had a wife whose Christian name was Joan. It is believed that the couple in the ballad were Woodfall's early master and mistress, who were known far and wide for their good works.

Dark. *A Leap in the Dark.* Thomas Hobbes on his death-bed said: "Now am I about to take my last voyage—a leap in the dark."

Davy Jones. *Gone to Davy Jones's Locker.* Dead. A sailors' phrase. One conjecture is that Jones is a corruption of Jonah, who was swallowed by a whale. But Jonah did NOT die! Another, an American version, is that the phrase is properly "Duffy Jones's Locker," Duffy being the ghost of the West Indian negroes, Jonah the Prophet, and the locker a seaman's chest.

Day of Rest. Every day of the week is a day of rest—somewhere. Christians set apart Sunday; the Greeks, Monday; the Persians, Tuesday; Assyrians, Wednesday; the Egyptians, Thursday; the Turks, Friday; the Jews, Saturday.

D-Day. The name given by the Allied Military Command to zero hour for the invasion of France, on the Normandy coast, on 6th June, 1944. It has been assumed that the "D" stood for Deliverance Day, the day on which the Allied Forces began the deliverance of France from the Germans. In point of fact, it represented nothing at all except "D" for day—the day fixed for the attack. "D-Day plus" represented days after D-Day, according to the plus number.

Dead as a doornail. The nail in this case is the large-headed one on which the door-knocker falls. Anybody knocked on the head with the regularity of this doornail would most certainly be dead.

Dead Head. The term applied to those people who for various reasons expect a seat in a theatre or concert hall, or any other performance without paying for it as an acknowledgment of services rendered, or to be rendered. It is by no means as new as protests of theatre managers would lead one to expect. In the Naples Museum there can be seen (or at least it could be seen before the War of 1939-45), a free pass for the theatres of Herculaneum and Pompeii. The pass was in the form of an ivory disc with the intaglio of a skull on it. Its description was "*cranio morto*," which is, in the language, "dead head."

Deaf as a Beetle. The beetle is not, in this case, the insect of that name, but the heavy wooden instrument used to drive in wedges, or to press down levelly paving-stones. It is full of heavy woodenness.

Dear, Dearest. The words, curiously enough, have two distinct and apposite meanings. When taken from the Anglo-Saxon *derian*, it means to hate, and from the Scottish *dere*, to annoy. It is in this sense that Shakespeare wrote in "Hamlet," i, 2: "Would that I had met my *dearest* foe in Heaven." But in the sense of someone beloved, the derivation is the Saxon *deor*, rare.

Death, Queer causes. Æschylus was killed when a tortoise, being taken by an eagle to its eyrie, fell from the bird's claws and struck the bald head of the sage.

Agathocles was killed by a tooth-pick after a meal, at ninety-six.

Chalchas, the soothsayer, who had predicted the date of his death, died from laughing at having lived past the date.

Gabrielle, mistress of Henri IV, died from eating an orange.

Otway, the poet, while starving, had given to him a guinea. He bought a loaf of bread, and died while swallowing the first mouthful of food he had had for days.

Philomenes died from laughing at seeing a donkey eating figs which had been prepared for himself.

George, Duke of Clarence, was drowned in a butt of malmsey (a sweet wine made in Greece and the Canary Islands).

Zeuxis, the painter, having just painted an old hag, was so amused at the character he had depicted that he began to laugh heartily and broke a blood-vessel.

Death-watch. Is the popular name given to a genus of beetle (correct name, *anobium*) which bores into dead wood. It makes a ticking sound; but the superstition that the noise foretells a death in the house is stupid.

Debut. To make a first appearance. It is composed of two French words which explain the origin very well: *de*, from, and *but*, the mark.

December. Those who ask how "dec" can signalize the twelfth month should be reminded that, until the change in the calendar, the year began in March, which made December the tenth month.

Decimate. A most misused word, particularly in newspapers. To decimate does not mean practically to annihilate a body of people. The word comes from the Latin *decem*, ten; and denotes a tenth part.

Dee, Dr. John. In his day a famous astrologer (1527-1608). He professed to be able to raise the dead. He possessed a magic glass, solid and tinted pink, in which it was claimed by him that all who looked into it could see their friends in foreign lands. The glass is now in the British Museum. Under the belief that Dr. Dee had dealings with the Devil, a mob on one occasion stormed his house, destroying the greater part of his magnificent collection of books and mathematical instruments. Dr. Dee died in poverty, and was buried at Mortlake.

De Foe, Daniel. Author of "Robinson Crusoe." Originally, his name was Foe. He and his father being active Dissenters, the son became known as Mr. D. Foe to distinguish him from his father. Later, he signed his letters Daniel De Foe, and joining the two latter together, he wrote as Daniel Defoe.

Dei Gratius. Usually written "D.G." Latin, "By the Grace of God."

Delirious. In this word, to describe a person out of his conscious senses, the soil has been used as a symbol. The word is derived from the Latin *de*, from, and *lira*, a furrow. Thus the analogy is one who goes out of the furrow in ploughing—out of the straight.

Deluge, The. Hebrew reckoning puts the flood that destroyed the world as having happened in the year 2348 B.C. By the Septuagint chronology, in the year 3155 B.C. The earliest reliable document of the event is the Babylonian tablet from the library of Assurbanipal, which dates from 660 B.C. It was, however, derived from an earlier Accadian original, composed so long ago as 2000 B.C. The story told in this document is almost word for word the Bible story. "*Apres moi la Deluge.*" *See* "After me . . ."

Delphi. A town at the foot of Mount Parnassus, famous for its Temple and the Delphi Oracle, celebrated in every age. The ancients looked upon Delphi as "the navel of the earth." In the temple was kept a white stone bound with a red binding-cloth, to represent the navel and umbilical cord.

Demise. Is one of the most misused words in the language. It is incorrect to speak of the death of a person as his demise. The meaning of demise is to "transfer, to bequeath"; and the term should apply only to the death of a monarch, whereby the Crown is "demised" to his heir and successor.

Democracy. It is as well in these days that the term should be properly understood and appreciated. It comes from the Greek *demos-kratia*, the rule of the people; and we cannot improve on Dr. Brewer's concise interpretation: "A form of government in which the sovereign power is in the hands of the people, and exercised by them, directly or indirectly; also a state so governed, and the body of the people, especially the non-privileged classes."

Den. As a suffix for many place-names in the southern counties, denotes a deeply-wooded valley. Most of the "dens" of Anglo-Saxon days were given over to pastures for pigs. A Court of Dens existed up to the seventeenth century to judge between disputes arising from the common pasturage.

Denarius. A Roman coin worth about 8½d. It is from this word that we take our initial "d" for pence.

Deo Volente. Is frequently attached in the form of the initials "D.V." to religious advertisements. An instance is: "A meeting will be held (D.V.) at . . ." The phrase means "God Willing," or "By God's Will."

Derby. The Blue Riband of the Turf, was first run in 1780, in which year it was started by the twelfth Earl of Derby. He had established The Oaks the year before.

Devil looks over Lincoln, As the. A statue of the Devil used to stand on Lincoln College, Oxford, which gave rise to the saying that the Devil looked over Lincoln. It was taken down in 1731.

Devil, To go to the. Or "*Gone to the Devil.*" A tavern of the name of "The Devil" stood in Fleet Street in close proximity to the Law Courts, and was much frequented by barristers. When a barrister was wanted and could not be found at his Chambers, the injunction from his clerk was: "Go to the Devil." This is probably the modern use of the phrase, though it existed long before in connection with the Devil in the fifteenth century mystery plays.

Devil to Pay. When money was lost in unsuccessful litigation it passed into the hands of lawyers. In London barristers spent a great deal of their time in the Devil Tavern, in Fleet Street. And, also, many of them took small briefs and other legal work because they "had the Devil to pay" for drink. The devil is, also, a seam in a ship, and to "pay" is to cover the seam with pitch.

Devil take the Hindmost. Legend had it that the Devil had a school at Toledo. Students, when they had reached a stage in their studies, had to run through an underground hall. The last man was seized by the Devil, and had to become his servant.

Printer's Devil. The messenger boy to a firm of printers is thus called, because, as one writer has put it: "They do so commonly black and bedaub themselves that the workmen do jocosely call them devils." The term originated, however, in Venice, when printing was commonly regarded as one of the Black Arts. Manuzio, a printer, employed a black slave, who was regarded as his devil imp.

Devil among the Tailors. The first use of this phrase was a description of a disturbance at the Haymarket Theatre, London, at a performance of a burlesque called "The Tailors: A tragedy for warm weather." A crowd of tailors caused a riot, as they considered the play an insult to their calling.

Devil, To Outdance the. The phrase comes down from the days of witchcraft. At the witches' covens, the Master of Ceremonies represented the Devil, disguised as a man or a goat. He challenged one of his more promising neophytes to dance and in the competition that followed the Devil of course, would win, his competitor usually dying of heart failure or exhaustion.

Diamond Sculls. An annual rowing match at the Henley Royal Regatta. It was first rowed in 1844. The award is a pair of crossed silver sculls a few inches in length, having a pendant of diamonds.

Dickey. The shirt front, once so popular, and now an object for mirth, was derived from the German *decken*, which meant to hide. Which is exactly what the Englishman's dickey *did* do.

Dictionaries. The word dictionary, a list of the words of a language or languages, is from the Latin *dicto*, "saying." The earliest Greek and Latin "lexicons," so-called, were mainly collections of unusual words and phrases; and the nearest approach to a dictionary as we know it, was the work of Valerius Flaccus, compiled in the time of Augustus (third century A.D.) on the meaning of words, of which an abridgement is still extant. The succeeding most important dictionaries were those of Calepino (1502), in seven languages, and Robert and Henry Stephanus (1572). The first real English dictionary was Dr. Johnson's (1755), and the standard work to-day is the *Oxford Dictionary*. A magnificent work, and probably the greatest one, is the *Century Dictionary*.

Die is Cast. The word "die" used in this sense is from the Latin *datum*, past participle of dare, meaning to give, to throw. In popular Latin, *datum* was taken in the sense of, "That which is given or decreed by lot or fortune," and was so applied to the dice determing fate. The phrase is as old as the method of determining by chance.

Dieu et mon Droit. The Royal motto of Britain (since Richard the Lionheart and the Battle of Gisors). It does not mean, as a reader once told us, "My God, I'm Right!" The interpretation is, "God, and my right."

Diggings. A colloquial name for lodgings. The name came from the Galena lead-miners of Wisconsin. They lived during the Winter months in underground dug-outs which they had "digged." The "origin" sometimes given that it was derived from the Californian gold diggings is not correct.

Digits. The first nine numerals (1 to 9) are so-called, because of the habit in all countries of counting as far as ten on the fingers. The Latin word for finger is *digitus*.

Dilemma. "*On the horns of a dilemma.*" The word is Greek *di* or *dis*, two-fold, and *lemma*, a thing taken or received. A dilemma, therefore, is a position before which there are two alternatives.

Diogenes. Is best known to fame as the man who lived in a tub. The evidence of this is, however, very inconclusive. He spent his youth in extravagant living until, meeting Antisthenes, he began to practice the most rigid asceticism, living in temple porches or in the streets. A cynic, he wrote nothing, but taught those he met, with complete contempt for time, place or other circumstances.

Forget the painting of the death of Diogenes in his tub; he was captured by pirates and sold for a slave to Corinth, where he died, still a slave.

"Dirty Dick's." A famous London tavern in Bishopsgate. It is popularly believed to have received its name from its association with the miser, Nathanial Bentley, who never washed himself. As a matter of fact, "Dirty Dick" was a Leadenhall ironmonger. There is another story that the proprietor of "Dirty Dick's" was to have been married, and a reception had been prepared in the dining-room of the inn. On the morning of the wedding (the story goes) the bride died. "Dirty Dick," in despair, vowed that the room should never again be opened or even touched, and so it remained thick with dust and cobwebs.

Dirty Dog. In the East the dog is still held in abhorrence as the scavenger of the streets. Hence the name describes anyone guilty of an unclean or despicable action.

Dished. *To be dished.* The word is contracted from the Old English *disherit*. A person is dished when something he expected to inherit is left elsewhere.

Dish of Tea. The theory recently advanced in a Sunday newspaper that the tea in a "dish of Tay" is from the French *the*, the original pronunciation of tea, is not correct. In the time of Queen Anne, when coffee houses in England were at the height of their popularity, both tea and coffee were sold only in shallow bowls without handles, and such vessels were called dishes. The author possesses a copy of *The Daily Courant*, of 8th August, 1712, which contains in an advertisement, "coffee at two-pence per dish and tea at three-halfpence a dish."

As for tay in place of our "tea," etymologists all agree that tea or te was pronounced tay. In his "Rape of the Lock," Pope three times spells it tea, but makes it rhyme with obey, stay, and away.

Diss. He knows nothing about Diss. Diss, in Norfolk, was so little frequented by visitors at one time that it became the custom at Cambridge to express indifference respecting trivial matters by the phrase, "He knows nothing about Diss."—*Apperson.*

Ditto, the word used for "again," comes from the Latin *dictum*, that which has been said before.

Ditty Box. One suggestion is that the sailor's "ditty box" is a shortened form of the proper name "commodity box," intended originally for the stowage of his clothes and hair brushes, comb, shaving outfit, writing materials, etc.; but now a compendium of writing materials and other things. The late Captain W. N. T. Beckett, M.V.O., R.N., gives the suggestion that it might at some time have been a bag made of "dittis," or Manchester stuff. He also added that it might have come from the word *dicht*. This is a variant of *dight*, to clean, repair or make good, a word which is still in common use in Scotland.

Divan. A long, low, backless couch which has come into great favour. The word is Turkish, signifying a Council of State or a Court of Justice. The Turkish councillors reclined on long couches ranged round the walls.

Dive, Highest and Shallowest. Because he "felt happy" on 12th January, 1941, a nineteen year old soldier, Keith Green, dived off a cliff in South Africa two hundred and sixty-five feet into the sea. He was uninjured, but a comrade, who then tried the dive, was killed.

The shallowest dive recorded was by Professor Powsey—from seventy-two feet, into four feet of water.

Dixie, Dixieland. "*I want to be in Dixie-land.*" There is much more behind the Dixie songs than is generally known. Mr. Dixie was a landowner on what is now known as Manhattan Island, New York. In common with most American landowners of that time, he possessed black slaves. But he treated his slaves with such kindness that Dixie's Land came to mean to the black people almost a second Heaven. When, because of the numbers to which they had grown, Dixie was compelled to sell some of his slaves to other masters, they looked back on the days in Dixie-land as days of happiness.

Doctor, To. To "doctor" wine means to strengthen it with brandy, or to make weak wine stronger with some other mixture. To "doctor" accounts in a book, is to falsify them to make them look stronger than they are.

Doff your hat merely means to "do off" your hat; in the same way that to don it means to "do on" your hat.

Dog and Duck. Another tavern name. Its presence on an inn-post indicates that duck-hunting with spaniels in a pond nearby was a popular pastime.

Dog-cart. Owes its name to the fact that it really *was* a dog-cart—the cart in which sportsmen drove their setters and pointers to the shoot.

Dog Days. Are supposed to be the days of the year with the greatest heat. The term comes from the Romans, who called the six hottest weeks of the Summer *caniculares dies*. It was their theory that the Dog-star (Sirius), rising with the sun, added to the heat, so that those days bore the combined temperature of the dog-star and the sun. The dog-days are from about 3rd July to 11th August.

Dog, Gay. Slang term for a philanderer. Dog is used here as a chap, or a fellow. A sad dog or a surly dog is used in the same sense.

Dog, Hair of. *See* "Hair."

Doggett's Coat and Badge. Prize given in a water match for Thames watermen. It takes place in August each year, and is so-called from Thomas Doggett, an actor of Drury Lane, who instituted the event in the reign of George I. It is rowed from the Swan Inn at London Bridge to the Swan Inn at Chelsea. The "coat" is an orange-coloured livery jacket.

Dogs, Isle of. *See* "Isle."

Dog-watch. It was a corruption of dodge-watch. A ship's crews is divided into two watches, starboard watch and port watch, each being alternately on watch for four hours. Now, in order to avoid the same men being on the same watch always, the afternoon watch, between 4 p.m. and 8 p.m., is made into two watches each of two hours, giving nine watches a day instead of eight, and thus changing the rota. The short watch is called the dog-watch, or, as it should be, the dodge-watch.

Doldrums. *To be in the Doldrums.* The Doldrums is a region in the Pacific Ocean between the trade winds, where calms and baffling winds are met, thus delaying the progress of sailing ships. Seamen in those old days, therefore, became depressed at the lack of progress of their ships in the region. Thus, the phrase to be in the doldrums came to mean out of spirits, in the dumps.

Dole. The name given to unemployment pay introduced into Britain during the depression after the 1914-1918 war. The word is from the Latin *dolar*, grief, sorrow, lamentation ; and the dole in Britain lived up to that description.

Dolly Shop. This was an old name for a rag, or second-hand clothes shop, from the black doll that was hung outside as a sign of the type of business transacted.

Dominoes. This popular game has a strange history. It was invented by two French monks, who played with square stones on which spots had been marked. The winner of each game signalized the event by reciting, "*Dixit Dominus, Domino Meo,*" first line of the Vesper service. When the game spread to all the monks in the monastery, the Vesper line was abbreviated to "Domino"—and the player of the game to-day still uses that word to signify that he has won.

Donkey's Years. "*As long as Donkey's Years.*" This is a corruption of a word because of the running on of the "s" of one word into the "y" of the following word. The phrase explains itself when it is pointed out that the original was, "As long as Donkey's *Ears*," the longest ears of any animal.

Don't care a damn. *See* "Dam."

Don't care a jot. The "jot" is in reality an Iota, the smallest letter in the Greek alphabet. It is equivalent to the English "i."

Doss. A slang name for a bed or sleep. Comes from the old word *dossel*, a bundle of hay or straw. A bed stuffed with straw was called a doss. Probably originally from Latin *Dorsum*, a back.

"Double Dutch." Talking Double Dutch, talking something unintelligible. In the seventeenth century, in Britain, "Dutch" was synonymous with "Foreign." Double Dutch was something excessively, and therefore aggressively, foreign.

Doughboys. The nickname bestowed on the American soldier, as Tommy Atkins was bequeathed to the British soldier. The American name came from the American Civil War, in which the U.S. infantrymen had large globular glass buttons to their uniform. They looked, so it was said, like doughcakes.

Downing Street. This street, famed as the centre of the Government of Britain by reason of the fact that it contains the official residence of the Prime Minister and the Chancellor, derives its name from Sir George Downing, a noted Parliamentarian and Ambassador, who served under both Cromwell and Charles II. He died in 1684.

Down to Bedrock. Bedrock is the hard, basic rock beneath a seam of coal in a pit. A miner says he is down to bedrock when a seam in the mine is exhausted of coal.

Doyley, the tea-table napery, was introduced to our afternoon teatable by two brothers named Doyley, who owned a linendraper's shop in the Strand, London.

Dragon's Hill. At this spot in Berkshire, legend has it St. George killed the Dragon. A bare place is shown to visitors on a hill where, they are told, the dragon's blood ran out, and on which nothing will grow. Nothing does grow there, but there are various ways of ensuring that foliage will not grow on any given spot !

Dragoons. There were seven regiments of Dragoon Guards in the British Army. The name arose from the short-barrelled firearms which these mounted infantry carried. The name description "dragoons" was given to these firearms from a fanciful comparison to a dragon spurting fire from his mouth. A dragon's head was also wrought on the muzzle of the earliest of the muskets.

Drat them. A corruption of the old-time oath, "God rot them." It was first corrupted to "Od rot it."

Drawing - room. Until quite recently was the *with*drawing room to which the ladies withdrew after dinner, leaving the men to their wine and cigars.

Draw it mild. An admonition to one inclined to exaggerate or use explosive language. The allusion is to beer : "A pint of beer, Miss, and draw it mild."

Drawn and Quartered. *See* "Hanged."

Draw the King's Picture. A crooks' term for coining money.

Draw the Nail. This is an old Cheshire phrase for the releasing of a person from a promise given. The writer has not heard of it for many years, but it was common in his earlier days. When a Cheshire man agreed to promise a certain line of action he registered the promise by driving a nail into the trunk of a tree. His oath was to keep his vow so long as the nail remained there. If, at any future time, he wished to retract, he had to "draw the nail" from the tree. It was not unknown for a person, who promised under moral duress, to leave enough of the head of the nail projecting as not to give undue trouble when he wanted to "draw it."

"Dreeing his Weird in the Backwoods." Dree, to perform, to endure, still lives in the Border Counties of Scotland. *Weird* meant Fate, Destiny. Readers will recall the "Weird Sisters," the Fates, of Shakespeare's "Macbeth."

Dressed up to the Knocker. Titivated up to the limit of his resources. In olden times doorknockers were placed high up on front doors to prevent them being wrenched off by sporting hooligans.

Dressing down, To give a good. In the sense of a good talking-to, or lashing with the tongue, the phrase is derived from the ore-mines. To dress down ore is to break it up, and crush and powder it in the stamping mill.

Drink, In the. Originally "the drink" was an American name expression for a large stretch of water, and particularly the Atlantic Ocean. Since the outbreak of the World War, however, it has been appropriated by the R.A.F. to describe any airman coming down on water, after a forced landing. To come down in the drink means to have been forced down in the sea.

Drum. Not the band instrument, but a party. In the eighteenth century the term was given to any large evening party, an allusion, apparently, to the drumming noise made by the conversation of hundreds of voices. The term was in great popularity among the military.

It is stated that the term "kettle-drum" was adapted from afternoon tea-parties, at which a kettle appeared—the little drum as distinct from the big drum. The origin is, however, a doubtful one.

Drunk. "*As a fiddler.*" Since the fiddler at a party was continually plied with drink by the guests, the allusion is obvious.

Drunk as a Lord. When George III was King and, indeed, for long afterwards, drinking was the sign of the gentleman ! To be as drunk as a lord was a sure mark of gentility. A "three bottle man" was a pattern of society. Few dinners but ended with all the guests helpless under the table in front of the chairs upon which they had been sitting. The temperance movement which set in towards the end of the nineteenth century put an end to heavy drinking.

Drury Lane. The street, and therefore the theatre, is named after Drury House, a mansion built by Sir William Drury on a site which would be now in the middle of the present Aldwych. The theatre now standing is the fourth of its name, the first having been opened to the public in 1663.

Dud. "It's a dud." The term, mostly used now in a military sense, such as "a dud shell," has no known origin. There is a Dutch word *dood*, meaning dead; and this may possibly be the derivation, though there is no etymological evidence of it.

Dudgeon. "*In high dudgeon.*" To have resentment. In "Macbeth," Shakespeare says: ". . . On thy blade and dudgeon gouts of blood." The handle of inferior daggers at one time were made of dudgeon wood—boxwood root, but a dagger with a wooden handle was considered what would to-day be called *infra dig.* A man forced by circumstances to be content with a dudgeon handle naturally felt some resentment at his fate.

Dukes. A common term for hands. It comes from the gypsy *duk*, which refers to palmistry. "It's in his duk," meaning it is his fate because it is in his hands. The word is also spelt "dooks."

Dumping. A word which came to fame during the lively Free Trade *v.* Tariff Reform election of 1906. The Tariff Reform policy initiated by Mr. Joseph Chamberlain, urged that the troubles of British agriculture were due entirely to the "dumping" into this country of cheap foreign food. The Liberal Party replied with a "Dear Food" battle-cry. The election was won by the Free Trade party. Actually, "dumping" came to be defined as the pouring into a country of the surplus supplies of the dumping country at a price which is lower than that at which the importing country can itself produce the commodity.

Dumps. "*Down in the Dumps.*" Out of spirits. There is a fable frequently quoted as the origin of dumps, which states that Dumops, King of Egypt, after building a Pyramid died of melancholia. Therefore, to be in the dumps is to be in the same state of mind as Dumops. It is, of course, nonsense. It is probable that the word is derived from the Dutch *dompig*, dull, low, misty. Another likely source is our own *damp*, to be damped down.

Dun. *To dun a person*; pursue him for a debt. Joe Dun was a famous London bailiff exceedingly efficient in catching defaulting debtors. "You had better Dun him for the money" was a popular phrase of the time.

Dunce. Name given to a poor scholar or a person dull in intellect, or unable to learn easily. The origin is beyond the usual interest. John Scotus was a schoolman who came from Dunse, in Scotland. At the time of the introduction of the new theology, he was an uncompromising supporter of the old theology. He opposed the new learning and the classics. He was accordingly regarded as the arch-opponent of progress and learning. The description "Dunse" was given to him, and his followers were called Dunsers. From that time Dunse was used to describe anyone who was an opponent of learning or progress. The name has since become "dunce" with a "c." Scotus died in 1305, and is buried in Cologne.

Dunderhead. A stupid fellow, with no spirit in him. "Dunder" is the name given to the lees or dregs of wine. Actually, it is the overflow of fermenting liquors. In other words, it has none of the spirit in it.

Dunkirk To do a. To evacuate a place. The allusion is to the withdrawal of the British Expeditionary Force from France in 1940. After the Belgians had laid down their arms in the World War of 1939-45, the position of the British Forces on the Continent became desperate. Arrangements were made for the Army to withdraw to the port of Dunkirk, the only port fitted for an evacuation. From Dunkirk, despite incessant bombing by hundreds of German planes, 211,532 fit men and 13,053 casualties, as well as 112,456 allied troops, were taken off and brought to Britain, between 26th May and 3rd June, 1940. Thousands of little ships carried out the operation, including many pleasure motor cruisers which had never before left the Thames and other inland pleasure waters. The operation was movingly described by Mr. Churchill as "a miracle of deliverance."

Dunmow Flitch. The origin of this well-known competition in conjugal bliss is as follows: A noble-woman of Juga instituted a custom, later restored by Robert de Fitzwalter one hundred and thirty years later (in 1244), whereby: "Any person from any part of England going to Dunmow, in Essex, and humbly kneeling on two stones at the church door, may claim a gammon of bacon if he can swear that for twelve months and a day he has never had a household brawl or wished himself unmarried."

After many vicissitudes, the custom still revives as a holiday spectacle.

Dun's in the Mire. Dun is, of course, the name for a horse—the old dun horse—and the mire referred to the mire of the unmade roads at the time the phrase was coined—about 1836.

Dutch Courage. Courage that is the result of bravado due to alcoholic liquor. So-called because at the time of its origin, in the seventeenth century, the Dutch were notoriously heavy wine drinkers, and were unduly boastful when the wine was in.

Dutchman. "*I'm a Dutchman if I do.*" During the long disputes between England and Holland, the word Dutch was synonymous with everything that was false. To say, "I'll be a Dutchman if I do," meant to have the strongest repugnance to do what was being asked.

Dutch My Old. Few songs have had a greater appeal than that written and sung by Albert Chevalier, the Cockney comedian:

"We've been together now for
forty years,
And it don't seem a day
too much.
There ain't a lady living in
the land,
As I'd swap for my dear
old Dutch."

The highest lady in the land (apart from the Queen) is a Duchess. To say that his wife is his Duchess was in those days a compliment of the highest order. "Dutch" is an abbreviation of Duchess.

Dutch Uncle Talking like a. An allusion to the days when the name Dutch was anathema to England and English people. *See* "Dutch Courage."

Dyed in the Wool. Said of a good fellow, a sport. The origin is that such a man is true right through. Cloth which is wool-dyed before weaving (not dyed in the piece afterwards) is true throughout, and will wash without the dye coming out.

E

Eagle. As an inn sign, the eagle was formerly a compliment to Queen Mary, whose badge it was. In Christianity it is emblematical of St. John the Evangelist because, like the eagle, he looked on the Son of Glory.

The Romans, regarding it as a royal bird, loosed an eagle from the funeral pile of a dead emperor.

Earl's Court. A fashionable district of London. So-called from the Earl of Warwick whose estate it was until, by the marriage of the Dowager Countess of Warwick with Lord Holland, it passed into the Holland family.

Ear-marked. Set aside for a special purpose. The allusion is to the marking of cattle with the owner's identification sign on the ears. The custom, however, is much older than that. In *Exodus* xxi, 6, it is written of a servant: " . . . his master shall bore his ear through with an awl; and he shall serve him for ever." If a Hebrew servant declined to be freed after six years' service, the master bored his ear, as described, in token of his voluntary servitude.

Earn. *To earn one's living.* The overwhelming influence of the soil is evidenced in this word as expressive of income. It is derived from the old German word for harvest. The Dutch *erne* also means harvest; and so does the Bavarian *arnen.*

Ears. The superstition that ears burn when one is being talked about is an old one. Shakespeare, in "Much Ado about Nothing," mentions it; but much earlier, Pliny wrote: "When our ears do glow and tingle, some do talk of us in our absence."

"*I'd give my ears.*" A reference to the old practice of cutting off the ears of such persons who refused to withdraw wrongful and offensive opinions.

Earwig. The popular belief is that the name is given to this insect because it crawls into the ears of sleeping humans and penetrates the brain. A second "origin" is based on the shape of the hind wings which, it is pointed out, resemble the human ear. The true origin is a simple one. The word is derived from the Anglo-Saxon *eor*, an *ear*, and *wic* (or *wick*), a hiding-place, not *wicga*, beetle, as Dr. Brewer assets. In Old English, the word ear meant an undeveloped flower-bud, particularly of corn. The favourite hiding-place of an earwig, as most people know, is in closely folded bud-ears. This was perfectly well-known in Old English times, which was the reason the insect was given the name of *eor-wic.*

East. The Christian custom of turning to the East, and building their churches with the altar on the East side of the church, is older by far than Christianity. The Greeks, for instance, buried their dead with their faces upwards, but with the feet turned towards the East—an indication that the dead was on his, or her, way to Elysium, and not to the place of eternal darkness. The custom is followed in this country, all graves being dug to allow the feet to point eastwards.

Easter. It will probably come as a shock to the devout to know that Easter, the most sacred season of the Christian Church, in its origin had nothing to do with the Risen Christ, but was in honour of a Heathen Deity. The word is from the Anglo-Saxon *Eastre*, through the Teutonic *Ostara*, the Goddess of Light, or Spring. As in Christmas (q.v.) the early Christian Church appropriated the feast, and the date, to the Christian festival. The Heathen feasting lasted for eight days; our Easter holiday, so far as schools are concerned, lasts for seven days.

Easter Eggs. Almost from the time that men began to think, the egg has been the symbol of Creation. The Phœnician, Hindu and Japanese mythology held that the world was hatched from an egg—the Mundane Egg, for which, according to Persian legend, Ormuzd and Ahriman, Angels of Light and Darkness, are to contend for ever.

Easter eggs had their custom originally in Persia. It was adopted by the Jewish race, and from them taken in a slightly different form by the earlier Christians as a symbol of the Resurrection. The red colour which marked the Easter egg in bygone days—and which in many parts of the country still exists to-day—is a token of the blood of the Redemption.

Dr. Brewer suggests as a more likely origin, however, the Roman rule that forbade the eating of eggs during Lent, but allowed them again on Easter Sunday. This rule, however, applied to many other things besides eggs, in connection with which no Easter custom has developed.

Eat Humble Pie. This phrase dates back to the old days of feasting off venison, when banquets were given in Baronial Halls. The lords and ladies dined off the flesh of the deer. The huntsmen and the servants of the household had to be content with what were called the "umbles"—the heart, liver and the entrails. These were made into huge pies. Hence, to eat Umble Pie meant that you were not of sufficient importance to sit with the household. You were, in point of fact, an inferior person.

Eavesdropper. *One who listens clandestinely to conversation.* The word comes from the Anglo-Saxon. In those times owners of houses were not allowed to build to the extremity of their land; they had to leave a space for eaves. This the Saxons called the *yfes drype.* Thus, an eavesdropper was a person who placed himself inside the eaves-drip in order to hear conversation in the adjacent house, or land.

Eccentric. Used to describe somebody or something a little queer. The word actually means to deviate from the centre, from the Latin *ex centrum*, otherwise, not according to rule. Scientifically, the term is applied to the planets which circle the earth, the earth not being in the centre of their orbit.

Eccles. *Eccles-cake.* This word is a contraction of the Latin *ecclesia*, a church. It forms a component of many name-places in the North of England, particularly Lancashire. Its origin is, thus, obvious. Eccles-cakes were first made in Eccles.

Echo. *To applaud to the echo.* To applaud so loudly as to produce an echo from the distance. According to Roman mythology Echo, a nymph, finding her love for Narcissus unrequited, pined away until only her voice was left.

Economy. Although the word is now used mostly for national or international politics, it belonged primarily to the house, being derived from the Greek *oikos*, a house, and *nomos*, a law. Even now, the principal "economy" in the minds of the ordinary man and woman is the true one—the relation to home expenditure and income.

Political Economy. The science of the laws and conditions which regulate the production, distribution and consumption of all products necessary, useful or agreeable to man. The principal topics are labour, capital, competition and governmental interference with the natural course of trade, demand and supply, international trade, including the questions of free trade or protection, the influence of government upon economic relations and the progress of civilization.

Ecstasy. A state in which the mind is exalted, or liberated, from the body. The word comes from the Greek *ek*, out, and *stasis*, a standing. Thus, the accurate description of ecstasy is out of standing, displacement.

Eden. The first home of man. There has been much speculation as to the site of the Garden of Eden. Recent discoveries have made it clear that *Edinu* was the Sumerian name for the plain of Babylon, at the southern end of which stood the city of Eridu, formerly on the Persian Gulf; and near it a beautiful garden, inhabited by the Gods, and containing the Tree of Life. This points to a district north of the Persian Gulf. The river with four heads, mentioned in the Bible, two of which are the Euphrates and the Tigris, must have been the Persian Gulf. The two other rivers cannot be identified with any certainty. The Pison, compassing the land of Havilah, may have been the Pallakut, the classical Pallacopus.

Eden Hall, Luck of. An enamelled drinking-glass in the possession of the Musgrave family at Eden Hall, Cumberland. It is supposed to be endowed with fortune-bringing properties. The story goes that a servant of the family once went to draw water from St. Cuthbert's Well in the garden, that the fairies had left the glass by the side of the well while they danced in a glade, and that the servant ran off with it.

Edmonton. In Anglo-Saxon days merely Edmund's Town.

Eel. Apart from the fish of that name, an eel was the name given to a rope's end used for scourging. The description dates back to the days when whips for scourging were made out of eelskins.

Eelpie Island. A pleasure resort on the Thames. The *piece de resistance* there was eel pie, from eels caught in the waters round the island.

Egg. *To egg on somebody.* Egg, used in this sense, is a corruption of the Anglo-Saxon word *eggian*, to prick, to spur on.

Eggs. "*Sure as eggs is eggs.*" The remark must have been coined by some ignoramus after hearing mathematicians discussing a mathematical, or algebraical, proposition, for there is no doubt that the original "eggs" was "x" (the unknown quantity) and the saying was: "As sure as x is x."

Ego, Egoism. *To believe too highly of oneself.* The word in Latin meant "I." It was introduced into Philosophy by Descartes to denote the whole man—body and mind.

Egotism. The habit of continually talking about oneself; in the first person "I."

Eisteddfod. Is merely Celtic for a gathering of Welsh bards. It is derived from *eistodd*, to sit.

Eldon Hole wants Filling. A retort to a braggart. Eldon Hole is a deep chasm in the Derbyshire Peak District, said of course, to be bottomless. It isn't! But it would take a lot of doing to fill it!

El Dorado. A wealthy or promising region; a desirable place in which to live. It is the name given to a country rich beyond all precedent in gold and jewels which the early Spanish explorers believed to exist on the Amazon, and called Manoa. It was originally given to the supposed King of Manoa. It was said of him that he had been so often covered with oil and then powdered with gold-dust that he had become literally gilded.

Eleanor Crosses. The name given to the crosses erected by Edward I at the spots where the body of his Queen, Eleanor, rested en route from Harby, Nottinghamshire, where she died, to Westminster, where she was buried. Crosses were set up at Lincoln, Newark, Grantham, Leicester, Stamford, Geddington, Northampton, Stony Stratford, Woburn, Dunstable, St. Albans, Waltham, West Cheap and Westminster. There was one, also, at the ancient village of Charing, which stood midway between the cities of Westminster and London. The cross in Charing Cross Station to-day is not one such cross. It is a copy of an original one that was demolished by the Puritans in 1647. The original stood in Trafalgar Square. It was not one of the Eleanor Crosses.

Elements, The. Aristotle taught that there were four elements—fire, air, water and earth. Subsequently, a fifth was added, and was called the *quinta essentia*; it was supposed to be common to the other four, and to hold them together. It is from this fifth element that we get the word quintessence.

Elephant. This is not strictly an "origin," except in the way of being an origin of life. But such astronomical figures have been given of the period of gestation of an elephant, that it may be as well to state, clearly, that the period is eighteen months, not years.

Elephant and Castle. The famous landmark in South London takes its name from the arms of the Cutlers' Company. The public-house of that name, however, derives its name from the skeleton of an elephant dug up in 1714 near Battle Bridge. By the side of the skeleton was a flint-headed spear. It is suggested from this that the elephant was killed in the battle between Queen Boadicea and the Romans.

Elephant, White. *The name given to an undertaking that has proved a total loss and has left a debit on the hands of the projectors.* The origin lies in Siam. A white elephant is regarded as a sacred animal, and its upkeep is, or was, expensive. The King of Siam, wishing to get rid of a courtier no longer in favour, used the device of giving him a present of a white elephant. The subsequent cost of upkeep of the gift usually ended by ruining the unfortunate fellow.

Elgin Marbles. Were brought from Greece by Lord Elgin, and consist of fragments of statuary from the Parthenon of Athens, famous Greek temple of antiquity. They were bought by the Government for £35,000, and are now in the British Museum.

Elixir of Life. A potion (supposed) of the alchemists that would prolong life and restore youth indefinitely. The word is the Arabic *el iksir*, the Philosophers' Stone.

Ell. The old measure, was like the measure, a *foot*, taken from a part of the body, for convenience. An ell (Anglo-Saxon *eln*) was the distance from the forearm to the tip of the middle finger. A "foot" was the length of the foot.

Elysium. The Elysian Fields. *The happy resting place.* In Greek mythology, the final abode of the Gods. It was held that the "Fields" were the paradise of the poets.

Ember Days. The days have nothing whatever to do with embers. It is still commonly stated that they were given the name from the practice of penitents sitting in ashes of repentance, or ashes, at these seasons. Nor is the term a corruption of the Latin *quatuor tempora*, four times, or its corruption through the Dutch *quatemper*. Ember Days came, undoubtedly, from the Anglo-Saxon *ymbren dagas*, "running days," because they came round at regular intervals.

Encore. "*Do it once more,*" in the sense in which we use it; again. For some curious reason this is regarded as a French word for "again." It is nothing of the sort. Our use of the word for appreciation of a performance is quite unknown to the French. If the French desire a thing to be repeated, they call out "*bis*" (twice). *Encore une tasse,* is another cup, and this is the correct use of the word.

Encyclopædia. A book containing all-round or general information. The word is derived from the Greek *enkylois*, in a circle, and *paideia*, learning.

End of the World, The. According to the Rabinical legend, the world will end in the year 6000. The reasons given are: (1) Because the name, Yahweh, contains six letters; (2) because the Hebrew letter "m" occurs six times in *Genesis*; (3) because Enoch, the Patriarch, who was raised to Heaven without dying, was the sixth generation of Adam; (4) because God created the earth in six days; (5) because six contains three binaries—the first two thousand years were for the law of nature, the second two thousand years the written law, and the third two thousand the Law of Grace.

Endorse. "*I endorse that.*" Meaning "I accept that," or, properly, "I back that." It is derived from the Latin *in-dorsum*, on the back. The correct example of the use of the word is the endorsing of a promissary note by a person who accepts responsibility for it.

End. *West End, East End.* It may seem a curious circumstance that in this country factories and other trappings of industry are invariably situated in the East end or on the East side of the city, and the more select of the residences in the West end or on the West side of the city. The explanation, however, is simple; the prevailing winds in Britain are West. Thus, the residential side of the city is that from which the winds usually come, preventing the smoke of industrial chimneys blowing over the houses.

Ends-a-wagging. A naval slang term. It means as announcement that any movement or transaction is drawing to a close. The idiom is borrowed from word passed that the end of a rope, which is being laboriously hauled along, coiled down or reeled up, is in sight.

Enfant Terrible. A French phrase meaning a precocious child, who is always saying or doing awkward things. In this country, it is frequently used to express the "nuisance" of young and enthusiastic newcomers to any body of government or executive responsibilities who want, like a new brush, to sweep clean.

England. In Alfred the Great's day was spelt Englaland, the land of the Angles, who came from Jutland.

Englander, A Little. Contemptuous name given to a person who would rather see England a small and wealthy country, than the head of a great Empire. The opposite to an Imperialist. The name first came into general use during the South African War of 1899-1902, when Shaw and G. K. Chesterton, with others, earned the sobriquet.

Englishman's Home is his Castle. Sir Edward Coke, in his "Institutes," wrote: "A man's house is his castle." Later, in a report on a noteworthy case, he wrote: "The house of everyone is to him as his castle and fortress, as well for his defence against injury and violence as for his repose." The reference is to the fact that a bailiff, though an officer of the law, cannot break into a house to arrest or to distrain upon goods. The house is the owner's castle or fortress.

Enough, Enow. Although the latter word is now little heard except among country people, it is the one which should be used when referring to numbers. Properly used, "enough" refers only to quantities. "I have enough of that," but, correctly speaking, "I have enow apples."

Entail. The word comes from the French *tailler*, to cut. It means a property, or estate, in which the rights of the present owner are *cut down* to the extent that he cannot sell the estate or bar his issue from inheriting it. To "cut the entail" means to put an end to the entail.

Entente Cordiale. The phrase is French. It means an understanding, but not an actual alliance, between nations; but is generally accepted as that between France and Britain arranged, largely, through the personal intervention of the late King Edward VII. Political opinions of late years have wondered whether it rendered much service to Britain!

Enthusiast. If the word is taken literally from the Greek *en theos*, it means one who is inspired by a God. But when it is used in connection with people who enthuse over Cubist, "Swing," and other such crazes, it seems to be out of line with the original meaning.

Entree. A "swagger" word for entry! Used, mostly, by people affecting a knowledge of the French language. Originally, when the Court spoke only French, the word meant access to Royal circles.

Ephesiam. A boon companion, a good fellow. Why such a fellow should be endowed with the name of Ephesus, the ancient city of Ionia, or with the Temple of Diana, or the Ephesian Council of A.D. 449, is a mystery.

Epic. One of the most misused word in the language, particularly by newspapers. Any brave action is described as an epic. Used correctly, an epic is an heroic poem. Aristotle's rule for an epic was that it must be on a great and noble theme; it must be one in itself.

Epicure. One devoted to the pleasures of the table. Sometimes, quite erroneously, described as a follower of Epicurus, the Greek philosopher who founded a school at Athens in 307 B.C. Epicurus taught that pleasure and good living constituted the happiness of life. But the pleasure meant, and taught, by Epicurus was tranquility of mind and freedom from want and pain which come from simplicity of life and self-control. His self-styled followers, however, corrupted his doctrine into: "Good living is all we should seek"; and called "good living" luxurious eating! Nothing is further from Epicurus.

Episode. A parenthetic addition. In the Greek, it meant "coming in beside." An episode was, originally, dialogue that was interposed between the choric songs in Greek tragedy.

Epoch. A check, cessation, stop or pause. A point of time. Derived from the Greek *epecho*. It is used to denote a period of time, and a sequence of events that date from such a period.

Epsom Races. Were instituted by Charles I.

Epsom Salts Sad to relate, the present purgative is no longer entitled to the name. The original Epsom Salts came from a natural mineral spring at Epsom, in the eighteenth century. Waters of the spring were evaporated, leaving behind the mineral salts. The salt, in point of fact, was magnesium sulphate, and it still is in the present salts, though it is now manufactured.

Equality State. This is the name given to the U.S.A. State of Wyoming where, first among the communities of the world, women were accorded the right to vote.

Era. A series of years beginning from some starting-point, which is usually an epoch. The origin of the word is in some doubt. It has been suggested that it is derived from A. ER. A, the initial abbreviations of *Annus erat Augusti*, words employed by the Spaniards to signify the year in which they became subjects of Augusta and adopted the Roman calendar. The more likely origin, however, is that the word is derived from the Latin *aera*, plural of *ae*, which was used to denote copper and was afterwards used to describe counters or items of calculation.

Dr. Brewer gives the following as the principal eras:

Era of the Greek Olympiads, 776 B.C.
Era of the foundation of Rome, 753 B.C.
Era of the Nabonassar, 747 B.C.
Era of Alexander the Great, 324 B.C.
Era of the Seleucidæ, 312 B.C.
Era of the Julian era, 45 B.C.
The Christian era begins from the birth of Christ.

Erk. Nickname in the R.A.F. for an aircraftsman of the ground staff. Wing-Commander F. W. J. Heading in 1920 wrote a song which he called "Airks." One verse of it ran:

"While Jack is on the quarter-deck, and Tommy rules the square,
We look to you, our boys in blue, to guard us in the air.
You fear no foe when up you go to keep the country free,
Give me an airk who doesn't shirk; he's the boy for me."

The R.A.F. Station at Uxbridge, Middlesex, adopted the name for aircraftsmen, but shortened it to "Erk." In 1944 someone added the "Christian" name Joe, so that an aircraftsman of the R.A.F. became Joe Erk.

Eros. The Greek God of Love, identified by the Romans with Cupid. He is the son of Mercury and Venus. The statue of Eros in Piccadilly is really not Eros, but Cupid. The legend of Cupid is that he wets with blood the grindstone on which he sharpens those deadly arrows!

Esquire. Is without doubt another of the most misused words in the English language. From the Latin *scutarius*, it was originally applied to one who carried the shield (escu) of a Knight. The Richmond Herald, C. H. Athill, Esquire, compiled the following as legally entitled to be called Esquires: "The sons of Peers, Baronets and Knights; the eldest sons of the young sons of Peers and the eldest sons in perpetuity; the eldest son of the eldest son of a Knight, and his eldest son in perpetuity; the Kings of Arms, the Heralds of Arms, Officers of the Navy and Army of the rank of captain and upwards, Sheriffs, J.P.'s while they are in commission, Sergeants-at-Law, King's Counsel, Companions of Knighthood, certain Officers of the Royal Household, Deputy Lieutenants, Commissioners of the Court of Bankruptcy, Masters of the Supreme Court, and those whom the King in any Commission styles Esquires."

And nobody else—legally!

Essays. The first English discursive compositions to be given the name of essays were those of Lord Bacon.

Et cetera Usually written *etc*. The literal meaning is "and the other things." Cetera is a neutral plural. It should not be applied to persons.

Ethiopia. The word is worth a place in a dictionary of origins because of its meaning. It comes from the Greek *aithein*, to burn, and *ops*, the face.

Etiquette. Is another remarkable example of a corrupted use. It is a French word meaning label. On ceremonial and other important occasions a ticket of instructions was issued to visitors detailing what they should do. The ticket, or label, was their etiquette. To-day, it is a code (mostly unspoken and unwritten) of rules governing behaviour and decorum.

Etna. The volcano. The name come from the Phœnician *attuna*, a furnace. The legend of Mount Etna, described by Virgil is that its eruption is due to the restlessness of Encealadus, the hundred-headed giant who lies buried under the mountain, where the Greek and Latin poets placed the forges of Vulcan and the smithy of the Cyclops.

Eton. Is the Anglo-Saxon *Eyton*, the island town.

Euphemism. Is an agreeable way of saying a disagreeable or unpleasant thing. Its origin is the Greek *eu*, well, and *phemi*, I say. "Light-fingered gentry" is an euphemism for thieves; and "fell asleep" for death.

Eureka. Properly should be Heureka, "*I have found it*." It was, as is pretty well-known, the exclamation of Archimedes, the Syracusan philosopher. King Hiero had had delivered to Archimedes his royal crown for the purity of the gold to be tested. The King, who had delivered a certain weight of gold to a smith to be made into the crown, suspected that the gold had been mixed with an alloy. Archimedes, at his wits' end to know how to test, was pondering over the problem when he went to his bath. As he stepped in the brimming tub some of the water slopped over the side. The story can be continued, now, by Vitruvius, who says that it at once occurred to Archimedes that a body must remove its own bulk in water. He further argued that as silver is lighter than gold, a pound-weight of silver would be more bulky than a pound-weight in gold and would, consequently, displace more water. "When the idea flashed into his mind," says Vitruvius, "the philosopher jumped out of the bath, and without waiting to dress himself ran through the streets naked, crying 'Heureka,' to try the experiment at home."

The result was that Archimedes found that the crown was actually deficient in weight of gold.

Hence, the corrupted word "Eureka" is now applied as an exclamation when anything hidden is at last found.

Eureka, as the motto of California, in allusion to the gold found there, is now obvious.

Europe. The name is derived from the Greek *euros*, broad, and *ops*, the face. In other words, Europe is "the broad face of the earth."

Euthanasia. A Greek word meaning an easy, happy death. It has been given the name of late years of mercy-killing. For some years in Britain debate has been raging on whether doctors should be given the power of putting to death persons who are suffering from a disease known to be incurable, and who are in extreme pain by reason of the disease. The House of Lords, in December, 1936, rejected a Bill to make Euthanasia possible. But doctors have practised it quietly for some years. A distinguished surgeon (un-named) described in a medical paper in 1936 how he had given easy death to four patients, and a country doctor, also un-named, stated that he had on five occasions administered Euthanasia. The stumbling-block to medical authorities supporting the "mercy-killing" is what can be said to constitute an incurable person, in view of the constant discoveries of medicine in illnesses previously labelled as incurable.

Evacuation Day. An American celebration of 25th November, and Britain's first "Dunkirk." It commemorates the evacuation of New York City by the British after the War of Independence, 1783.

Evans, William. Although not strictly an origin, the name of this giant porter of Charles I is given because of the many times the author has been asked whether it is true that there was so small a man in England that he was carried in the pocket of another man. There was! The dwarf was Sir Jeffrey Hudson, known as the King's Dwarf. He was carried in the pocket of William Evans, who stood nearly eight feet, and was broad in proportion.

Every man Jack of them. The old form of every was "everich," and everyone was written "everichon." The word, passed down in speech to the corruption, "every-John." When the name John became familiarly corrupted to Jack, the old meaning of "everi-chon" was forgotten, so we came to the phrase "every man Jack of them."

Evil Communications corrupt Good Manners. Although this phrase is usually attributed to St. Paul (1 *Cor*. xv, 35), the rightful author was Menander. The correct wording is: "It must be that evil communications corrupt good dispositions."

Evil Eye. The term springs from a belief held through all the ages that certain persons could cast a curse on objects upon which they looked malevolently. The ancients held that the first morning look of such eyes was certain destruction to man or beast. Virgil has blamed the evil eye for the leanness of cattle.

Ex. A Latin prefix for "out of," or "by reason of." In other words, after. Thus, an ex-Minister means one out of office; ex-cathedra means by reason of; and *ex post faco* means from what is done afterwards.

Exception that proves the rule, The. Does not mean that any exception proves the correction in general of any rule. In the days when the phrases was coined, *proved* was interpreted as "tested." Thus, St. Paul said, "Prove all things," when he meant the word prove in its original meaning, "test all things."

Exchequer. Was originally (in the days of Edward I) a court to look after the revenues of the Crown and to recover debts due to the King. Its name came from the "chequered" cloth which covered the table of the court. *Chequered* is derived from the Old French word *eschequier*, a chess board.

The Latin root is *scaccum*, a chess-board.

The original Exchequer is described by Foss in "Lives of the Judges." "All round the table," he wrote, "was a standing ledge, four fingers broad, covered with a cloth, and this cloth was black-rowed with strekes about a span, like a chess-board. On the spaces of this cloth, counters were arranged marked for checking computations."

Exeter. Was called by the Saxons Exancester, or the Roman town on the Exe.

Eye. Was the Anglo-Saxon word for island. It was sometimes spelt *Ey* or *Ea*. Used principally as a suffix, they enter into the names of many places by the side of the Thames, which are now joined to the mainland, such as Batters*ea*, Bermonds*ey*, Moles*ey*, and so on.

Chelsea was originally spelt *chesel-ea*, meaning a shingle island.

Eye of a Needle. "*It is easier for a camel to go through the eye of a needle than for a rich man to enter the Kingdom of God.*" The interpretation of this phrase is one of exceeding difficulty. Various origins have been given to the meaning of "needle." An "eye" was at one time the name given to the gateway in an Eastern city wall. Camels were forbidden to enter through certain of these eyes. But there is the stumbling-block that there is no evidence to show that the name *eye* for such a gate existed in Biblical times. It is probable that Christ, in using the term, was emphasizing the impossibility of a camel going through the eye of a needle, and therefore of the rich man going into the Kingdom of God.

See "Camel."

Eye-opener ! The word, coming from America, was originally a concoction of mixed spirits taken as a cure for drowsiness. An "eye-opener" in very truth !

Eye-teeth. Are so-called because their fangs extend upwards nearly to the orbits of the eyes.

F

Fabian Policy. So-called after the Roman, Quintas Fabius Maximus, who, appointed by the Romans a dictator in order to combat the disasters which had overtaken the Roman armies at the hands of Hannibal, adopted a policy not of attacking the Carthaginian army, but of following it and delaying and harassing it in every possible way. From this he was nicknamed Cunctator, or delayer ; and from it comes the expression "a Fabian policy" for one of caution or deliberation.

Fabian Society. The *Daily News*, describing the Fabian Society in 1894, stated : "Fabian tactics lie in stealing inches, not in grasping leagues." And that was exactly the object of the association of Socialists founded in 1884 by Bernard Shaw (G.B.S.), Sidney Webb (afterwards Lord Passfield), and others. The name they took from Quintas Fabius, the Roman general (275-203 B.C.), who won his war against Hannibal "by wariness and caution, not by violence and defiance."

Faction. A party of persons having some common end in view, but usually seeking to obtain that end by irregular means. The origin is of more than passing interest. The Romans divided the charioteers in the Circus into factions, or classes, one of each contending in a race. The four regular factions, distinguished by their dresses of green, red, blue and white represented Spring, Summer, Autumn and Winter. Domitian added purple and yellow factions, making six contestants in each race. A dispute in Constantinople, in 532, between the green and blue factions and their partisans (the Emperor Justinian favouring the latter), led to a civil war of five days which cost thirty thousand lives and nearly upset the government. It was this particular faction fight which led to the term being mainly applied to parties opposed to the government in power.

Factory King. The name applied to Richard Oastlet, of Bradford, promoter of the "Ten Hours' Bill."

Factotum. Its derivation explains the meaning of the word—the Latin *facere totum*, to do everything required. Which is exactly what a factotum does to-day. It is one of the few uncorrupted meanings of Latin words !

Fag, Fag-end. The modern slang for a cigarette and for the stub of a cigarette, respectively. The origin, which seems to have left so many etymologists in doubt, is perfectly simple. It was born in the cloth-weaving industry. Fag or fag-end was the name given to the selvedge, or coarse end, of a piece of cloth. It thus came to mean the end of anything. Thus, fag-end of a cigarette means the stub. The custom of calling a cigarette a "fag" arose from small boys, at first in the weaving towns, calling to smokers : "Chuck us the *fag*, guv'nor," using the word they knew for "end."

Faggot. Can be either a bundle of sticks, or a savoury made from the offals of pigs seasoned with sage, onions and other herbs, and fried or baked in tins.

Faggot Votes are those obtained by transfer of property, temporarily, to a person whose already owned-property is not sufficient to qualify him for a vote. The "faggot" was a "bundle" of property divided into small lots for the purpose given above.

Fair. A description bestowed on many people famous in history or story. Among them are :

Fair Maid of Anjou. Lady Edith Plantagenet, who married David of Scotland.

Fair Maid of Brittany. Eleanor, grand-daughter of Henry II, and at one time the rightful Queen of England. The usurper, King John, imprisoned her in Bristol Castle, where she died.

Fair Maid of Kent. Joan, the beautiful and only daughter of the Earl of Kent, who married Edward the Black Prince.

Fair Maid of Norway. Margaret, daughter of Eric II. Being recognized as successor to the throne of Scotland (she was grand-daughter of Alexander III) she set out for her kingdom, but died from sea-sickness during the journey.

Fair Maid of Perth. Kate Glover, said to have been the most beautiful woman in the city. She is the heroine of Scott's novel of that name.

Fair Rosamund. According to the story she was the fayre daughter of Walter, Lord Clifford, the concubine of Henry II, and was poisoned by the Queen in 1177. Henry is said to have built for her a house named Labyrinthus, wherein no man or woman might find their way to her, save himself. As a fitting end to the story, the inscription on her tomb, at Godstow, is of interest :

"Here, Rose the graced, not
Rose the Chaste, reposes.
The smell that rises is no
smell of roses."

The fair above is derived from the Anglo-Saxon *faeger*.

Fair, A Day after the. In this case fair is from the Latin *feria*, which means a holiday. In other words, to arrive a day after the fair is to arrive too late and miss the fun. It is used, also, as expressing wisdom after the event.

Fairy Rings. At the cost of annoying those who still believe in fairies, and despite those grown-ups who see them dancing at the bottom of the garden, the writer must truthfully explain the fairy rings. They were never made by dancing feet, but by perfectly natural means. The circle is caused by a fungus which seeds circularly. The decay of the fungus year by year renders the soil unfit for a new crop of fungus, but increases the fertility of the ground, and hence there appears a gradually increased circle of grass, brighter and greener than the surrounding turf.

Fake. To defraud. Despite the evidence of several dictionaries, the word has nothing whatever to do with the Indian fakir. The Indian word means "poor." Mohammed cried *el fakr fakhri*, "poverty is my pride." Nor does the word come from the Latin *facimentum, facere*, to make. In fact, all the evidence goes to show that it has no pedigree at all, but is a corruption of old Dutch or old German thieves *argot*, and was originally feague. To *feague* a horse was to make it look younger and stronger than it actually was, by such devices as blowing up the skin and painting it here and there.

Fall. *To fall short of*. In this sense the Latin root is *excido*, to fall. It is used in the sense of a missile projected but falling to earth before reaching its object. To fall short of one's endeavour is to just miss attaining the object.

Fall foul of. Means really to impede. The metaphor is from the sea. A ship falls foul of another when it impedes her progress. A rope is foul when it becomes entangled.

Fall, In the. "American ism for Autumn," says one authority. It is nothing of the sort. The word "fall" for the Autumn can be found in the very English works of Drayton, Raleigh, and many other Elizabethan writers. It is the correct English name for the Autumn ; the fall of the leaf.

Fall into a Snare. Is really the Latin phrase, *insidias incidere*.

Falling Bodies. We have received this question at the rate of four or five times a day for months. The answer to which of two bodies of varying weights would reach the ground first if dropped from a height is this : All bodies, whatever their weight, fall at the same speed from a height. If a feather and a ton weight were dropped together in a perfect vacuum both would reach the bottom at the same moment. Dropped from a height over land in the open air, two objects fall together until what is termed "terminal velocity" is reached. At that point air resistance takes effect and invariably the lighter of the articles, presenting less resistance to the pressure, lands first.

The formula for ascertaining the speed of falling bodies is as follows :

First second, 16 feet.
Second second, 16 by 2^2.
Third second, 16 by 3^2.
Fourth second, 16 by 4^2.
And so on.

This is without taking into consideration air resistance.

Falling Stars. We like best the Mohammedan belief and origin. They hold that a meteor (falling star) is a firebrand flung by the good angels against evil spirits who approach too close to the gates of Heaven.

Fame, Temple of. The most noted temple of fame is the Pantheon, erected at Rome by Agrippa. It was dedicated to all the Gods. Another, erected in Paris in 1790, is the shrine of Frenchmen honoured by their country.

But in this country it is usually a temple of memory only, where immortality lies in the writings or the Science in which the fame was won. To have a niche in the temple of fame means that one's works will live in the memory of the people.

Familiarity Breeds Contempt. The Latins used the proverb ; and its quotation in English literature goes back as far as Udall (1560-92), the Puritan, of Kingston-on-Thames, who was sentenced to death for tracts attacking the Bishops, but was subsequently reprieved.

Family Circle. The phrase has lost much of its meaning these days ; but in the Norman period the family circle was, indeed, a circle, since the fire occupied a space in the centre of the floor and the smoke found a vent through a hole in the roof. Those were the days when to "sit round the fire" meant exactly what it said. Similarly, in Russia and in many parts of Germany, an enclosed stove in the centre of the living-room gave warmth to the occupants.

Fanatic. Properly applied, this word should be used only in connection with religion. It is derived from *fanum*, a temple, and related to people who, in Roman days, attended temples and there, falling into strange fits or seances as they would be termed to-day, were said to be able to see the past and foretell the future.

Fanny Adams. Whatever the phrase "Sweet Fanny Adams" may mean to-day, there is no doubt as to the origin of it. Fanny Adams was the name of a young woman who was murdered in 1810, and whose body was found, cut into pieces, and thrown into the river at Alton, Hants. The murderer, a man named Fred Baker, was afterwards publicly hanged at Winchester. In the Navy, Fanny Adams was, after this crime, the name by which tinned meat was vulgarly described. Barriere's and Leland's slang dictionary gives the explanation : "Fanny Adams (Naval) tinned mutton" ; and the *Blackwood Magazine* of February, 1927, gives : "Fanny Adams (or preserved mutton) from a ship."

Farce. The now popular entertainment of the stage has a queer origin. It is derived from the Latin *farcire*, to stuff. Like episodes (q.v.) a farce was originally an interlude, inserted in the main performance, hence the farce—"stuffed in."

Fare. From the Anglo-Saxon *faran*, to go. It meant, originally, a journey for which passage money was paid ; it has come to mean the money paid for the passage, and the person paying the money is also called the fare.

The secondary meaning of fare—food and provisions—is difficult to understand. It has no origin, so far as can be discovered.

Farewell. An expression of goodwill to a traveller starting out on the fare (journey)—the wish that the journey would end in all well. *See* "Fare," above.

Farm. The most probable of two suggested origins of the word farm is the Anglo-Saxon *feorm*, which meant a feast. The corruption to its present meaning makes intriguing reading. The first step is connected with the word itself—feast. Lands were let by the Lord of the Manor to tenants on condition that such tenants supplied the lord with a certain number of nightly entertainments for his household and guests. The authority for this appears in the Saxon Chronicle of A.D. 775. It is there recorded that the Abbot of Peterborough let land on condition that the holder of such land should pay annually fifty pounds and *anes nihtes feorme* (one night's entertainment). Frequently, similar conditions appear in the records of Domesday Book. The next step towards the present farm occurred when the providing of such entertainment became difficult of provision, or impossible of achievement. (It should be interpolated here that the entertainment meant, principally, provisions for the household.) Consequently, money payment was substituted and the payment was then called *firma alba*, or *blanche ferme*, signifying that payment was being made in white money instead of victuals. When the practice became universal, and there was no longer the need to supply entertainment, the rent became known as *firma*. By the process of substitution of words, the land itself came to being called the firma. And the further change to farm grew into being.

The other suggested origin comes from the Latin *firmus*, meaning firm or durable. It is held by the supporters of this derivation that the land thus let was held on a firm and durable agreement. It is, however, a very doubtful origin, with nothing in actual existence to warrant it being accepted.

Farmer George. George III, because of his dress, manners and bucolic sporting habits.

Faro. The card game (illegal in England), was so-called from a representation of Pharoah on the cards, originally.

Farrago. "*A farrago of nonsense.*" A confused mass, or jumble. The word is Latin, and means in that language a mixture of corn or fodder for cattle together with meal—Latin *far*.

Farthing. Britain's smallest coin. It was the Anglo-Saxon *feorthing*, "a little fourth." In those days the silver penny was deeply impressed with a cross (something like the Good Friday hot-cross bun) and was broken into four pieces to make farthings. Later, a silver farthing was introduced. The first copper farthing was coined for Charles II. Farthings are now made of bronze.

Farthingale. A hooped petticoat of Elizabethan days. It is worth mentioning as an instance of a fashion introduced by a Queen's vanity. Elizabeth wore this hooped petticoat in order to disguise her figure. The name is not a corruption of *Verdingale*, from the French *vertugarde*, a guard for modesty. Instead, it came from the Spanish *verdugads*, green rods, of which the frames were made before whalebone was introduced.

Fate. "*The cruel Fates.*" From the Latin *Fatum*, usually in the plural *fata*. It was held by the Greeks and Romans that there were three Fates who controlled the birth, life and death of man. They were Clotho (who held the distaff), Lachesis (who spun the thread of life), and Atropos (who cut the thread at the appointed end of life). They were referred to as "cruel," because they were arbitrary and paid no heed to the wishes of anyone. Pope wrote:

"For thee the *Fates*, severely kind, ordain
A cool suspense from pleasure and from pain."

Fat's in the Fire. Meaning trouble, misfortune. The origin is obvious; if the fat in the frying-pan is spilt on the fire a column of flame and smoke spoils the food which is being fried.

Feast of Lanterns. A Chinese festival held on the fifteenth day of the first moon of the year. The origin is interesting as showing how customs are derived from small beginnings. Walking by the side of a lake one evening a daughter of a Mandarin fell in, and was drowned. The father, told of the tragedy, gathered his household together, and with them, carrying lanterns, hurried to the scene. The body was recovered, and buried. On the anniversary of the tragedy the Mandarin caused fires to be lighted by the side of the lake, and invited all who attended to offer up prayers for her soul. In course of time the reason for the feast of lanterns was forgotten, but the ceremonial was not only continued, but was made the occasion of a national holiday.

Feast of Tabernacles. Commemorative of the forty years' wandering of the Israelites in search of the Promised Land. During the wandering they dwelt in huts or tabernacles formed of tree branches covered with leaves. Strict Jews still take their meals in temporary structures covered with leaves during the festival, which lasts nine days.

Feather in his Cap. From the custom of the Red Indian, who stuck a feather in his head-dress for every enemy slain in battle.

Feather one's nest. The allusion is to the habit of birds which line their nests with feathers to make them *soft* and *comfortable*.

Feather, White. *To show the white feather.* To be branded a coward. The allusion is to the old cock-fighting days. Fighting cocks, game birds, were highly bred, and had no white feather in their plumage. The presence of such a white feather indicated a cross-breed, and the likelihood that the cock might not fight to the death.

Feathers. As the name of a public-house, first appeared as a tribute to Edward the Black Prince, whose crest was the plume of feathers ever since associated with the Prince of Wales.

Fee. This is another of those words which, like so many purely British names, spring from the soil with which, in olden times, all commerce in Britain was bound up. It comes from the Anglo-Saxon word *feoh*, cattle which, in those days, was one of the principal means of making payment. It is interesting to note, in passing, that the Latin *pecunia*, money, was derived in similar way from *pecus*, which also meant cattle, and capital from *capita*, head of cattle. Those were the days of barter, before money held the significance which it holds to-day.

Feed of Corn. When, in these days of few horses, you ask an ostler to give your animal a "feed of corn," it means no more than just a meal. But in olden days it was a definite measure of fodder. A "feed of corn" was a quartern of oats, and was charged for as such.

Fee-Simple. This phrase, which all owners or renters of property find in agreements, means that a tenant in "fee-simple" holds land and tenements for himself and his heirs absolutely and simply, without mentioning what heirs.

Fell. The name in the North of England for a hill. A Norse word, it means the place where the ground is on the fall, as on a hill-side. Snae-fell, the snow mountain, is an example.

Fell, Doctor. His chief claim to fame is the fact that he was the Dr. Fell, Dean of Christ Church College, Oxford, of whom Tom Brown wrote the couplet:

"I do not like thee, Dr. Fell,
The reason why I cannot tell;
But this I know, I know full well,
I do not like thee, Dr. Fell."

The Doctor expelled Tom Brown from Oxford.

Fellow Feeling. The phrase was written by the actor, David Garrick, in his "Epilogue on Quitting the Theatre," in June, 1776: "A fellow feeling makes one wondrous kind." Byron, misquoting him in "English Bards and Scotch Reviewers," wrote "us" for "one."

Felo-de-se. Self-murder. A suicide. Because a suicide, or man committing deliberate felo-de-se, cannot be buried in consecrated ground, coroners and juries have of late years adopted the practice of returning verdicts in most cases of "Suicide while the balance of mind was disturbed," thus avoiding the stigma of murder of one's self, and leaving the way open to Christian burial.

Fetish. The word comes from the Latin *facticius*, made by art. Its origin was West Africa, where Portuguese sailors and traders applied it to objects worshipped by the natives. They also sold the fetishes. The Portuguese word for the charms was *feitco*. Tylor, in his "Primitive Culture," describes a fetish as follows: "To class an object as a fetish demands explicit statement that a spirit is considered as embodied in it, or acting through it, or communicating by it, or at least that the people it belongs to, do habitually think this of such objects."

Fettle. Has a number of meanings. It may be ale seasoned with sugar-ginger and nutmeg, known as fettled ale; it may also be a thrashing, or "fettle" somebody. Morris used it in the sense of being prepared, "When the Ark was *fettled* and forged." But the sense in which the word is used to-day, being "in good fettle," comes from the Anglo-Saxon *fetel*, a girdle. In other words being girded up, ready for anything.

Feud. It may seem a simple word to class, since the Anglo-Saxon *fah* meant hostile, and *fahman*, a foeman. But there is also another feud, from the Latin *feudum*, sometimes spelt *feodum*. This word was connected with fee (q.v.). It is from the latter derivation that we get feudal system. A *feud* was land held by a limited or conditional estate, the property being in the lord, and the usufruct in the tenant. A dispute may be over a *feud*, tenancy, or over a *feud* of hate.

Feudal System, The. *See above,* "Feud." The feudal system was introduced into Britain by William the Conqueror. He seized all the land of the country and portioned it out to nobles in return for their homage and the raising and maintaining of an army and other service. In this way they held *feuds,* see above.

Palgrave, delving into the origin of feudal tenure, considered that it might be traced to the grants made by the Romans to the barbarian Læti occupying the Limitanean or Ripuarian territories, upon the condition of performing military service.

Few. "*Never in the field of human conflict, was so much owed by so many to so few.*" Speech in the House of Commons by the Prime Minister, Mr. Winston Churchill, on 20th August, 1940, referring to the fighter pilots who had fought the Luftwaffe in the Battle of Britain, between 8th August and 31st October, 1940. They destroyed 2,375 German planes in daylight alone, and saved England from an undoubted invasion, planned for when communications had been destroyed throughout the country.

Fiasco. Dr. Brewer states that the Italian *fiasco* means a flask, and it is uncertain how it came, in Venetian slang, to mean a failure. He tells the story of a harlequin, noted for his clever harangue who, on one occasion, improvizing over a flask, and gaining no applause, said: "It is thy fault, fiasco." Hence any failure became a fiasco.

The story is quite fanciful. It is true that the word came from Venice. The origin is as follows: When Venice was famed for its glass, the utmost care was taken by the makers of Venetian glass to ensure that their ware was perfect. If any flaw developed in the delicate work, it was the practice of the workmen, in order to avoid waste, to turn the article into a common flask—a *fiasco.* Hence the Venetian glass-makers regarded a fiasco as something which had failed to come up to their standard.

Fib. "*That's a fib.*" The word fib is derived from fable. "That's a fable," in other words, not true.

Fiddle, Fit as a. The usual origin given is fit as a fiddle tuned to concert pitch. We have never regarded this as a good origin, since a fiddle is, of itself, an inanimate object. In old pugilistic days the name, Fiddler, was given to a boxer who depended more on his activity than upon his strength to win. Thus, to wear down his opponent, he had to be exceptionally fit. Again, the fiddler who usually supplied the only music at Irish dances, played unceasingly from dusk till dawn—a feat of endurance which could only come from fitness. The author suggests that the original phrase was "Fit as a Fiddler."

Fiddler's Money. A threepenny piece. It was originally a small coin paid to the fiddler by each of the dancers at a merry-making.

Field. Was originally the Anglo-Saxon *feld*, a place from which the trees had been felled, or cleared. The origin is interesting, for the reader, turning over in his mind the large number of name-places with the suffix feld or field, can gain a good idea of the extent to which Britain was at one time forest land. Shef-field, Chester-field, Earls-field, are examples.

Fiend. The origin is the Anglo-Saxon *feond*, a hater. It was usually applied not to fellow citizens, but to express Satan. The Danish and Swedish *fiende,* was an enemy.

Fifth Columnist. The words, or phrase, so frequently used in the second Great War as expressing a traitor within the gates, originated in the Spanish Civil War between the Falange (Fascists) and the supposed Communists. It was stated in Madrid that four columns of enemy were attacking the city from outside, and an invisible Fifth Column was attacking from the *inside.* From this, forces antagonistic to a country, and living in that country, came to be called Fifth Columnists. There is no doubt that "Fifth Columnists, paid by German money, were responsible for the capitulation in France."

Fig (slang). Here is a word for which it is difficult to find an authentic derivation. In one usage it represents perfection, such as "in full fig," full or official dress; in another a state of full readiness, such as used by Thackeray: "Is not one of the Queen's pyebalds (horses) in full fig." Yet in a third it is made to suggest something entirely worthless, in "I don't care a fig." Again, to *fig* a person is to hocus him. It has been stated that "I don't care a fig" comes from the Spanish *fico*, a contemptuous gesture which consisted of thrusting out the thumb between the first and second fingers.

Fight. "*He who fights and runs away, lives to fight another day.*" The tag is not, as it sounds, more or less modern English copy-book. Reproached for fleeing from Philip of Macedon at Chærona, Demosthenes made reply: "A man that runs away may fight again."

Fight on the Beaches . . . in the Streets." On 4th June, 1940, Mr. Winston Churchill, Prime Minister, made what was probably the greatest speech of his career. Following is the vital text: "That is the resolve of His Majesty's Government. . . . We shall fight on the seas and the oceans . . . we shall fight on the beaches, we shall fight on the landing-grounds, we shall fight in the fields and in the streets, we shall fight in the hills; we shall never surrender. . . ."

Finger, To lift the little. Said of a man known to he a heavy drinker. You can see the derivation of this in any café or hostelry—a person lifting a cup or glass invariably sticks out the little finger, and the finger lifts thus with the glass.

Fire. "*To go through Fire and Water.*" A reference to the ordeals of fire and water which were the common methods of trial in Anglo-Saxon times. In the ordeal by fire the accused had to carry a red-hot bar of iron nine yards from the fire, or to walk, bare-foot and blind-fold, along a path strewn with red-hot ploughshares. The water ordeal was to plunge a hand into boiling water.

Greek Fire. A combustible composition, the constituents of which are supposed to have been asphalt, niter and sulphur. It would burn on or under water, and was used with great effect in war by the Greeks of the Eastern Empire, who kept its composition secret for several hundred years. Upon the conquest of Constantinople the secret came into the possession of the Mohammedans, to whom it rendered valuable service. It is sometimes called "Grecian Fire."

Kentish Fire. See "Kentish."

Thames on Fire. See "Set."

Fire Away. Say what you have to say. The allusion is, of course, to firing a gun, which is waiting, fully primed, the command.

Fire Dogs. These adjuncts to the fender, which still remain in many households, were once real dogs who were imprisoned in a wheel at one end of a roasting spit. Their job was to run round the wheel, thus turning the spit. It took three hours of this canine exercise to cook the Roast Beef of Old England. Should the dog not exert himself sufficiently it was the custom to put a live coal inside the wheel to accelerate his movements.

Fire of London. The Great Fire of London broke out in the baker's shop of Master Farryner, in Pudding Lane, and burned for three days and nights, spreading to Pie Corner, where it was at last halted. St. Paul's Cathedral, eighty-nine other churches, thirteen thousand two hundred houses, and other property was burned down.

Fish. As the symbol of Christ, *see* "Ichthus."

Fish. "*He eats no fish.*" In Elizabethan times a way of saying that a man was honest, and could be trusted. The allusion was to the Roman Catholic custom of banning meat and eating only fish on Friday. Roman Catholics of the period were naturally opposed to Protestantism, and therefore to the Government. They were looked upon as intriguers, not to be trusted.

Fish, A Pretty Kettle of. Dr. Brewer says that "Kettle of fish" was an old Border name for a picnic by the riverside, in which newly-caught salmon was the chief dish. The salmon was boiled on the spot, and when fit for eating was partaken of by the company in gipsy fashion. The discomfort of this sort of picnic, says the Doctor, probably gave rise to the saying, "A pretty kettle of fish," meaning an awkward state of affairs, a mess or muddle. It is, the present writer fears, an entirely fanciful origin. How the picnic party could, in the first place, rely upon catching a salmon for the picnic, we fail to see!

In point of fact, the origin of the phrase is quite simple, if one bears in mind the habit of the English people of corrupting words in passing them down by phonetic sounds, and then spelling the phonetics. The pretty *kettle* of fish was, in fact, a *kiddle* of fish. And a *kiddle* was a basket placed in a river for catching fish. It was perfectly well-known in the time of the Plantagenets.

One of the perquisites of the Warder of the Tower of London was the right to trap fish in his *kiddles* outside Traitors' Gate. Citizens made periodical raids on his kiddles and destroyed them. "A pretty kiddle of fish" he would exclaim on seeing the damage done; in the same way that to-day one might say, "Here's a pretty state of affairs."

Flak. The name given by all nations to anti-aircraft shells bursting round attacking aeroplanes. It arose during the World War (1939-). It is German in origin, the letters Fl-a-K forming the initials of Flieger-Abwehr-Kanone, German for, "The gun that drives off raiders."

Flagellants. Were a sect of enthusiasts in the middle of the thirteenth century, who went in procession through the streets inflicting on themselves scourgings, or flagellations in order to merit, by it, the favour of God. They were put down soon after their appearance, but were revived during the Black Death.

Flagellation in Britain during recent years has revived among a certain class of sexual perverts; and there have been a number of prosecutions in the courts.

Flame. Word for a lover. "An old flame," a discarded lover. The simple derivation is that the Latin for love is *flamma*, and the French word *feu* is also used to express love.

Flaming onions. The name given by pilots of the R.A.F. to green, fiery spheres shot up by German anti-aircraft defences, and intended to set fire to an aircraft.

"Flannelled Fools." Term bestowed on cricketers by Rudyard Kipling. It gave rise to much criticism at the time, and doubtless mitigated against him in his prospects of becoming Poet Laureate.

Flapper. Colloquial name for a young, girl, properly applied to one who has not yet "put up her hair." The allusion is to the large bow which in the days that the term was coined usually adorned the hair. It flapped in the breezes! A young duck not yet able to fly is also called a flapper.

Flat-foot Floogy with the Floy-floy. This title of a "Swing" tune popular over here shows the debasement to which the art of music has descended through American composers, if the term may be used. Enthusiastic singers of the words may be surprised to know that in America a "flat-foot floogy" is a prostitute, a street walker, "first-class"; and "floy-floy" is slang for a certain type of venereal disease. How the words were ever allowed to be published is remarkable.

Flea. The name is the Anglo-Saxon *fleah*, to jump. The insect is well-named, for it can leap thirty times its own height, and draw eighty times its own weight. Socrates and Chærephon once spent a considerable time working out the problem of the flea's capacity for jumping!

Sent off with a Flea in the Ear. The allusion is to the distress of a dog with a flea in its ear.

Flesh-pots. "*Sighing for the Flesh-pots of Egypt.*" Means, of course, regretting the good things you formerly possessed. The origin is *Exodus* xvi, 3, where the children of Israel, wandering in the desert after being freed by God from the Egyptians, wished that they had died when they sat by the flash-pots of Egypt, rather than undergo their present trials in the dreary wastes.

Flogging a Dead Horse. The phrase was first used by John Bright in a speech on the Reform Bill of Earl Russell. He declared that the Bill was "a dead horse," and any attempt to recreate interest in it was "flogging a dead horse."

Flotsam and Jetsam. The names applied to wreckage at sea. From the Old French *floter*, to float, and jetsam, the French *jeter* and English jettison, to throw out. Flotsam is wreckage of a ship, and jetsam things thrown from a ship by the crew to lighten it.

Flummox. *To flummox him completely.* The origin of the word is obscure, but probably is allied to the Old English *flummocks*, to maul or mangle; or perhaps to *flummock*, which stood for bewilderment.

Flying Bomb. On 16th June, 1944, during an air raid by the Germans, an aeroplane crashed in Southern England. The explosion damaged by blast a large number of dwellings, but there was no crater, such as had always been the case when bombs were dropped, or planes crashed. Investigation showed that the plane was unusually small—about thirty feet long. For some time it had been known that the Germans were experimenting with a pilotless plane, which was to be sent from emplacements in the Pas de Calais area of the French coast, and it was conjectured that this plane was the first to be tried out. This proved to be the case, and on subsequent days and nights a large number flew over Southern England.

The robot-planes were jet-propelled, and the system seemed to be to load them with sufficient petrol for a flight of a certain duration and start them from catapult emplacements on a set course, on which they were kept by compass and gyroscope arrangement. When the petrol became exhausted—or perhaps there was a device for cutting off the petrol at a given time—the plane fell to earth. It carried a load of explosive equal, so R.A.F. experts said, to a 1,000 lb. bomb. The planes were of varying speeds, some two hundred and fifty miles an hour, and others four hundred miles per hour.

The first name given to them was that of Robot-plane. This proved too cumbersome for the bright gentlemen of the British newspapers, who promptly christened this secret weapon "The Flying Bomb." The fighter pilots of the R.A.F., who shot hundreds of them into the Channel as they came over, nicknamed them "The Doodle Bug."

F.O.B. A commercial contraction for "Free on Board." It means that from the time of shipment, the shipper is legally free from all risks.

Fool. The word comes from the Latin *follis*, a windbag, with the plural *folles*, puffed-out cheeks.

Fool all the People all the Time. The tag runs as follows: "You can fool some of the people all the time, and all the people some of the time, but you can't fool all the people all the time." It is generally ascribed to Bill Barnum, the Circus King, who lived up to it; but in some quarters is said to have been first uttered by Abraham Lincoln at Clifton (Ill.) on 8th September, 1858.

Foolscap. A sheet of paper measuring 13½ by 17 inches. The name is derived from an old watermark in the paper, the first known specimen of which occurred in 1540. The watermark was in the form of a fool's cap and bells.

Fools, Feast of. A feast of the Middle Ages designed to honour the Ass upon which Christ rode into Jerusalem. It developed, however, into blasphemous foolery. The prayers for the day were intoned in traversty, and in place of the Amen the entire procession brayed like an ass.

Court Fool. Up to the seventeenth century licensed fools or, as they were called, jesters, were kept at Court and by the more important of the noble houses. They had great privileges, and could, within reason, poke fun at the King or his guests. Probably the best known Court Fools of England were Will Somers, Henry VIII's jester, and Robert Greene, jester in the Court of Elizabeth.

Foot. A measure of length. *See* "Ell."

Right foot foremost. The allusion is to the superstition that it is unlucky to leave one's house or chamber with the left foot foremost. The Emperor Augustus held this superstition very strongly. Pythagoras taught that it was necessary to put on the right shoe first; and this was supported by Iamblichus on the ground that it symbolized that man's first duty is to God. The symbol seems a little hazy.

Football. A form of football was played in Derby and Chester in A.D. 217. Many generations before that, however, football, very much like our game, was played by the ancient Greeks. The Romans must have played a version of the Rugby Code, for their name for the game was *harpasto*, "I seize!" Their game was played by two large companies of men who endeavoured to *throw* the ball into the opposing goal.

Footing. *On good footing.* Well in standing. During the reign of Bluff King Hal the rank of a man was designated by the size of his shoe. The higher rank he held, the bigger the shoe he wore.

To pay one's footing. The phrase was born during the old apprenticeship days. It was the custom for a newcomer to the trade to pay for drinks for his fellows on the first day at his job.

Footpad. From the padded shoes worn to deaden his steps as he approached his victim.

Fop. Has nothing to do with the actual clothes, in relation to which we use the word to-day. The word is derived from the German and Dutch *foppen*, to jeer at. It was in use so far back as 1697, when a character in a comedy was given by Vanburgh the title of Lord Foppington.

Forecastle (of a ship). Now referred to as fo'castle. It was shortened from afore-castle. The "castle" in the old days was the state cabin which was built high in the centre of the ship.

Forget-me-not. The "remembrance" legend of the little flower is derived from a tragedy of the Danube, which may or may not be true. Anyway, a German Knight to please his lady climbed down the bank of the Danube to pick the flower, fell into the swift-flowing stream and, impeded by his armour, was swept away and drowned. But not before he was able to throw the flower he had picked to his lady on the bank with the words (his last), *vergess mein nicht*, "forget me not."

Fork. Although gold and silver forks were made in the thirteenth century, the fork did not become a table implement in England until the seventeenth century. Queen Elizabeth was the first English Sovereign to use a fork at table, a fact which led to a famous Divine preaching a sermon, in which he said: "It is an insult to the Almighty not to touch one's meat with one's fingers."

Previous to the use of forks meat was eaten with the fingers, picked, usually, out of a common bowl. Most houses of quality had a small fountain in which host and guests could wash their hands before eating. When forks became in use they were at first made of precious metals, and were carefully guarded, each person bringing his own.

Fork Out, To. Thieves' slang for "pay over." In their argot forks meant fingers. You will notice how the old custom of fingers for forks (see above) survived in slang.

Forties, The Roaring. That part of the Atlantic Ocean between forty degrees and fifty degrees N. latitude. So-called because of the wild weather usually experienced there.

Foul Weather Jack. The nickname bestowed on Commodore John Byron, navigator of the eighteenth century, because whenever he put to sea he was sure to experience bad weather. The name is now sometimes bestowed on ships known to roll badly in strong weather. One of the newest liners was so-called by regular passengers.

Fourth Estate. The Press. The other three Estates of the Realm are: the Lords Spiritual, the Lords Temporal, and the Commons. The Press is believed to have first been so described by Burke in a speech in Parliament in which he said: "Yonder (pointing to the Press gallery) sits the Fourth Estate), more important than them all."

Foxtrot, a dance. The suggestion is that the short steps of the dance were called foxtrot from the short steps of a horse in breaking from a walk into a trot. A horse in this operation is said to be foxtrotting.

Free House. Most public-houses of the present day are owned by large brewing companies, and only the brand of beer brewed by them is on sale at the bars. A free house is a house independent of any brewing firm, which can purchase for sale the wares of any brewer.

Free Lance. The term applied to any person, not attached to any particular firm, but who supplies wares on approval to all firms. More particularly, it is applied to a journalist who writes for the Press generally, submitting his articles for acceptance. The name is derived from the knights who, after the Crusades, were ready to enlist under the banner of any country for a monetary consideration. The lance is, of course, a reference to their weapon—the Knightly lance.

Freemason. The name as applied to the Society is well-known, and needs no explanation. It is not so well-known, however, that there was one—and only one—woman Freemason. The Hon. Elizabeth St. Leger, daughter of Lord Doneraile, when a Lodge was held in her father's house in the early eighteenth century, hid herself in the empty case of a grandfather clock and witnessed the proceedings. A sneeze is said to have revealed her presence, and she was compelled to be initiated as a member of the craft in order that its secrets should be kept violate. The story is authenticated.

French Leave, To take. To take a day off without permission. In France they return the compliment by calling it *S'en aller a l'Anglaise*—English leave!

Fringe. On the Fringe of. Nearly there, as on the fringe of

Society. The allusion is to the Jewish priests. The fringes of their garments were accounted as sacred. They were touched by the people as a charm. To be on the fringe of the garment was to be next to Holiness.

Froebel Teaching Method. A system of education for young children instituted by Frederick Wilhelm Froebel, German educator. Briefly, the system is that children between four and six years of age should not be taught by rule, but according to their natural instincts and activities. Play was the basis of his teaching.

"Froggies." A popular nickname for Frenchmen. But it applies only to Parisians—from their ancient and heraldic device, which bore three frogs or toads.

From Pillar to Post. In its meaning, actually from pillory to whipping-post. A reference to the old-time custom of crowds in following a convicted person from the pillory to the whipping-post. Usually, however, the whipping-post was the tail-end of a cart, the offender, stripped to the waist and his hands tied to the tail of the cart, being whipped through the streets, followed by the hooting crowd.

Fub. *To fub, or fob, someone off with a story.* The word is best spelt *fob*, since it comes from the German *foppen*, to hoax, or jeer.

Fudge. "Oh, Fudge." An exclamation of disgust, or disbelief. Actually, it is not so meaningless as it sounds, for the Low German word *futsch* meant "begone!"

Funeral. The Latin name was *funus*, with which word is connected *fumus*, smoke; and it is suggested that the words together have reference to the practice of burning the dead (cremation). It is not true, as one authority has it, that the Latin word for funeral was *funis*, a torch, and that the word means a torchlight procession, since Roman funerals were always held at night, although it is correct that funerals did take place at night. It was held that for magistrates or priests to see a corpse made them ceremoniously unclean, hence the night burials. *See* "Sin-eaters," "Shovel Offertories."

Funny-bone. Is a play on the name of the bone in the upper arm called the *Humerus*. The funny-bone is the spot at the elbow where the ulnar nerve passes by the internal condyle of the humerus. The nerve there is unprotected.

Furbelow (of woman's dress). Is a corruption of *falbala*, Spanish for flounce.

G

Gab. "*The gift of the gab.*" There is no direct connection, as Dr. Brewer says, with the Celtic or Irse *gab*, the mouth. A better etymology is the Mediæval English *gabbe*, idle talk.

Gabriel's Hounds. Wild geese. The noise of their flight is described as like that of a pack of hounds in full cry. The legend is that geese are the souls of children who died before being baptized, and are wandering through the air until Judgement Day.

Gadabout. Name given to a person, usually a woman, who spends her time paying frivolous visits. The word *gad* in this sense is Gaelic, meaning to rove. *By Gad.* A euphemistic way of saying the old oath, "By God."

Gadget. The name given to any device which is of use in almost any circumstance. It began its service as an expression among the men of the Royal Air Force. The origin is unknown, a surprising fact in view of its recent application. There is nothing to suggest that it is derived from the Scottish *gadge*, an early form of our present word gauge.

Gaff. Has been for many years a term for humbug. To "blow the gaff" meant to expose the humbug. It was also the name given to the entertainment in a cheap music-hall in earlier days. *Crooked as a gaff*, however, is an altogether different word. It is derived from the Spanish *gafa*, a boathook. The crooked part is identifiable by any fisherman who has used a gaff to land a salmon or a pike. *Penny gaff.* A rude entertainment of the old days for which the entrance charged was a penny. *Penny Dreadful.* Name given to the old "blood-and-thunder" boys' books. It needs no further description.

Gaffer, An old. Although now used as a term of contempt for an old man, it originally denoted respect, and indeed love, being a corruption of grandfather, or god-father.

Gag. A stage term to describe the "filling-in" of an actor when another of the company has missed his cue of entrance, or has forgotten his words. It was, however, originally a device to disconcert or stop the mouth ("gag") of another actor by the unexpected speaking of words not in the script of the play.

Galaxy, *of Stars.* This is the correct meaning, but the stars alluded to are not theatrical or cinema stars, or any other style of stardom except the stars in the sky. The word comes from the Greek *galaktos*, akin to the Latin *lac, lactis*, milk—the Milky Way.

Gall *of bitterness; gall and wormwood.* The origin is obvious when it is considered that the gall is the bitter fluid secreted by the liver. To "gall anyone" is to render him bitter against the offender.

Galley. *A galley slave.* The worst form of slavery. The origin of the word seems to be unknown. It is said, however, to have been coined by the Corinthians seven hundred years before the Christian era. The galleys were huge boats of some two hundred feet long, with as many as five rows, or banks, of oars, and frequently comprising fifty oars in each tier. The oars were worked by one, and sometimes two, men, who were chained to them with permanent gyves, welded on.

Galligaskins. Were a loose, wide kind of breeches worn by men in the seventeenth century. The name still survives in parts of Cornwall, where a wide pair of field trouser is still given that description.

Gallivanting. The origin of this word becomes apparent when it is split into its component parts. "Galli" is a contraction of gallant, a amorous person of the male sex, and "vaunt," to make a vain display. To go gallant-vaunting was to spend one's time making a vain (a proud) display of love to members of the opposite sex.

Galvanise. The science of electrical currents produced by chemical agency, discovered by Louis Galvani, of Bologna. Galvanized iron is sheet-iron coated with zinc to protect it from disintegration by the elements.

Game not worth the Candle. *See* "Candle."

Gammer. The female equivalent of Gaffer. A corruption of grandmother, through gran'mer.

"Gammer Gurton's Needle." One of the two earliest comedies of the British stage. The earliest by eighteen years, was "Ralph Roister Doister," produced at Eton. But if viewed from its freedom from dependence on foreign sources, and its sketching from contemporary life, "Gammer Gurton's Needle" is our earliest regular English comedy. The action turns on the loss of a needle (which was an implement of considerable value in those days) and the manner in which knavish Diccon, of Bedlam, sets the village by the ears about it. A conclusion is reached by Gammer Gurton finding the needle at last exactly where she had left it—in the seat of Hodge's breeches. The author of the play has never been satisfactorily established; but it has been variously ascribed to Bishop Still, Dr. John Brydges and William Stevenson. It is more likely by the latter.

Gammon. "*It's all gammon.*" The word has nothing to do with bacon, but comes from the Anglo-Saxon *gamen*, a game. There is still a reminder of the original meaning in the game of Back*gammon*, in which the player has to go back on the board. "It's all gammon" means, literally, "It's all a game." The word as "game" was known in earliest days. In the *Chester Plays*, i, 102, it states: "This *gammon* shall begin." Centuries later Dickens wrote (in "The Pickwick Papers"): "Lord bless their little hearts, they think it's all right, and don't know no better, but they're the wictims of *gammon*, Samivel, they're the wictims of *gammon*."

Gamp. Slang term for an umbrella. Its origin was Sarah Gamp, the disreputable monthly nurse in Charles Dickens's "Martin Chuzzlewit," who carried with her everywhere an umbrella. There is no truth in the oft-repeated statement that Dickens was influenced in his choice of the name Gamp by the town of Gaingamp, in Brittany, where gingang (now called gingham) was made into umbrella covers. *See* "Gingham."

Gamut. *To run the Gamut.* To go through the whole scale. Guido d'Arezzo (born about 991) is said to have called the seven notes of the musical scale after the first seven letters of the alphabet—a, b, c, d, e, f, g; whence the name gamma, taken from the last of the series, applied to the whole scale. He is also said to have invented the names of the notes used in singing (ut, re, mi, fa, sol, la, si), after certain initial syllables of a monkish hymn to St. John, in a stanza written in sapphic metre, namely:

"*Ut* queant laxis *re*sonare fibris
*Mi*ra gestorum *fa*muli tuorum,
*Sol*ve pollutis *la*biis reatum,
*S*ancte *I*ohannes."

In music the gamut is the first or gravest note in Guido's scale of music; gamma ut. Thus, to run the whole gamut is to go from the top to the bottom of the scale, the whole range or compass.

Ganger. The word is formed from the verb *to gang*, derived from the Anglo-Saxon *gangan*, to go or to travel together. The derivative is retained to-day, in that a gang is a body of people who go together. Therefore, a ganger is the leader of the gang.

Garden, Gardening. The oldest known representation of a garden is shown on an Egyptian relief from Tel-el-Amarna, which dates back to 1500 B.C. Then there were, of course, the Hanging Gardens of Babylon, 600 B.C. But actually, private individual gardens and the art of gardening are believed to have been introduced into Athens by the philosopher Epicurus (342-270 B.C.). For his sins, he has a potato named after him—Epicure!

Garden of England. A highly disputed title. Kent, Worcestershire and the Isle of Wight all claim the distinction. Perhaps the Isle of Wight, as the more mild in climate on the whole, and with its luxurious vegetation, has the prior claim.

Gargantuan. Great beyond credulity. From Gargantua, hero of Rabelais's satire, a giant of inconceivable size, who could drink a river dry, and once ate five pilgrims with their staves in a salad. The word comes from the Spanish *garganta*, gullet; and is used to describe a voracious guzzler.

Gargoyle. Properly, a spout for rain-water, of the Gothic period of architecture. It was built projecting from the wall, so that the water falls clear. Its origin is an interesting study. The word comes from the French *gargouille*, the throat, or gullet (down which the water flows). But the grotesque carving of the gargoyle comes from Gargouille, the ferocious dragon that lived in the Seine and ravaged Rouen, and was slain by Romanus, Bishop of Rome, in the seventh century. A wealth of imagination went to the designing of the name of the gargoyle!

Garraways. A famous coffee house in Change Alley, Cornhill, London. It was kept by Thomas Garway, a tobacconist and coffee merchant, in the sixteenth century. With Old Jonathan's Coffee House, Garraways was the forerunner of the present Stock Exchange. Stock-brokers foregathered in the coffee houses to do their business over cups of coffee. The origin is commemorated even to-day in the term "The House" used by members to describe the Stock Exchange, and also by the name of the Stock Ex*change*, after Change Alley.

Garret. Though the top room of a house is now little more than a limber room, garret in Mediæval English meant a look-out, or a watch tower. Shakespeare in 2 *Hen. VI*, i, 3, says: "He did speak them to me in the *garret*, one night, as we were scouring my Lord of York's armour." The word garrison comes from the same root, meaning a supply of soldiers for a *fortified* place.

Garth. The Norse equivalent for the Anglo-Saxon *yard*. In place-names it is allied to "ton," denoting a guarded place, or a place girded round. Apple-garth in Yorkshire, and Fish-guard in Pembrokeshire, are examples.

Gas. The inventor of gas, van Helmont (1577-1644), in naming his discovery, was influenced by the word chaos, says Dr. Murray. We prefer the likelihood that he had in mind the German word *geist*, spirit. After all, he WAS German!

Gat. American slang for a revolver. There is no doubt that it is short for Gatling, the machine-gun invented by Dr. R. J. Gatling, and first used in the American Civil War. Its use for revolver is doubtless due to the American predilection for words which exaggerate size.

Gate. Where it appears in place-names, meant just what it says—a gate to the town or city, from the period when most cities were walled round for defence. It was usually a passage through the town wall. Aldgate (Old Gate), Cripplegate (the gate where cripples sat), in London, are examples.

In the North of England, however, it was used to describe a road through the town, such as Briggate (Bridge Road) in Leeds, and Kirkgate (Church Road).

Gate of Tears. The passage into the Red Sea. Called thus by the Arabs, because of the number of shipwrecks that took place there.

Gauntlet, To run the. The phrase dates from the Thirty Years' War. It was then *gantlope*; and gantlope came from the Swedish *gata*, a passage, and *lope* (which meant leap), a course. The passage was a double line of soldiers, the course was the way between them—and it was also the leap! The delinquent ran down the course, each of the double line of men giving him a blow with a rope-end as he passed. Nowadays, the phrase is applied to anyone standing up amid criticism from all sides, such as a Minister in the Commons.

To throw down the gauntlet. To challenge anyone. In the mediæval ages a Knight, challenging another, threw his gauntlet (mailed glove) on the ground. A Knight accepting the challenge picked it up.!

Gazette. According to Dr. Brewer this name for a newspaper was derived from the smallest Venetian coin, a gazetta (less than a British farthing) charged for hearing read out in a public place a manuscript newspaper issued by the Venetian Government once a month. It may be so, but it may be as well to consider the fact that a magpie was known as a *gazza*, and its chatter was described as *gazetta*. A newspaper certainly chatted the news.

Gee-Gee. "*To have a bit on the gee-gees.*" Rather a humorous origin to this. The commands to a horse have always been "Gee-up" and "Gee-whoa." So children named the animal, in their childish way, a "gee-gee." Grown-ups adopted the word as a colloquialism.

Geewhiz. Used as an exclamation of surprise. "*Bill got married to-day.*" "*No! Geewhiz!*" The users may, or may not, be horrified to learn that the word is another of the many euphemisms for the oath, "By Jesus."

Gentleman. In feudal days there was a strict class distinction between the labourer, the yeoman, and the man "of gentle birth," though not noble birth. The gentle birth entitled him to bear arms.

Geometry. Euclid is reputed to have formed a school of mathematics at Alexandria between the years 323 and 248 B.C., and most of the principles of mathematics and geometry now used were calculated by him. But who *first* invented geometry is unknown. The Egyptians must have had a knowledge of it, because such knowledge was obviously necessary to erect the Pyramids. The derivation of the word is Greek, *geometria*, from *ge*, the earth, and *metron*, a measure.

George. This, as a name for a male person, goes back to the Greek *Georgos*, a farmer, literally an earth-worker. Virgil's *Georgics* describe his activities.

Geranium. The first red geranium grown in England was raised by a florist in King's Road, Chelsea, in 1882. The Mohammedans believe that the geranium was a common mallow, which was changed by the touch of Mahomet's cloak as he passed it.

Gerrymander, To. So to arrange results as to give an entirely wrong idea of the real position. To hocus-pocus. The story has been told that Elbridge *Gerry*, Governor of Massachusetts, U.S.A., prepared a map of a new electoral distribution of the constituency, to give his party an unfair advantage over the others. An artist, shown the drawing, remarked that it looked in outline like a salamander. "Why not a gerry-mander?" was Gerry's reply.

Actually, there is no truth whatever in the fact that it was a scheme of Gerry to secure an advantage. A reliable American authority states, emphatically, that he opposed the measure of redistribution. But the name lives on.

Get one's back up. The allusion is to the cat's habit of arching its back when angry.

Get out of bed the wrong way. From the old superstition that to get out of bed with the left foot first was a harbinger of ill-luck for the whole of the day. *See* "Foot. Right foot forward."

Get the Bullet. A variation, quite understandable, of being "fired," shot off, as it were.

Get the Sack. *See* "Sack."

Get your Dander Up. Dander here is a corruption of dandruff, the scurf of the head. Why it should have come to be applied to the hair over the dandruff is not known. To get the *hair* up is, of course, in allusion to the raising of their fur straight up by enraged animals. "Dandy," for a fop, comes from a totally different source—it is a corruption of Andrew, but why, etymologists have never discovered.

Ghost Walks. "*Wages are now being paid.*" The phrase originated in the theatre, through an actor who was an outstanding success as the ghost in "Hamlet." The company was in sore financial state, after the manager and proprietor had annexed their share of the takings. Ultimately, the "ghost" presented himself before the manager and demanded his wages. Told that there was not any money in the exchequer with which to pay, he replied: "Then the ghost won't walk to-night." He was paid! For the remainder of the tour the company gathered outside the manager's office each Friday, the while "Hamlet's" ghost interviewed the manager to see whether or not the ghost was going to walk that night!

"G.I." A nickname common during the Great War of 1939-45 for the American soldier. Its meaning was "Government Issue," from the fact that everything he wore, from socks to tunic, trousers and hat, and everything he ate, or was paid, was issued to him by the Government of the United States—he was, in fact, a complete "Government Issue."

Gibberish. "*It's all gibberish to me.*" Despite the contrary opinions of other etymologists the writer holds that this word for unintelligible conversation is derived from *Geber*, the Arabian alchemist of the eleventh century, who wrote in mystical jargon in order to avoid the death penalty for sorcery, which he might have incurred from the Ecclesiastical authorities of his day had he written, plainly, such heretical opinions. It seems a far-fetched theory to our mind to endeavour to connect it with *gibber*, a variant of jabber. Gibber did not come into use for many years after gibberish.

Gift of the Gab. *See* "Gab."

Gilderoy's Kite. "*To be hung higher than Gilderoy's Kite.*" To be punished out of all proportion to the offence. Gilderoy was a notorious Perthshire highwayman. He robbed Cardinal Richelieu in the presence of the King, and picked Cromwell's pocket. He was hanged in 1636. His real name was Patrick Macgregor.

Giles. The nickname given to a countryman. It is derived from the French *gilles*, stage name for a stage simpleton.

Gilly-flower. Countryman's name for the wallflower. It is incorrect to say that the name is derived from July-flower, the month in which it blooms. It is derived from the French *giroflee*, a clove, and was called by Chaucer, gylofre.

Ginger. Name given to people with red hair. Guinevre, Queen of the Court of King Arthur, possessed red hair.

Gingerbread, Taking the gilt off the. In olden days gingerbread cakes were made in the shape of animals, men and birds, and were profusely decorated with gold leaf. These were commonly sold at fairs all over the country. None would be sold by the vendors if it had not the gold leaf decoration, such being regarded as not so good value. Hence, anything inferior was said to have had the gilt taken off the ginger-bread.

Gingham. Name given to a striped material, at one time very popular for the making of working frocks for domestic servants, and for the clothes of children in orphanages. The "derivation" widely spread is that the name is derived from the town of Guingamp, in Brittany, where gingham was dyed and made into umbrella covers before the introduction of silk covers. It is added that Dickens had the town in mind when he called his character Sarah *Gamp*. The derivation is a false one. The word's real origin is the Malay word, *ging-gang*, meaning striped. Thus, both Gamp and Gingham, as nicknames for an umbrella, are falsely used.

Gipsy. The name is the British description of the nomad race. In other countries they are called Abzigans, Ziqeuner and Zingari. When they appeared in England, about the beginning of the sixteenth century, they were thought, from their dark skins, to have come from Egypt, and were therefore called Egyptians. This quickly became shortened to gypcians, and then came to gipsies. Whence exactly the gipsies came is unknown. Their language undoubtedly had its origin in a debased Hindu dialect, with added words from the Persian, Armenian and other languages. According to legend, their wandering is due to the fact that they refused to shelter the Virgin Mary and her child in the Flight to Egypt, and must, therefore, be waifs and strays on the earth.

Girdle. "*A Good Name is better than a Golden Girdle.*" The meaning is obvious. The origin was the old custom of carrying money in a belt, or in a purse suspended from the belt. In this country a girdle of gold meant a belt of sovereigns or half-sovereigns. In France, the origin of the proverb was slightly different. In or around the year 1400 women of known bad character were forbidden to wear girdles of gold tissue assumed by other women.

Give Him a Baker's Dozen. Give him all he is owed and then one more in addition. Said of an offender against the code of conduct. *See* "Baker's Dozen."

Give him Beans. Derived from a French proverb : "If he gives me peas, I will give him beans,' meaning to get quits with him.

Give him plenty of rope. Let him do what he likes because we can always check him in the end—like a horse tethered ; it can always be brought to hand, no matter how much grazing space the rope may give it.

Give the Cold Shoulder. To show a lack of hospitality, such as, for instance, to a visitor who, turning up after a meal, and not being especially welcome, is presented with a cut off the cold joint, the put-away shoulder of lamb, as a meal.

Gladstone bag. In compliment to William Ewart Gladstone, the great Prime Minister, though he was never known to carry one of them.

Glamour. A popular and far too common term to-day for attractive and seductive. The word seems to have been changed entirely from its first meaning, for it comes from the Icelandic *glam*, which meant dimness of sight ; and from *glamr*, a mythical ghost. Certainly, to-day, much of the vaunted "glamour" of film stars is mythical ! Scott popularized the word in literature ; and his supporters claim that it is a corrupt form of grammar.

Glass. In the Middle East, before Egypt was a mighty power, a caravan of Phœnician merchants built a pile of stones in the desert on which to support their cooking vessels. The stones were of what is called *natron*. When their meal was ready and the pots were removed, the merchants found a clear transparent substance under the pots which, when cold, could be picked up and looked through. It was the first known piece of glass. Natron is an impure form of carbonate of soda and this, under the heat of the fire, combined with the desert sand to form silicate of soda, which is a form of glass. And pretty much the same stuff is used to make glass to-day, combined with other ingredients, including red-lead. That is the story told by Pliny. There is no doubt that it happened ; but whether it was the origin of glass is doubtful. Remains of glass have been discovered in the ruins of Assyrian cities ; and glass was certainly known in Egypt as early as 1740 B.C. It was not manufactured in England, however, until 1556.

Glastonbury Thorn. A tree in the Somersetshire town, where Joseph of Arimathea built a church. The legend is that when he saw the spot, Joseph decided to build a church there, and stuck his staff in the ground. The staff took root and burst into leaf on Christmas Day. And it still flowers about Christmas-time (not 25th December, but the old Christmas date before the calendar change).

Glory. The Hand of Glory. Was a charm much sought after by highwaymen, thieves and other criminals. For the charm to work, the hand had to be taken from the corpse of a man executed by hanging. It was prepared in a certain way, and was said to ensure that the possessor of it should never hang. So potent was it regarded that large sums were paid to gaolers to cut off the hands of a gibbetted malefactor and sell them to others.

According to Scott in "Antiquary" XVII : "De hand of glory . . . is hand cut off from a dead man as have been hanged for murther, and dried very nice in de smoke of juniper wood."

Another legend of the Hand of Glory was that a candle placed in a dead man's hand gave no light to anyone but him who carries the hand. Hence thieves adopted the dead hand as a candle-holder during their nefarious operations.

Glove. Comes to us without any deviations from the Anglo-Saxon *glof*, the palm of the hand.

"*Hand and Glove Together.*" On terms as intimate as a glove is to the hand.

To Bite the Glove. On the Border (of Scotland and England) to bite the glove was considered a pledge of vengeance which could only be ended by death. The custom is mentioned by Scott in "The Lay of the Last Minstrel" :

"Stern Rutherford right little said,
But bit his glove and shook his head."

Gloves were worn at one time by the clergy to indicate that their hands were clean and not open to bribes.

Glow-worm. Actually, only the female beetle has the glow. The male is winged and is not phosphorescent. He flies about in the evening and is attracted by the light of the female. Scientists for centuries have puzzled over the mystery of the light borne by the glow-worm. The nearest they have arrived to a solution is that it seems to be caused by certain chemicals in the fat tissues, which become luminous when combined with the oxygen drawn in through the breathing tubes. All attempts by scientists to reproduce an artificial light of similar quality and brilliance have so far failed.

Glutton. A gourmant, a greedy feeder. The original glutton is usually given as Vitellius, Roman Emperor (A.D. 15-69), but the writer is of opinion it might more fittingly be applied to Apicius (A.D. 14-33) who, having spent in luxurious living so much of his wealth as to leave him an income the equivalent of only £70,000 hanged himself rather than have to exist on such plain living !

Go. "*All the Go.*" The phrase came from drapers, who when a particular line of goods was introduced and were selling well, stated that they were "all the go."

"Go and Chew Coke." A retort or a reproach to a person who has caused offence. Seemingly a meaningless remark, it yet comes from one of the best-known of Shakespeare's "exclamations." It is a corruption of Cæsar's words of reproach to Brutus : "Tu quoque, Brute !"—"And thou, too, Brutus !"

Goat. "*To play the Giddy Goat.*" The allusion is to a goat frisking and butting about—a comical sight, to say the least.

Goat and Compasses. In spite of many denials, the writer insists that the origin of the public-house sign, the Goat and Compasses, is that it is a corruption of "God en-Compasses (us)." To those who hold that it is taken from the arms of the Carpenters' Guild, it may be pointed out that their alleged "compass" is a chevron.

God, Gods. Following is a list of the Gods of Classical Mythology, together with their names. They number twelve Greater and four Lesser Gods :

Greek.	Latin.
Zeus (King)	Jupiter
Apollon (The Sun)	Apollo
Ares (War)	Mars
Hermes (Messenger)	Mercury
Poseidon (Ocean)	Neptune
Hephaistos (Smith)	Vulcan
Hera (Queen)	Juno
Demeter (Tillage)	Ceres
Artemis (Moon, hunting)	Diana
Athena (Wisdom)	Minerva
Aphrodite (Love and beauty)	Venus
Hestia (Home life)	Vesta
Lesser	
Dionysos (Wine)	Bacchus
Eros (Love)	Cupid
Pluton (Of the Inferno)	Pluto
Kronos (Time)	Saturn

In the time of Hesiod (properly, Hesiodus), roughly about 860 B.C., the Gods numbered thirty thousand, and in order that none might be angered by his omission, the Greeks observed a Feast of the Unknown Gods.

God and Mammon. "*You cannot serve God and Mammon.*" Mammon is from the Syrian word, *mamona*, meaning riches. It is believe that there was a god of that name, but direct evidence is lacking.

God Tempers the Wind to the Shorn Lamb. It would be a very curious state of affairs if God did—for a lamb is *not shorn*! The phrase was coined by Sterne in his "Sentimental Journey." He took it from an earlier phrase—some one hundred and forty years before. But the earlier phrase was: "To a close-shorn *sheep*, God gives wind by measure." Which is more accurate.

Gods, Among the. The name given to the gallery of a theatre, not from their elevated position, an allusion to the Gods of Olympus, but because, when the phrase was coined, the roof of Drury Lane Theatre was embellished with carvings and paintings of the various Deities; and the gallery was in very close proximity to them.

Gog and Magog. Dr. Brewer describes the British legend thus: The sole survivors of a monstrous brood, the offspring of the thirty-three infamous daughters of the Emperor Diocletian, who murdered their husbands; and being set adrift in a ship reached Albion, where they fell in with a number of demons. Their descendants, a race of giants were extirpated by Brute and his companions, with the exception of Gog and Magog, who were brought in chains to London, and made to do duty as porters at the Royal Palace which stood on the site of the present Guildhall, where their effigies have been at least since the reign of Henry V.

The old giants were destroyed in the Great Fire of London, and the present ones, fourteen feet high, were carved in 1708 by Richard Saunders.

Golden Gate. The name given to the entrance to San Francisco Harbour by the Spaniards, because they regarded it as the gateway to the Land of Gold. Centuries later, in 1847, the great gold rush took place from San Francisco.

Golden Wedding. *See* "Weddings."

Gone to Pot. Vanished for good. The allusion is to the melting-pot.

Gone to Rack and Ruin. The phrase should properly be "wreck and ruin," when it explains itself.

Gone to the Devil. *See* "Devil."

Gone to the Dogs. In the East the dog is regarded as a pariah. The remains of food are thrown to him in the gutter.

Gone up the Country. Insolvent. Vanished to avoid paying one's debts. The phrase was introduced into England from the Colonies. When a man could not make a living in the Colonial towns, he usually went prospecting for gold up-country.

Good-bye. The word "good"—here used in its correct sense is Holy. The Bible was for centuries known as the Good Book—a better word than Bible, since bible is the Greek *biblos*, meaning *any* book. In most country village Bethels, even to-day, the Bible is still referred to as "the Good Book."

Good-bye is actually a contraction of God be with you. The French say *a Dieu* (I commend you to God).

Goodman's Croft. The name given in Scotland to a strip of land, or the corner of a field, left untilled. It is a popular superstition that unless some such place is thus left, the Spirit of Evil will damage the crop.

Good Wine needs no Bush. In former days, houses in which wine was sold usually displayed an ivy bush at the end of a stake outside the house. Travellers who had once tasted good wine in the house were generally careful enough to take good stock of its position before leaving. Hence, they needed no bush to direct them when next they were in the neighbourhood.

Note.—The bush displayed, as stated above, was of ivy, because the ivy is sacred to Bacchus, God of Wine.

Goodwin Sands. Were, originally, the Goodwin Lands. They comprised more than four thousand acres, and Earl Goodwin fenced them in on the sea side with a stalwart wall. William the Norman presented the lands to the Abbot and Abbey of St. Augustine at Canterbury. The Abbot allowed the wall to fall into so great disrepair that the sea burst through and flooded the lands, which became the dangerous, low sandbanks they are to-day.

Goose. *To cook one's goose.* The story of this phrase is: Eric, King of Sweden, arrived at a certain town accompanied with only a few soldiers. The townspeople, feeling reasonably safe against the number, and not expecting the King to attack with so small a force, hung out a goose in derision for him to shoot at. Finding, however, that the King meant business, they sent out envoys to inquire what he wanted. "To cook your goose," was the royal reply.

Gooseberry. Was not derived from a goose, nor from gorze, the "gorze berry," as is so often stated. It was originally *grose* or *groise*, from the Old French *groisele*, or *groselle*. There was, also, the Irish *grosaid*, but one and all of them meant simply what the word still is—just, gooseberry.

Gordian Knot, To cut the. In Greek legend Gordian tied a knot in the cord that connected the pole and yoke of the ox-cart in which he was riding when he was chosen King of Phrygia. The knot was so intricate as to defy all attempts to untie it. The Oracle in the Temple in which the ox-cart was preserved declared that whosoever should succeed in undoing it would become master of Asia. Alexander of Macedon solved the difficulty by cutting the knot with his sword, and the Oracle was fulfilled. Hence, to "cut the Gordian knot" is to overcome a difficulty in a bold way.

Gotham, The Wise Men of. The story goes that King John approached the town of Gotham with the idea of inspecting and buying the castle and grounds. The townspeople had no desire to be saddled with the expense of keeping a Royal resident. Accordingly, the King's messengers, whenever they appeared, found the populace engaged in idiotic games. Told of this, the King abandoned his project and returned to London. "We ween there are more fools pass through Gotham than remain in it," was the comment of the "wise men."

Another story of the men of Gotham is that they built a wall round a cuckoo in order to shut the bird in, and thus keep the season of Spring.

Gossip. *Sib*, or *gesib*, was the Anglo-Saxon for kinsman; and gossip was originally *god-sib*, related to one in the service of God, such as a sponsor in baptism. Dean Hoare suggests that the present use of the word gossip arose from the practice of God-parents meeting together to have a chat. It sounds a fanciful "origin" to us.

Go the Whole Hog. To go full out, neck or nothing. It is said to come from a poem by Cowper, entitled: "Of the Love of the World Reproved," in which the eating of pork by the Turks is discussed.

Go-To. An old country expression, and one which has outlived most of the phrases. The author heard it in a Surrey village quite recently (1945). "You're a fine old woman, so you be," said a man of an aged lady sitting by her cottage door.

"Aw, *go-to*," was the reply, meaning "get along with your flattery."

Go to Bath. Nonsense. Bath was the fashionable health resort. The inference was that the person thus consigned needed medical care.

Go to Battersea (to be cut for the Simples). The phrase was used to one not overburdened with wits. Simples, or medicinal herbs, were cultivated in the days that the phrase was coined (the early 1700's), hence the pun on the word Simples, for a daft person.

Go to Jericho. If the story told is true, the admonition has nothing to do with the city of the Bible. Jericho was the name given by Henry VIII to the Manor of Blackmore, near Chelmsford, to which he was wont to retire from State troubles. His courtiers, who knew their Harry, very naturally suspected some fresh gallant-ry, and announced with some glee that he had gone to Jericho. The phrase now means not gallantry, but annoyance; get out of my way. Go somewhere else.

Go to Putney. With all deference to Putney, now a quite desirable place, the waterside borough was in the days when the phrase was coined, something quite different. To be told to go to Putney was as bad as being sent to Coventry—put outside the pale.

Gouk. Name for a cuckoo, which is another name for a fool, or a simpleton. A "gouk" is the term bestowed upon someone who lacks intelligence. Why the gouk, or cuckoo, is regarded as simple the writer has never been able to understand, since the bird is clever enough to induce other birds to bring up its own family, while it enjoys life free and unfettered.

Graces, The three. In Classical Mythology the Three Goddesses who, being so blessed themselves, bestowed beauty and charm. They were sisters—Aglaia, Thalia and Euphrosyne.

Grand Tour. The name given a hundred years or so ago to the tour made by each of the sons of gentlemen in their turn through France, Germany and Italy, in the same way that, to-day, the daughters of gentlemen are presented at Court, as the preliminary to moving in fashionable circles.

Grass Widow. Term given, colloquially, to a married woman separated from her husband but not divorced. It is not a corruption of Grace Widow, a widow by grace or courtesy, as Johnson, and other etymologists, have stated. Its origin lies in the custom of European husbands in India sending their wives to the cool hills during the hot season, while they remained behind in the parched cities. On the hills, in the cool, the grass grew greenly, hence a "Grass" widow.

Grave, One Foot in the. The original version was coined by the Greeks, who had it, "One Foot in the Ferryboat" (that of Charon. The "grave" version was said by Julian (who altered the calendar) in the words, "I will learn something, even if I have one foot in the grave."

Great Scot! Is not, as has been stated, a contraction of "Great Scotland Yard." General Winfield Scott (U.S.) was a man of enormous dignity and military style, who was nicknamed "Old Fuss and Feathers." His dignity and demeanour when he stood as a candidate for the U.S. Presidency was such that he earned the additional sobriquet of "Great Scott." The phrase came into use in America as a humorous ejaculation for the extraordinary or unusual.

Great Unwashed, The. The politician Burke first characterized the working-class thus. But it was Sir Walter Scott who popularized the description—if popularized can be regarded as the right word.

Greek Calends. Until the Greek calends means "never." There were no Calends in the Greek months.

Greek meets Greek. "*When Greek meets Greek, then comes the tug-of-war.*" The allusion is to the obstinate resistance of the Greek cities to Philip and Alexander of Macedonia.

Greenacre. Is a term used by London stevedores when a set of goods falls out of the slings while being loaded or unloaded. It is a tragic-humorous skit on James Greenacre, who was hanged up for murder in 1837.

Green-eyed Monster. Jealousy. It is suggested that the term green-eyed for jealousy was taken from the green eyes of the cat tribe. Shakespeare makes Iago say:

"Oh, beware, my lord, of jealousy;
It is the green-ey'd monster which doth mock
The meal it feeds on."

We give it as the only origin we know, though it cannot be regarded as at all satisfactory.

Greengage. Was so named after the Reverend M. Gage, who introduced the plant into this country from the monastery of La Chartreuse, France.

Green Man. As the name of a public-house, indicated that the house was kept by a former game-keeper. Game-keepers in mediæval times were always attired in green.

Grenadiers. Originally throwers of grenades. Half-a-dozen of height, strength and good service were chosen from each company to throw grenades, which weighed from two to five pounds. The throwers, grenadiers, were foremost in assault. They proved successful and, later, companies of grenadiers were formed (about 1670). And so the Grenadier *guards* came into existence. When hand grenades went out, the name was retained for the company—and so was the height of the chosen men! Ironically enough, the hand grenade came back as a mighty weapon in the 1914-1918 war, and has pretty well gone out again in the present (1939-45) one.

Greyhound. Has nothing to do with "grey." Originally the word was grehound in this country. In Scandinavia it was grei-houndes. But the term is really Icelandic, where "grey" means a dog, and "hundre," a hound. Thus, a greyhound was originally a cross between a dog and a hound. The colour "grey" in Iceland is spelt "grar."

Greyhound. As the name of an inn is in honour of Henry VII, whose badge it was.

Greyhound (in silver). Is the badge of a King's Messenger, worn hidden round his neck attached to a silver chain, and surmounted with a crown.

Grey Mare is the Better Horse. The saying is believed to have originated in the preference at one time given to the grey mares of Flanders over the finest coach-horses of England. At least, that was the view of Macaulay.

Grin like a Cheshire Cat. The origin usually given is that it came from the custom of selling cheese in Cheshire in the form of a cat made in moulds. The cat was invariably grinning. But the grinning Cheshire cat was no pussy. "He" was Mr. Caterling, of Chester, who was appointed forest warden by Richard III. In his numerous sword fights against poachers his terrifying facial contortions became famous, and to "grin like the Cheshire Caterling" became a local saying which, in time, became abbreviated to "Cheshire Cat." Incidentally, Mr. Caterling is the cat referred to in the nursery rhyme, "Hi, Diddle-Diddle."

Groaning Chair. A country name given to the chair in which a woman sat to receive congratulations on her safe delivery after confinement.

Groat. For the many people who have asked the value of the old *groat*, it may be stated here that it was a silver fourpenny-piece.

Grocer. A grocer was originally a wholesale dealer, from Old French *grossier*, through *gros*, one who sold goods by the gross. There is no record of the change from the old grocer to the present retail grocer.

Grog. The spirit, usually rum, served on board Naval ships. The name comes in a roundabout way from Admiral Edward Vernon (1684-1757). He was nicknamed Old Grog by his men from his habit of walking the quarter-deck in all weathers in a grogram cloak. When he introduced into the Navy the practice of serving rum mixed with water, instead of neat rum, with a view to economy, his concoction was at once named by the personnel, "grog." The name has stuck.

Groundlings. Was the name given to those people who, in Elizabethan times, occupied the cheapest part—the bare ground in front of the stage, without seats. As showing the topsy-turvy world, the present "groundlings" sit at the top of the theatre, in the Gods (q.v.).

In this connection, it should be borne in mind that the earliest theatre of the times stated were in the inn yards, and plays were acted by bands of strolling players, so that the groundlings' seat really was on the ground—the bare yard of the inn, while the quality occupied the balconies which ran round the yards of Elizabethan inns.

Grouse, To. To be always grumbling, mostly without any real justification. The first recorded mention of the word in this connection was in military circles about 1892; but it is probable that it originated in the Crimea and Indian Mutiny period. It was popularized as a word, however, during the Great War of 1914-18. There is no connection between it and the game bird of that name; the origin is probably the French *groucier*, which has a similar meaning.

Growlers. Older readers will remember the growlers of their youth — the four-wheel cabs. They were not called growlers at their advent; the surly manners affected by the drivers gave them the cognomen.

Gruel. "*Give him his gruel*," or "*To take his gruel*." Gruel as an article of food is mentioned in the Bible; but the expression "Give him his gruel" as a punishment is an allusion to the practice, in which Catherine de Medici was the acknowledged mistress, of giving poisoned drink to an enemy under the guise of friendship and hospitality. The drink was, in France, mostly gruel.

Grundy. Mrs. Grundy first appeared in "Speed the Plough," a comedy by Thomas Morton, which was produced at Covent Garden on 8th February, 1800. In the play Mrs. Grundy, who has since become the symbol of propriety in this country, is constantly referred to by a neighbour, wondering what Mrs. Grundy will do or say—but Mrs. Grundy never herself appears.

Guildhall. The meeting-place of the trade guilds. Founded in the days when the Guilds conducted industry, and congregated members in very much the same way, but better and with more authority, than the trade unions do to-day. They were, in fact, the earliest trade union. The old Guilds are still represented to-day in the various Livery Companies of the City of London.

Guillotine. The execution apparatus of France was in use in the Middle Ages, when it was known as the "Maiden." But it was not named after Dr. Guillotin, as most philologists insist. Dr. Guillotin's share in the instrument was as follows: On 10th October, 1789, he proposed in the French Chamber that a more merciful instrument of death should be devised. The Chamber left the mechanical details of a device to a Dr. Louis. The result was that what is now called the guillotine was for long called the louisette, or louison. Why it suddenly became changed to guillotine is not known. Nor was Dr. Guillotin executed on it, as is so often stated; it was an altogether different Dr. Guillotin.

Guinea-fowl. Have nothing to do with the coinage. They were introduced into England from Guinea, West Africa.

Gunner's Daughter, To Kiss the. In olden days, to be flogged on board ship. Sailors in the Navy who were to be flogged were fastened to the breech of a cannon.

Gunter, According to. *See* "Cocker."

Gutter. "*It all goes down Gutter Lane*." Gutter Lane, London, in the thirteenth and fourteenth centuries was known as Guthrum Lane, and as the home of the chief gold and silver smiths of the capital. *Guttur* is the Latin name for the throat. "It all goes down Gutter Lane" means that such a man turned all his gold and silver down the guttur "lane"—i.e., down his throat and into his stomach. In other words a glutton.

Guy's Hospital. Was founded by the generous benefaction of Thomas Guy, a Lombard Street bookseller, in 1732. He made his fortune largely by buying up, at a large discount, seamen's prize-money tickets, and investing the proceeds in Stock.

H

Habeas Corpus. An Act passed in 1679 commanding the producing of the body of one detained in prison in order that the court may judge whether such detention is valid. The Act was rendered necessary in order to end the scandal of the unlawful arrest of persons, and their incarceration for unlimited time without trial and, in many cases, without being told what charge was made against them. During the World War (1939-45) the Act was suspended by Parliament, and a number of people who were suspected of what might be termed Fifth Column (q.v.) activities were incarcerated without charge or trial, some of them for several years.

Habeas Corpus means, "You are to produce the body."

Haberdasher. There seems little doubt that originally the word was the French *hapertus*, a mixture of silk and wool. A very dubious origin is that the phrase was the Anglo-Saxon *habihr das*, "Will you buy this?" A third conjecture, often put forward, connects it with the French *avoir*, to have. It should be remembered that the haberdasher formerly sold only cloth, hence *hapertus* is the writer's choice.

Hack. Short for Hackney, a horse let out on hire. *See* "Hackney," below.

Hackney. A London district. Dr. Johnson, insisting that the district belonged to a Danish chief named Hacon, with *ey* added as expressing an island, observes: "The suggestion that coaches were first let out for hire in this district is not correct." It is not correct; but then neither is Dr. Johnson correct! The name is properly derived from the fact that the fields in the district were those in which the horses (not coaches!), sold at the great Smithfield Horse Fairs, were turned out to grass while waiting for the sales. Dr. Johnson overlooked the fact that in the same district is *Mare* Street, leading to Smithfields, along which the horses were driven to the sales—and Mare Street cannot be connected with Hacon in any way!

Hackney was also the name given to a breed of medium-sized horses, as distinguished from horses used for war purposes. It dates to the fourteenth century.

Hackney Carriage. The first Hackney conveyance plying for public hire dates to 1637, when King Charles I licensed fifty hackney-coachmen (each to keep twelve horses for about two hundred coaches) in London and Westminster.

Haddock. The tradition of the haddock is that it was the fish in the mouth of which St. Peter found the piece of money, and that the two marks on its neck are the impressions of the finger and thumb of the Apostle. Dr.

Brewer rightly points out, however, that haddocks could not have lived in the fresh waters of the Lake of Gennesaret.

Hades. According to Homer, the god of the nether world—Pluto of the Romans. The name came, later, to be adopted for the nether world itself, where dwell the spirits of all the dead ; the world of shades. In olden days the souls in Hades were believed to carry on there a counterpart of their material existence ; those of the righteous without discomfort amid the pale, sweet blooms of asphodel, or even in pleasure, in the Elysian Fields, and those of the wicked amid various torments. The lower world was described as surrounded by fiery and pestilential rivers, the solitary approach being guarded by the three-headed dog, Cerberus, to prevent the shades escaping to the upper world.

Hag-knots. The name given in country districts, particularly in the New Forest, to the tangles found in horses' manes, when the animal is groomed after its night's rest in the field. The superstition is that the knots were tied by hags (witches) to use as stirrups when they rode the horses in the night. In Bourne's " Popular Antiques " it states : " Hagges are said to be made of sweat, or some other vapour issuing out of the head ; a not unusual sight among us when we ride by night in the Summertime. They are extinguished like flames by shaking the horses' manes."

Ha-Ha ! Probably the most peculiar origin of any word we have. The sound which is written " Ha-Ha ! " to denote laughter is thus described by Walpole in his " Modern Gardening " : " The destruction of walls for boundaries, and the invention of fosses (ditches), an attempt then deemed so astonishing, that common people called them *Ha-Ha's* to express their surprise at finding a sudden and unperceived check to their walk."

Hail. A greeting. Its origin is the Icelandic *heill*, Anglo-Saxon *hal*, and the English *whole*. It is thus an abbreviated way of saying " be whole," in other words, be in good health.

Hair. " *Hanging by a single hair.*" One single tuft of hair is left on the shaven crown of a Musselman—for Mohamet to grasp hold of when drawing the deceased to Paradise.

Hair. " *His hair stood on end.*" Hair can, literally, stand on end. Each hair of a person's head has a tiny muscle by which the hair can be erected. The muscle is remarkably efficient in certain animals, such as the cat, when facing attack, or the porcupine. In the human species, however, it acts only feebly. The sensation known as " goose-skin " is due to the contraction of these muscles when, on sudden fright, the human hair, true to our original animal instinct, does try to " stand on end."

Without turning a hair. Meaning not to show any signs of distress. The allusion is from the stable, where the first sign of distress in a horse is sweating, which roughens the animals' coat.

Hair-breadth Escape. How narrow is an hair-breadth escape can be judged by the official measure. In measurement the forty-eighth part of an inch is referred to as a hair-breadth.

Hair, Locks of. Probably the custom of giving locks of hair was a continuance of the ancient superstition that a person could be bewitched, or influenced for good or evil, through another who possessed his hair or nail trimmings. An instance is recorded of an old man who carried round with him a bag supposed to contain his precious savings, and which was much envied by his neighbours. At his death it was found to be full of hair and nail cuttings, so that nobody should wish him harm.

Hair of a dog that bit you. Means take the same again. If you have hang-over, take another drink of the alcohol which gave you the hang-over. The saying arises from the old-time belief that the burnt hair of a dog is an antidote to a dog-bite.

Hair, Red. The idea that a person with red hair cannot be trusted is said to arise from the fact that Judas, who betrayed Christ, had red hair.

Hairs. Dr. Hans Fredenthals has recorded that a red-head has on the average 83,000 hairs on the head, a brunette 102,000, and a blonde 104,000.

Hake. " *To lose in Hake but gain in Herrings.*" An old fishermen's saying, in keeping with " What you lose on the swings you gain on the roundabouts " of the shore-man. Hake feed on herrings, and are therefore driven away from the herring fishing grounds, though they are saleable fish.

Halcyon Days. Days of peace and plenty. It was the name given to the seven days before and after the shortest day because, according to the fable, there were always calms at sea during this period. Pliny wrote : " They (halcyons) lay and sit about midwinter, where daies be shortest ; and the times whiles they are broodie is called the halcyon daies ; for during that season the sea is calm and navigable, especially in the coast of Sicilie."

Note.—Halcyons were kingfisher birds.

" Half is more than the Whole." Excellent legal advice, and true even to-day, though it comes from Hesiod (about 860 B.C.). He used the words to his brother, Perseus, with whom he wished to settle a dispute without going to law. Lawyers seem to have been much the same in those days as now.

Half-penny. Because the original penny piece was deeply indented, crossways, so that half pennies, and farthings (q.v.), could easily be separated when necessary.

Half Seas Over. When a sailing ship had all her sails set, a sudden change in the wind often threatened to lay her over on her side and bring the sea swishing over her gunwales half-way up the slant of the deck. Sailors described as " half seas over " any one of them rolling along the street drunkenly, and in danger of falling over sideways at any moment.

Halifax. Camden states that the name of the Yorkshire town is derived from *halig*, holy, and *fax*, hair ; and he tells this story in support of it : The town was formerly called Horton. A clerk there who had been jilted, cut off his false sweetheart's head and hung it in a yew tree. The head came to be reverenced as a holy relic and when, in time, it rotted away, little filaments of fine thread could be seen beneath the bark. These were regarded by the Hortonians as the *fax*, or hair, of the murdered girl, and the town was renamed Halig-fax.

But another story says that because an image of John the Baptist was kept in an hermitage there as a holy relic, the town was named Holy Face. Which, however, does not explain how the face became fax.

Halifax Gibbet Law. Owing to widespread thefts of the woollen material supplied to them, woollen manufacturers in the town found their completed fabrics lacking in body and weight. Accordingly, a law was passed making the theft of anything to the value of thirteen-pence-halfpenny subject to the death penalty. On conviction, a thief was executed, publicly, the same day. The method of execution was not that in general used throughout the country—the rope—but a type of guillotine. The Law is thus put on record by Taylor, the Water Poet :

" At Halifax, the Law so sharpe
doth deale,
That whoso more than
thirteen pence doth steale,
They have a jyn that
wondrous quick and well,
Sends thieves all headless
into Heaven, or Hell."

Hallelujah. From the Hebrew, *halelu-Jah*, Praise ye, Jehovah. It occurs only once in the

Bible—in *Rev.* xix, 1, 3, 4, 6; and then in the Greek form, *alleluia.*

Hallelujah Victory. That gained by the newly baptized Britons over the Picts and Scots near Mold, Cheshire, in A.D. 429. As they attacked, under Bishop Germanus, of Auxerre, they shouted "Hallelujah."

Hallmark. The test mark of Goldsmiths' Hall stamped upon gold and silver as a guarantee of its purity. The marks are a leopard's head for London; anchor for Birmingham; sword between three wheat sheaves for Chester; castle with three towers for Exeter; five lions on a cross for York; a crown for Sheffield; three castles for Newcastle; castle for Edinburgh; tree and salmon ring for Glasgow; hibernia for Dublin. These are accompanied by the standard mark, date mark and the carat figure.

Hallowe'en. Like most of the Christian feasts, Hallowe'en is a Heathen festival which Christianity took over. The date, 31st October, was at one time, before the reformation of the calendar, the last day of the old year. Now the Romans had a feast about this time in honour of the Goddess Pomona, in which nuts and apples, representing the Winter store of fruits, played an important part. (In Scotland to-day the roasting of nuts and "apple ducking" are still the main fun of the festival.)

The Druids appropriated some of the Pomona customs for their great Autumn festival, when they lighted fires in honour of the Sun-God. And they believed that on the eve of this festival Saman, Lord of Death, called together the wicked souls that, within the past twelve months, had been condemned to inhabit the bodies of animals. This is the origin of the present belief, particularly in Scotland, that witches and ghosties are abroad on this night.

When Christianity came to us it promptly confiscated the feasts of Pomona, the Sun-God, and Saman, and changed the departed wicked souls into the good souls of the departed Saints, christening it the Feast of All Hallows—Hallow in those early Anglo-Saxon days being the word for Saint. Thus we came to All Hallows' Eve, or Hallowe'en Eve.

Hallucinations. The apparent perception of some external thing to which no real object corresponds. From the Latin *alucinari*, to wander in mind.

Ham. An Anglo-Saxon word prevalent in many English place-names. Chiefly written with a long "a," it meant in this sense a home. Thus, Hampton was the home town, and Hampton Wick the home town on the creek. Where it appears in the names of families, it may be interpreted the home of (example) Wolsingham, home of the Wolsings. It is an interesting commentary that ham (*heim*) also denotes a home in German, and the suffix appears in the same way—Mannheim.

Hammer and Tongs. "*To go it hammer and tongs.*" With reiterated force. The origin is obscure. One authority says: "A corruption of hammer and tongues, a wordy warfare." The most probable derivation is the continual hammering, until he has the article in shape, by a blacksmith with his hammer as he holds the article with his tongs.

Hammercloth. Was the covering hanging below the box seat of a coach, or the old-fashioned carriage. The suggestion that it derived its name from the fact that the hammer, bolts and nails to remedy a breakdown were kept there is a fallacy. One of two possible origins is correct; either it was because hammering played a part in the preparation of the cloth, to improve its strength, or that the true name was "hammock-cloth," the driver's seat being slung, after the form of a hammock. Probably the latter is the more likely.

Hammersmith. The town by the Thames was so-called because in its early Saxon days the place, then a village, had an abnormal number of smithies. The Saxon name was Hammerschmiede.

Hammock. Columbus, in his account of his first discovery voyage, wrote of Indians who bartered their cotton and *hamacas*, "or nets in which they sleep."

And in Hawkins's "Voyage to the South Sea" is recorded the fact that the Brazilians called their beds *hamacas.*

Hampshire Hogs. The nickname for people born in Hampshire. The allusion is to the county's reputation for breeding the best pigs.

Hand and Glove. So intimate, as the hand is to the glove, or vice versa.

Hand, Bloody. The device in armour of Ulster. It appears in armourial bearings of a number of families, and in such cases is usually connected with murder. Dr. Brewer says that in a church near Aston, Birmingham, is a coat of arms of the family of Holt, which bears the "Bloody Hand." Sir Thomas Holt, he explains, murdered his cook in a cellar with a spit, and on being pardoned for the offence by the King, was enjoined, by way of penalty, to wear ever after a bloody hand in his family coat.

Hand, Bloody (trial). *See* "Bloody Hand."

Hand, Dead Man's. *See* "Glory."

Hand-fasting. A marriage of approval once popular on the Border, and once a common practice among the Jews, and still to be found in parts of the East. A man, by hand-fasting, was permitted to choose a woman to live with him for twelve months. If the co-habitation proved agreeable to both at the end of that period, they were pronounced man and wife.

Hand in your Checks. A phrase from America, meaning to die, to settle your account. It arose from the custom in many restaurants of giving a certain amount of credit to known patrons. The customers departed with their bills (checks) without paying. Periodically, they were requested to hand in their checks for settlement. Another version is that it comes from card games, when counters were used for money, and the counters (checks) were handed in for cashing at the end of the game.

Hand that rocks the Cradle rules the World. The line comes from the poem, "What Rules the World?" by the American, William Ross Wallace (1819-1891), beginning: "They say that Man is mighty"; and ending:

"But a mightier power, and stronger
Man from his throne has hurled.
And the hand that rocks the cradle
Is the hand that rules the world."

Handicap. Is a corruption of "hand in cap," from the drawing of lots out of a hat or cap.

Handkerchief. Was originally 'kerchief, a corruption of cover-chief (French *couvrir*, to cover, and *chef*, the head). When the kerchief came into use for the face and was accordingly carried in the hand, "hand" was added to its name. In the North of England the miner still refers to the scarf he wears round his neck as a neckchief.

Hands (plural). It should be noted that the plural of "handfull" is "handfuls," and not, as is so frequently written, "handsful."

Hands Down, To Win. A horse-racing metaphor. To win hands down means that the jockey has not had to urge his mount forward, by working his hands.

Hands, on Head. In a religious sense, the ordination of priests by a Bishop, or in the act of confirmation. But in Roman days it indicated the right of property in the person thus laid. A Roman who laid his hands on the head of a slave before the prætor, indicated that he laid claim to such person as a slave. *See* "Ear-marked."

Hands. To wash one's hands. An allusion to Pilate's washing of his hands at the trial of Jesus, after he had said that he found no fault in Jesus, but yet yielded to the clamour of the mob for his condemnation.

Hanged, drawn and quartered. Formerly the capital, or death, sentence. It should read, correctly, drawn, hanged and quartered. The convicted criminal was drawn to the place of execution on a hurdle, hanged, and his body cut and chopped into quarters, which were spiked in a public place as an example! During the reign of George III, the quartering was substituted by the dis-embowelling of the victim while he was still alive.

Hanging. Was originally by suspension, not by a "drop" as at present. The first person to be executed by the drop was Earl Ferrers, in 1760.

It is an interesting commentary that a Peer, should he come to the scaffold, can claim the privilege of being hanged with a silken rope.

Hanging Gardens of Babylon. One of the Seven Wonders of the World (q.v.). Nebuchadnezzar married a woman of Median, a hilly country. She found the flat plains of Babylon wearisome to her. To gratify her wish, the King built the hanging gardens to remind her of her native mountains. The gardens are said to have been four hundred feet square, with terraces rising from the river one over the other, each being planted with trees and flowers. The terraces were provided with sufficient soil to give root space to trees of a great size.

Hang Out. "*Where do you hang out?*" A slang term for "Where do you live?" to-day; but in earlier days a very natural inquiry, since it was the custom to hang over one's premises a sign indicating the nature of the wares sold within. The custom is perpetuated to-day in public-house signs.

Hang Out the Broom, To. This is an old country phrase, dating back to 1820, for the absence of a wife from her home. To hang out the broom meant that, the good wife being away, the good man's friends and cronies might come and make merry in the kitchen!

Hansom Cab. The street public-hire conveyance so popular in Edwardian days, with the driver perched high above it at the back. It is not true, as is invarably stated, that the vehicle was invented by Joseph Aloysius Hansom. It is true that Hansom patented the cab in 1834, but he did not invent it. It was invented by Edward Bird, secretary to the Misses Gotwaltz, nominal post-mistresses of Birmingham, and he presented his invention to his brother-in-law, Edward Welch, who was a partner of Mr. Hansom. Bird received no remuneration, and the cab was first known as "Bird's Patent Safety Cab." Hansom sold his patent rights for £10,000 to a company of which he was appointed manager. It was a disastrous transaction; he never received a penny of the money, and before long returned to his profession—that of an ecclesiastical architect, designing Roman Catholic churches. In 1944 only one Hansom Cab remained for hire in London to excite comment from the younger generation.

Hara-Kiri. The Japanese way of suicide in cases of official disgrace, or when sentenced to death. The method is sufficiently explained by the translation—*hara*, the belly, *kiri*, to cut. The first recorded instance of hara-kiri was that of Tametomo, brother of the ex-Emperor Sutoku, in the twelfth century.

Harbinger. The word is interesting because of the curious corruption that has made it a bearer of good tidings, as in the phrase "Harbinger of Spring." Its original meaning was one who provides or obtains lodgings, or harborage, allied to "harbouring" a person. It is derived from the Old High German, *hari*, an army, and *bergan*, to lodge. In Mediæval English it was spelt *herbergeour*. Hawkins, in "Bishop Ken," wrote: "Bishop Ken's house . . . was marked by the harbinger for the use of Mrs. Eleanor Gwyn."

Hard Up. In difficulties; short of money. The term comes from the sea. During a storm, the captain of the old sailing ships would order "Hard up the Helm," the reply to which was to put the tiller as far as possible to windward, in order to turn the ship's head away from the wind and thus aid her to weather the storm.

Hare. "*Mad as a March Hare.*" It is suggested that the phrase should be as mad as a *marsh* hare, because hares are wilder in marshes from the absence of hedges and other cover. On the other hand, March is the rutting (breeding) season, when the hare naturally disports itself for the benefit of his love-making.

Harliquinade. More elderly readers will remember the harliquinade as that part of the old pantomimes which followed the transformation of characters, and in which the harlequin and clown played the principal parts. Harlequin was a sprite supposed to be invisible to all but his faithful Columbine. He was fated to dance through the world and frustrate the knavish tricks of the clown, who was supposed to be in love with Columbine. It was harlequin who in this frustration of tricks effected the great transformation scenes of the old pantomimes. Greatest of all harlequins was John Rich (at one time owner of Drury Lane), in the days when pantomime was in dumb show—mime. He introduced pantomime to England purely from his inability to speak on the stage, so uncouth was he. But his power of expression by mimicry is said never to have been equalled.

Harmonia's Necklace. To be given Harmonia's necklace means to hold an unlucky possession. Harmonia, daughter of Mars and Venus, in Mythology, was given as a wedding present a necklace which proved fatal to all who possessed it.

Harmonious Blacksmith. The grave of the blacksmith whose hammerings led to Handel composing the famous air, can still be seen in the churchyard at Whitchurch, Middlesex. Handel was, at the time, organist in the church.

Harmonium. The musical instrument, first patented in Paris by Debain, was so-named from the sustained harmonies produced by the effects of the wind by which its reeds are played.

Harvest Festival. One professed "authority" on origins makes the remarkable statement that this observance by way of thanksgiving for the fruits of the earth, really grew out of the Harvest Supper which landlords were accustomed to give their tenants after the harvest had been gathered in. A more astonishing "origin" has seldom been put forward. The antiquity of the custom appears even in *Exodus* xxiii, 16: "The feast of Harvest, the first-fruits of thy labours." Cain, it is recorded, brought of the fruit of the ground, and offered it to the Lord. If that is not a harvest festival comparable with our religious festival, words have lost their meaning.

Calimachus affirms that: "The first-fruits were sent by the people of every nation to the Temple of Apollo, in Delos, and by the Hyperboreans in particular, the most distant that enjoy the happiness of corn and harvest."

The ancient Jews, by command of their laws, offered a sheaf (*Lev.* xxiii, 10): "Ye shall reap the harvest, then ye shall bring a sheaf, first-fruits of your harvest, unto the priest."

Of our Harvest Feasts in country areas, where after the corn has been safely gathered, the farmers give a supper to the harvest workers, Hone says: "For should they (the farmers) refuse them (the workers) of this much-expected time, this festal night, the youth, especially of both sexes would decline serving him for the future, and employ their labours for others who would promise them the rustic joys of the harvest supper, mirth and music, songs and games. These feasts appear to be the relics of Pagan or Jewish ceremonies."

Hat. "*To hang up one's Hat.*" To denote that you are the master. Visitors usually hold their hat in their hands.

Hat-Trick. Properly the taking of three wickets at cricket in successive balls. It was thus called, because at one time any bowler performing the feat was entitled to a new hat at the expense of the club. The term should not be employed outside the realm of cricket.

Hat's Off. The mark of a pleasurable occasion, "Hat's Off to So-and-So." The phrase is said to belong to the Navy, where hats are doffed to receive pay. The money due is waiting the parade of the men. As the sailor steps forward to his name, he repeats his name and number, and his pay is placed on the top of the hat which he extends to the officer.

Hauled over the Coals. *See* "Coals."

Hautville's Coit. The name given to the huge stone rear Stanton Drew, Somerset. Tradition holds that it was a coit, or quoit, thrown by Sir John Hautville

Haversack. Was, originally, an oat-sack, from the German *hafer*, oats, and *sack*. Haver is a common name for oats in Westmorland; *haver-cake*, meaning oat-cake.

Havoc *To cry havoc.* The original meaning becomes clear when it is remembered that the havoc is the Anglo-Saxon *hafoc*, a hawk. To cry havoc was to cry hawk—to call encouragement to the hawk loosed upon its prey, in the days when hawking was a British sport. Dr. Brewer's definition of the phrase may, therefore, he a later extension of the cry to humans; he describes it as "an old military command to massacre without quarter, which was forbidden in the ninth year of Richard II, on pain of death."

Hawker. Often also referred to as a huckster, and this was probably the original word. In Low German, *hukke* meant a bent back. From his back bent under the weight of the goods carried in a pack, the travelling pedlar came to be called a *hukkester*. The word by corruption came to hawker. To hawk, even from earliest English, was used in connection with the bird, the hawk.

Hawthorn. In Mediæval English *hawe* meant a hedge, and hawthorn was a hedge-thorn. In the Language of Flowers the hawthorn means "good hope" because of its promise of Spring. In ancient Greece, the hawthorn was used as a crown for girls at weddings. The Romans regarded it as a charm against sorcery, especially where babies were concerned, and hawthorn leaves were laid in the cradles of new-born babies.

Hay, where it appeared in place-names, signified a place surrounded by hedges, usually for the purposes of the chase. A variant of the word is haigh. Horsehay, is an example; and The Hague, in Holland, was properly Gravenhage, meaning the Count's hedge, a hunting-seat of the Counts of Holland.

Haymarket. One of the busiest parts of London's West End, situated just off Piccadilly Circus. It is so-called because up to 1831 hay was sold there in open market!

Health. "Good Health." According to Rabelais, the giant Gabbura was the inventor of the drinking of healths. Gabbara was the ancestor of Gargantu, a giant of mediæval (most likely Celtic) legend, and famous for his appetite. He is commemorated in "Gargantuan appetite."

"Hear-Hear." The murmur of approbation so common at public meetings, was originally "Hear him! Hear him!" and was meant as an admonition, to call special attention to the sentiments the speaker had expressed, hence an agreement with his opinions. The "him" was apparently dropped for the sake of brevity.

Hearse. In its beginning, a hearse was a *herce*, a French word meaning a harrow. Shaped like a harrow, the *herce* was a framework, holding candles, which was placed over the bier or coffin. Later such a frame, fitted for candles, was used to carry a corpse from the house to the church.

Heathen. Dr. Brewer gives as the origin of the word: "Literally, a dweller on a heath, i.e., some remote part where Christian doctrines would not penetrate till long after they had been accepted in towns." But people were classified as heathen long before there was any Christian doctrine! The Romans classified as heathen those dwellers in the country who were thus cut off from all knowledge of their complicated system of Mythology.

Heaven, Seventh. *See* "Seventh Heaven."

Heavy Man. An actor who plays foil to the hero, such as Iago to Othello. "Heavy" because they are usually robust men both in physique and in the nature of the manner in which they must play their rôle.

Hector. To hector a person is to badger, or bully, him. The origin usually given is that it is derived from Hector, the Trojan warrior killed, and his body insulted, by Achilles. Nobody familiar with the Iliad would fall into such a mistake, for Hector was the noblest and most magnaminious of all the Trojan heroes of the Epic. It is far more likely that "to hector" is a corruption of to heckle.

Heel of Achilles. When Thetis, mother of Achilles, dipped her son in the River Styx to make him invulnerable, she held him by one heel. This, being untouched by the water, remained vulnerable to a wound. It was from a spear wound in the heel that he died.

Heir. Heir-Apparent, Heir-Presumptive. The arguments over the meanings are legion. Yet the answer is perfectly simple. The heir-apparent is one whose right of inheritance is indefeasible provided he, or she, outlives the immediate ancestor. The heir *must* be the heir, whatever happens.

The heir-presumptive is one who, snould tne ancestor die immediately would, in the present circumstance of things, be the heir; but whose right of inheritance may be defeated by a nearer heir being born.

Princess Elizabeth is the heir-presumptive to the British throne, because should a son be born to the King and Queen, he would inherit—a male heir having the prior claim.

Hell. Anglo-Saxon *helle*, the abode of the dead. The Greek Hades, and the Latin *infermum*. In Scandinavian mythology, the Ogress Hel, the Prosperpine of Scandinavian mythology.

Christianity itself has never seemed able to make up its mind as to the meaning of Hell. In the Old Testament "hell" is used to denote "Hades," a resting-place of the dead to await judgment. Whereas, in the New Testament it is regarded as a place of torment (*Luke* xvi, 23: "He lifted up his eyes—from Hades—in torment").

The Greeks believed Hell (under the name of Tartaros) to be a deep and sunless abyss as far under the earth as Heaven is above the earth, where the wicked received their punishment.

Hellfire. In 1863, a clergyman named Williams was charged under the Clergy Discipline Act with "publishing heretical doctrines" in a periodical called

"Essays and Reviews." The main piece of heretical doctrine alleged against him was that he had written of his disbelief in everlasting fire after death.

Lord Westbury delivered the judgment of the Judicial Committee of the Privy Council—and he is said to have done so with great relish — acquitting the defendant. Following this, a legal wag suggested that the epitaph of the Lord Chancellor when he died should be:

"In the Judicial Committee of the Privy Council, he dismissed Hell without costs, and took away from the orthodox members of the Church of England their hope of everlasting damnation."

Hell Kettles. Three deep, water-filled pits at Oxenhall, Durham. They are, of course, by local repute, bottomless. In point of fact they are three coal-pit shafts.

Hell or Connaught. A phrase in use all over Ireland. It is attributed to Cromwell and arose when, under the Commonwealth, the native Irish were dispossessed of their lands in three provinces and ordered to settle in Connaught under penalty of death.

Hemp. Is connected with a prophecy: "When hempe is spun England is done." Lord Bacon interpreted it thusly: "Hemp is composed of the initial letters of Henry, Edward, Mary, Philip, and Elizabeth." Curiously enough, if this is so, the prophecy came true, because at the close of the reign of the last-named, England was, indeed, done—for the next Sovereign was described not King of England, but "King of Great Britain and Ireland."

Henchman. Anglo-Saxon *hengest*, a horse and man. Originally, an attendant who looked after his squire's horse or horses.

Heroic Age, The. The legendary period when the Gods of Olympus were said to have married the daughters of men, so that the offspring partook of the two-fold character of Gods and Humans. The decline, in fact, of the Gods.

Hick. A term for a simple-minded person, obsolete in England, but still flourishing in America, was a pet form of Richard. Richard II is called Hick Heavyhead in "Richard the Redeless." When the word was used in England Hick was stood for much the same as Giles or Hodge—simple-minded.

Highgate Horns. Highgate was, originally, a village that sprang up round the old toll-gate on the road from Barnet to London. Passengers wishing to pass through the gate were subjected to an absurd ceremony of "swearing on the horns." The horns were those of an antler, fastened on a stick, and held over the head of the person taking the oath.

According to Dr. Brewer, the terms of the oath were:

(1) Never to kiss the maid when he could kiss the mistress.
(2) Never to eat brown bread when he could eat white.
(3) Never to drink small beer when he could get strong beer—unless he preferred it.

High Old Time. "*To have a high old time.*" Thoroughly to enjoy oneself. The phrase probably came by way of a traveller in Germany, where the word for a wedding was *Hochzeit*, which means, literally, a high time!

Hip Hip Hurrah! "Hip" is said to be derived from the initials of *Hiersosolyms est perdita*, Jerusalem, is destroyed. When German knights started a hunt for Jews in the Middle Ages (the German was not much different then from now!) they ran shouting "Hip, Hip."

Hurrah, as explained elsewhere in this volume, was an invocation, later corrupted to *Hurra*, Paradise. Thus, says Dr. Brewer, "Hip, Hip, Hurrah would mean, 'Jerusalem is destroyed, or lost to the infidel, and we are on the road to Paradise'."

Hipped. A person who is in the state of being hipped is in low spirits, suffering from what our American cousins would call a fit of the blues. The word was derived by corrupting the first syllable of hypochondria, which the *Oxford Dictionary* gives as "a morbid state of causeless depression."

Hippocratic Oath, The. Hippocrates is generally acknowledged as the Father of Medicine, and his oath was taken, and still is taken in some universities, by medical students when they take their degree. It is far too long to give here; but some paragraphs will be sufficient to reveal it as probably the noblest oath ever sworn:

"I will look upon him who shall have taught me this Art even as one of my parents. I will share my substance with him, I will supply his necessities, if he be in need. . . . I will teach this Art, not only to my own sons, but to the sons of him who has taught me, and to disciples . . . without fee or covenant. . . .

"Whatever house I enter, there will I go for the benefit of the sick, refraining from any wrong-doing or corruption, especially from any acts of seduction. Whatever things I see or hear concerning the life of men in my attendance on the sick, or even apart therefrom which ought not to be noised abroad, I will keep silence thereon, counting such things to be as sacred secrets."

"Without fee or covenant" is seen to-day in the hospital "walking" training; the "seduction" clause rules to-day in the B.M.C.; the "silence" is practised to-day even in the face of the law.

Hippodrome. In the beginning was a race-course. The word is derived from the Greek *hippos*, a horse, and *dromos*, a course.

History Repeats Itself. A remarkable instance of the interpretation of this phrase occurred in the Second Great War (1939-45).

216 B.C. The greatest disaster in the history of the *Ancient* world befell the Roman armies on the Plain of Cannhæ in Southern Italy. There eighty thousand Roman attackers were themselves encircled and annihilated by the Carthaginian forces under Hannibal. THE COMMANDER OF THE ROMAN FORCES WAS ÆMILLIUS PAULLUS.

A.D. 1943. The greatest disaster in the history of the *Modern* world befell the German armies on the plain around Stalingrad, in Southern Russia. There three hundred and thirty thousand attacking Germans were themselves encircled and annihilated by the Russian forces under Marshal Rokossovsky. THE COMMANDER OF THE GERMAN FORCES WAS FIELD-MARSHAL PAULUS.

Hoax. A contraction of hocus-pocus, which see.

Hobnob. Is a corruption of Hab-nab, have or have not, which can be interpreted as "give and take together," or hob-nob together.

Hockey. The name is derived from the diminutive of *hook*, the club used in the game being hooked slightly at the end.

Hocus-Pocus. This name for a trick, or fraudulent claim, is said to have been derived from Ochus Bochus, a wizard and demon of Northern Mythology. Another "origin" is that it is a vicious corruption by Protestants of *Hoc est corpus*, uttered by Roman Catholic priests at the Raising of the Host, during which it is claimed by the Roman Catholic Church the bread and wine is changed into the Body and Blood of Christ.

Hodge. Was a pet name for Roger, and has been a contemptuous name for a rustic since the sixteenth century.

Hoist with his own petard. The petard was an ancient infernal engine filled with gunpowder. The attendant filled it with gunpowder and then fired it—at the peril of his life! Hence, caught in his own trap, or hoist with his own petard.

The list of people who have been "hoist with their own petard," is a remarkable one. Some of them are:

Hugues Aubriot, Provost of Paris, who built the Bastille, was the first person to be confined in the fortress.

Perillus of Athens made a metal bull for Phalaris. Criminals were shut up in its interior, and fires were lighted under the belly. Phalaris tested the invention on Perillos himself, who was the first person to be baked to death.

The Earl of Salisbury was the first to use cannon. He was also the first Englishman to be killed by a cannon-ball.

Enguerrand de Marigni, Minister of Finance to Phillipe, erected a gibbet at Montfaucon for the execution of criminals. He was himself hanged on it.

Matthew Hopkins, called the witch-finder, was himself tried by his own test for witchcraft, and was executed.

The Bishop of Verdun invented the Iron Cage—which was too small for a person either to stand up or lie down in. He was the first man to be shut up in one.

Ludovico Sforza invented the Iron Shroud, a terrible instrument of torture. He was the first to be tortured in it.

Regent Morton, of Scotland, devised The Maiden—a kind of guillotine, and was the first to lose his head to her.

Dr. Guillotin proposed the idea of the execution machine named after him. He did not die by it. The Guillotin who was executed was Dr. J. B. Guillotin, of Lyons.

Verily, invention is a dangerous occupation.

Hold the Fort. The phrase is immortalized from its use by General Sherman, in 1864, during the American Civil War. He signalled the message to General Corse from the top of Kenesaw.

"Hole-in-the-Wall," The. Many public-houses throughout Britain have this name as a tavern sign. The suggestion has been made that it may have been derived from inns built in the thickness of the city walls. In "Notes and Queries" (Vol. 182, p. 319), reference is made to William Kent's theory of its origin—that the name was derived from the holes made in the walls of debtors' prisons, through which those incarcerated received gifts of money, food and drink from the charitable. The presence of so many of the inns of this name near prisons or on the sites of prisons lends colour to this version.

Holm. A word found in place-names of Scandinavian origin. It denotes an island situated in a lake or river. Ling-holm, in Lake Windermere, for instance; and Stock-holm in Sweden.

Holocaust. Though now applied to any great loss of life, its proper use is in connection with fire. The derivation is the Greek *holos*, whole, and *kaio*, I burn. In its Biblical sense it was a sacrifice completely consumed by fire.

Holt. An Anglo-Saxon word denoting a wood. Though in numerous places now bearing the name of Holt there is no sign of any wood or trees in any number, they did exist when it received its name. *Hot* was another version of it, as in the case of Alders-hot, the wood of alders.

Holy Maid of Kent. The name given to Elizabeth Barton. A Kentish servant-girl, she was subject to trances, and foretold events. Entering a convent as a nun, she (so she said), under inspiration, incited Roman Catholics to resist the Reformation. She pronounced against the divorce of Catharine of Aragon, and when Henry VIII did divorce her and marry Anne Boleyn, she announced the "doom" of Henry—and was accordingly hanged at Tyburn.

Holy Stone. The soft sandstone used for scrubbing the decks of ships is said by some authorities to have derived its name from the one-time practice of scouring the decks for Sunday service. Another suggestion is that it comes from the fact that sandstone, being porous, is full of minute holes, and that the name is really holey-stone.

Homage. The word is from the Latin *homo*, a man. It signified the service made by a vassal to his lord.

Home, Sweet Home. This, one of the best-loved songs in the England language, was first heard in the opera, "The Maid of Milan," produced at Covent Garden in 1823. The words were written by John Howard Payne, and the music by Sir Henry Bishop. Payne was an American! And the music by Bishop is said to have been taken from a Sicilian air. In fact, this typical British song has very little that is British about it.

Homer. It is little known that the poet to whom is assigned "The Iliad" and the "Odyssey," monuments of poetry, in all probability never existed. The name Homer means, "One who puts together"; and the probability is that Homer's works were the writings of a group of poets between the twelfth and ninth centuries before Christ.

Honey. It is a mistake to suppose that the bees collect honey. They obtain nectar from the flowers, carry it to the hive, and there change it into honey. It is said to take thirty-seven thousand bee-loads of nectar to make one pound of honey.

Honeymoon. "The month when all is sweetness; the first after marriage, especially the part spent away from home," says Brewer's "Dictionary of Phrase and Fable." The truth, however, is that the name is derived from the custom in Northern Europe of drinking hydromel, or diluted honey (mead), a fermented liquor made from honey, for thirty days (a *moon*, month) after the marriage feast.

Honi soit qui mal y Pense. The generally accepted translation is: "Evil be to him who evil thinks." The more correct one is: "Dishonour be to him who thinks evil of it."

There are several stories of its origin. One is that at a State function, the Countess of Salisbury accidentally dropped her blue garter. Edward III, seeing her predicament, picked it up and slipped it round one of his own knees, with the phrase quoted above. The incident, so the story goes, led him to institute the Order of the Garter, instead of an Order of the Round Table, which he had in mind.

The other story is that it was Edward's Queen herself who dropped the garter, whereupon it was adopted by the soldiers going to the war with France as their badge. The story continues that the "it" (y) of the motto referred not to the garter, but to the war with France: "Dishonoured be he who thinks ill of it (the war)." The doubtfulness of this version lies in the fact that soldiers would hardly be likely to know what had happened in the ballroom of the Royal Palace.

Hoodlum. A newspaper reporter in San Francisco, in attempting to coin a name for a gang of young ruffians who were infesting the streets of the town, hit upon the idea of taking the leader's name and reversing it. The leader was one, Muldoon. The reporter, accordingly, wrote Noodlums. Like the majority of reporters his writing was not particularly decipherable, and the compositor in setting it up in type, made it *H*oodlums. And Hoodlum has been the name for a street rough ever since.

Hook or by Crook, By. More "origins" have been given to this phrase than any other the writer has come across. One is that it is a shepherd's phrase, meaning that rather than lose a sheep he will make use of a hook cut from the hedge it he has not his crook with him. Another is that more than a hundred years ago there were two famous K.C's, one named Hook and the other Crook. Both were equally noted pleaders, and both equally successful, so that people determined to go to law, vowed that they would win either by Hook or by Crook.

Then there is the story of the thieves who stole washing from lines by means of a hook, and *objets d'art* from tables beside open windows with a crook. Lastly, there is the explanation that the poor of the manor were allowed to go into the forest with a hook or a crook to get wood for the Winter. What they could not reach they could pull down with the hook, and gather it together with the crook.

If the writer may be permitted to sum up, he would point out that the phrase is used by Spenser in "The Færie Queene"; that Spenser wrote the epic poem earlier than its published date of 1589, which was about three hundred years before Messrs. Hook and Crook, K.C's; and that much of Spenser's writings was about shepherds!

Hoot, Don't care a. It was, originally, a "hooter." And hooter was a corruption of Iota, the smallest letter in the Greek language. *See* "Jot."

Horn of Fidelity. An "enchanted cup" which Morgam la Fay sent to King Arthur. Its enchantment consisted in the fact that no lady could drink out of it who was not true to her husband. An unfaithful wife who so attempted to drink would spill the contents. The horn, coming to King Mark, his Queen and a hundred ladies essayed the test. Only four managed to drink from the horn without spilling.

Hornpipe. The hornpipe was an old wooden wind instrument, native to Wales, each end being finished off with horn. The dance of the same name was so-called because it was first danced to the music of the hornpipe.

Horoscope. From the Greek *hora*, an hour or season, and *skopeo*, I observe. Those who profess to cast horoscopes do so by this hour-observing, or scrutinizing, because it is the disposition of the heavens at the exact hour of birth which is examined.

Horse. According to Classical Mythology, the horse was created by Poseidon (Neptune). The first being to drive a four-in-hand was, says Virgil, Erichthonius.

Horse-racing. Was known in England before the days of Boadicea. But on the Turf, as we know it to-day, Newmarket is probably the oldest race-course. King James I attended a meeting there in 1605.

Hose. The term is now applied exclusively to stockings (men's socks are called half-hose); but in Saxon days and for generations afterwards any leg covering, even including tight breeches, were known by the original name of *hosa*. The plural was *hosan*.

Hostler. The man who looks after the horses at a hostelry (or did so before the motor car drove them off the road) was in the days that the word was coined the hotel-keeper himself; *hostelier*, keeper of an hostelry.

Hotch-potch. Comes from the French *hochepot*; *hocher*, to shake together, and *pot*.

Houri. Among the Mohammedans a black-eyed nymph of Paradise, beautiful virgins endowed with perpetual youth. Their task is to form the chief felicity of the Faithful. Every believer, it is stated in the faith, will have seventy-two hours in Paradise.

Hull, Hell and Halifax. Taylor, the seventeenth century "Water Poet," quotes this saying as an old beggars' and vagabonds' prayer: "From Hull, Hell and Halifax, Good Lord deliver us." And it might well be so, for Hull in those days was so well governed in vagrancy laws, that beggars had little chance of acquiring sustenance by begging without doing hard labour for it; and anyone caught stealing property to the value of thirteen-pence halfpenny in Halifax was hanged (*see* "Halifax Gibbet Law"). Hell, of course, speaks for itself.

Humble Pie, To eat. *See* "Eat."

Humbug. Has been a slang word since 1735; but there are divided opinions as to its origin. The one finding most favour is that of Dr. Brewer in his "Phrase and Fable," that the word is composed of *hum*, to hoax, and *bug*, a false alarm. *Bug* is of greater antiquity that the compound word, signifying something to be shunned. The frequently given origin of *uim bog*, Irish for a spurious coin, can be dismissed; the word humbug, with the meaning given above, existed long before.

Hundred-eyed. Argus, in Greek fable. Juno appointed him guardian of Io, the cow, but Jupiter had him put to death; whereupon Juno transplanted his eyes into the tail of her peacock. Which is the story of the peacock's tail.

Hundreds. A Hundred was a sub-division of the English shires, said originally to have been introduced by Alfred the Great, though this is doubtful. Each "Hundred" comprised a colony of "Ten times Ten" families—ten divisions of ten freeholders and their dependents in each. In all there were one hundred champions to defend the common cause.
See "Chiltern Hundreds."

Hung in the Bellropes. Throughout Cumberland, Leicestershire, and in Worcestershire, a betrothed couple are said to be "hanging in the bellropes" during the three weeks which elapse between the first and third calling of their banns in church. If the marriage does not come off, then the deserted one was, and still is, said to be "hung in the bellropes."

Hurly-Burly. Is derived from the tumult of ancient warfare, with especial reference to the excitement of *hurl*ing spears, and the *burly*ness of men who could wield mighty battle-axes.

Hurry. "*Don't Hurry, Hopkins.*" The term has become better-known over here since the arrival of American soldiers. It was coined in their country. The story goes that a man named Hopkins, of Kentucky, borrowed a sum of money giving, in acknowledgment, a promissory note. On the note he wrote: "The said Hopkins is not to be hurried in paying the above."

Husband. A husband has somewhat declined in social standing from the original. In Anglo-Saxon days *hus* was a house, and *bondi* was Norse for a freeholder or yeoman. A husband was a householder from his position as head of the household. And so, says Dr. Brewer, the term came to be applied to a man joined to a woman in marriage, he being, naturally (*sic*) the head of his household. But, in the true sense of the word, a man could in Anglo-Saxon days he the "husband" of his mother, or sister, so long as he was the head of the house.

Hussar. The Hungarian word for twentieth was *huszar*. When Matthias Corvinus ascended the Magyar throne, he raised a corps of horse soldiers by decreeing that one man out of every twenty in each village should be chosen by lot. Each twenty families had to equip the chosen man free of all cost to the State. There is no proper connection between Hussar and the Slavonic *hussar*, goose-herd.

Hussy. This word is a curious example of corrupted use. It means, to-day, an ill-behaved woman, a jade or a flirt. Yet the word was the mediæval English hussif (housewife), a perfectly reputable woman.

Hustler. Another word more commonly used in America than over here. It was taken there by Dutch settlers, for the word is derived from the Dutch *hutselen*, to shake together, to and fro.

Hymen. The Hymenal Altar. Properly speaking Hymen should be regarded as a marriage *hymn*, a giving praise to the Deity, who was the God of marriage. It was from the Greek *Hymen*, song of praise to a God, that the English word *hymn* is truly descended. The first hymn for Christian worship is said to have been composed by Hilary, Bishop of Arles, about A.D. 431.

The Hymenal Altar is the marriage altar.

Hythe. Where it appears in name-places signified a harbour, a haven. Rother-hithe is an example.

I

Iambic Verse. An *iamb*, or *iambus*, is a metrical foot consisting of a short syllable followed by a long one. Iambic Verse are poetical satires written in Iambics, or two-syllable foot measure. They are so-called after Iambe, an attendant upon one of the Queens of Sparta, who kept a book of lively, free and satirical pieces. Iambics were used among the Greeks from earliest times in popular poetry, especially of a festive or a vituperative character.

I am Escaped by the Skin of my Teeth. Contrary to its appearance, there is nothing of slang in the phrase. Users of it may be surprised to know that it is derived from the Bible; what is more, from the *oldest* book in the Bible—*Job* xix, 20.

Ianthe. When Lord Byron wrote "Childe Harold," he dedicated it to "Ianthe," She was subsequently identified as Lady Charlotte Harley, who was only eleven years at the time.

Ibid. Is a contraction of *ibidem*, Latin, meaning "in the same place. It appears very frequently in dictionaries of poetical quotations. Where following a quotation the word appears, it means that the quotation is taken from "the same" source as the quotation immediately above it.

Icarius. An Athenian who, according to Greek legend, was taught the cultivation of wine by Dionysus (Bacchus). He gave of his wine to some peasants. They, becoming intoxicated, believed that Icarius had poisoned them, and slew him, burying his body under a tree. His daughter was led to his burial place by the howling of his dog and, overcome by grief, hanged herself. Icarius is not to be confused with:

Icarus, son of Dædalus who, with his father, fled from Crete to escape the resentment of Minos. He flew too near the sun which melted the wax cementing his wings, and he fell into that part of the Aegean Sea which is called after his name.

Iceberg. Means ice *mountain*, the word *beorh*, or *berg*, being Anglo-Saxon for a hill, or mountain. An iceberg starts its career as a glacier, moving slowly down the mountain-side until it reaches the cliffs, and glides into the ocean. For each cubic foot of the iceberg above the water, there must be eight cubic feet below the water. Collision with an iceberg sank the liner *Titanic* in April, 1912.

Ice-Blink. A peculiar appearance in the air caused by the reflection of light from the surface of an ice-pack or floating mass of ice, or from land covered with snow. By it the presence of ice may be recognized at a distance of twenty miles or more.

The Danish name for the great ice cliffs of Newfoundland is "The Ice-Blink."

Ice-brook Temper. The allusion is to the ancient practice of Spaniards of hardening the steel of their swords by plunging them while still white-hot from the forge into the ice-cold water of the rivulet Salo, near Bibbilus (now Calatyud, in Aragon).

Ice Saints. Are those whose festival days fall in what is called the Blackthorn Winter — the second week in May.

Ichabod. Generally interpreted, "The glory has departed." Correctly translated the word means, "Where is the Glory?" Ichabod was the son of Phinehas, one of the three men who had charge of the Ark of the Covenant (*Samuel* i, 4). Israel fled before the Philistines, who captured the Ark. Phinehas was killed, and on hearing that the Ark was captured his father, Eli, died. Phinehas's wife gave birth to a son and gave him the name I-chabod, saying: "The glory has departed from Israel, for the Ark of God is taken" (1 *Sam.*, iv, 22).

Ich Dien. The motto of the Prince of Wales, and the German for "I serve." It was adopted by the Black Prince after the Battle of Cressey. The generally accepted theory is that the Black Prince found the motto under the plume of John, King of Bohemia, slain by him at Cressey. This origin is very doubtful. Verstegan maintains that the origin is Anglo-Saxon, from *Ich thian*, the latter word being derived from *theyn*, a free servant.

Ichthus. The word is the Greek for "fish"; and a fish was used by the early Christians as a symbol for Christ because Ichthus is formed of the initial letters of *I*esous *Ch*ristos *Th*eou *U*ios *S*oter, meaning, "Jesus Christ, Son of God, Saviour." The author has on numerous occasions seen drawings of a fish in the Catacombs of Rome, as they had been drawn by the earliest Christians.

Iconoclasts. The name given to those who systematically attack cherished beliefs. The word is Greek, "breakers of images"; and the original Iconoclasts were a party in the Eastern Empire in the eighth and ninth centuries who opposed all use and honour or worship of images (icons), and destroyed them during the period they were in power. The Iconoclasts were originated by the Emperor Leo the Isaurian, and were continued by Constantine, Copronymus and other Emperors, notably Leo the Armenian, and Theophilus. The Emperors treated those who honoured icons with great cruelty, and after the death of the last of them the Iconoclasts became extinct.

Idea. Comes from the Greek *idien*, to see. It is used, however, not in the sense of seeing something visually, but of seeing in the *Platonic* sense.

Ides. "*Beware the Ides of March.*" In the Roman calendar the eighth day after the Nones (q.v.), that is, the 15th of March, May, July and October, and the 15th of the other months. "Beware the Ides of March" is used as a warning of impending and certain danger, the allusion being, of course, to Julius Cæsar.

Idiot. The word is from the Greek *idios*, private, one's own, the Greek *idiotes* signifying a man in private life, as distinguished from one holding an official position. The assumption was that the latter would be of higher intellect and better education. The meaning to-day has gone a little further over to the left, representing one who is weak in mind or deficient in common sense.

Ignoramus. Its present use, in describing someone ignorant of knowledge of something, or everything, is a corruption of the word. Ignoramus meant, in its original Latin, *ignore*, to take no notice of. For a great many years in our Law Courts the word was used in that correct sense. Grand Juries wrote "Ignoramus" on the back of a bill of indictment which they threw out, meaning "not found," not to be sent into Court, or, more briefly, "ignored."

I.H.S. Does not and never has meant *Jesus Hominum Salvator*, "Jesus, Saviour of Men." Nor has it ever meant *In hoc Salvus*, "Safety in this (the Cross)." The letters are the first three letters of the Greek word, *Ihsous*, Jesus, the "h" representing the Greek long "e."

I Know a Trick worth Two of That. The age of this seemingly modern piece of slang is the interesting feature of the phrase. It comes from "King Henry IV," part I, act ii, scene 1.

Ilk, Of that. Probably few words are so misued as these. Ilk comes from the Anglo-Saxon *ilca*, meaning "the same." It is used correctly only when the surname of the person spoken of is the same as the name of his estate. An example is: Kinloch of that ilk—meaning

Kinloch *of Kinloch*. It is not correct to use the phrase as meaning all of that name or spelling.

Ill-Starred. Unlucky. The word is a survival of the days when men believed that the stars influenced the fate of humans. Among the credulous the belief still exists, to the extent of providing a good living for alleged horoscope preparers, whose victims are mostly stupid women.

I'll take my Davy on it. The word davy here is a corruption of affidavit. (*Affidavit*, Latin, " He has stated on faith.")

Imbecile. A curious word, the origin of which has never been satisfactorily traced. It would seem to mean weak in strength (not in mind), coming from the Latin *in*, on, and *bacillus*, a staff, thus one who leans on a stick. That it was formerly used in this sense is obvious from a passage in Jeremy Taylor's " Holy Dying," which runs : " It is a sad calamity that the fear of death shall so *imbecile* man's courage and understanding that he dares not suffer the remedy of all his calamities." In this connection, the word obviously means " weaken."

Immaculate Conception. The dogma that the Virgin Mary conceived without original sin was first mooted by St. Bernard, but was not received by the Roman Catholic Church as an article of faith till 1854. It was stoutly asserted by Duns Scotus, nearly six hundred years before that. *See* " Dunce."

Immaculate means " without spot," from the Latin *macula*, spot, and *im*, not.

Immolate. The word means to sacrifice, after the manner of a sacrificial victim. Its original meaning was to sprinkle a victim with sacrificial meal mixed with salt, from *in* (or *im*), on, and *mola*, meal mixed with salt.

Imp. " *He's an Imp.*" A mischievous child is the present interpretation. But the original word was *emphuo* (Greek), to graft, literally, to produce ; and the Anglo-Saxon for it was *impian*, a shoot. From this came off-spring, a child, shoot of his father. The Anglo-Saxon is still retained in the phrase : " He's the living shoot of his father."

Imposition. From impose, as the task was an imposed one. An illustration is an imposition as a punishment for school children.

In a Crack. At once. The allusion is to the short space of time it takes for a gun to go off.

In a jiffy. At one look. The word " jiffy " is a modern spelling of the old *gliff*, which meant a mere glance.

Inch of Candle. In older days a candle was used to time the acceptance of bids at a sale by auction. The auctioneer would announce the depth of candle to be burned, up to which time bids would be accepted. Where such sales were frequent, candles of an inch length were prepared, and bidding went on until the candle spluttered out.

In Clover. To be in comfortable, or enjoyable, circumstances—like a cow in a clover field, recognized as the best grazing for cattle.

Incubus. Firstly a nightmare, secondly an oppressive influence on the mind. Originally (in mediæval times), it was an evil spirit which was supposed to consort with women in their sleep. In the Middle Ages this belief was accepted by Church and Law, and deformed children were said to be the result of such association. The word comes from the Latin *incumbare*, to lie on.

India-rubber. The first recorded instance of the use of india-rubber which we possess is from Herrara who, more than five hundred years ago, wrote of having seen (during Columbus's second voyage) the natives of Hayti play a game with balls made of the gum of a tree, which bounced. Torquemada mentioned the tree by name in 1615, and added the information that the Spaniards used the juice of the tree to make their cloaks waterproof. But nobody troubled to introduce rubber into England until many years afterwards.

Indian File, i.e. (as is well-known), walking one behind the other in a line. The origin is not, however, so well-known. It involved, among the Red Indians, each man stepping carefully into the footsteps of the man in front ; and the last man in the file was under the obligation of obliterating the footsteps, thus leaving no tracks and no trace of the number of men who had passed by.

Indian Ink. Has never come from India, but is made in China of fine lamp-black baked with a glutinous substance. It is used by both the Chinese and Japanese for writing with small brushes.

Indian Summer. The Autumnal Summer generally occurring in the first fortnight of October. It is frequently the mildest and driest part of the year.

Infantry. There is no truth in the supposition that the name came from the body of soldiers of foot raised by an Infante of Spain. Even before that time the foot-soldier in Spain was known as a soldat. Its real origin is the Latin *infans*, an infant. In the days of chivalry youths of good family, with their attendants, marched on foot in the rear of the *mounted* knights. They thus became the forerunners of the infantry of the army.

Inferno. *See* " Hell."

In Flagrante delicto. Caught in the very act ; red-handed. In Latin, " while the offence is flagrante."

In for a Penny, in for a Pound. It means that as I am in the thing anyhow, I might as well go the whole hog, since it cannot be any worse. A variation is : " I might as well be hanged for a sheep as a lamb."

In forma pauperis. As a pauper. It is under this phrasing that a person accused of a criminal offence can ask the free services of learned Counsel to defend him.

Infra dig. A clipping of the Latin *infra*, beneath or below, and *dignitatem*, dignity ; thus, beneath one's dignity. Something one cannot do without losing one's self-respect.

Ink. Was invented by a Chinaman, named Tien-Tcheu, about two thousand years before Christ. That is the earliest ink man has been able to trace. It was apparently made of charcoal, or soot, mixed with gum. And it was also a Chinaman who invented paper to use with it.

In loco parentis. Latin, meaning to be in the place of parents to a child.

Innocents' Day. 28th December. Sometimes called Childermas Day. It was formerly the custom in England to whip up the children on this day in order that the memorial of Herod's murder of the children, after the birth of the Infant Christ, might stick the closer, says Hone, in his " Every Day Book."

In Quad. In prison. The phrase is less slang than a corruption of quadrangle. Debtors confined in the old London debt prisons were allowed to receive visitors in the quadrangle, or exercise yard, so that friends went to see them " in the quad " ! And " quad " is still the schoolboy's contraction for the quadrangle of the school. Incidentally, *quaid* is the gipsy word for prison.

In re. Latin, " in the matter of." In re our telephone talk—in the matter of (regarding) our telephone talk.

In statu quo. In the condition things were before the change. Thus, if a country invaded another and seized some of its lands, peace could be restored *in statu quo ante*—that is, with the borders as they were before the invasion.

Ins and Outs of the Matter. A debate on the matter. The hearing of both sides, for and against. The " ins " represented the party in government, and the " outs " those in opposition. Hutton wrote : " There was then (1755) only two political parties, the ins and the outs. The ins strove to stay in, the outs strove to get in and turn the ins out." In-side out is another version of the phrase.

Insult. The word means to "leap on," from the Latin *insultare, saltus,* a leap. The priests of Baal, it will be recalled, to show their indignation against their gods, "*leaped* upon the altar which they had made."

In the Jug. Another term for prison. "Jug" is derived from the old Scottish word *joug,* an iron yoke or pillory for the head, in which rogues and vagabonds were exhibited as punishment. When, half a century after their innovation, a stone house of detention was built to hold these offenders, the name given it was "the stone joug," and "the stone jug" is still a slang term for gaol.

In the Nick of Time. The phrase dates back to the days of Tallys—sticks of wood, which were both an acknowledgment of money owing, or paid, and a way of registering a person's attendance. Nicks, or notches, were made in the stick. To be in the nick of time meant to arrive at the place in time to have the attendance "nicked" or recorded on the tally.

In the Odour of Sanctity. Said of a person of strong religious beliefs who has died; but more often, we fear, used as a term of contempt. It arose from the idea that the bodies of saints after their death emitted a fragrant odour. They frequently did; but the odour usually arose from the profuse employment of incense at the last solemn rites of the Viaticum.

In the Soup. In a mess. An American phrase imported here after we had exported the word "soup" as meaning water.

In the Straw. A coarse expression indicating that a woman has been brought to bed in readiness for her labour. It has, however, a background of social history; for straw was the usual stuffing of a bed among the poorer sections of the community.

In the Swim. Well in with the right people or in the right circles for gain to oneself. A fisherman probably invented the phrase; for in the swim is the term an angler uses when he is securing a good creel of fish. River fish invariably keep together in what is called "a swim."

In the Wrong Box. The story told of this phrase (by Johnson) is that when Vauxhall was an alfresco pleasure garden, rows of comfortable boxes existed for the convenience of those who wished to do their courting in private, while having at the same time a view of the illuminations and a hearing of the strains of the bands. But they being all alike, a lover leaving a box for a space frequently had difficulty in identifying his particular rendezvous, and often made himself a nuisance to other lovers by finding himself "in the wrong box."

Intrepid Fox. Was the name of a famous and historic tavern in Soho, named after Fox, the great Whig Minister. During the election of 1784 the landlord, the redoubtable Sammy House, served all customers free, and also entertained notable Whigs.

Iota. *See* "Jot."

Ipso facto. The translation from the Latin is "by the very fact"; without doubt. An example of how it should be used correctly is Dr. Brewer's, "By burning the Pope's Bull, Luther *ipso facto* (by the very deed itself) denied the Pope's supremacy."

Irish Stew. In effect, poverty stew. Stew, in the usual sense of the word, consists of fragments of meat stewed together with a variety of vegetables. Irish Stew, when the name was coined, consisted of onions and potatoes only, the Irish peasantry being too poor to purchase meat to go in the stew.

Iron. *The Iron Chancellor.* Sobriquet of Prince Bismarck, Chancellor of the German Empire, because of his iron will.

The Iron Duke. The Duke of Wellington, also distinguished for his iron will.

Iron Maiden of Nuremburg. An ancient instrument of torture used in Germany for heretics, traitors and parricides. It consisted of a box large enough to admit a man standing up. The folding-doors were thickly studded with iron spikes which, when the doors were closed on the prisoner, were forced into his body. He was left thus to die.

Iron Rations. Were so-called, not from the hardness of the fare, but from the iron box in which they were contained to keep them from the air.

Irons in the Fire, Too many. The allusion is to the practice of laundresses who, in order not to waste time, kept two or three flat-irons in the fire when ironing clothes. The warning means that if she had too many irons in the fire some would become too hot *and burn* the clothes.

I's. "*To dot the I's, and cross the t's.*" To round the thing off; to complete. The "i" and the "t" are the only two letters (except the little used "j") in the English language which require additions after the word containing them has been written. Thus, to "dot the i," is to complete.

Isle of Dogs. A small peninsula between the Limehouse and Blackwall reaches of the Thames at London. So-called because Edward III kept his greyhounds there. There may or may not be some grounds for the suggested alternative "Isle of Ducks," from the numbers of wild fowl which nested and thrived there.

Is there no Balm in Gilead? A quotation frequently made use of in literature these days as a rebuke; a request to know why things have not been done that ought to have been done. The origin is *Jeremiah,* viii, 22: "Is there no balm in Gilead? Is there no physician there? Why, then, is not the health of the daughter of my people recovered?"

The biting rebuke of the question lies in the fact that Gilead was famous for its balm. Balm, incidentally, is the gum of a fragrant tree.

"It's a Long Way to Tipperary." Probably the best-known and most popular song ever written, sung by British troops on the march in all parts of the world. It was written for a wager. The author and composer, the late Jack Judge, while with other artists in a public-house in the Midlands on New Year's Day, 1912, accepted a challenge that he could not write a song, and the music, and "produce" it the same day. He sat down and wrote and composed "Tipperary," and sang it the same night at Stalybridge Grand Theatre.

J

Jack. To use this name as a substitute for John—which is a common occurrence—is incorrect. The derivation is the French *Jacques,* through the Latin *Jacobus,* through the Hebrew *Yaago,* which is equivalent to James. Dr. Brewer denies this; but the fact remains that Jacob-ites was the name given to the supporters of *James,* the Pretender to the Throne; and on the death of his father, he was proclaimed King *James* of England, by Louis XIV of France.

What is more difficult to discover is why the name Jack has come to be applied in contempt, such as jackanapes, Jack-in-office, and so on. It has developed, or rather retrogressed, as a sobriquet for a humble servitor. Take, for instance, the tag: "Jack will never be a gentleman."

Jackanapes. An insolent or pushing young man. The description is said first to have been applied to the Duke of Suffolk, whose crest was the clog and chain of a tame ape. But the word existed long before that in a monkey—a Jackanapes being a "jack" (monkey) imported from Napes (Naples). Another version gives the word as Jack-of Apes, Jack being explained as a male monkey. There is more authority for "Napes" as Naples.

Jack-Boots. The name is derived from the French *jacque*, a leather jerkin, or jacket; and they were called "Jack" boots because they, too, were made of leather when first brought into use. They were worn almost exclusively at that time by cavalry.

Jack Horner. "*Little Jack Horner sat in a Corner.*" This is the only nursery rhyme said to have a stratum of fact. "Jack" is stated to have been steward to the Abbot of Glastonbury at the time of the dissolution of the monasteries. He became possessed of the deeds of the Manor of Mells, which was in the neighbourhood, and retained them. The story is that the deeds were sent to Henry VIII concealed in a pasty, and that Jack Horner put in his thumb and pulled out a plum—the deeds of the property, which made him the virtual owner. Whether it is true or not, the fact remains that his descendants owned the Manor for generations.

Jack Ketch. The name usually given to a hangman. It is said to have been derived from Richard Jaquette, Lord of the Manor of Tyburn, where felons were executed up to 1783. On the other hand, another version is that he was himself a hangman of that name, known for his barbarity. He was the executioner of Lord William Russell, and of Monmouth. Ketch was commemorated in a ballad, but it is still not clear whether his name was Ketch, or whether that was the name given to the hangman, as it has since been generally applied to an executioner.

Jack Robinson. Quickly, "Before you could say Jack Robinson." According to Grose, the saying had its origin in the habit of a very volatile gentleman of that name in paying flying visits to his friends' houses, and flying off again almost as soon as he had been announced. It is, however, to be regarded with grave suspicion.

Jack Straw. Was the nickname of one of the leaders in the Peasants' Revolt of 1381, which is why, in this world where money and position is power, he came to be synonymous with a worthless sort of fellow.

Jack Straw's Castle, the noted hostelry at Hampstead, London, is said to be built on the site of Jack Straw's habitation on the hill-side.

Jack-Tar. Has nothing to do with the popular belief of his tarpaulin rough-weather coat. The term dates back to the wooden hulk days of sail when, on reaching port, the ship was caulked and tarred. The filthy job left Jack's hands and face tar-grimed for many days afterwards.

Jack the Ripper. An individual who, in 1888-89, committed a series of murders, the victim in each case being a prostitute. He afterwards mutilated the bodies. He was never apprehended, and his identity, though suspected, has never been proved.

Jack up the Job. This phrase, meaning to throw up one's employment, is probably a corruption of "chuck up one's job."

Jacket. From the French *jacquette*, a diminutive of *jacque*, a jack or coat. The *jacque* was a leather, sleeveless coat, sometimes quilted, worn over the hauberk, a coat of mail of interwoven steel rings. At a later stage the *jacque* was itself made sword-proof by metal plates on its underside.

Jacob's Stone. The Coronation Stone brought to England from Scone, near Perth, Scotland, and on which the Kings of Scotland had been crowned. The monks claimed that the stone was that on which Jacob rested his head when he had the vision of the angels. The tradition of the stone is that wherever it may rest, there will reign one of the royal line of Scotland.

Jacquerie. The name given to an insurrection of the French peasants in 1358. *Jacques* is the name given to the artisan class in France from the sleeveless cotton jacket worn by them. This may be one derivation of the name Jack for a lower-class person. *See* "Jack."

Jail-bird. For certain offences in olden days women were imprisoned in a large iron *cage*. That they were, therefore, jail *birds*, was a natural collorary!

Jamie Duff. Scottish nickname for a mourner at a funeral. There existed a James Duff, who took pleasure in attending funerals as a mourner, because he enjoyed the ride in the mourning coach.

Janissaries. The word means a soldier, from the Turkish *yeni*, and *'askari*, soldier. When the Turks captured Constantinople, they ordered every fifth Christian boy to be surrendered to the service of the Sultan. He was trained for war. In time these men acquired a magnificent reputation for courage and discipline. In consequence, they came to occupy high position; and so great was the reputation of the corps, that Turks bargained with Christians to take their children and give them for enlistment in the Janissaries.

January, because the Romans dedicated this month to the Deity Janius. The God presided over the beginning of things, being the patron of births, and thus of the first month of the year. He was also the tutelar deity of doors and gates. The door of his Temple in Rome stood open in times of war and closed in times of peace. Janius possesses two heads, so that he could look backwards at the past year, and forwards into the current year.

Jarvey. English coach or cab drivers were given this nickname from, it is said, an original driver whose name was Jarvis. The origin is doubtful, however, and it should be pointed out that the symbol of St. Gervaise is a whip.

Jazey. The name by which all stage people call a wig. The allusion is to the fact that wigs were originally made of *Jersey* flax and fine wool.

Jazz. The name given to irregular rhythm in music. It is of negro origin. The origin of the name Jazz, says Dr. Brewer, is uncertain. One account is that it is an adaptation of one Razz, a band conductor in New Orleans, U.S.A., in 1904. Another account is that it has long been a common word to the negroes on the Barbary coast, where it means to "mess 'em up, and lay it on thick"—and that seems to fit Jazz perfectly!

Jeep. During the World War of 1939-45, the American forces which came to this country for training brought with them a small, high, but exceedingly powerful open motor car of a general utility model. It was named by them a "Jeep." The name is said to have been given to it by a private soldier of the American Army. It began, according to the story, as a "reconnaissant car." But that was too technical. "Quad car," because it carried four people, ran for a time, but that, too, faded out. Then the soldier before mentioned noticed the letters "G.P." (general purposes) painted on the sides of one of the cars, and called it a "Jeep." The name was adopted.

Lance-Corporal Jacques, of the Canadian Army, however, suggests that the name had already been given to a similar vehicle in 1937. He says that in the Summer of 1937, a vehicle was delivered to a small village in Manitoba, Canada, called Douglas, which was the rail point for the large Artillery Camp at Shilo, four miles away. The Army was notified, and three sergeants went down to bring the car up. About this time the cartoonist, Seegar, creator of "Pop-eye," brought into his strip a strange animal which he called "The Jeep," and which was delivered to Pop-eye in a box. When the sergeants saw their vehicle in a freight car, one of them said, "I'll bet it's a Jeep."

As regards this story, however, it should be pointed out that the vehicle which the sergeants found waiting for them was a large truck with heavy caterpillar luggs instead of wheels—not a bit like the Jeep of the American Army.

On 9th February, 1945, the Controller at the Industrial and Commercial Property Registration Office, in Dublin, refused an American motor manufacturer's claim to use the name "Jeep" as a trade mark, on the ground that it had become a common noun, and that, as a result of common usage, the word "had fallen into the public domain."

Jenkins's Ear, The War of. Robert Jenkins was an English sea-captain. In 1738, he appeared before the House of Commons and alleged that Spaniards had boarded his vessel and cut off one of his ears. He explained: "I commended my soul to God, and my cause to my country." The incident led to the war between Britain and Spain in 1742, which came to be nicknamed "The War of Jenkins's Ear."

Jericho, Go to. *See* "Go to Jericho."

Jerry-builder. Few words have so remarkably diverse theories of origin. One such, suggests the Prophet Jeremiah, is the "jerry" in the sense of jeremiad—foredoomed to decay and ruin speedily, such as the prophet foretold.

A second theory suggests that it is a reference to Jericho, the walls of which fell down when a number of people shouted!

Still a third alludes to a builder named Jerrey, said to have been infamous for his cheap and rubbishy houses.

But we prefer to the view that the word is a corruption of *joury*, derived from the French *jour*, a day, meaning for a day—temporary, unsubstantial.

Jersey Lily, The. The name given to the actress, Lily Langtry. It was a pun on her name, Lillie, and her birthplace, Jersey.

Jesus Paper. Large-size sheets of paper mostly used for engravings. It derived its name from the fact that it was originally stamped with the initials, I.H.S. (q.v.).

Jew's Harp. It is a moot point whether the name should be Jeu's Harp, from the French *jeu*, to play; or jaw's harp, from the method of extracting music from it. The frame of the instrument is held between the lips and the spring twitched with the fingers, the sound thus produced being altered in pitch by means of the mouth and tongue.

Jib. "*I know him by the cut of his jib.*" A jib is the triangular sail borne in front of the foremast. And "sailors" recognized the nationality of vessels at sea by the cut of their jibs. In connection with the use of the phrase for a human person, the lower lip is referred to as a jib.

Jib, to refuse a fence, as a jibbing horse; applied to a man or woman who tries to back out of a bargain which is turning out badly.

Jiminy. An exclamation of surprise: "By Jiminy, I will." It is merely a contraction of *Jesu Domine*—Jesus, Master.

Jingoes. The name given to a war party in Britain during the Russo-Turkish War of 1877-78. There was a strong move in Britain for intervention in the struggle. The term "Jingo" was made popular by the famous song, still heard even to-day:

"We don't want to fight, but,
by jingo, if we do,
We've got the ships, we've
got the men, we've got the
money, too."

The Russophobes became known as the Jingoes, and such war-mongering policy has been called Jingoism ever since.

Joan, The Pope. The woman who, it is repeatedly alleged, became Pope of Rome in the ninth century. There is little doubt that the story is a pure invention. However, the woman is said to have been one, Joannes Anglicus, who was born in England and educated at Cologne, in Germany.

Jockey. The name for a rider of horses in races comes from Scotland, where *Jock* is the diminutive Scottish form of John or Jack. It is also used to describe a servant. The first jockeys engaged in horse-racing were boys, hence the term *jock*eys.

Joe Miller, A. Name called out when a member of the company, especially among stage people, is telling an old story. Joe Miller was a witty comedian, with a host of stories. A book of his sayings was compiled by John Mottley in the reign of James II. For very many years it was the only book of jokes extant, and was called upon by those who fancied themselves as after-dinner entertainers. Hence the cry "Joe Miller," when a story was recognized. In point of fact, "Joe Miller's" book even to-day forms the basis of many jokes coming to us over the radio.

"John Anderson, My Joe." The well-known poem by Burns was founded on an eighteenth century song, unfit for print, which was itself a parody of a sixteenth century anti-Roman Catholic song in ridicule of the Sacraments of the Church.

John Audley. An old phrase of the days of the portable theatre, and one which still exists in the theatre world of to-day. It was used as a kind of code. For instance, the travelling or fairground theatre of the old days depended for its revenue on the number of shows it could get in during the period of the fair. If, while a performance was proceeding, a queue gathered outside which would fill another "house," the showman called out from the door: "Is John Audley here?" This was a hint to the people on the stage to finish quickly and get rid of the audience to make room for those waiting outside. The sentence is said to have been the invention of an old showman named Shorter, who was famous as a booth player at country fairs.

John Bull. This universal name for an Englishman came from "The History of John Bull," first published as "Law is a Bottomless Pit," by Arbuthnot. A satire on the prolonged war with France, it threw ridicule on the Duke of Marlborough. The Englishman in the satire was named John Bull, the Dutchman Nicholas Frog, and the Frenchman Lewis Babou.

John Doe and Richard Doe. Fictitious names for a plaintiff and defendant in an action for ejectment. They came into use during the Protectorate, when they were introduced by Lord Chief Justice Rolle, to overcome a difficulty due to faulty drawing up of a Writ of Ejectment Law. The necessity for them was swept away by the Common Law Procedure Act of 1852.

John o'Groat's (house). Everyone knows the name as the starting-point of from one end of Britain to the other (Land's End). There is not, of course, a house there. But there was one, originally, belonging to Jan Groot. The story told is as follows: Jan Groot, with two brothers, came from Holland and bought lands on the present site of John o'Groats. This was in the reign of James IV of Scotland. The family increased, until there were no fewer than eight of the name, each with their own children. Once every year they held a family gathering in the house of the founder. Then a question of precedency arose and led to a quarrel. Old John promised that by the time of the next gathering he would find a way of avoiding any quarrel over precedency. He built an eight-sided house, each side with its own entrance door, and in the room of this put an octagonal table! A small green knoll is still shown as having been the site of the house.

John Roberts. A large-size jug. In 1886, Sunday closing of public-houses came into effect in Wales, mainly through the efforts of Mr. John Roberts, M.P. So an outsize tankard was evolved which, it was claimed, would hold sufficient beer to carry the thirsty customers over from

Saturday night until Monday morning! It was only natural that the tankard should be nicknamed with the cognomen of the Sunday Closing apostle.

Jolly-boat. The small boat usually hoisted at the stern of a ship. There is nothing "jolly" about it; its name is derived from the Danish *jolle*, the Dutch *jol*, and our own yawl.

Jonathans. A famous coffee house of London, which was situated in Change Alley. With Garraways, it was the forerunner of the Stock Exchange.
See "Garroways."

Joss. The house-god of the Chinese. Every family has its joss. A joss-house is a temple; and a joss-stick the strip of scented wood burnt to the joss in the joss-house.

Jot. *See* "Don't care a Jot."

Journeyman. The explanation that a journeyman is a person travelling in search of work is obvious. The word, however, meant a little more than that. It is derived from the French *journee*, which meant also a day's work, from *jour*. A journeyman was, then, one who travelled from place to place offering his labour from day to day, or for as long as the job lasted. The custom is still in existence in this country in the large number of Irishmen who, throughout the harvest season, travel through the Fen Country picking potatoes, and moving from farm to farm in the task.

Jubilee Plunger. The nickname given to Ernest Benzon, who lost a quarter of a million pounds on horse-racing within two years of beginning to bet, in 1887, the year of Queen Victoria's Jubilee.

Judgment of Paris. *See* "Apple of Discord."

Jug. This, from the point of view of a delver into the origin of words, is one of the most remarkable words in the language. Though the article has been in use for centuries, and though there is hardly a household which does not possess one, there is still no reliable trace of the origin of the word "jug."

It seems to have first been used in the sixteenth century; and in trying to trace it, Wedgewood suggested in his dictionary of etymology that it was identical with the female name, Jug, a pet form of Joan or Jane.

It is a fact that in early days a soldier's wench was called a jug, or jugge; and what does seem to link the name jug with the female name is the fact that the large leathern drinking vessels of the day, and of earlier days, were known as *jacks*, or *black-jacks*. It may well be that Jack's Joan became a more dainty black-jack and called a jug.

Juggernaut. A Hindu God and the second in the Hindu trinity. The name means "God of the World," and is one of the thousand names by which Vishnu (or Vishnoo) is known. It will be known to most as the God under the wheels of whose car thousands of people threw themselves and were killed—a form of sacrifice which they believed secured them a place in Heaven. The practice was prohibited by the British Government. Juggernaut's car was forty-three feet high and was pulled on sixteen wheels, each six and a half feet in diameter.

Juggins. "*A silly Juggins.*" Mr. Juggins was a misguided gentleman who in, or around, 1880 squandered his entire fortune in reckless gambling on race-courses. The popular verdict of the populace, "Silly Juggins," has survived.

Jumper. Although the name is now given to any kind of knitted, slip-on outer garment, it meant, originally, a kind of loose jacket with sleeves worn by seamen and stevedores, usually with overalls, reaching to the thighs and buttoned the whole length in front. Its derivation is *jump*, a short coat worn by men more than two hundred years ago, and connected with the French *jupe*, a petticoat.

Jump Over the Broomstick, To. The phrase means to marry informally. Broomstick, however, is a corruption of "brom," the name for the bit in a horse's bridle. Thus, to jump the brom is to avoid the restraint of a full marriage service, and to wed quietly and informally.

June Weddings. The popularity of June as a wedding month, and the belief that marriages in that month will be lucky, dates from ancient days. The Romans dedicated the month to the *Juniores*, or young people.

In Mythology, June is the month of Juno, guardian of the female sex from birth to death.

Junior. The name given by Americans to the son of the house is not the modern description which it is claimed. The Romans dedicated the month of June to the young people, particularly of the male (or soldier) sex. They called them juniores.

Junk. This term for any unwanted material really belongs to the sea. Junk is the sailor's name for rope-ends. It is derived from the Latin *juncus*, a bulrush, from the fibre of which in ancient days ropes were made.

The sailor's description of salt beef as "junk" probably means that it is, or was, as tough as rope to eat!

Junket. So-called because it was originally made in a rush basket manufactured from the rushes of the bulrush—Latin *juncus*.

Jury-mast. The name should really be "joury"-mast, from the French *jour*, a day, because a jury mast is one rigged up temporarily, to replace one carried away by bad weather.

Justice is Blind. It is pretty well-known that the figure of Justice over the Old Bailey Criminal Court in London bears a bandage over her eyes, in order that she may not see the scales of Justice which she holds in a hand. But the phrase is much older than the figure of Justice. The ancient Egyptians conducted trials in a darkened courtroom in order that the pleaders, witnesses and the defendants, being all unseen, the judges could not be moved in their judgment by sympathy, or knowledge, of the people concerned.

Juvenile Lead. A stage description of those men who play leading rôles as lovers in dramatic, or light comedy, productions. And they need not be, and seldom are, juvenile in years.

K

Kaaba. The stone building inside the great Mosque at Mecca. The name is Arabic for "square house." The Kaaba is said to be erected over the spot where Adam first worshipped after he had been expelled from the Garden of Eden.

Kaffir. Name given to natives in South Africa. It comes from the Arabic *Kafir*, an infidel, and belonged originally to Hottentots who had rejected the Moslem faith. It was further given to the people of Kaffristan (the country of the Infidels) in Central Asia.

Kailyard School. The description given to a body of writers whose works were principally about Scottish humble life. Some of the Kailyard School were: J. J. Bell, Sir James Barrie, S. R. Crockett. The name is due to the motto: "There grows a bonnie brier bush in our kailyard."

Kaiser. Just the German form of Cæsar; and it came to the same end as Cæsar. Cæsar, Kaiser, Czar and Shah are all forms of the Babylonian *Shar*, meaning king. It can be noted that Belshazzar, familiar in Bible history, was most likely originally Bel-Shar-Usur, God-the-King-save.

Kaleidoscope. A combination of three Greek words—*Klos*, beautiful, *eidos*, appearance, and *skopeo*, I behold. Its only presence now is in the form of the word as a description of any gay and colourful spectacle. The original kaleidoscope was a long instrument which, by means of mirrors fixed at suitable angles, presented a seemingly endless variety of beautiful forms of colours. Its invention is credited to Baptista Ports, in the sixteenth century; but it was perfected by Sir David Brewster in 1817.

Keelhaul. Keelhauling was a wicked punishment practised in olden times in the Navy. Weighted and tied at the end of a rope, the sailor was thrown into the sea from one side of the ship and hauled under the keel and up the other side. The unfortunate man seldom survived the ordeal.

Keen. When we use the word to-day, it is in the sense of sharp—a keen man of business is a sharp man. But the original word, the Anglo-Saxon *cene*, meant bold, and the Icelandic *kaenn*, meant wise.

Keep it Dark. The phrase meant, originally, a hiding-place for treasure. It was kept safe from sight, in a dark place.

Keep the Ball Rolling. An expression which came from the game of Bandy, once very popular. It was very much like our present Hockey, being played by two sets of players having hooked sticks. The object was to keep the ball rolling between and towards the opposite goals.

Keep the Pot Boiling. An allusion to the days when the meal was meat boiled or stewed in a pot, which remained slung by a chain over the fire in the wide chimney-piece. To keep the pot boiling meant not only having it on the boil, but putting something in to boil—in other words, to keep enough in it to live on.

Keep, To. Few words in the English language have so varied a meaning. Keep (guard) the door of my lips, says the Psalm. Keep (retain) the memory. Keep (restrain) me from presumptuous sins—the Psalms. Keep (tend) a garden. Keep (do) accounts. To keep (carry out) one's promises.

The one use of the word which seems out of place is to "keep" a shop, which obviously should keep (in necessities) the shop-keeper! The explanation is simple: The shop-keeper keeps a shop because the Anglo-Saxon keep, *cepan* (pronounced keepan) meant to traffic, to trade; and *sceoppa*, Anglo-Saxon, from which we get shop, meant a treasure store. So that *cepan-sceoppa*, shop-keeper, meant a trader in stores.

Keep your Pecker Up. Pecker was a slang term for the mouth. If you kept your head up you kept up, also, your mouth.

Keep your Powder Dry. During his campaign in Ireland, Cromwell addressed his troops prior to crossing a river to attack on the opposite bank. He concluded his address with the exhortation: "Put your trust in God, but be sure to keep your powder dry." There is a later version, of the present war: "Praise the Lord—and pass the Ammunition" (q.v.).

Keep your Weather-eye Open. Means to be on the watch in the right direction. It is a seaman's allusion. A sailor looks towards the wind when he wants to forecast the weather.

Kelpie. A spirit in Scottish folk-lore, and frequently met with in Scottish verse and literature. Represented as a spirit of the waters in the form of a horse, it is supposed to delight in drowning travellers.

Ken and Kin. Where they appear in place-names, denote a head or promontory. In Scotland they appear in Kenmore and Kinross, and in England in Kenton and in Kent.

Kennel. Is aptly retained. It comes from the Italian *canile*, a dog. But where it means a gutter, it comes from the Latin *canalis*, a pipe, through which water is carried. Our word channel is a corruption of the word, and so is canal.

Kent. Derived its name from Cæsar Cantium, after the *Cantii*, who peopled the *Kenn*, headland or corner. *See* "Ken," above.

Kentish Fire. Rapturous applause and the stamping of feet. Whatever it may have meant in older days, it certainly did not more latterly indicate approval; its sound in a theatre was usually ironic.

Kernel of the Matter. Kernel is the Anglo-Saxon *cyrnel*, the diminutive of corn. And it is surely on the kernel, or corn, that the crop depends.

Kersey. The wool cloth is so-called because it was made at the village of Kessey, near Hadley, in Suffolk, where a woollen trade was once carried on.

Kettledrum. In the eighteenth century, and particularly in military circles, a "drum" was the name given to a crowded evening party, the allusion being to the noise made by the party and the noise made by a drum in the band. Later, in India, when tea-parties became popular, a wag christened afternoon tea-meetings "kettle-drums," i.e., little drums, as compared with the "big drum" evening parties. It is assumed that he had in mind the tea-*kettle*.

Kettle of Fish, A Pretty. *See* "Fish."

Kew Gardens. In ancient documents, Kew was described as Kay-hoo—a quay, or *hoo*, Danish for an island or a spit of land at the mouth of a river or creek.

Key and Bible. An old custom of divination in England. The Bible was opened at *Psalm LI* (where it says: "For I acknowledge my transgresstion") or at *Ruth, I.* A door key was placed inside the book with the handle projecting. A string was then tied round the Bible, and it was held both by the accused and the accuser, who were bound to repeat the words touched by the wards of the key. The key was then supposed to turn towards the guilty person and the Bible to fall to the ground.

Keys! Cross Keys. This name for a public-house sign represents St. Peter's Keys, which were the sign of the supreme authority vested in the Pope as successor to St. Peter himself.

Keys! The King's Keys. An old legal phrase for the crowbars, hammers and other instruments used to force an entrance to premises so that a warrant might be executed.

Khaki. (Hindustani, *Khak*, colour of the soil, dusty.) The origin of the khaki uniform of the British soldier is told here for the first time from information given by Mr. J. Leeman, son of the inventor. In 1883, Mr. J. Leeman was travelling in India for a Manchester cotton firm. A Colonel Kinlock suggested to him that he could acquire a fortune if he could produce a cotton drill, khaki-coloured, which would be fast to the sun and to washing. At that time some regiments in India were dipping their white uniforms in mud as a means of concealment. Back in England, Mr. Leeman approached a Lancashire dyer, Mr. F. A. Gatty, and together they carried out experiments. Samples were prepared and were boiled by Mrs. Leeman in a copper pan. When dried in the sun, however, the colour faded. More samples were prepared for test. On this occasion, however, the copper pan was cooking the dinner, so Mrs. Leeman boiled the cloth in an old rusty pan. This "did the trick," as the dye used (oxide of chromium) was fastened by the oxide of iron from the rusty pan. A private company, F. A. Gatty and Company Ltd., was formed, and has since clothed the troops of the British Empire for more than half a century.

Kick. "*Quite the Kick.*" A corruption of the word *chic*; not the French *chic*, which means smart, fashionable, but the Italian, meaning a dandy.

Kick the Bucket. *See* "Bucket."

Kickshaws. The word, meaning odds and ends, was once written "kickshose." Its origin is the French *quelqe chose*.

Kidnap. Should not properly be used in relation to the "kidnapping" of an adult. "**Kid**" is, of course, slang for a child (a kid is a young goat); and "nap" (nab) is slang for steal.

Kil. The prefix "kil" so often found in Scottish and Irish names was a Gælic word signifying a hermit's cell; and a hermit's cell in those days was usually the foundation of a subsequent church. Most of the "kils" mark where Christianity flourished exceedingly. Examples of the prefix are Kil-Marnoch, Kildonan, I-colm-kill (The Island of Colomba of the Church).

Killed by Kindness. Strange though it may seem, this fate did actually overtake the Athenian (Greek) legislator Draco. A popular man, he was smothered to death in the theatre at Aegina, in 590 B.C., by the mass of cloaks and caps showered upon him by the spectators.

Killing no Murder. This was the title of a pamphlet sent from Holland to England in 1636 recommending the murder of Cromwell. It was written by a Colonel Sexby, who had "ratted" to the Royalists; and who, a year earlier, had only just failed in his own attempt to assassinate the Protector.

Kindly Fruits of the Earth. In case any reader is in doubt as to what particular fruits of the earth are "kindly" and which are unkindly, it may be as well to say that the word used in the Bible quotation means the *varied* fruits of the earth—all the *kinds* of fruit, kindly being used as the adjective of kinds.

Kine. The word for the plural of cows is now little used, except in poetry. But it is interesting to recall as showing how throughout the years and among the tongues words are built up. The Anglo-Saxon for cow was *cu*, the plural being *cy*. The Scottish word was *ky*. This, being pluralled by adding *en*, became *kyer*, from which we English got kine.

King. In the Anglo-Saxon tongue *cyn* meant a people, or a nation. The suffic *ing* meant "of," in the sense of "son of." Thus, put together, there emerged *cyning*, son of the nation, or of the people. And that is the story of our word, King. It might, perhaps, be added that the Anglo-Saxon *cyn* became also our word kin.

King Cotton. The expression, to describe the paramount cotton industry, was first used by James H. Hammond in the United States Senate, in 1858.

King-Maker, The. Richard Neville, Earl of Warwick (1420-71) because he was instrumental in placing Edward IV on the Yorkist and Henry VI on the Lancastrian side of the throne, after supporting each of them in turn.

King of Misrule. Name given to the leader of the Christmas-time horseplay of mediæval times. In some documents he is referred to as the Abbot of Misrule. The festivities were derived from the Pagan Saturnalia, and consisted in processions through the streets on hobby-horses and other mock animals, to the accompaniment of music. They even proceeded thus to church.

King's Bench. One of the three divisions of the High Court of Justice. It dates from the Norman times, and is so-called because at one time the King himself presided over it. When it was held in the Royal Palace, it moved its sittings to wherever the King stayed.

King's Evil. The ancient name given to *Scropula*, a disease of the scalp. It derived the name King's Evil from the belief that the disease could be cured by the touch of Royal hands. In Macauley's "History of England," it is recorded that Charles II "touched" ninety-two thousand one hundred and seven persons. The largest number at one time was in 1684, when many people were trampled to death in the rush. The practice ended with Queen Anne, and one of the last persons to be touched was Dr. Johnson.

King's Picture, The. To paint the King's picture is coiners' slang for counterfeit money, because money bears the image of the King.

King's Weather. Warm, sunny and rainless weather. It became a by-word in the latter part of the reign of George V—George, the Well-beloved—because of the invariably fine state of the weather whenever he drove abroad in State or on official business.

Kingston-on-Thames. The Thames-side Royal Borough. It was thus named because of the stone on which the early Saxon monarchs knelt when they were appointed to their kingly rank. The stone **is** preserved within railings near the present town hall. Edward the Elder, Athelstan, Edmund, Ethelred and Edward the Martyr are said to have knelt on the stone for the Royal Unction.

Kinless Loons. This was the uncomplimentary name given to judges whom Cromwell sent to Scotland. Its allusion is to the judges' lack of relatives in Scotland, and the consequent belief that that would guarantee their impartiality in judgment!

Kiosk. The present wooden hut from which one purchases cigarettes or newspapers, is somewhat of a come-down from the original kiosk, which was a Turkish Summer-house, or pavilion, supported with pillars. These were usually covered with flowering creepers, and the whole kiosk not invariably enclosed a fountain.

Kiss the place and make it better. This phrase, so often used by mothers to soothe a child who has hurt itself, is not so stupid as it sounds. Sorcerers affected to kiss adder bites to make them better. It usually resulted that way—because the kissing was, in fact, a sucking out of the adder's poison!

Kiss the Scavenger's Daughter. The Scavenger's Daughter was the name given to an instrument of torture invented by William Skeffington, Governor of the Tower of London in the sixteenth century. He himself gave it the name of his "daughter" because, he said, it emanated from his own brain. Anyone put to torture by it was said to be kissing the Scavenger's Daughter.

Kissing. Although from earliest Biblical days kissing was a means of salutation between men ("He fell on his neck and kissed him"), kissing *between the sexes* was entirely unknown in Ancient Hebrew times.

Kissing Goes by Favour. The author suggests that, though this is more or less an accurate description of the act (!), the proverb is due to a misreading of folk-lore. By favour would seem to imply "choosing." Now the Anglo-Saxon "to kiss" was *cyssan*, while "to choose" in Anglo-Saxon was *coesa*. The varied words may possibly have been confused.

Kissing the Bride. Came from the "Pax" rubric of Salisbury. The kissing took place immediately before the Communion of the newly-wed couple. It is still practised in a number of South country churches.

Kissing the Pope's Toe. At one time those who were granted audience of the Pope were offered the Papal Hand to kiss. But on one occasion a woman, taking the hand, kissed *and also squeezed it*. "The Pope, seeing the danger to which he was exposed," says Matthew of Westminster, "cut off the hand thus sacrileged, and was thus compelled to offer his foot." The custom has prevailed since.

Kit. The word, for one's immediate needs in the way of clothing or gear, has retained its original meaning. From the Dutch *kitte*, it was a wooden receptacle, made of hooped staves, into which articles were placed for keeping, such as the tools of workmen, and so on.

Kit-Cat. This is the name given by artists to a three-quarter length portrait and, accordingly, to a canvas measuring twenty-eight by thirty-six inches. The origin is interesting. In the eighteenth century a number of leading Whigs of the day formed a club in the house of Christopher Catt, in Shire Lane, upon which the High Courts of Justice now stand. The club was named the

Kit-Cat Club. The rooms were on the low side in height, and when Sir Godfrey Kneller painted the forty-two portraits of the members, he was obliged to restrict the size to that given above. Thus, kit-cat size came to portrait canvases. Steele, Addison and Congreve were among the members of the club who refreshed themselves principally on the mutton pies made by Mr. Catt, who was a pastry-cook.

Kite, To fly a. In Stock Exchange language a " kite " is a worthless bill. To " fly a kite " is to raise money by means of worthless bills.

Kith and Kin. It is a little difficult to reconcile the joining of the two words for though they have a " kindred " meaning they are, at the same time, quite distinct. Kith comes from the Anglo-Saxon *cunnan*, to know, meaning in effect an acquaintance or a friend, while kin is derived from the Anglo-Saxon *cyn*, a people, in its turn derived from *gan*, to beget, thus meaning relationship.

Kleptomania. That word, the usefulness of which to people with an urge to obtain something for nothing, is becoming more and more pronounced in our police - courts, means " thief-madness," from the Greek *kleptes*, thief, and *mania*, madness. London magistrates may well think that the Greeks had, indeed, a word for it.

In passing, it may be pointed out that *klepts* (thieves or robbers) was the name given by the Greeks to their fellow-countrymen who, after the conquest of their country by the Turks, in the fifteenth century, refused to submit, and maintained their independence in the mountains. They later degenerated into brigands and lawless marauders.

Knackerman. Comes from the Icelandic *knakkr*, a saddle, hence a man who deals in horses.

Knapsack. A knapsack was usually a bag in which provisions were carried, such as a soldier might need on a march. The word came from the Danish *knappen*, to eat, and *zac*, a bag.

Knave. How this word evolved into a term for a rascal is a mystery that philologists have not yet discovered, for the Anglo-Saxon *knave* was a boy (the German *knabe* still is), especially a boy in someone's employ. Even in Biblical days he was a boy, as instance *Ex.* i, 16, in Wycliffe's Bible : " If it is a *knave* child sle ye him." And Piers Plowman (1400) wrote : " He bid his *knave* knele."

At the time that a *knave* was a boy servant, so was a *knight* a man servant (as, again, the German *knecht* still is). Now, knight has become an honour, and knave a dishonour. This is one of the minor problems of the searcher into folk-lore.

Knickerbockers. The name for the garment came from the George Cruikshank's illustrations of " Knickerbocker's History of New York," a burlesque published by Washington Irving in 1809. Dutch worthies were shown in very loose knee-breeches.

Knight. In Anglo-Saxon days a knight (*eniht*) was a boy, youth, or attendant or servant. During the Middle Ages he became a person of noble blood trained to arms and chivalry, first as a page and afterwards as a squire to his Sovereign or his superior Lord.

See " Carpet Knight."

Knock. As a place-name, it is frequently found in Scotland. A Gælic word, it implies a hill or knoll. Kilmar-nock is an example.

Knocked 'Em in the Old Kent Road. Since the song of this name by that great Cockney artiste, Albert Chevalier, the " knock 'em in the Old Kent Road " has meant to create an impression, to astonish the natives with admiration.

Knocked into a Cocked Hat. *See* " Cocked."

Knots in wood are the remains of dead branches. When a branch dies or is broken off the dead stump becomes grownover with a healing tissue, and as the stem which bears it increases in thickness the dead stump is gradually buried in the newer wood.

Know Thyself. The advice of the Oracle at Delphi, and attrbiuted to many of the great philosophers of Greece.

Knowing the ropes was originally a sailor's term, in the days of sailing ships, for an able seaman. He would not have been an able seaman if he had not known all the ropes belonging to a ship.

Knowledge is Power. The author knows few words so misconstrued as this word knowledge, particularly when used in connection with power. Knowledge is not altogether what it is assumed to be—book-learning. Men possessed knowledge before there were any books worth speaking of open to them. The writer suggests that the " ledge " was derived from the Anglo-Saxon *lac*, a gift ; and that *leche* signified the gift of having knowledge. To the man to whom the gift is given of being able to acquire knowledge from eyesight, from mental activity, and from keen observation of the world, power is most likely to come. Many of the great leaders of Labour who have risen to power assimilated very little knowledge from books ; but their knowledge carried them to power.

Knuckle under, To. To give up. To yield. In both Mediæval English and in Anglo-Saxon, knuckle referred not only to the finger-joint but also a knee-joint. To knuckle under, therefore, meant to bow the knee.

Krieg. A word with which, since 1939, we have become exceedingly familiar. It is the German name for war. Although the Latin language had *bellum* and the French *guerre*, all meaning war and strife, the Teutons, although exceedingly warlike, had no such general name. It was not until the Mid-High German period that *krieg*, meaning striving after, came to stand for war in Germany. To *krieg* has since been added words expressive of the manner of " striving after," for instance, *blitz*krieg, striving after from the air.

Kudos. Greek for glory.

Ku-Klux-Klan. The secret society wh ch grew up in the Southern States of America about 1866. Its activities were directed mainly against negroes. An Act of Congress in 1871 suppressed it, but it was still in evidence as an underground movement forty years later. Its victims were marked with the letters " K.K.K." on their foreheads. It is said that the name was taken as spelling the sound of the cocking of a gun, which was the Society's principal method of murder.

Kursaal. The name given to the place of entertainment at Southend-on-Sea, where all kinds of amusement are provided. Whoever invented the slogan, " Southend is *so* bracing," came very near to investing the Kursaal with its original meaning. It comes from the German, and is literally " cure-all " expressing the purpose of the public rooms at a *Kurhaus*, a hydropathic establishment.

L

Labyrinth. Most of the works of reference on Philology describe the word as Greek, denoting a mass of buildings, or garden walks, so complicated as to puzzle strangers to extricate themselves. Maybe it is so, but those are mazes, not labyrinths. The proper name of labyrinth is the Cretan maze constructed by Dædalus, and from which Theseus escaped by the help of Araidne's thread. Not, please, *skein* of thread, as Dr. Brewer puts it, but a *clew* of thread ; hence the present " clue " of the popular detective stories.

Lackadaisical. To do something in a half-hearted or careless manner. The origin is obscure. It may have come from the old wail "A-lack-a-day," which really meant "a lack (loss) to-day," or it may be connected up with the Latin *lassus*, wearied, in the sense of "alas, this day." The *Oxford English Dictionary* does not trace it satisfactorily.

Laconic. To express much in a few words. It comes from that land of stoicism and simplicity, Sparta, with its alternative name Laconia. The best example is the retort of the Sparta magistrates to Philip of Macedon. Philip had sent a message: "If I enter Laconia, I will level Lacedæmon to the ground."

The magistrates replied, simply, "If."

A modern laconic reply is the famous *Punch* admonition: "To those about to marry—DON'T."

Lacrosse. Is said to be the name given to the game by Charlevoix who, seeing it played by Alonquin Indians with a stick, between Quebec and the Three Rivers, called it *le jeu de la Crosse*. We give the origin for what it is worth.

Lady. It may come as a shock to many to learn that they are entitled to the title of lady only if they are housewives and bread-kneaders. The word is, literally, the bread-kneader, as lord is bread-guarder. The word is derived from the Anglo-Saxon *hlaef-dige* ("*lae-dige*"). Girls, in those days, were literally spinsters, while a "daughter" can be traced back to Chaldean origin in words meaning cow-girl. The duty of the sons of the house was to perpetuate the family, as will be noticed from the origin of the word, the Sanscrit *sunu*, derived from *su*, to beget. The present definition of a lady infers that she is neither a bread-kneader nor a working housekeeper!

Lady of England. The title conferred by the Council of Winchester on the Empress Maud, daughter of Henry I of England, and wife of the Emperor Henry V of Germany. The date of the honour was 7th April, 1141.

Lady of the Lamp. Name given by wounded soldiers of the Crimea to Florence Nightingale (1820-1910), because she went the rounds of hospital wards in the Crimea with a lantern, bringing relief to pain during the night.

Laisser Faire. A French phrase meaning "Let us alone." It was first used in France to designate that principle of political economy which would leave industry and trade free from taxation or restriction by government, except so far as required by public peace and order.

Lammas Day. A corruption of its old name, *hlaf-maesse*—loaf feast. The date is 1st August, when, in Anglo-Saxon days, it was the custom to offer loaves of bread to the Church as representing the first fruits of the earth. There is another suggested origin, that the name was originally Vincula-mass, the feast to commemorate the deliverance of St. Peter from chains, which was also celebrated on 1st August. It is a far-fetched theory.

Lampblack. When first used, this pigment was obtained by burning resinous substances over the flame of a lamp.

Lampoon. Used strictly, the word means to abuse vitriolly with personal satire. Its origin lies in drink. The Anglo-Saxon *lapian*, and the Old French *lapper*, each meant drink; and the French *lampon*, derived from them, was a drinking song. Which proves, again, that the proverb "when the drink is in, the wits are out," is pretty near the truth.

Lan, Llan. These are Celtic words denoting an enclosure—in a later period a sacred enclosure. It is, of course, a common component in Welsh place-names.

Land. "*See How the Land Lies.*" Spy out the position before we decide to do anything. The origin of this very sensible piece of advice is Joshua, in the Bible, who sent spies "to view the land" before he attempted to cross the Jordan. In modern war communiques it would doubtless be recorded as, "Our patrols pushed forward, but made no contact with the enemy."

Land of Green Ginger. Despite all efforts of etymologists to disperse the canard, it is still maintained that a square at Hull is thus named because it was there that ginger was landed from the river and sold in open market. The story is nonsense. In 1685, Sir Willoughby Hickman was a candidate for the borough's parliamentary seat. A letter is extant in which, referring to this, he wrote that the stage coach took him from the waterside to the George Inn "at the corner of the land of Moses Greenhinger." And the "land of Mr. Greenhinger" has come to-day to the "Land of Green Ginger."

Larder. When the careful housewife, returning from her shopping-places her supply of bacon in the larder, she is using the storeroom in its original capacity. For the Latin *laridum*, and the Old French *lardoir*, meant a store-place for bacon. An interesting commentary on this is the fact that it is the only store-place for meat recorded in ancient times, a circumstance which would seem to imply that the pig was the chief animal slaughtered and laid down in salt as meat.

Larder. "*The Douglas Larder.*" Scott, in "Tales of a Grandfather," tells this story of the "Douglas Larder": He (Lord James Douglas, in 1307) caused all the barrels containing flour, wheat, meat and malt to be knocked in pieces, and their contents mixed on the floor. Then he staved the great hogsheads of wine and ale, and mixed the liquor with the stores. Last of all, he killed the prisoners and flung the dead bodies among the disgusting heap, which his men called, in derision of the English, "The Douglas Larder."

The prisoners were the English garrison in Douglas Castle, Lanark, which Douglas had seized.

Lark. A spree. The origin is doubtful, but may be a corruption of the Middle English *laik*, play, and the Anglo-Saxon *lac*, a contest. There is no connection between the word and the bird of that name.

Larrikin. The word is used to describe a rowdy one who engages in rough play. Like Mrs. Harris, there "ain't no sich" word. It arose from a one-man corruption of the word larking—to lark (*See* "Lark," above). The habit of Irishmen, like Scotsmen, of rolling their "r's" is well-known. "Notes and Queries" tells this story of the invention of larrikin: James Dalton, a Melbourne police sergeant of Irish extraction, was giving evidence against a number of youths. "They were a'larrikin' down the strate, your Worship," he said. The Bench, not understanding the rolling "r's," asked for the word to be repeated. It was—and so often that it passed into a catch-word, and was soon applied universally to all rowdy youths.

Last Man, The. This title was bestowed upon Charles I by the Parliamentarians, meaning that he would be the last King of Great Britain. When his son, Charles II, came to the throne, he was jestingly referred to by the Royalists as the Son of the Last Man.

Last Words. Following are some of the more famous "last words" of great men and women of all ages:

Anaxagorus, the Philosopher, who had a school: "Give the boys a holiday."

Archimedes, after being told by a Roman centurion to follow him: "Wait till I have solved my problem."

Henry Ward (Beecher): "Now comes the mystery."

Anne Boleyn: "The executioner is, I believe, very expert; and my neck is very slender."

Julius Cæsar, to Brutus, his friend, who stabbed him: "Et, tu, Brute."

Charles I, at the moment of putting his head on the block, speaking to Bishop Juxon: "Remember." (What the Bishop was to remember has remained a mystery to this day.)

Danton, speaking to the executioner: "Be sure you show the mob my head. It will be a long time ere they see its like."

Elizabeth, Queen: "All my possessions for a moment of time."

Elizabeth (sister of Louis XV): "I pray you, gentlemen, in the name of modesty, suffer me to cover my bosom." (As she was on the way to the scaffold, her kerchief had fallen from her neck.)

Garrick, the actor: "Oh, dear."

Garth, Sir Samuel, a doctor, to his physicians: "Gentlemen, let me die a natural death. (The writer fears that this is an invention.)

Hobbes: "Now I am about to take my last voyage—a leap in the dark."

Julian (The Apostate): "Thou hast conquered, O Gallæan." (Victisi, O Galilee.)

Marie Antoinette (to her children: "Farewell for ever. I am going to your father."

Martineau, Harriet: "I see no reason why the existence of Harriet Martineau should be perpetuated."

More, Sir Thomas: "See me safe up (as he went to mount the scaffold). For my coming down, let me shift for myself."

Palmerston: "Die, my dear doctor? That's the LAST thing I shall do."

Rabelais: "Let down the curtain. The farce is over." The same words, with the alteration of curtain to comedy, is ascribed to numerous other people.

Richard III, after his men had deserted him for Richmond at Boswell): "Treason! Treason."

Roland, Madame: "Oh, Liberty. What crimes are committed in thy name."

Simon de Montfort (at the Battle of Evesham): "Commend your souls to God, for our bodies are the foes."

Socrates: "Crito, we owe a cock to Æsulapius."

Tenterden (Lord Chief Justice): "Gentlemen of the jury, you may retire."

Victoria, Queen: "Oh that peace might come." (She was referring to the South African War.)

Wolsey, Cardinal: "Had I but served my God with half the zeal that I have served my king, He would not have left me in my grey hairs."

Laudanum. Opium gives, as a rule, a headache; but not such a headache as this word gave those who first endeavoured to trace its history. Laudanum, an extraction from the poppy, is not the laudanum of the Latin *ladan* and the Persian *ladanum.* This was a resinous substance which exuded from a shrub in Syria, much valued by the ancients for its healing properties. When opium was first brought to Europe from the East it was thought, from its appearance, to be this gum, and was named laudanum. The name, though wrong, has never been changed. Laudanum is the name first given by Paracelsus to a quack elixir. He probably derived the name from laud (Latin, praise), in relation to the cures which he claimed for it.

Laugh and grow fat, in allusion to Democritus, the "laughing philosopher." He had the habit humorously of revealing the absurdities of his countrymen. He laughed continuously and he certainly grew fat, in addition to living to be one hundred and nine years of age!

Laugh Best that Laughs Last, He. The proverb is first found in Vanbrugh (1706). It is referred to by Scott as a French proverb: "Rira bien qui rira le dernier."

Laugh up your Sleeve. In the days when this phrase was coined the sleeves of outer garments were very wide. A person covering his or her face with the sleeve was suspected of hiding a smile at someone's expense.

Laureate, The Poet. In classical times the poet who came to fame by reason of his heroic verse was publicly crowned with a wreath of laurel or bay leaves. The Latin name of the bay tree was *laurus,* hence the name Laureate for the Court, or leading, poet of the country. Homer and Virgil, Plutarch and Tasso are all represented in sculpture with their heads crowned with laurels. It was the belief of the ancients that laurel communicated the spirit of prophecy and poetry.

Lavender. When the housewife associates lavender with clean sheets, she is wiser than she knows, for the name comes from the Latin *lavendula,* the root of which is *lavare,* to wash. Our word laundress and the French washer-woman, *lavandiere,* come from the same root. Lavender was at one time used in the washing of linen which was too delicate to be beaten on the stones in the streams. It was accordingly rinsed well in soap and water, laid across a line, and beaten gently with long sprigs of lavender.

Law. Relatives "in-Law." A great deal of misapprehension exists in regard to a brother or sister in-law, and to the other "in-laws." The Law in question has nothing whatever to do with the Law of the country. An in-law is no relation whatever. The Law concerned is Canon Law, a body of law applicable to the government of the Church. It has reference to the degrees of affinity within which marriage is prohibited.

Lawyers' Treat. A lawyer never treats his clients at a place of refreshment. They defray the costs of the refreshment between them.

Lead Pencil. The lead pencil does not, and never did, contain any lead. The writing medium is composed mostly of graphite and clay. In some cases it is plumbago. The name lead pencil was given to it in the sixteenth century, when it was supposed that the contents were, in fact, lead.

Lead up the Garden Path. The meaning is to "Blarney" a person. (*See* "Blarney.") To entice. There is no record of when the phrase was first used, or of how it came into being. But the probability is that it arose from "affairs of the heart." From time immemorial the swain, wishing for a few moments alone with his inamorita, has led her gently into the garden, particularly in the dusk; and certainly on her introduction to her prospective parents-in-law, she was led up the garden path!

Leading Article, Leader. That article in a newspaper which, as distinct from the news, expresses the personal opinions of the newspaper in politics or on any matter of national or political importance. It is designed to "lead" the opinions of the readers into a line of thought advocated by the newspaper. It was not called a leading article because, as one authority puts it, the lines of print were separated by a "lead," a narrow strip of metal, "so as to give the print more importance and more space in the paper." This is sheer nonsense.

Leaf, Leaves (of a book). Before the invention of paper, writing was recorded on the leaves of certain plants. The name still stands for a page of writing. Moreover, the word folios, for a number of pages of Ms., comes from the Latin *folium,* a leaf.

League of Nations. A league of the nations of the world formed, with headquarters at Geneva, after the 1914-18 war, with the object of preventing war in the future. Its birth was due, in the main, to the exertions of the President of the U.S.A., Mr. Woodrow Wilson. His action, however, was repudiated by that country, and America did not become a member of the League. Under its constitution, all the nations bound themselves not to resort to war, and to take steps to impose sanctions by the others on any nation which resorted to force. Political and trading agreements, and two-nation agreements, negatived entirely the objects of the League; and when Japan seized a large part of Chinese territory (Manchuria), Great Britain herself did not oppose the seizure. Following that encouragement came the seizure of Abyssinia by Italy, similarly accepted by Britain, and the territorial aggrandisement by Hitler for Germany. It is doubtful whether in the centuries of history there has been a greater failure than the League of Nations.

Leaning Tower of Pisa. Was never meant to lean. It was built for a campanile (bell tower). Because of bad building, on too small a base and too shallow a foundation, one side of the base subsided, thus making the tower famous. It proved exceedingly useful this way to Galileo, who spent his time dropping balls of various weights from the top to prove that articles of different weights reach the ground at the same time from the same height—which, of course, they do, unless they are at such a height as to attain terminal velocity, and encounter air resistance.

The Pisa tower is one hundred and seventy-eight feet high, fifty-seven feet in diameter, and is sixteen feet out of the perpendicular. The building began in 1174.

Ganot has stated that the reason that the tower continues to stand, despite its lean, is because the vertical line drawn through its centre of gravity passes within its base.

The Leaning Tower of Pisa is NOT one of the Seven Wonders of the World.

Leap Year Proposals. As this superstition seems to be a vital one for the female sex in these days of surplus women, it may be as well to get its terms plainly expressed. The saying is that during Leap Year the ladies may propose and, if not accepted, can claim a silk gown. Now, apart from the fable connected with St. Patrick (given below), the authority given for this is a Law of the Scottish Parliament which enacted the following:

"It is statut and ordaint that during the rein of hir maist blissit Megeste Margaret, for ilk yeare knowne as lepe yeare, ilk mayden ladye of bothe highe and lowe estait shall hae liberte to bespoke ye man she likes, albeit he refuses to taik hir to be his lawful wyfe, he shall be mulcted in ye sum ane pundis or less, as his estait may be; except and awis if he can make it appeare that he is betrothit ane ither woman he then shall be free."

There was, however, another saver for the men, either introduced at that time, or later. The writer is indebted to Mr. Henry Hollebon, of Eastbourne, for the transcription of a document which adds: "Everie ladie that goes a'wooing must weare a scarlet flannel petticote, the edge of whiche must be clearlie seen; else noe man neede paie forfeit."

Now the date of this Act is given as 1288 or 1228. In those years, however, there was no "blissit Megeste Margaret" on the throne of Scotland. Margaret's reign was somewhere between 1045 and 1093, and the Maid of Norway, another Margaret, acknowledged Queen of Scotland, died on her journey from Norway to Scotland in 1285.

The Fable of Leap Year has been ascribed to St. Patrick. It runs like this (quoting Dr. Brewer): "He was told by St. Bridget that a mutiny had broken out in her nunnery, the ladies claiming the right to 'Pop the question.' St. Patrick said he would concede them the right every seventh year. St. Bridget threw her arms around his neck, and exclaimed, 'Arrah Pathrick, jewel, I daurn't go back to the girls wid such a proposal. Make it one year in four.' St. Patrick replied, 'Bridget, acushla, squeeze me that way again, and I'll give ye leap year, the longest of the lot.' St. Bridget, upon this, popped the question toSt.Patrick himself who, of course, could not marry; so he patched up the difficulty as best he could with a kiss and a silk gown."

Which seems a strange going-on for an abbess, nuns and a Saint!

Leather. "*Nothing like Leather.*" The quotation should not end there. The concluding words are "for administering a thrashing." The proverb then explains itself. There is, however, an Aprocyphal story of a town, in danger of a siege, which called a defence council of the leading citizens to solicit ideas. A mason suggested a strong wall, a ship-builder proposed wooden walls, and a currier (a curer of skins) arose and said, "There's nothing like leather."

Leave no Stone Unturned. This popular and very much over-used cliche of the politician to-day, was hackneyed in the year A.D. 1! It dates back, in fact, to 475 B.C., when the Persian general, Mardonius, was defeated at *Plataea*. Believing that the general had left treasure in his tent, Polycrates sought for it for many days, without success. He consulted the Oracle of Delphi, who told him: "Leave no stone unturned." Polycrates returned to the tent, obeyed the injunction, and discovered the treasure under the stone floor.

Leave Some for Manners. The custom has always prevailed in polite society of leaving a portion of wine in the bottom of one's glass. In older days this was supposed to be the perquisite of the servants. The same applied to the remnants in the bottom of the bottle—which was never completely emptied. The custom dates back to the earliest banqueting days of England. But whether it has any foundation in the passage from *Ecclesiasticus*, "Leave off first for manners' sake and be not insatiable," is doubtful.

Leek. The leek is *not* the official national emblem of Wales, though it is popularly supposed to be, and most Welshmen wear it on festive occasions, and at sporting events. The Welsh emblem is the daffodil; and it appears as such on the bottom left-hand corner of British postage stamps.

Left. From the earliest times the right hand has played a predominant part in man. "He raised his right hand," says the Bible. All forms of salutation, from the time of the Cuniform writings of Babylon and Assyria down to the present day, are shown as coming from the right hand. "A strong right hand," to quote again the Bible. We speak of a left-handed compliment as being a reproach; a morganatic marriage is a "left-hand" marriage; a left-handed oath is one not considered binding. In view of this, it is remarkable that no etymologist has sought a reason for such preponderance. The writer has searched diligently down the ages for any explanation. The result has been a failure to discover any trace of the word "left" as meaning opposite to "right." But there was in Anglo-Saxon the word *lef*, weak, and *lefan*, to weaken. Long years after, in North Friesland, there appears the word *lefter-hond* for left-hand. The opinion of the writer is that the left hand was never so named as the opposite to right, but meant that the hand was the *weaker* hand. The obvious cororally is that our present rule of referring to the left—take the first turning on the left—as a direction is grammatically, and etymologically, incorrect, unless the left is a weaker body. This does not, of course, apply to the word left in the sense of leaving, the derivation of which is from another source.

Left Alone with His Glory. The words were first used in Wolfe's poem on the burial of Sir John Moore.

Left in the Lurch. Is actually a term from the card game of Cribbage. One is left in the lurch when one's opponent has run out his score of sixty-one holes before one's-self has scored thirty-one, or turned the corner.

It is probable, however, that the real meaning of the word was earlier, and was "purloined" by the card-game. A poacher "lurches" when he lurks about laying traps for game. If a poacher found himself deserted by his fellow poachers when an alarm was raised, he considered that he had been left in the "lurch."

Legend. By the use of the word to-day, we infer that the object thus described is one which is fiction and not the truth. A legend is a fable. The meaning is in complete variance with the origin of the word. Legend is the Latin *legenda*, from *legere*, to read; and the Legenda was a book containing the narratives of the lives of the Saints, read in the religious houses of olden days. These narratives, with their tales of miracles, and their exaggerations and wealth of flowery language so beloved of the East, are the reason for the word legend being regarded as a mythical story.

Legion. The word came to mean many, an unspecified number, because in ancient Rome a body of soldiers numbering up to several thousands was called a levy, from the Latin *milites legere*, troops raised by levy.

Leigh, Ley. A suffix frequently met with in English place-names. It is derived from the Anglo-Saxon *leah*, from the verb "to lie." Leys were open glades in the forests where cattle could graze and lie. Some idea of the extent of the forest lands in many parts of the country can be gathered from the frequency with which the word leigh, or ley, appears in its names; taken in conjunction with other names of which *hurst* forms a component. Hurst was the more thickly wooded parts of the forest; leys were those parts of the forest which had been cleared by hand, or had been left clear by Nature.

Lemon sole. This fish-course delicacy has nothing whatever in common with the lemon. The name comes from *limande*, a dab or fish. But where *limande* developed is not definitely clear. It may have been derived from the Old French word *limande*, meaning a board, in reference to the flatness of the fish, or it might be an allusion to the mud in which the fish generally lies, from the Latin *limus*, mud.

Lens. Is Latin for a bean. The double convex magnifying glasses, the most perfect of all such, is of bean shape. It is a suggestion that this may be the explanation of the term lens for such glasses.

Lent. The name for the beginning of the Church's holy season has, as in the other instances, nothing to do with Christianity. It is a shortened form of *lencten*, the Anglo-Saxon word for Spring. From the same root comes the word lengthening; and lencten marked for the Anglo-Saxons the beginning of the lengthening of the days.

Galeazzo's Lent. A form of torture invented, or perhaps devised is the better word, by the Duke of Milan (Galeazzo Visconti). It was calculated to torture without destroying life for a period of forty days.

Leopard. The jungle cat's name arose from the belief, quite erroneous, that the animal was a cross between a lion and a pard—the name given to a white panther which had no spots on the skin—in other words, *leo-pard*.

Let the Cat out of the Bag. *See* "Cat."

Lethe. The classical name for forgetfulness, oblivion. From the Greek *letho*, "to cause not to know." In Greek mythology, the Lethe was one of the rivers of Hades, of which all the souls of the dead were required to drink in order that they might forget all their past life.

Let-Up. The word is of interest because it is to-day what the educated person refers to as bad English. It is, in fact, used as a colloquism for going slow, or stopping any operation on which one was previously engaged. Yet the word is only a continuation of the old Anglo-Saxon *lett-an*, which meant slow, to hinder. Although the phrase is now archaic, it is perfectly permissible to use the term "let-up" to describe someone hindering, or slacking, at his task.

Levant, To. To decamp. There seems no reason why the word should have come into the language in place of the perfectly good English word of decamp; for it is a normal Spanish word. *Levanter la casa* is Spanish for break up the house. The word seems to have induced one philologist to search diligently round for some abstruse meaning. He eventually arrived at the idea that it referred to the grand tour taken by the scions of noble houses in the old days, who were all expected to go to the Levant, i.e., the Orient or the East. So that, the ingenious fellow explains, when the scion had departed he was said to have Levant-ed!

Levee. This name, given to a reception held by the King, was derived from the practice of the French Queens of receiving their doctors, messengers and friends on their *levee*, that is, in its French meaning, on their rising from bed—i.e., during their toilet.

Liars should have good Memories. Many writers have used the phrase throughout the centuries; but the original was Quintillian in his "Mendacem memorem esse Oportet": "It is fitting that a liar should be a man of good memory."

Libel. "*The Greater the Truth, the Greater the Libel.*" This dictum was laid down by Lord Ellenborough. He proceeded to explain the conundrum by saying: "If the language used were true, the person would suffer more than if it were false." The word libel comes from the Latin *libellus*, a little book; and is, in truth, a writing of a defamatory nature.

Lich. This word, frequently used as a prefix of names and places, is the Anglo-Saxon *lic*, a corpse. Examples of its modern use in that sense are Lich-gate (or lych-gate), the covered gate at the entrance to a churchyard where the corpse is rested waiting the arrival of the clergyman to precede it into the church; and lich-owl. The significance of its application to the owl is the belief, which has existed for centuries, that the owl is a creature of ill-omen, and that its screeching forebodes death.

Lichfield. From the derivation of "Lich," above, it will be apparent that Lichfield must mean the corpse field, or the field of the dead. And, indeed, the Staffordshire town derived its name from a massacre of Christians during the persecution by Diocletian in, or around, the year 304. Something of the same nature lies behind Lichfield in Hampshire.

Lick into Shape. The origin of this phrase is the old belief (quite erroneous) that bear cubs are born shapeless and are licked into their proper form by the mother bear.

Lieutenant. Though most people are aware that *locum tenens* means one who holds the place of another in the performance of any duty or function, probably not one in a hundred is aware that lieutenant is *exactly the same thing*. Lieutenant is the Latin *Locum*, account of, and *tenens*, from *tenere*, to hold, coming to us through the French *lieu* for locus, meaning "instead of." The word is more rightly used in the sense of Lieutenant-Colonel, the holder of that position being the Colonel's deputy.

Light as a Feather. Few phrases in common use in England can have so remote an origin, or one so little known as this one. It dates back to the earliest of the Pharoahs, and is part of the ceremony of Egypt's dead. Perhaps it is best explained by the following scene from the papyrus of one, Hunefar, an official in the service of the King during the fourteenth century B.C.:

"Osiris, the Eternal Lord, is presiding over the weighing of the heart (or conscience) of Hunefar, who is dead, and attending the ceremony of his soul. The ceremony is held in the Court of the Two Laws, in the centre of which stand the Great Scales. On one side of the scales is a feather, and on the other the heart of Hunefar. Hunefar has been conducted to the scales by Anubis, God of the Dead (with the head of a jackal). The bust of Ma'at, Goddess of Truth, is superimposed on the centre of the scales. It is the duty of Anubis to inspect the scales and make sure that the feather (representing Right) is not outweighed by the heart of Hunefar.

"Thoth, Writer to the Gods, stands by to record the result of the weighing. Twelve of the great gods and goddesses of Ancient Egypt are in attendance at the test. Hunefar, praying, specially asks that his heart be allowed to go with him on his eternal journey; that the weighing be just; and that no false witness may come against him.

"*If the heart should be heavier than the feather it will instantly be devoured by that being called The Devourer* (*a mixture of lion, crocodile and river-horse*), who is sitting near the scales, waiting. The test goes well, and Hunefar's heart is pronounced as being tried in the balance and found *as light as a feather*.

"This fact is communicated to Osiris, who announces that Hunefar's conscience has been found free from wickedness."

And from this we say to-day when we meet a man who is happy and conscious-free, that "his heart is as light as a feather."

The above scene is from the "Book of the Dead."

Light that never was on Sea or Land. The story told of this sentence is that a visitor, admiring one of Turner's landscape pictures of a sunset, remarked: "I never saw anything quite so wonderful as that in nature." Said the great Master, in reply: "No, but don't you wish you could?"

Wordsworth, the poet, who was a contemporary of Turner, is said to have heard the remark, and to have embodied it in the line quoted. It appears in "Elegiac Stanzas."

Lighthouse, Pharos. *See* "Seven Wonders."

Limb of the Law. The allusion is that as the limbs of the human body are directed by, and obey, the head, so the limbs of the law—the police, the lawyers, and so on—also carry out and obey the directions of the head—the Law.

Limehouse. The term which came to be applied to violent abuse of an opponent, especially in politics. On 30th July, 1909, Mr. Lloyd George in a violent speech attacked bitterly, and with considerable invective, the Dukes, landlords, capitalists and, in fact, the whole of the upper classes. The speech was delivered at Limehouse—which town at once became the adjective for speeches of a similar nature.

Limerick. These little nonsense verses were not called "limericks" until long after they were first popularized by Edward Lear in his "Book of Nonsense." What connection the improvized verses to-day have with Limerick is hard to see. Dr. Brewer states that the name arose from the practice of singing the chorus, "We'll all come up, come up to Limerick," after each verse; but the author has never heard such a chorus sung, although he has invented and sung as many Limericks probably as anybody else.

Limousine. This name existed many years before the motor car body with that name was thought of. *Limousine* is a French word signifying a cloak. The idea was, you see, a "cloaked" car, cars having previously been open.

Lincoln Green. So-called, because at one time the city was famous for its light green. Other cities, equally noted for colours, were Yorkshire for its grey and Coventry for its blue.

Line. "*The Thin Red Line.*" The term has been used to describe the British infantrymen since Balaclava, where the 93rd Highlanders were given that title by the great war correspondent, W. H. Russell, because they did not form into the usual hollow square, but met the enemy in a line. It must be borne in mind that the infantrymen in those days wore red jackets.

Lines. "*Reading Between the Lines.*" There were times in English history when more could be got from a letter by reading between the lines than by reading the writing. It is said that the Gunpowder Plot was revealed by this means, the letter to Lord Mounteagle giving a warning to that nobleman in the form of a message contained in alternative lines of a perfectly innocuous letter. That his Lordship must have known that such cryptogrammatic writing was used is shown by the fact that he read it correctly. Writing by invisible ink is also done between the lines of the visible writing. From this actual writing between the lines, the phrase came later to mean a reading of an *inference* within the writing.

Lingo. This word for language is not quite such slang as it sounds. It is the modern interpretation of the Latin *lingua*, the tongue.

Lining the Pocket. A bribe. It is said that the expression dates from the days when Beau Brummel was the fashion plate of England. A tailor, wishing to obtain his patronage and recommendation, sent the Beau a fashionable coat, the pockets of which he lined with bank-notes. Brummell is said to have acknowledged receipt in a letter to the tailor stating that he approved of the coat, and especially admired the lining.

Link-men. Link is derived from the Latin *linum*, through the Mediæval English *lin*, signifying flax. Links were torches made from tow or flax (linen also was made from flax), and when so made were given the name of *lunts*, meaning a torch, and also a match. Links were in olden days the only illumination in London's streets. A Link-man could be hired to lead a party through the streets during darkness. He went ahead with his flaming torch, or *lunt*, link.

Linn or Lynn. These component parts in many place-names are derived from the Celtic *lleyn*, a deep pool. Lin-coln and King's Lynn are examples.

Lion of the Party! Lionise. Before the days of the popular travelling circuses with animals, a lion was little more than a name to most people in the Provinces. In London, on one occasion a show of lions was held in the Tower of London. Country cousins, coming up to Town, were taken to see the lions. Huge numbers of people visited the animals during their stay, and led to the term "lionising" and the "lion of the party" becoming incorporated into the language to express a centre of attraction.

Live and Let Live. First appeared as a proverb in Fergusson's "Scottish Proverbs," 1641, and in Ray's "English Proverbs," 1670.

Live like Fighting-Cocks, To. To live well. Good living, such as was fed to fighting-cocks from the Early Greeks down to the days when cock-fighting was abolished in Britain. The good living was an essential in order that the birds might fight with greater endurance.

Liver. "*A white-livered person.*" A coward. It was anciently believed that the liver of a coward contained no blood, a belief which should have resulted in his being guiltless of his crime, since he obviously couldn't help it. But hence the allusion "white-livered."

Both the Greeks and the Romans before battle sacrificed an animal to the Gods. If the liver of the sacrifices was blood-red it was a favourable omen; if it was pale and unhealthy, it foretold defeat.

Liverpool. Few words have afforded philologists more laughter at amateur attempts to find it an origin than the city of Liverpool. The most popular fiction is that it was named after some mysterious Liver bird. But it was not until the seventeenth century that this mythical bird was invented, and "Liverpool" existed before that. The town was already named Leverpool in 1190.

A second "origin" is that it comes from the Welsh *Llyr-pwl*, the sea pool. Then there are those who assert that the English *lither*, stagnant pool, gave the name. Carlyle, for instance, wrote, "The creek of the Mersey is a *lither* pool, a lazy or sullen pool."

Finally, there was an extraordinary gentleman who asserted beyond contradiction that Liverpool owed its name "to the occupation of that part of the Mersey shore on which Liverpool now stands by an Irish outcast and his followers in the fifth century, Leaoir Macmannimin, and caused the pool of the Mersey to be named Lear's Pool."

Some of the best brains in the world of learning have busied themselves in searching for the origin of Liverpool, and have failed, among them Mr. Ernest Weekley. If Weekley cannot trace the origin, the writer doubts if anyone can—or will.

Llanfair Pwllgwyn gyll gogerychwyon-dnburl-Uantysdiogogogoch. The name of this Welsh village, in Anglesey, means: "The Church of St. Mary in a Hollow of White Hazel near to the rapid whirlpool and to St. Tysillid's Church near to a red cave." The place is called "Llanfair" because time is too short to say the name in full. It is, of course, the longest name in Britain.

Loafer. Attempts have been made to prove that this word is derived from the Spanish-American. The early settlers of Mexico, it is added, gave the name of *gallofo* to a vagrant. Well, maybe they did, but a century or two before that the Germans had *laufer* to describe the person who idled away his time; and the Dutch had *loopen* for strolling idly, without purpose.

Lobster. In peace-time was the name given to a soldier on enlisting because, in the days when the red tunic was his dress, he was said to have turned red! There had been "lobsters" (soldiers) before that, however. They are described in Clarendon's "History of the Rebellion." Speaking of a fresh regiment of horse received by Sir William Waller, he says: "They were called by the King's party the regiment of lobsters, because of their bright iron shells with which they were covered, being perfect cuirassiers, and were the first seen armed on either side."

Lock, stock and barrel. Everything. The whole lot. A gun is made in three parts—the stock, lock and the barrel.

Lode Star. In Mediæval English *lode* or *lod* meant a way, a course, or a path. In Anglo-Saxon, *lad* meant the same, with the addition of carrying. The Mediæval English word has never lost its meaning—a lode star is a leading star. In the days before compasses and maps existed for the mariner, he found his way by the leading star, or lode star—exactly as did the Wise Men of the East find their way to the Infant Christ.

Loggerheads, At. This is another of those words for which no satisfactory, or generally accepted, origin can be found. Logger was the name given to the heavy wooden clog fastened to the legs of grazing horses to prevent them from straying far—a logger on their heads, so to speak.

A Canadian version of the meaning concerns the quarrels of the loggermen over whose timbers, or logs, should be first away down the river.

On the other hand, a man who had spent many years on a whaler wrote to the author to assure him that a loggerhead was the channel in the bow of the boat through which ran the rope attached to the harpoon. This rope, he explained, sometimes ran so fast through the loggerhead that water had to be continually poured on to it to prevent the friction firing the rope. When such an eventuality was seen there was a shout, "At loggerheads"—and the dispute with the harpooned whale went on. Of the three, we like the last-described best.

Log-rolling. A slang term for the giving of mutual help, usually in a secret or underhanded way. It is an allusion to the lumber camps where lumberman of different camps will give each other a hand in rolling logs to the water's edge in time for the flood. It must be remembered that time meant everything when it came to catching the flood down stream, so any help given to a rival camp might be of enormous benefit to the helper in leaving the bank free for his own logs.

London Bridge is Built on Wool. The origin of this old saw, and popular "catch," lies in the fact that the first of the stone London bridges was paid for by a tax on wool. After several wooden bridges had been destroyed, Peter, Chaplain of St. Mary Colechurch, in the Poultry, London, began, in 1176, to build a stone bridge. Money becoming short, he appealed to Henry II, who gave towards the expenses the proceeds of a tax which he imposed on wool.

London Stone. Whether this historic stone marked the centre of the town, as was common in Roman times, or whether it had some earlier importance, is not now known. It was fixed deep in the ground within a few feet of the wall of St. Swithin's Church, Cannon Street, against which it is now preserved. There is mention of the stone as early as Athelstan. And it was struck by Jack Cade in front of the mob when he exclaimed, "Now is Mortimer lord of London."

Longest Life. The oldest man of whom there is authentic record in England was Thomas Carn. In the parish register of St. Leonard's, Shoreditch, it is recorded that he died in the reign of Elizabeth, aged two hundred and seven. Born in 1381, he lived in the reign of ten Sovereigns, and died in 1588.

Longest Word in the English Language. Is undoubtedly "ultraantidisestablishmentarianism." It was coined by Mr. Gladstone during a political speech at Edinburgh. We are not counting as long words scientific names given to various drugs and preparations, which are not genuine names, but a joining together of three or four separate names. Nor do we accept "Smiles" as the longest word, because there is a mile between the first and last letter!

The longest English surname is said to be Featherstonehaugh.

Lord Mayor's Show. The first London Lord Mayor's Show was that of 1458, when Sir John Norman went in state by water to be sworn in at Westminster.

Lords Cricket Ground. Was named after Thomas Lord, who owned the site of what is now the Holiest of Holies of Cricket, in St. John's Wood. Lord founded the first private cricket club in London in 1780, at Dorset Square. Later, he removed it to Lords.

Lothario, A Gay. This name and description of a seducer of women was first used by Davenport in his "Cruel Brother," written in 1630.

Lotus Eater. One living in luxury and ease. The lotus-eaters in legend were a people who ate of the lotus tree, the effect of which was said to make them forget home and friends and desire only to live in lotus land in idleness. (*See* "Odyssey," xi.)

The classic myth of the lotus is that Lotis, daughter of Neptune, flying from Priapus, was changed into a tree, which was called lotus after her.

Love me Little, Love me Long. Was first used in a play by Christopher Marlowe, who lived 1565-1593.

Low. Used as a component part of a place-named, is derived from the Mediæval English *lowe*, meaning to lie low. Mar-*low* is an example. The word should not be confused with the Anglo-Saxon *hlaw*, which meant the lowing of a cow. The Anglo-Saxon language had no word for the low-lying ground which can be construed into a place-name suffix.

Lucre, Filthy. Unconsciously, the "filthy" is exceedingly apt, for lucre is from the Latin *lucrum*, gain; and is linked with the Greek *leia*, booty. Akin to it are also the Sanscrit *lotra*, stolen goods, and the Hindu *lut*, loot—in other words, filthy lucre is dirty gain.

Lucullus, The Feast of. A luxurious spread of good things. Lucullus (110-57 B.C.) was a wealthy Roman who expended enormous sums on feasting and entertainment. It is said that on one occasion he spent £1,800 on a single meal. The phrase, "Lucullus will sup with Lucullus to-night," to illustrate a gourmand who eats his luxurious meal alone, occurred as follows: Lucullus on one occasion ordered a particularly lavish supper to be prepared, and when asked who were to be his guests, replied, "Lucullus will sup to-night with Lucullus."

Luggage. Some confusion over the origin of this word to describe personal baggage has arisen over a mistake in an Anglo-Saxon word *gelugian*. The word did not exist in that tongue; it was an invented word by Somner. In Mediæval English *luggem* meant to pull (by the hair). In Norwegian *lugg* also meant the hair. Later, in England, *lug* came to mean the ear, and is still used for that article. But the word luggage was not coined because the luggage is pulled about by the ears (handles). Luggage is luggage merely because it is lugged, or pulled.

Lukewarm. Came from *lewk*, Old English word meaning tepid. The qualification "warm" should not be added to it. Luke water is sufficient.

Lumber-room. The word is a corruption of Lombard Room. The Lombards were the first pawn-brokers in England. Their rooms, packed with all manner of goods not wanted by their original owners, were known as the Lombard rooms.

Lunatic, and Lunar (the moon), have always been connected in the minds of man. Lunacy is a form of madness formerly supposed to be affected by the moon. And a lunatic is a sufferer from lunacy. But lunacy, to-day, is classified as madness of all kinds without reference to the moon.

Lydford Law. Lydford, in Devonshire, was a fortified town, in which were held the courts of the Duchy of Cornwall, but so foul were the dungeons in which alleged offenders were held awaiting trial, that the unfortunate persons usually died before they could be heard. Thus, Lydford Law came to mean punish first and try afterwards.

Lynch Law. A lot of nonsense has been written about this phrase. The truth is easily referable. Lynch Law was, originally, the type of law administered by Charles Lynch (1736-96), a Virginian planter (afterwards a Colonel in the army of General Greene), who in the early days of the Revolution, in company with his neighbours, Adams and Calloway, undertook to protect society in the region where he lived, on the Staunton River, by punishing with stripes or banishment such lawlessness as was alleged against persons. The penalty of death was never inflicted by Lynch. Lynch was a Quaker, and the origin of Lynch Law has sometimes been attributed to his brother, John Lynch, founder of Lynchburg, in Virginia.

Thirdly, the idea that the term Lynch Law originated in the action of the Mayor of Galway, James Fitzstephen Lynch, in hanging his son in 1493, is erroneous. But how Lynch Law came to its present meaning of death by the mob, is not clear.

M

Mac. This prefix to Scottish names is Gælic for "son of." Thus, MacGregor is the son of Gregor.

Macabre. The history of the word, though it has been widely discussed and searched, has not been clearly traced. But the ultimate source of the Danse Macabre (Dance of Death) may be the Apocrypha. It was called *Chorea Machabaeorum* in the fifteenth century.

Macadamised Roads. This system of road-making was introduced in 1820 by John Macadam, a Scottish engineer. The method was to crush with a heavy roller successive layers of broken stones. Subsequently an improvement was effected by covering the surface with tar; and roads are now generally tar-macadamised. More lately, concrete roads have become general; but the concrete is still poured on the "macadamised" base.

Macaroni, Macaronis. It may seem strange to have to state that macaroni is not grown. But the writer during the past twelve months has been asked to settle the argument on no fewer than thirty-two occasions. Macaroni is a dough, or paste, prepared from the glutinous granular flour of hard varieties of wheat pressed into long tubes or pipes and afterwards dried in the sun. It is manufactured principally in Italy.

Macaronis was a word given to dandies in London about 1760, when there sprang into being a society called the Macaroni Club. Its members were flashy individuals who had travelled through Italy, and the only good thing they ever did was to introduce macaroni to English tables. These hooligans (there is no less word for them) were the pest of Vauxhall Gardens (q.v.). They have handed down their name to any type of flashy or foppish dress.

It is not the case that the Macaronis wrote and gave their name to Macaronic Verse. This is best described as verse in which foreign words are jumbled together with English words. It was originated by Odaxius of Padua about 1480.

Macdonalds. Parasites. The story goes that Lord Macdonald, son of the Lord of the Isles, raided the mainland with his men who, stripping the captured enemy of their clothes, donned them in the place of their own rags, with the result that they were over-run with parasites.

Mace. The mace owes its name to the days when men went about in armour. The mace was then an iron club, generally with projecting spikes, and was used in war. But now it is a staff of dignity of office, associated with the Speaker of the House of Commons and with Mayors of Corporations.

MacFarlane's Geese. The MacFarlanes lived on the banks of Loch Lomond, but never returned after their house was destroyed. When James VI visited the chieftain, he was entertained at the sight of the gambolling of a flock of geese, but on tasting one for dinner and finding it exceedingly tough, remarked, "MacFarlane's geese like their play better than their meat."

MacGirdle's Mare. Most schoolboys who have a smattering of Greek will know the story of the MacGirdle mare, whose diet was reduced by her owner until it had reached a single straw a day, upon which she died. It is an old Greek joke.

Machiavellian. Unscrupulous methods, evil ways. It came from Niccolo Machiavelli, the Florentine statesman, who was notorious as a underhand schemer and intriguer. He wrote "Il Principe" (1573), which taught that rulers may resort to any kind of treachery to uphold their power; and that a dishonourable act of theirs was as nought against their continuing to hold that power. The doctrine seems to have been adopted in all its Machiavellian ferocity by Adolf Hitler.

Mackay, The Real. The phrase is used to describe excellence. A real Mackay is a genuine or excellent friend. Its origin is the United States boxer of old, Kid McCoy, and it was coined when McCoy was at the head of his profession. To be, in the United States, the best of a kind, was to be a real McCoy. The phrase was coined about 1929.

Mackintosh. The raincoat is so-called after the Scotsman who invented the waterproofing of material.

Macon. A word which had the briefest life of any word coined in the English language. It signified bacon taken from the back of a sheep instead of from the back of a pig. "Macon" remained in the news a few months shortly before the 1939 war. Then it became "dead mutton." There was another Macon, however, of much earlier origin—a poetical, romantic name for Mecca.

MacPhersons. The name means sons of the parson. It arose, according to the fable, in this way: A young brother of the chief of the powerful clan Chattan became a monk, and subsequently Abbot of Kingussie. On the death of the eldest brother, without children, the chieftainship of the clan fell on the abbot. He obtained a dispensation from the Pope, and married. A large number of Kingussies was the result. The people of Inverness-shire, accordingly, called them the Mac-Phersons—the sons of the parson. That is the fable—in case any MacPhersons have not heard it.

Mad as a Hatter. The reproach has nothing whatever to do with hatters. They are as sane as anybody else. It was, originally, "Mad as an atter." Atter was the Anglo-Saxon for a viper or adder; and mad was anciently used in the sense of venomous. Thus, the expression "mad as an atter" meant as venomous as a viper, or an adder.

Mad as a Tup. Dates from 1883. Burne, in "Shropshire Folk-Lore," says, "As Mad as a tup in a halter." A tup is a ram, and since a ram generally runs loose with the ewes, he *would* be mad in a halter. "Notes and Queries" comments: "In Derbyshire . . . there is no commoner saying to express anger shown by anyone than to say that he or she was 'as mad as a tup'."

Maffeking. To celebrate with wild and extravagant rejoicing. During the South African War of 1889-1902, Mafeking was besieged by the Boers from 11th October, 1899, to 18th May, 1900. When the news of the relief of the town was received in London, scenes of uproarous rejoicing broke out. Such scenes have ever since been referred to as mafficking.

Magazine. A curious word this. Its original meaning was the Arabic *makhzan*, a storehouse; and in the English language came to mean a place where arms and munitions were stored by the Army. In 1731 it suddenly came into the language as the description of a periodical, containing stories and articles. The first of these periodicals was "The Gentleman's Magazine," and the name is described in its first number as, "A monthly collection to treasure up as in a magazine, the most remarkable *pieces* on the subjects above-mentioned." (*Note.*—Arms in the military magazine were described as *pieces*.)

Magi. The Magi were at one time a sacred cast of the Medes and Persians, the priests and "Wise Men" reputed to be skilled in Enchantment. It is from them that we get magic and magicians. It will be remembered that the Magi were the Wise Men who came to the Infant Christ.

Magnifique. "*C'est magnifique, mais ce n'est pas la guerre.*" The phrase was the comment of the French General Bosquet to Mr. A. H. Layard on the charge of the Light Brigade. Its English meaning? Well, splendid achievement, but not according to rules; a deed the only justification for which is the success it achieves.

Magnun opus. The chief or principal of one's literary, dramatic, artistic or musical work.

Magpie (in shooting). The score made by a shot striking the outermost division but one of the target. It was given the name "magpie" because it was signalled from the butt by a black-and-white flag."

Mahogany, Under the. Under the table. "I had hoped to see you three gentlemen with your legs under the mahogany in my humble parlour," says Dickens, in "Master Humphrey's Clock." It was also a slang term in the Northern counties for a wife. The origin lies in the wood commonly used in those days to make dining tables. For a man to discuss it over the mahogany meant to discuss it with his wife over the dining table. But the North Country man, with his gift of shortening phrases, fell into saying that he would discuss it "with the mahogany," meaning by that with his wife! The phrase "Under the Mahogany" still maintains its meaning of a friendly gathering round a table in many North Country areas.

Mahomet. "*If the mountain won't come to Mahomet, Mahomet must go to the Mountain.*" The Arabs had asked for miraculous proof, and Mahomet ordered Mount Sagon to come to him. When it did not move he said: "God is merciful. Had the mountain obeyed my words it would have fallen on us to our destruction. I will, therefore, go to the mountain and thank God that he has had mercy on a stiff-necked people." Mahomet, or Mohammed, "the praised one," Founder of Islam, or Mohammedanism, was born at Mecca about 570, and died at Medina in A.D. 632.

Maid of Norway. The name given to Margaret, daughter of Eric the Second and Margaret of Norway. On the death of her maternal grandfather, Alexander III of Scotland, she was acknowledged Queen of Scotland, but she died from sea-sickness on her journey to Scotland. The date was 1285. *See* "Leap Year."

Maiden. A type of guillotine used in Scotland in the sixteenth and seventeenth centuries for execution. It was introduced there by the Regent Morton, some say from Yorkshire (which is doubtful) and others from Italy. It is not true that Morton was himself the first to suffer death by it. He was not executed until more than fifteen years after he had introduced the instrument.

Maiden is also the name given in country areas to the last handful of corn cut by the reapers on a farm. It was the custom to dress this sheaf with ribbons and bring it home with rejoicings.

Maiden Speech. Is the first speech of an M.P. in the House after his election; and Maiden Stakes in racing is an event for horses that have never raced before.

Mailed Fist, The. William II of Germany, when bidding adieu to Prince Henry of Prussia on his start to the East, said: "Should anyone essay to detract from our just rights, then up and at him with your mailed fist." Since that day the phrase has, with aptness, been used to describe military might used aggressively.

Main Chance, The. *An eye to the main chance* means an eye to the money! The phrase is derived from the game of "Hazard." The first throw of the dice is the main (which has to be between four and nine). The player then throws the "chance" which determines the "main."

Mainbrace, To splice the. This order, given in the Navy, means the serving out of an extra tot of rum to those on board. The "splicing" is usually a special occasion, such as a Royal visit. There is actually a mainbrace—the rope by which the main-yard of a ship is kept in position. The origin seems to have been lost in antiquity.

Majesty. The first English monarch to be addressed by the title of Majesty was Henry VIII. Previous to that the monarch was referred to either as the King, or as "Your Highness."

Make a Bad Break, To. An American expression for a blunder. It is derived from the game of billiards.

Make a Pile, To. The origin lies in the Californian gold diggings, where one's fortune, if made at all, was in the nature of a pile of washed gold.

Make and Mend. A naval term, which really means an afternoon off. One of the Navy's traditions is to give a half-holiday one day a week for the purpose of making and repairing clothes. On these occasions the last thing that a man does is to attend to his wardrobe! If he doesn't write a letter home, he may produce his "corker" and seek a well-earned rest. In fact, make and mend has become a synonym for a siesta.

Make Bricks without Straw. The wail of the Children of Israel, after Pharoah had told them that he would no longer give them straw for the making of bricks, but that the tale of bricks must be maintained, was: "How can we make bricks without straw?" They would seem to have solved the problem, however, for it has since been discovered that many of the bricks found in Egyptian excavations were made from mud or clay mixed with papyrus.

Make Things Hum. The origin is the hum of machinery when it is in full speed.

Make Tracks For ——. The phrase means to set out for a destination. It belongs, for its beginnings, to the early settler in America. When he left civilization to seek a living as a pioneer in unknown places, he set out in his covered waggon, and the wheels "made tracks" which showed the direction of his journeying.

Make-up. The "make-up" of a person is his combined habits, temperament and behaviour, all of which go to show his character. It is easy to recognize, therefore, that the word came from the theatre—from the make-up box of the actor, whereby he could turn himself into the appearance of the character he was to portray on the stage.

Make-up (women). A speciality of the female sex in assisting Nature to present an appearance of beauty and elegance in themselves. Since earliest times women have thus adorned themselves. Ancient records of make-up extant come from Egypt, in Cleopatra's time. Egyptian ladies favoured henna for dyeing the finger-nails, palms of the hands and soles of the feet. They also used eyelash black, and painted the underside of the eyes with green.

The Romans were lavish with rouge, chalk to whiten the skin, and a special hair bleach. Britain's ladies developed the habit of make-up when the Crusaders thoughtfully or unthinkingly brought back with them cosmetics and beauty preparations from the harems of the East.

Mall. A place in which the game of pall-mall was played. Malls were mallets with which balls were knocked through iron hoops. *See* "Pall Mall."

Malthusian Doctrine. The doctrine propounded by the Reverend T. R. Malthus (1766-1834, the English Economist. In his "Essay on the Principle of Population," he held that population, unless hindered by positive checks, such as wars, famines, etc., or by preventive checks such as social customs that prevent early marriages, tends to increase at a higher rate than the means of subsistence can be made to increase. He advocated that Society should aim to diminish the sum of vice and misery and check the growth of population by the discouragement of early and improvident marriages, and by the practice of moral self-restraint.

Mamma. A child's first name for its mother. The word is both Greek and Latin for "breast." All animals that are suckled at the breast are mammals. The mamma of mammals is a conglomerate gland secreting milk.

Mammom. "*Ye cannot serve God and Mammon.*" The word comes from the Syriac *mamona,* meaning riches.

Man. Man's body, according to Sir Wilfred Grenfell, is composed of as much fat as would make seven bars of soap; iron enough for one medium-sized nail; sugar enough to fill a shaker; lime enough to whitewash one chicken-house; phosphorus sufficient to make two thousand two hundred match-tips; magnesium enough for one dose of salts; potash sufficient to explode one toy cannon; and enough sulphur to rid one dog of its fleas. At pre-war rates (1938) the whole lot was priced five shillings at current market value.

Heaviest Man in Great Britain was Daniel Lambert, of Leicester, who weighed 52 stone 11 lb. Born at Leicester on 13th March, 1770, he was 5 ft. 11 in. tall.

Man in the Iron Mask, The. No living soul knows the identity of this mysterious individual who, for more than forty years, was held a prisoner by Louis XIV in various prisons, ultimately dying in the Bastille in 1703, with his face still shielded from identification. Among the identities put forward are: A twin brother of Louis; Count Mattioli, who had once refused to give up the fortress of Casale to Louis; Louis, Duc de Vermandois, natural son of Louis XIV; Mattiolis's secretary, Jean de Gonzague. But the most likely was General du Balonde, who had raised the siege of Cuneo against orders.

Man of Desitny. Napoleon. Sir Walter Scott described him as "The Man of Destiny, who had power for a time to bind kings with chains and nobles with fetters of iron."

Man of Kent. A man born in the county of Kent, but east of the Medway, as distinct from a Kentish man, born west of the Medway.

Man of Ross. This name was given to John Kyrle, of Ross, Herefordshire, because of the improvements he effected in his native town, in spite of the fact that there was little money to spend on them. Pope wrote of him: "Richer than miser, nobler than King or king-polluted lord." The Kyrle Society, which aims at the improvement of homes for the poorer people, is named after the Man of Ross.

Man-o'-Straw. Without substance, having nothing to lose. Its original meaning was slightly variant. The term was derived from men who hung round the Law Courts (then at Westminster) and who were ready to give any evidence required, for a bribe. They were identified by displaying a wisp of straw in their shoes. When a witness was required to swear to anything wanted by Counsel, he sent a clerk of look for a "man of straw," knowing that there would be no prosecutions, since the man had no money with which to pay any damages.

Man-o'-War. Everyone knows, of course, that this is a term for a warship, of whatever calibre. But what the writer has never been able to discover, and what intrigues him, and he is sure others, is why we call warships "men-o'-war," and then refer to them as "she"?

Mandarin. The remarkable thing about this word is that it is universally believed to be essentially Chinese. It is nothing of the kind. The word was the Portuguese *mandar*, to command. It was applied by early Portuguese settlers of Macao to Chinese officials of that colony, and became an European designation for a Chinaman of high rank.

Mandrake. Of all the plants of the earth the mandrake is surely the plant to which is attached the greatest superstition. Chief among them is that it promotes fecundity in woman. (Read the story of Rachel and Leah, *Gen.*, 30.) Another superstition was that a small dose made a person vain of his beauty, but a large dose induced madness.

Figures of human likeness cut out from the root were believed, in ancient days, to possess a charm and virtues. It was held that the mandrake could not be dragged from the ground without fatal effects to the person uprooting them; and it was at one time the custom to fix a cord round the root and attach the other end round the neck of a starved dog. The dog being urged forward by the sight of food, pulled out the mandrake but throttled itself in the doing. Newton, in his "Herball to the Bible," states that the mandrake "is supposed to be a creature having life, engendered under the earth of the seed of some dead person put to death for murder"; and the plant was supposed to scream on being uprooted.

The name is derived from man (due to the seeming appearance of a human form of the roots) and drake. Why drake is not apparent.

Manna. One of the mysteries of the ages is the composition of the manna which the Children of Israel found each morning outside their tents, except on the Sabbath. The name is a corruption of the Hebrew *man-hu*, "What is this?" Attempts have been made over the centuries to identify various substances as the manna from Heaven, but without success. All that can be said of it is that it resembled nothing so much as hailstones, that it melted with the heat of the sun and then bred maggots.

Mansion. In its original Latin, *mansio*, from *Manere*, to remain, was a tarrying-place, or resting-place, more often than not applied to a tent pitched in the desert. It is in this sense, beyond doubt, that Christ spoke of, "In My Father's house are many mansions" (i.e., resting-places). Because of the "tarrying" the word has been interpreted, also, as meaning a day's journey. Subsequently, it became the name given to a roadside house for the accommodation of travellers. It is probably from these houses, which grew into large buildings, that the original mansion became prostituted to meaning a palace of a building.

Mantelpiece. Our present mantelpiece with its ornate carving and, in the cases of Adams' creations, its value, came to a similar glory with mansion, in which the best mantelpieces are built. It was, however, originally a shelf with pegs above a fireplace on which wet mantles, or other garments, were hung to dry.

Manure. A contraction of the Old French *manœuvrer*, to work with the hands, to cultivate with manual labour, develop with culture. It was, of course, an easy step to arrive at the improving of the land by adding some substance.

Maps. The first people to invent and use maps were probably the Ancient Egyptians. In the museum of antiquities, at Turin, Italy, are several Egyptian papyrus maps more than three thousand years old. They are regional maps only. The first attempt at a map of the world, so far as is known, dates from the sixth century B.C. It is believed to have been prepared by Anaximander of Miletus. His map makes the Aegian Sea the centre of a circular world, the extremities of which were the Caspian Sea in the East, and the Cassiterides or Tin Islands (presumably the Scilly Isles) in the West.

What are claimed to be the oldest maps in the world date from about 2300 B.C. They were said to have been made in Babylonia, and are on clay tablets, circular in shape. One specimen, defining Lower Babylonia, is in the British Museum in London. Without doubt the most famous mapmaker in history was Ptolemy, the Greek astronomer of the second century A.D. He was not accurate; for instance, he drew Albion (Britain) practically upside down! But he got the bearings correctly!

Margate. Not the least of the troubles facing the earnest delver into name-lore is the necessity for persuading the public from a belief in the host of fanciful "explanations" of names and places written by amateur philologists. One such instance is in connection with Margate. Here is the "origin" of Margate by one of the species: "Margate is the gate of the Thames Estuary; and the Latin name for the sea was *mare*—thus Margate, the sea gate."

Why this elucidator should go to Latin for his search, when there is a perfectly good Saxon word close to his hand, is a mystery to the writer. In the thirteenth century, Margate appears in documents as Meregate or Mergate. Now the Anglo-Saxon *mere* was a pool (we still call a deep, tree-lined, pool a mere), and the Anglo-Saxon *geat* was a road, and Margate was the road by the mere, or pool. That the pool is no longer there in evidence, having long been filled in, does not excuse the amateur philologist by-passing the Anglo-Saxon for Latin root.

Marigold. The pretty yellow flower was at one time dedicated to the Virgin Mary, and windows having depicted in them the flower may frequently be seen in Lady Chapels.

Mariner's Compass. The compass as a guide to sailors was known to, and used by, the Chinese as far back as 2364 B.C. But its first *recorded* use in sea travel was made by a Chinese writer in about 750 B.C. It was brought to Europe by Marco Polo.

Marines. "*Tell it to the Marines.*" The phrase never fails to infuriate any Marines hearing it. But they can take comfort in the news that the phrase does not mean that the Marines are liars. The story of the saying is that during a dinner the King, on being told by a naval officer that he had seen flying fish, remarked, "Tell that to my Marines." An officer of the Marines present took umbrage at the remark. The King, surprised (so the story goes), apologized for an offence unwittingly given, and explained that what he meant was that his Marines had travelled in every part of the world, and if they accepted the story, so would he.

Mark, Up to the. The mark in this sense is the standard fixed by the Assay Office for gold and silver articles. To be not up to the mark means not up to standard, unwell.

Marmalade. There is a strange story of the "origin" of marmalade which has been going round for several years. According to this the preserve was first heard of in Scotland, where the cook of a noble house served some orange jam to guests. One of them, asked what he thought of it, replied, "Mair, ma Lady" (more, my lady); and from this the jam came to be called marmalade.

As an instance of guessing at the origin of words, this will take some beating. There is no mystery about marmalade. The Portuguese word for quince is *marmelo*. The jam which the

Portuguese housewives made from the quince fruit was termed *marmelada*. Marmalade is, properly, jam made from quinces. The marmalade we know is merely orange jam.

Maroon, To. To maroon a person is to put him alone on an inhospitable shore. It is said by some to have come from the Spanish word *Cimaroon*, meaning wild or unruly. It is doubtful how this word came to be applied to castaways, for the Spanish word does not concern itself with any such habit, except in the wild, adjectival, sense. On the other hand, the name Maroon, as a noun, is applied to the descendants of negroes in South America and the West Indies. These ran away from their slave masters and found refuge between Dutch and French Guiana in the neighbourhood of the *Marony* river. It is claimed by some sources that the term Maroons was derived from the name of the river. There is no direct evidence to confirm either source, but the latter seems the more probable.

Marquis of Granby. This name on public-house signs is in tribute to John Manners, Marquis of Granby, eldest son of the Duke of Rutland. Second in command of the British forces at the Battle of Minden, during the Seven Years' War in Germany, he was later appointed Commander-in-Chief of the British Army. He was greatly beloved by the men.

Marriage is a Lottery. Smiles in "Thrift" wrote in 1875: "The maxim is current that 'marriage is a lottery'."

Marriage knot. In the English marriage service the knot is tied invisibly, and the phrase has no significance other than metaphor. But in the Hindu marriage service the bridegroom ties a ribbon in a knot on the bride's neck. Before the knot is thus tied the father of the bride may refuse his consent, but not afterwards.

The Parsees bind the hand of the bridegroom with a seven-fold knot. The Carthaginians tied the thumbs of the couple with leather. The Roman custom was for the bridegroom to *loosen* the knot on the bride's girdle. Even in Britain to-day, a gipsy wedding is accompanied with the tying together of the hands of the couple.

Married at Finglesham Church, To be. Finglesham is in Kent, and the point of the saying was that there was no church at Finglesham, but there was a chalkpit celebrated for casual amours. The sense of the sentence is thus made plain.

Married Women. The practice of a married woman taking the surname of her husband originated in Rome, but with a slight difference to our present form. Supposing that Julia married Cicero, her married name would have been Julia *of* Cicero. To-day, the "of" has been dropped; she would under our rule be Julia Cicero.

Marry in Haste. . . . This phrase first appeared in Painter's "Palace of Pleasure" (1652): ". . . . leaste in making hasyte choice, leasure for repentaucnce shuld folow."

Marshalsea Prison. Was thus called because its governor was a Knight Marshal, that is, an official of the Royal Household. The prison stood in Southwark, London, and was used to confine debtors who, through non-payment, had committed contempt of court, and also Admiralty prisoners. Life in the Marshalsea is described in Dickens's "Little Dorrit." The prison was pulled down in 1849.

Martello Towers. The amateur etymologist has been very busy on these towers, a few of which still linger at various spots along our south coast. Writing in the correspondence column of a Sunday newspaper a year or two ago, he announced that the towers derived their name from Martello, a Corsican engineer, "the first inventor." Another proclaimed that the reason for the "Martello" was the striking by a sentry of a bell with a *martel* (hammer) as often as he discerned a pirate ship at sea.

The simple truth of the matter is that the name is a corruption of Mortella, from Cape Mortella where was a tower which gave British ships and troops much trouble to capture it. And, remembering this, the Government thought it might give our enemies similar trouble if ever they tried a landing. So they scattered them round vulnerable places. So much for the fancies of the amateur.

Martin, St. The patron saint of innkeepers, drunkards and beggars. (*See* "All my Eye and Betty Martin.")

St. Martin's Beads. Counterfeit; the first "Brummagem" jewellery. The jewellery had nothing really to do with the saint, but crept in because sale of counterfeit gems was carried on by cheap-jacks, or hucksters, on the site of the old collegiate church of St. Martin's le Grand, which had been demolished at the Dissolution.

Martinet. The name applied to a strict disciplinarian. It is said to be so-called from General Martinet, who reformed the French infantry in the reign of Louis XIX, and was killed at the Siege of Doesbourg in 1672. If this is so, it is strange that there is no French use of the word in a strict disciplinarian sense.

On the other hand, a martinet is also the name given to a Cat o' Nine Tails, dating back to Old French; and this seems a more likely origin of a word meaning discipline. The writer cannot connect the latter "martinet" with the old military engine of the Middle Ages.

Marylebone. This name for a London area is a corruption, not of St. Mary the Good, as is so often stated, but of St. Mary of the Bourn—the parish church of St. Mary beside the bourn, or stream, which descended from Kilburn to Tyburn. The "burn" at the end of both these names also means "bourn," a stream.

Masher. A lady-killer. A suggested origin is that the description arose from the *machinaw*, an embroidered blanket worn by the North American Indians. A male, thus arrayed in extravagant colours, it is said, captured the admiration of the squaws. If this were correct, it is strange that the word should have been coined not in America, but in England, where a *machinaw* is hardly likely to have been seen. The likely derivation is that it is a corruption of the Romany (gipsy) word *masha*, a fascinator.

Mason and Dixon's Line. This is an American expression for the old-time boundary line between the slave states and free states. It was fixed by Charles Mason and Jeremiah Dixon, English surveyors, and lies in 39 deg., 43 ft. 26 in. North latitude. The states on the one side became nicknamed Dixie's Land, and it is to these that the American songs refer, but only in name!

Mast, Before the. To serve before the mast. A common or ordinary seaman, because in the days of sail the seamen's quarters were in the forepart of the ship. The phrase is often used to refer to beginning at the bottom rung of the ladder.

Masterly Inactivity. The phrase was used by Sir James Mackintosh in his "Vendicioe Gallicioe," where he states: "The Commons, faithful to their system, remained in a wise and masterly inactivity."

Maudlin. Snivelling, stupidly sentimental. The word is a corruption of Mary Magdalen, from the fact that painters of old invariably represented the Magdalen with eyes swollen as the result of penetential tears.

Maundy Thursday. Christ at the Last Supper on the day before the Crucifixion, washed his disciple's feet. He also enjoined them: "A new commandment I give unto you, that ye love one another." The first words of his injunction, in Latin, are, *Mandatum novum.* The French form of Mandatum is *maunde*. Now all this became mixed with the Saxon word *maund*, which was the name applied to an alms basket in which the lady of the manor carried bread for distribution to the poor.

In monasteries it was the custom, on the day before Good Friday, for monks to wash the feet of as many poor persons as there were monks in the monastery; and in England the King, as a token of Royal humility, did the same. This Royal humility was retained up to the reign of James II. It is now replaced by the King's Maundy Money, distributed by the Royal Almoner to as many poor people as the Sovereign is years old.

Mausoleum. This name, now given to any large and stately tomb, rightly belongs to the tomb of Mausolus, a large and magnificent edifice adorned with sculpture, and built at the order of his Queen, Artemisia. Erected at Halicarnassus about 350 B.C., it is ranked as one of the seven wonders of the world. Parts of the sepulchre can be seen in the British Museum.

Mavournin. In Irish, "my darling" (*mo mhurnin*). Thus, the words of the popular song, "Kathleen Mavournin," are "Kathleen, my Darling."

awkin. A bedraggled, untidy erson. It is a slight corruption of Malkin, used in the thirteenth century as a disparaging term for a woman or girl, especially a slut or slattern, or a maid-servant. ". . . And malkyn, with a dystaf in her hand."—*Chaucer*.

May. Gardeners will be interested in the origin of the name of this gardening month. The budding of plants at this time of the year led to the Romans calling it *magius*, which was later shortened to *Maius*, from the Sanscrit *mah*, to grow. Later still, however, it was held sacred to *Maia*, mother of Mercury, and sacrifices were offered on the first day of the month.

May Day. May Day celebrations, a feature of the English countryside, go back to the days of ancient Rome, when Roman youths went out into the fields and spent the Calends of May dancing and singing in honour of Flora, Goddess of fruits and flowers.

Olaus Magnus wrote: "After their long Winter, from the beginning of October to the end of April, the northern nations have the custom to welcome the returning splendour of the sun with dancing, and mutually to feast each other, rejoicing that a better season for fishing and hunting hath approached."

In honour of May Day, the Goths and Southern Swedes held a mock battle between Summer and Winter. And until quite recently the battle was retained in the Isle of Man.

In England, Maypole dancing was the main celebration, though Chaucer records that there was a time when the custom going May-ing was observed by noble and royal personages. In his "Court of Love" he states: "Early on May Day fourth goth al the Court, both most and lest, to fetche the flouris fresh and braunch, and blome."

There was another side of May Day in these old times. Stubbes, in his "Anatomy of Abuses" (1583), refers to "men, women and children, olde and young, spending the night in woods and groves on the hills, and returning next morning, bringing with them birch bowes and braunches of trees to deck their assemblies withal. I have heard it credibly reported," he adds, "by men of great gravitie, credite and reputation, that of fortie, three score or a hundred maides goying to the woode ouer night, there have scarcely the thirde parte of them returned home againe undefiled."

The May Queen revels and dancing are all that remain to us of the old May Day revelry, and even these have died away except in scattered places. Instead, the day is now celebrated as a Labour festival.

Mayfair. Odd though it may seem to-day, this ultra-fashionable London area came to be so-called because Edward III ordered that each May there should be held at that spot a six days' fair in aid of the Leper Hospital of St. James' the Less. The hospital occupied the site on which St. James's Palace now stands.

Mealy-mouthed. Comes from the Greek *melimuthus*, honey-speech. On other words—sweetness in speech in order to avoid giving offence, or in order to obtain a favour.

Meander. To follow a winding course. Now used as a verb, it comes from *Maeander*, the winding river of Phrygia.

Meat. *One Man's Meat is another Man's Poison.* Originally from *Lucretius* iv, 638: "Iantaque in his rebus distantia, differitasque est, Ut quod aliis cibus est, aliis fuat acre venenum."

Medals. There is no known origin of the award of medals for deeds of distinction. The Chinese are said to have used military medals during the Han Dynasty (first century A.D.). But, so far as the Western part of the world is concerned, it was not until the sixteenth century that the custom of wearing medals as decorations of honour became recognized. Probably, the first medals bestowed as a reward for military services rendered to the Crown were the "Armada" medals of Queen Elizabeth (1588-89). There were two of them.

Mediterranean. The name means the sea in the middle of the earth, from the Latin *medius*, middle, *terra*, land. The earth must be taken to mean the Roman earth.

Melancholy. Mental depression, lack of cheerfulness, from the Greek *melas chole*. The Greeks put the depression down to an excess of black bile.

Melodrama. In its present form, melodrama has come to a marked corruption. The word is derived from the Greek *melos*, a song, and *drama*, a play; and melodrama was originally a play in which music was used, but was of minor importance. The two earliest melodramas in the English language were "Deaf and Dumb" (1801) and "A Tale of Mystery" (1802). The late Wilson Barrett was probably the first of Britain's great melodrama actors.

Menial. An inferior servant, from Old French for household, retinue, whence the Shakespearean *meiny* (*Lear* ii, 4) and our present derivative, menial.

Mentor. An inexperienced person's guide. A guide, philosopher and friend. It is so-called from Mentor, the friend and counsellor of Ulysses.

Mercenaries. Back in the times of the Greeks, and probably much earlier, there were men who sold their services as soldiers. The Romans gave them the name mercenaries, from *mercenarius*, meaning fighting men who, although declaring themselves "the friends of God and enemies of all the world," sold themselves to the highest bidder and accepted *merces* (pay) for their services. By the Greeks they were termed *Xenoi*, foreigners.

Mercer. Was in older days what we now call a draper. The name came from his wares or merchandise, called in Latin *merx* (*mercis*).

Mercerise. Has nothing to do with the term mercer. It was the name given in 1850 to the new way of treating textiles, invented and patented by John Mercer, an Accrington dyer.

Mere, Moor. Frequently found as component parts of place-names. The words mean a lake, or a marsh, of Anglo-Saxon times. Winder-mere, Blackmore are examples.

Merlin Chair. You may not recognize the self-propelled "Bath" chair under this name; but it was at first called by the name from J. J. Merlin, who invented it. It is not so modern as may be supposed. Merlin died in 1803.

Merry. A word of warning to those whose love is for old books. The word merry very frequently in such books has a meaning at variance with that given it to-day. Its old sense was cheerful, happy, not jollily happy. An instance is in the old Christmas morning greeting, "God Rest your Merry Gentlemen," in which the comma is invariably inserted after the word "you." This is incorrect. The proper parsing of the line is, "God rest you merry, gentlemen." In other words, "Gentlemen, God rest (keep) you happy."

Merry Andrew. The usual explanation of the term Merry Andrew is that it was derived from Andrew Borde (died 1549), physician to Henry VIII, who added facetiousness to his healing, and whose quips were a by-word. It is a very doubtful origin. Andrew was the stock name for a man-servant, as Abigail was for a female servant; and it should be borne in mind that Abigail figured as a waiting-woman in Beaumont and Fletchers' "Scornful Lady." The cognomen Merry Andrew came later to be applied to the assistant to a conjuror, who talked in order to distract the attention of the audience from the conjuror's hands!

Mesmerism. So-called after Franz Anton Mesmer (1733-1815), an Austrian doctor, who introduced into Paris a theory of animal magnetism as a cure. He began by stroking his patients with magnets, but later, becoming convinced that the power lay not in the magnets but in himself; he abandoned the magnets and introduced the system of imposing his will on the patient and projecting him into a trance. Dr. Brewer asserts that mesmerism has long since fallen into disuse. On the contrary, it is now being used to a greater extent by medical men of reputation for treatment in certain mental cases.

Mess. Much has been written of the origin of this term for the meal gathering of officers in the Army or Navy. By some it has been stated that the word comes from the Italian *messa*, a meal. Others give it as dating to the Biblical "mess of potage." A tracing of language and customs, however, would seem to make it clear that it is derived from two sources: First from the Latin *mensa*, a table, and secondly from the French *mets*, meat, allied to the Anglo-Norman custom of setting a dish of meat for *four* people at each table, or in front of each four people at a large table. Thus, four became synonymous with mess. Shakespeare speaks of the "mess of sons" (four) of Henry VI; and in "Love's Labour Lost" there appears, "You three fools lacked one . . . to make up a mess." It is doubtful whether the phrase, "to make a mess of things," has any connection with the mess of the table.

Metal Horse Shoes. These shoes for the hooves of horses were first mentioned in the second century before Christ. They were not common until the fifth century A.D., but became in regular use in the Middle Ages. Before that, shoes of straw or material had been used to protect horses' hooves against crumbling.

Methodists. The name given, in 1729, to the brothers Wesley and their religious supporters. It is said to have been the idea of a student of Christchurch, Oxford, because of the methodical way in which the Wesleys observed their principles.

Primitive Methodists were seccessionists from the Methodists, led by Hugh Bourne in 1810. "Primitive" because they reverted to the original Wesley teachings.

Methuselah. "*As old as Methuselah.*" Those who commonly use the phrase may be interested in knowing exactly how old Methuselah was. He died at the ripe old age of nine hundred and sixty-nine.

Meum and Teum. A Latin phrase, meaning "mine and thine." To say that a man does not know the meaning of meum and teum, is to accuse him of taking what was not his—in other words, to call him a thief.

Mews. A place where horses were stabled, when London had horse vehicles, of course. Yes; but that was a corruption of its real meaning. A "Mew" was a cage or enclosure, from the Old French *meute*, a pack. It meant, also, in the same language, to moult, or change, as hawks, and was sometimes spelt in this sense *mue*. A Mews was thus, originally, a place of confinement for hawks, or falcons, and in which they were kept confined during their moulting. Possibly, the earliest of its spellings was the Low Latin *muta*, a disease with moulting. From a stable for hawks, or falcons, its transformation to a stable for horses, when hawks were no longer there, was easy.

Michaelmas Day. The feast of St. Michael and All Angels, and one of the quarter and rent days. It is also the day when, in Britain, Justices of the Peace are appointed.

Michaelmas Goose. The custom of eating a goose at Michaelmas is said to have originated as follows: Queen Elizabeth, on her way to Tilbury Fort in 1588, dined at the house of Sir Neville Umfreyville. Goose was served. As the dinner ended, she gave the toast: "Death to the Spanish Armada." Almost at once a messenger arrived with the news that the Armada had been destroyed by a storm. The Queen at once gave a second toast and added: "Henceforth shall a goose commemorate this great victory." Unfortunately for the story, the custom of eating a goose at Michaelmas was quite well-known ten years earlier!

Mickey Mouse. A popular little figure in cinema film cartoons, invented and drawn by Walt Disney.

But also the nickname given by the R.A.F. for the bomb-dropping mechanism of a bombing plane.

Middle Ages. The period from the fall of the Roman Empire, about 476, to the capture of Constantinople by the Turks in 1453. The earlier part of the period, up to 1200, is sometimes referred to as the Dark Ages.

Midwife. Not from the Mediæval English *medewife*, meaning *mede*, reward, and wife; but from the Anglo-Saxon *mid*, with, and *wife*, woman—the nurse who is *with* the mother in her labour.

Milliner. The name given to a designer and maker of women's hats is a corruption of Milaner, after the city of Milan, in Italy, which at one time set the fashion throughout Europe for elegance in dress. The fashions of the Milaner was not then confined to women or hats. In "A Winter's Tale," Sheakespeare makes a character say, "No milliner can fit *his* customers with *gloves*."

Mind your P's and Q's. There are two explanations of this phrase. (1) The letters denote pints and quarts "chalked up" on the slate at country ale-houses. When a customer's account was getting too large for the innkeeper's liking, he chided the customer with: "Mind your p's and q's." (2) Refers to the Louis XIV period of huge wigs and deep curtseys. The formal curtseys required a "step" with the feet and a deep, low bend of the body in the course of which the wig might become deranged. French dancing masters, therefore, cautioned their Court pupils with "Mind your Pieds (feet) and Queues (wigs)."

Miniature. In modern usage is descriptive of a greatly reduced scale, style or form. But it was originally *miniatori*, name given by the monks to the illuminated rubrics they produced, and in which the head of the Madonna formed the initial letter. The paint used by the monks for this illumination was made out of *minium*, or red lead.

Mint. *See* " Money."

Miser. Possibly the greatest family of misers Britain has ever had was that of the Elwes. Sir Harvey Elwes died worth £250,000. He had never been known to spend more than just over £100 a year. His sister-in-law inherited £100,000—and starved herself to death trying to double it. Her son, an M.P. and a brewer on a large scale, never bought new clothes, never had his shoes cleaned, and almost starved *himself* to death, as well. A coincidence is that William Jennings, contemporary with Sir Harvey Elwes, and who lived near him, was also a miser of renown, and left £200,000.

Misfortunes Never Come Singly. The origin of this is *King* Alisaunder : " Men tellen in olde mone (remembrance), the qued commth nowher alone."

Mistletoe. The plant we call mistletoe was used in the religious services of the Ancients, particularly the Greeks. Virgil compares the golden bough in Infernis to the mistletoe. The Saxon *mis-el-tu* is a compound of three Sanscrit words, i.e., *Mas vishnu* (the Messiah), *tal;* a pit (metaphorically the womb), and *tu*, a movement to or from. The ivy and mistletoe, being evergreens, denote the everlasting life through faith in the promised Messiah. Williams maintains that the " Guidhel Mistletoe," a magical shrub, appears to be the forbidden tree in the middle of the trees of Eden ; for in the Edda the mistletoe is said to be Balder's death, who yet perished through blindness and a woman.

Mistletoe was regarded by the Druits as sacred because not only its flowers, but its leaves also, grow in clusters of three united to one stock. It is, however, the one evergreen never included in Church decorations.

Kissing under the Mistletoe. Is an English Christmastide custom dating back to the early seventeenth century. Its original ceremony, however, was that each time a man kissed a girl under the mistletoe he plucked a berry, and there could be no more kissing when the last of the berries had gone.

The association of mistletoe with kissing came about in this way. It is a story from Greek mythology. Balder, one of the Gods, was the son of Odin. His mother, Freya, loved her son so much that she persuaded all things living to protect him. Unfortunately, she forgot mistletoe, with the result that Loki, God of Evil, slew Balder with a spear made of mistletoe wood. The other Gods restored Balder to life, and mistletoe promised that it would do no more harm to their favourite, provided it was kept from touching the earth. The Gods accordingly placed mistletoe in the keeping of Freya, the Goddess of Love, hence its association with kissing. Incidentally, the pledge that mistletoe should not touch the earth rules to-day—the plant is a parasite growing on other trees.

See " Thirteen," " Unlucky."

Mistletoe Bough, The. Everyone knows the sad ditty, immortalized in song, of the bride who, playing at hide-and-seek on her wedding day, hid in an old oak chest, the lid of which closed on her with a spring lock, and in which her skeleton was found many years afterwards.

The usual identification is that she was the daughter of a Lord Lovel. There are, however, other claimants. One is that of Collet in his " Relics of Literature," another is included in the " Causes Celebres." A third states that the tragedy took place of Marwell Old Hall, the residence, in turn, of the Seymour and Dacre families. Of this hall, it is stated that " the very chest became the property of the Rev. J. Haygarth, a rector of Upham."

But, before all of them, came Rogers in " Italy," where the lady is Ginevra, only child of Orsini, and the bridegroom Francesco Doria, her playmate from childhood. The chest is circumspectically described as a heirloom richly carved by Antony of Trent, with scripture stories from the life of Christ. " After the tragedy, it is added, Orsini went mad and spent his life in quest of his daughter, while Francesco threw away his life in battle with the Turks."

We fear that the Old Oak Chest is mythical.

Strangely enough, the myth was enacted in real life in May, 1944, when two children were found suffocated in the tool locker, or chest, of a Southern Railway delivery van at Leicester Station. They had stepped into the locker in play—it measured 29½ in. by 20 in. by 13 in.—the lid had closed down on them, and the fastening hasp in front had locked. The boys had been missing for eight days when they were discovered.

Mob. From the Latin *mobile vulgus*, the vulgar (or fickle) crowd. It came into use in this country during the reign of Charles II. North, in an article at the time, refers to the fact that the rabble had changed now its name to mob.

Mob-Cap. Has nothing to do with the fickle crowd or mob. It belongs to Queen Mab of the Fairies, once a dainty apparition in gossamer wings, but later, in the sixteenth century, to be reduced to a slattern (you will remember Shakespeare's " mobled queen, *Hamlet* ii, 2), and to a disorderly dress. It is from the latter, dishevelment, that the mob-cap belongs.

Moke. Slang name for a donkey or ass. The word was first used in this connection in 1848. But forty years or more before that date *moxio* was the gipsy name for a donkey.

Mole, Blind as a. *See* " Blind."

Molly-coddle. The description was, in the early eighteenth century, *Miss Molly* for the type of person we now call a molly - coddle, an effeminate fellow. It would seem to contain a punning allusion to the Latin *mollis*, soft.

Monastery. The word comes from the Greek *monos*, alone ; whereas convent, the feminine correlative, means in the Latin *convenire*, to come together, a curious mixture of diverse meanings for the Roman Catholic faith.

Money. The name for our coinage is derived from the Latin *moneta*. The word is more plainly recognizable in our word used to describe financial transactions—moneta-ry. Moneta was the surname of Juno, in whose temple, erected to her in Rome by either Lucius Furius or Camillus, the first Roman coins were minted.

Money makes money. An allusion to usury interest, which dates back even to Hebrew Biblical days.

Monger. Though, to-day, the word is qualified by various adjectives, such as " coster," " iron," and others, its meaning has remained very much the same. The word is derived from the Mediæval English *mong*, a mixture, an association, and the Anglo-Saxon *mangere*, one who trades. Thus a monger in those days—and even in Shakespeare's day—was one who traded, or sold, a mixture of commodities, or commodities in association with one another.

Costermonger is properly one who sells costards, the apple introduced into this country by the Dutch in 1736.

Monkey. It must be a moot point whether the word monkey was derived from a little old Italian woman, the name for which was *monicchio* (diminutive of *monna*, a nickname for an old woman) or whether the little old Italian woman was so-named after the monkey !

Monmouthshire. The writer has over a period of years been asked many hundreds of times whether Monmouthshire is in England or Wales. He is obliged to the Librarian of Newport, Mon., an authority on the county's history, for the following authentic explanation of the position of the county.

The facts are as follows: Up to the time of Henry VIII (1509-1547), Monmouthshire was under the rule of the Lord Marchers. Owing to their misrule, Henry decided to subdue them, confiscate their lands and rights, and bring Monmouthshire within the English realm. This transference was further strengthened by Acts of Elizabeth and subsequent rulers, and stands good to-day. There are certain recent changes, however, bringing Monmouthshire within the law as applying to Wales—for the Church, Education, Public Health and Licensing Laws. With regard to Law itself, Monmouthshire is still retained in the Oxford Circuit, and the Assizes are held at Newport. Present-day Acts and Charters definitely refer to "Wales and Monmouthshire." This in itself is confirmation that Monmouthshire is still officially not included in Wales. Therefore, Newport being in Monmouthshire, and Monmouthshire, by law, still being an English county, Newport is in England. Historians would say that ethnographically Monmouthshire is in Wales, but ethnologically in England.

Monroe Doctrine. The doctrine, in American politics, of non-intervention of European Powers in matters relating to the American continent. It received its name from statements contained in President Monroe's annual message to Congress in December, 1823, at the period of a suspected concert of the powers in the Holy Alliance to interfere in Spanish America on behalf of Spain. It also laid down that the United States were never to entangle themselves in the broils of the Old World. It has, of course, been abrogated by the American participation in the European War of 1914-18, and also in her entry into the World War of 1939- But its terms were raised as late as 1940 as an argument why the U.S.A. should take no part in the war.

Monument, The. The two hundred and two feet high column near the north end of London Bridge, was built by Sir Christopher Wren to commemorate the great London Fire in 1666. Its position is close to where the Great Fire started.

Moon, The Man in the. Born of a fancied resemblance of a man walking with a dog, and with a bush near him. Also, sometimes, of a human face seen in the disc of the full moon. The origin of the fable is from *Numbers* xv, 32-36. In the prologue to "A Midsummer Night's Dream," Shakespeare says, "This man, with lantern, dog and bush of thorns, presenteth moonshine."

Moonrakers, The Wiltshire. The story goes that in the old smuggling days, the inhabitants of a Wiltshire village, seeing the Revenue men approaching, sank their smuggled whisky in the pond on the village green, and at once commenced to rake in the water with long hay-rakes. Asked by the Revenue men what they were doing, they explained, pointing to the reflection of the moon in the water, that they were trying to rake the great big cheese out of the water. The story, of course, ends with the announcement that on the Revenue men going away laughing, the "moonrakers" recovered their whisky unmolested. The writer has been shown no fewer than a dozen pools where the incident "authentically" occurred.

Moot. The Anglo-Saxon assembly of townspeople, of freemen in a township. The Anglo-Saxon parliament was the *wirena-gemot*, meeting of the witty—wise, not humorous. The idea of the meeting passed into that of litigation and argument, and so we came to use the word in the sense of a moot point—that is, a point for argument. An attempt is being made (1944) to raise the old idea of the moot as a People's Parliament nationally, in the form of an ordered society of discussion groups at which votes are taken on questions of local or national moment, after debate. A start has been made in the Esher district of Surrey, where are the headquarters of the new People's Moot.

Mop Fair. The usual derivation of mop given is from the Latin *mappa*, a towel, and Old French *mappe*, a napkin. It is with some misgiving that the writer publishes the traditional etymology. The napkin is hardly a mop, and the Old French *mappe* is a rare word, and he sees no reason why we should go to a foreign language to name so elementary an implement.

However, the Mop Fair was a statute fair for the hiring of agricultural workers. Carters fastened a piece of whipcord to their hats to show that they were carters seeking a master, shepherds a tuft of wool, and women servants a small *mop*. When hired for the coming year, a cockade or ribbons were worns. The day was regarded as a holiday by masters and servants alike. As recently as 1912 these hiring fairs were still existing in parts of Lincolnshire.

Moratorium. From the Latin *morari*, to delay. It is a legal permission to delay payment of an account. It was adopted, nationally, for the first time in 1891, in South America, during the panic which resulted from the default, to the tune of many millions of pounds of the Baring Brothers. It was also invoked during the 1914-18 war and after the end of the war, when Germany pleaded inability to pay the reparations imposed on her under the Versailles Treaty.

More Haste, Less Speed. Udall's translation of Erasmus's "Apophthegmata" (Sayings of the Ancients) transcribes him: "Soche persones as to make moste hast in the beginning, haue commonly (accordyng to our Englishe prouerbe) worst spede towards the endyng."

More Kicks than Halfpence. Older readers will remember the old hurdy-gurdys which toured the streets playing, and with a monkey attired in a red coat on the top to solicit the alms. If trade was not good in the way of contributions for the music supplied, the monkey generally got a kick or two. The "organist" got the half-pennies. It is from this that the phrase, "More kicks than halfpence," comes. It was referred to sometimes as "monkey's allowance."

Morganatic Marriage. Is one between a Royal person and a woman of less station, in which the wife does not acquire her husband's rank, and neither she, nor any of her issue, have any claim to his title or inheritance. George, Duke of Cambridge (1819-1904), cousin of Queen Victoria and uncle of Queen Mary, married morganatically in 1840. His children took the surname Fitz-George. It may be recalled that King Edward VIII (now Duke of Windsor) asked permission to wed Mrs. Simpson morganatically; but the Prime Minister, Mr. Baldwin, said that this would not be acceptable. *See* "Left-hand marriages."

Morgue. How the name morgue came to be given to the death-house where corpses are placed awaiting identification is a mystery. There is no known origin connecting the name to the duty. It is first mentioned in this connection in Paris. Originally, the word was used to describe the inner wicket-gate of a prison where the identification marks of new arrivals were taken before their cells were assigned to them. Dr. Brewer suggests that the derivation may be from the genuine word *morgue*, which meant a stately, or haughty, mein. It seems hardly likely of a prisoner at the gate of a prison.

Morris Dances. Are not, as seems widely believed, typical English folk dances. They were the ancient military dances of the *Moriscoes*, or Moors of Spain, and were introduced into England by John o' Gaunt.

Morton's Fork. This was the name given to a plan devised by Archbishop Morton in the time of Henry VII for increasing the Royal revenue. It was a tax. Those who were rich were compelled to contribute because they could well afford it. Those who lived modestly, and without show, had to make their contribution on the ground that their economy must mean that they had considerable savings !

Mother Carey's Chickens. The stormy petrels. There is no question that the stormy *petrel* is connected with St. Peter, who attempted to walk on the water. Sailors gave the birds the name of Mother Carey's Chickens, why is not known. A correspondent in *The Times* recently explained it as a corruption of the Latin *Mater Cara* ; Dr. Brewer does the same. And *The Times'* correspondent added that the French sailors' name for the bird was *avis Sanctae Mariae*. We leave the retort to Latin scholars.

Mother Earth. The name was dramatically initiated by Junius Brutus. After the death of Lucretia he went with two others to Delphi, the Oracle, to ask which of the three should succeed Tarquin. The Oracle replied: "He who should first kiss his mother." Junius at once threw himself on the ground, exclaiming, "I kiss thee, Mother Earth." He was elected Consul.

Mother of Presidents. The name bestowed on the U.S.A. State of Virginia, because of the many Presidents which that State has given to the American Republic.

Mother Shipton. There is no evidence that such a person ever existed. However, the Prophetess is SAID to have lived in the time of Henry VIII, and to have foretold the deaths of Wolsey and Cromwell, as well as a host of lesser lights. She is said also to have predicted in rhyme that ships would go without sails and vehicles without horses.

Mothering Sunday. This Sunday in mid-Lent is an illustration of how an ancient custom changes with the passing of ages, and yet retains much of its original meaning. In former days, when the Roman Catholicism was the established religion, it was the custom of the people to visit their "Mother Church" on mid-Lent Sunday, and to make offerings of gifts at the High Altar. As early as 1607, however, Cowel, in his "Interpreter," observed that the remaining practice of Mothering Sunday was a visit of the children to their homes when they ate "Mothering Cake." Later, it became a holiday for school-children in order that they could spend the day at home. Of late years it has been very little observed.

Mountain, Highest. The world's highest mountain is Everest, 29,140 feet. To the purists, who have on numerous occasions informed the writer that they understand that Mount Chimborazo, in the Andes is the highest mountain, it may be pointed out that Geography counts height only from the earth's surface. It is true that, taken from the centre of the earth, Chimborazo would be the highest because of the bulging of the earth at the equator, which results in twenty thousand feet above sea level being very much further from the earth's centre than twenty-nine thousand in the tropics. But, geography being what it is, Chimborazo is returned officially as 20,498 feet.

Mountebank. The name given to a boaster, or a quack, selling his remedies to the crowd in the open-air ; a charlatan. The word came to us from the Italian *montambanco*. Divided into its component parts the Italian word gives *montare*, mount, *in*, on, and *banco*, a bench—"mount on a bench." They still exist, and are frequently to be seen on their *banco*, now usually a box, in the little square in front of the Garrick Theatre, and at the foot of the Irving Statue in London.

Mourning. Is not always black. South Sea Islanders use black and white stripes. Syrians and Armenians use sky-blue in the hope that the deceased has gone to Heaven. Rome and ancient Sparta mourned in white ; and it should be noted that Henry VIII wore white for the death of Anne Boleyn. Ethiopian mourning is greyish-brown, Turkey is violet, Egypt yellow, and Persian pale brown.

MS. The initials stand for manuscript. But if you sent an MS. to a publisher to-day he would in all probability return it to you ! He wants typed matter, whereas manuscript is the Latin *manuscriptum*, "that which is written by hand."

Muff. "*A poor muff.*" "*He muffed it.*" Muff was originally an expression of contempt for a dandy who carried, like the ladies, a muff with which to keep his hands warm, thus mitigating against his defending himself with his sword. A "muff" was, therefore, easily taken advantage of.

Mug. Like jug, this word for a vessel to hold liquids is a mystery. Its origin is quite unknown. It first appeared, apparently, in the sixteenth century, and somewhat similar words are found in the Low German and in the Scandinavian languages. The Swedish *mugge* and the Norwegian *mugge*, for instance, meaning an earthenware cup. Pot, another name for a drinking vessel, is in the same category. And from the fact that all three allied vessels—mug, jug and pot—are still a puzzle to etymologists, suggests that in each case they sprang from personal names.

Mugging-Up. The term meant, in the first place, the operations of an actor making up his face (mug) for the part he was to play ; getting the appearance and the part perfect. From this, however, "mugging-up" was appropriated as meaning anyone studying, or going over his matter before an examination in any subject.

Mug-house. Was the name given to beer-houses in the eighteenth century. These mug - houses were the venue for regular companies of people who were served beer in their own mugs. In time music was introduced into them, and to ensure order during the performances the company elected a chairman. From this there developed the "Free and Easy," which in turn developed into the modern music-hall.

Mugwump. The idea that it is a slang term is not correct. It is, in fact, an Indian word for "wise chief," a captain, leader. It was in use as such among the Indians and Whites of Massachusetts in the seventeenth and eighteenth centuries. That was the original meaning. It has come to mean in this country, however, someone who thinks himself of consequence and puts on airs accordingly. The word has recently been defined by an English nobleman as "an animal that sits on the fence, with its mug on one side and his wump on the other." Mr. Ernest Weekley, that authority on words, quotes the jest in his "Something About Words."

Mulberry. The botanical name for the berry is from the Greek *moros*, meaning a fool, so-called, according to the Horus Anglicus, because it is reputed "the wisest of flowers, never budding until the cold weather is past." According to a fable the flowers were originally white, but became red from the blood of Pyramus and Thisbe.

Mulberry Harbour. The name given to the prefabricated harbour by means of which the Allied Forces were landed on the Normandy coast on D-Day (6th June, 1944). The harbour, made of concrete and steel, was fabricated in hundreds of workshops all over Britain, towed to the French coast, and there assembled, with quays, etc. On it and from it the entire Allied Army was landed and supplied. It was given the name

"Mulberry" because that was the code word used in all messages referring to its building, in order that no suspicion of its manufacture might leak out and reach the enemy. The Germans, who were counting on the difficulties of landing an army on the coast, were completely bamboozled by the appearance of the harbour.

Mumbo-Jumbo. This word for a farrago of nonsense is said to be a native African name, but it is more probably a mere loose rendering in English of African jargon. It is frequently used to describe any senseless object of popular idolatry. In "Travels in Africa" Mungo Park says that in the African villages Mumbo-Jumbo is a pseudo idol invented by husbands of unruly wives to subdue them. When trouble is rife among the various wives of a household, either the husband or a friend disguises himself as Mumbo-Jumbo, and with a following of accompanying devils parades in front of the dwelling to the accompaniment of noises. When the wives have been sufficiently scared, "Mumbo" seizes the chief offender, ties her to a tree, and gives her a sound whipping. How much truth there is in this story the writer would not like to say.

Mummy Wheat. From time to time stories have been circulated that wheat stored in mummy cases in Egypt at the burial of the Pharoah have, when planted, sprouted. There is not a word of truth in the statement. The writer has investigated all such stories which have been mentioned, without being able to confirm one of them. Wheat will not retain its fertility over a period of centuries, although it will sprout after a great number of years out of the ground. In one instance which appeared genuine, wheat said to have been taken from an Egyptian tomb did, indeed, sprout. It produced a type of wheat not grown for nearly five hundred years after the period of the tomb from which it was reported to have been taken; and wheat which was not Egyptian wheat at all.

Mum's the Word. Because "mum" is the sound of M-m, which can only be produced with closed lips. If you do not open your lips, you cannot talk.

Muses. The Nine Muses. In Greek mythology the daughters of Zeus and Mnemosyne. Originally, they were Goddesses of memory only, but later became identified with individual arts and sciences. They are: *Clio*, heroic exploits and history; *Euterpe*, Dionysiac music and the double flute; *Thalia*, gaiety, pastoral life and comedy; *Melpomens*, song, harmony and tragedy; *Terpischore*, choral dance and song; *Erato*, the lyre and erotic poetry; *Polyhymnia*, the inspired and stately hymn; *Urania*, celestial phenomena and astronomy; and *Calliope*, the chief of them all.

Museum. The home or seat of the Muses (see above) and of the Arts. The first building to be given the name was the university built at Alexandria by Ptolemy about 300 B.C. The largest and most important museum in Britain is the British Museum in London.

Muslin. The name comes to us from the French *Mousseline*, from Mosul, in Mesopotamia, whence, during the Middle Ages, the fabric was sent to all the markets of the world.

Mustard. In 1382 Philip, Duke of Burgundy, granted to the town of Dijon, famous for its mustard, armoural bearings with the motto, "Moult me tarde." The motto was adopted by mustard merchants, and in time became shortened to *moult-tarde*, which means "much burn"! That, at least, is the story. It is hardly likely to be true; and it must be mentioned that in much earlier days a condiment was mixed into paste with *must*, new wine, from the Latin *mustus*, fresh or new. The use of mustard in its present form for making into a paste is said to have originated in Durham. John Timbs gives an account of the way in which an old woman, named Clements, living in Durham in 1720, invented a method of extracting the full flavour from the mustard, details of which she refused to impart to anyone. George I, and various notabilities, are said to have patronized her, for she travelled to London twice a year and to the principal towns of England for orders. From this, says Timbs, arose the name Durham mustard.

My Lady Nicotine. As a name expressing the delights of tobacco, was first used by the late Sir James Barrie, the dramatist, in an essay on smoking which he wrote for the London *St. James's Gazette*.

Myrmidions of the Law. Bailiffs, sheriff's officers, policemen, and other inferior administrative officers of the law, but the Myrmidions were originally ant men (Greek *murmes*, ant), and belong to some nature myth far older than the *Iliad*. In Greek times they were a Thessalian tribe who accompanied Achilles to the Siege of Troy. Thus, a myrmidon has been with gradual decline a faithful attendant, an unscrupulous hired ruffian, and a police officer of the baser sort.

Mythology. From the Greek *muthos*, a fable, and *logos*, a discourse. A religion built upon fable; but some of the greatest reading in literature.

N

"N. or M." This answer to the first question in the Catechism in the Prayer Book must have puzzled many people. The meaning is that the person being catechized gives, at that point, his or her name or names. The letters are the initials of the Latin *nomen vel nomina*, name or names. The abbreviation for the plural *nomina* was the usual double initial (as Ll.D., Doctor of Laws) and this, when printed closely together as in the old Prayer Books, came to be taken for "m."

Nab. To seize suddenly, without warning. From the Swedish *nappa*, and the Danish *nappe*. A nabman was formerly a police officer.

Nabob. The old-time contemptuous name for one who has acquired wealth in the East, and uses it over here ostentatiously. It is a corruption of the Hindu *Nuwab*, plural of *naib*, meaning a deputy-governor of the Mogul Empire.

Nagging. Continual grumbling or fault-finding, particularly of a husband or wife. It comes from the Anglo-Saxon *gnag-an*, to gnaw or bite. Hence a dull, continuous pain, is a nagging pain.

Nag's Head Consecration. This was a story, circulated by Roman Catholic writers, that Matthew Parker, Archbishop of Canterbury (1559-1576), was consecrated at the Nag's Head Tavern in Cheapside. The incident arose on the passing of the Act of Uniformity in the reign of Elizabeth. All the Sees became vacant. Llandaff refused to officiate at Parker's consecration and the problem was how to obtain consecration in order to preserve the apostolic succession unbroken. To find a way out of this, the story says, a deposed bishop, one Scory, was sent for, and officiated at the tavern.

The story is, of course, denied. The official register shows that Parker was consecrated at Lambeth. Unfortunately, some semblance of truth was given to the story by the fact that all those who took part in the consecration afterwards *dined* at the tavern, including Scory.

Nail, Nails. There are many and curious superstitions connected with nails. In ancient Rome a nail was driven into the wall of the temple of Jupiter on 13th September. Originally done to tally the year, it later became a ceremony for warding off evil spirits, calamities and plagues.

The Romans invariably pared their nails upon the Nundinoe, observed every ninth day; they considered it unlucky to do so on certain days of the week. In

England, in the early seventeenth century, a similar superstition prevailed, and is believed to have been taken from the Romans. In the neighbourhood of Bottesford Moors, children's nails were bitten off, and not pared, for the first twelve months, lest the child should grow up a thief. In parts of Dorsetshire, around the same period, mothers pared their children's nails over the family Bible, in order that they should grow up honest. To cut nails on a Friday or a Sunday was considered unlucky. Lodge, in 1596, wrote, "Nor will he paire his nailes White Monday to be fortunate in his love."

The nails with which Christ was crucified were objects of great veneration in the Middle Ages. "On one of theise," says Sir John Maundeville, "the Emperor of Canstantynoble made a brydille to his hors, to bere him in batylle." It is added that through the virtue of this he overcame his enemies.

In olden times a nail was a measure of weight for wool, hemp, beef and cheese. It corresponded to eight pounds. It was also a measure of length—the sixteenth part of a yard, or two and a quarter inches.

Nail. *Hung on the Nail.* Pawned. The reference is to the old custom in pawnbrokers' shops of hanging each pawn on a nail, with a number attached, the customer holding a duplicate. The custom later gave way to shelves.

Nail. *To pay on the Nail.* In Bristol market-place are a number of carved pillars about waist-high, ornamented, and each having a bronze, flat top. At the Liverpool Stock Exchange there was a plate of copper. In the centre of Limerick is a pillar with a circular plate of copper about three feet in diameter. Now all these are called *nails*; and the story told is that these were the origin of "paying on the nail." It is stated that all things bought and sold were paid for before the market closed over these *nails*. The writer has no doubt that bargains were thus paid; but they were not the *origin* of paying on the nail. The phrase was quite common in the sixteenth century, long before these nails were in existence.

Nailed to the Counter. "*Another lie nailed to the Counter.*" The origin is said to have been the practice of a general store keeper in America, greatly afflicted with counterfeit money. He adopted the practice of nailing every such piece imposed upon him on the counter where it could be seen, to the accompaniment of the words, "Here's another lie nailed to the counter."

Naked Possessor, Naked Overdraft (legal). Naked possession is the Far West description of the possessor of a piece of land for a long period without any real title to it. He is the naked possessor because his title is not clothed in the set form of words recognized, and required, by a Court of Law.

A naked overdraft means one which is not covered by security.

Naked Truth, The. The old fable goes that Falsehood and Truth went together to bathe in a river. Falsehood came first out of the water and dressed in Truth's garments. Truth, not willing to don the raiment of Falsehood, herself went naked.

Namby-Pamby. The name given to something weakly sentimental, insipidly pretty or affectedly simple. It is a fanciful play on the name of *Ambrose* Philips (died 1749), author of pastorals ridiculed by Carey and Pope. Philips had written some verses for the children of Lord Carteret; of them Carey said, "So the nurses get by heart Namby-Pamby's Little Rhymes."

Names. Names in all countries and ages have been principally derived from localities, callings and personal aspects. Thus, in Britain we get *Johnson*, the son of John. *Watson* is the son of Wat, otherwise Walter, from the Old Norman French *Wautier*. The original *Lockhart* is said to have taken the heart of the Bruce to the Holy Land in a "locked" casket. *Bell* was probably the verger of a church who rang the bell. *Smith* was a blacksmith. *Bridgeman* was a man who either lived near or had something to do with a bridge. *Pullman* was the poolman. A family with the surname *Cant*, *Chant*, lived originally in Kent; *Lankshear* and *Willsher*, respectively, signify an original dwelling in Lancashire and Wiltshire. A volume almost as thick as this dictionary could be written on the "origins" of names alone, but the above will suffice to show how names came into being.

Nant. This Celtic word, where it appears in place-names, signifies a valley. Nan-cemellin, in Cornwall, is the valley of the mill. Trenance is the town in the valley.

Nap. A short sleep, not taken in bed. It is derived from two Anglo-Saxon words meaning, respectively, to nod and to bend oneself. Its application to sleep will be realized when one remembers the nodding head and bent figure of a person having a "nap" in a chair.

Nap. *Game played with hands of five cards.* It was so named after Napoleon.

Nap, To take the. A theatrical term for a pretended blow. Mayhew, in "London Labour," wrote: "Then Pantaloon comes up . . . and I give him the rap." The *Era Almanach*, 1877, records: "I don't think though, I shall be able to take the nap much longer." The word is often corrupted to "take the *rap*."

Napier's Bones. A mechanical contrivance, invented by Napier of Merchison, for multiplying and dividing numbers. It was one of the first calculating machines.

The bones were narrow strips of bone in the first place, but afterwards made of wood or ivory, or other material, and were divided into compartments, marked with certain digits.

Napoo. What the word really means is "Il n'y en a plus"—there is no more of it, in other words, "Nothing." Napoo came into use by British soldiers during the 1914-18 war.

Nappy Ale. This name has been given to strong ale for centuries. So long ago as 1529, Skelton wrote of a woman "who breweth nappy ale." It refers to ale which has a foaming head—the allusion being, apparently, to the nap on cloth.

Narcissa. In Pope's "Moral Essays," Narcissa is Mrs. Oldfield, the actress (1683-1730). She was buried in Westminster Abbey in a magnificent Brussels lace head-dress, a holland shift with ruffles of the same lace, and new kid gloves.

Narcissism. Morbid self-admiration, such as that which resulted in Narcissus being changed into a flower.

Narcissus. The story of the Spring flower is this: Narcissus, a beautiful youth, son of Cephisus and the nympth Liriope, born at Thespis Bæotia, saw his image reflected in a fountain, and became enamoured of it, thinking it to be the nympth of the place. His fruitless attempts to approach this beautiful object so provoked him that he grew desperate and killed himself. His blood was changed into a flower, which still bears his name. The nympths raised a funeral pile to burn his body, according to Ovid, but they found nothing but a beautiful flower.

Nark. The term for a spy for the police, current in criminal circles, is from the Romany word *nak*, a nose.

See "Nosey Parker."

Narrowdale's Noon. To put off doing something until Narrowdale Noon, is to defer it for ever. Narrowdale is a local name for the narrowest part of Dovedale, Derbyshire. The few cotters who dwell there never see the sun throughout the Winter, and when its beams pierce the deep dale in the Spring it is only for a few minutes in the late afternoon.

Naseby. There is a fable that this Northamptonshire town was thus named because it was considered in Anglo-Saxon times the navel or centre of England, as Delphi was considered the "navel of the earth" in the time of the Greeks. Unfortunately for the story, the town appears in the Domesday Book as Navesberi, showing that it belonged at that time to one, Hnaef, a Dane, a name hardly recorded, except in heroic poetry.

Nation of Shopkeepers. Term applied to Britain by the Kaiser. The phrase appears in Adam Smith's "Wealth of Nations." But Samuel Adams is believed first to have used it during a speech in the State House, Philadelphia, in August, 1776.

National Anthem. Whoever originally wrote and composed "God Save the King," Henry Carey, in 1740, reset both words and music for the birthday of George II. In point of fact, there is little doubt that the words were altered to suit the times on several occasions. "Send him victorious," is usually agreed to be Jacobite. "Frustrate their knavish tricks" is beyond doubt a reference to the Gunpowder Plot.

As to who started the Anthem, one name put forward is Dr. John Bull, organist at Antwerp Cathedral (1617-28); and Henry Carey is another. Dr. Brewer suggests that the air and opening words were probably suggested by the "Domine Salvum" of the Catholic Church.

National Debt. The National Debt of Great Britain is money borrowed from the Government on the security of the taxes, which are pledged to the lenders for the payment of the interest. The portion of the National Debt which is converted into bonds or annuities is called the Funded Debt, and the portion that is repayable at a stated time, or on demand, is called the Floating Debt.

The National Debt began in this way: In 1694 the Government granted a charter to the Bank of England, in return for the receipt of the whole of its capital—£1,200,000, lent at eight per cent. In return, the Bank was allowed to issue paper money to that amount. The sum was later increased by another million pounds, the Bank augmenting its note issue to this extent. Similar charters were granted to other companies, notably the East India Company, on like terms.

See "Paper Money."

Nativity of Christ. Although Christmas Day, 25th December, is set apart as the birthday of Christ, it is not the date on which Christ was born in Bethlehem. The actual date of the birth of Christ has been varyingly given, and ranges from May to August. The latter is probably correct. Christmas-time as a sacred season was recognized in times long antecedent to the time of Christ; and it was not until the fourth century that the Western Church adopted the present date as the birthday of the Saviour. It is noteworthy that the Roman Winter solstice festival was celebrated on 25th December; and there is little doubt that this pagan festival was among those "adapted" by the Christian Church to its own needs.

See "Easter."

Natter, To. The word is sometimes referred to as slang; but it is of old-established and quite reputable Scottish origin. It means to chatter peevishly, and is derived from—or, at least, is closely allied to—the Icelandic *knetta*, meaning to grumble, and *gnadda*, meaning to murmur.

Naughty. It is a curious misnomer that the word should have become the description of a wilful child. It was never meant as such. The word is composed of the Anglo-Saxon *na* (ne) *wiht*, thing, and originally naught and naughty meant worthless, good for nothing. It is in this sense that in *Jeremiah* xxiv, 2, is written the sentence, "The other basket had very naughty figs."

By Shakespeare's time the word had come to mean corrupt or evil. In Act V of the "Merchant of Venice," he refers to "a good deed in a naughty (evil) world."

Navvy. Few labouring jobs of work have so romantic an origin. The navvy is derived from navy. Navy comes from the Roman *navis*, a ship. When England decided to extend its inland *nav*igation by canals and railways, the men thus engaged to dig the beds of the streams that were to carry ships (even though they were only barge ships) were called "navigators." Inns sprang up near the scene of the work, and were given the name of Navigation Inn. They were used by the navigators. Before very long the public, with its genius for cutting names short and crisp, nicknamed the navigators *navvies*, and navvies they have been ever since, although there is little connection between them and the navy and navigation to-day.

Naze, Ness. A component in many place-names, meaning a nose of land, a headland, a promontory. It is of Scandinavian origin.

Ne plus ultra. Latin for "nothing further." In other words, absolute perfection; the most perfect state to which a thing can be brought.

Nearer the Bone, the Sweeter the Meat. First appeared in Percy's "Ballads," 1559, where it was rendered, "The higher the bone the flesh is much sweeter."

Necessary Woman. In the late eighteenth and early nineteenth centuries, the privy was known in private houses as "the necessary house." A "necessary woman" attended to the cleaning of the house. In a churchyard at Rickmansworth there was quite recently, and may still be, a tombstone bearing the inscription: "Here lyeth the body of Mary Laight, wife of Nathaniel Laight, of the Parish of St. James', necessary woman to His Majesty George II, who departed this life, November 1st, 1754, aged 32 years."

Necessity knows no law. The phrase was made most famous (or infamous) by the German Chancellor, Bethmann-Hollweg, in the German Reichstag on 4th August, 1914, when, in attempting to justify the German invasion of Belgium he said, "We are now in a state of necessity, and necessity knows no law."

The phrase was not, of course, new. Cromwell used it in a speech in Parliament, in 1654, and it occurs also in Milton's "Paradise Lost."

Necessity, the Mother of Invention. The earliest trace of this tag in print is in Farquhar's "The Twin Rivals"; but it was likely to have been in common use before that time.

Neck and Crop. The Mediæval English *croppe* and the Anglo-Saxon *cropp* both meant the top or head of a plant; the Old French *croupe* meant the top of a hill. Thus crop has come to mean the top of anything, including ears of corn at the top of the stalk, and the head of man. The Norwegian *nakk* meant a knoll, or top of a hill. Thus neck and crop is simply a strengthening of the idea of "top" by duplicating it. To fall neck and crop is to crash completely.

Neck-verse. The beginning of the fifty-first Psalm used to bear this name, from the fact that in all capital cases within benefit of clergy, the prisoner, by repeating the Neck-verse, saved his neck—or life. "Benefit of Clergy" was, originally, the privilege of exemption from trial by a secular court for the clergy, if arrested for felony. It came to mean, however, not only the ordained clergy, but all who were able to read and write and might, therefore, be *capable* of entering Holy Orders! It is suggested that Benefit of Clergy was based on the text in *Chronicles*, "Touch not mine annointed and do my prophets no harm."

Such a person as claimed Benefit of Clergy when before the court had to read the verse. If he was able to do so, "Legit ut clericus" was called, and the prisoner saved his neck, being only burnt in the hand and set free. It was abolished in 1827.

There is in doggerel verse the following lines, illustrating the benefit:

"If a monk had been taken for stealing of bacon,
For burglary, murder or rape;
If he could but rehearse (well prompt) his neck verse,
He never could fail to escape."

There is reference in the old play, "Gammer Gurton's Needle" (q.v.) to devices (according to the length of purse) whereby certain people charged with felony, and unable to read, were coached in the Neck-verse, and satisfactorily passed, in some cases, the test.

Nectar. The drink of the Gods in Classical Mythology. Like their food, Ambrosia, it conferred immortality.

The nectarine gets its name from Nectar of the Gods, because it is as sweet as nectar.

Needle in a Bottle of Hay. The *Oxford English Dictionary* has something like a dozen different bottles; but the one with which we are concerned is the Old French *botel*, a diminutive of the masculine form of *botte*, a bundle. A botle (bottle) of hay was, therefore, a *bundle* of hay. The phrase goes back many generations, for Chaucer, in 1386, referred to something as "nat worth a Botel hey." In 1578, in Lincolnshire records, there is an instruction that "No mann shall gett anie bottells of furres" (i.e., furze).

Francillon, in "Mid-Victorian Memories," uses the word *pottle* in this sense, stating, "I discovered what had hitherto been the proverbial needle in the *pottle* of hay." Both in Mediæval English and in Old French *pottle* was a measure of capacity for corn and dry goods.

Needle's Eye. "*It is easier for a camel to go through the eye of a needle* . . ." Because the postern gate in the wall of a city in the East was called the needle's eye, and camels could negotiate it only with great difficulty, it has been decided by amateur philologists that this was the "eye of a needle" to which Christ referred as being easier to go through than for a rich man to enter the Kingdom of Heaven. In point of fact, this name for a postern did not exist in Biblical days.

Nem Con. A contraction for the Latin *Nemine contrad icente*, no one contradicting. A motion passed by a meeting *nem con* means that there was no vote against it.

Nemesis. The word in Greek means "to give what is due." In the *Iliad* the word denotes any cause of anger, or righteous wrath. In the Hesiodic theogony, it is the name of a daughter of the night, who gradually became the punisher of the favourites of fortune. Nemesis was, in Greek mythology, the Goddess who doled out to men their exact share of good, or bad, fortune, and was responsible for seeing that everyone got his dues and deserts.

Nephew. Strange though it seems, a nephew really means a grandson, from the Latin *nepos*. It meant grandchild, or descendants in Early English. In I *Tim* v, 4, of the old edition of the Bible, is: "If a woman has children or nephews." But in the present revised edition, nephews has been changed to grand-children. Niece, from the Latin *neptos*, means a grand-daughter.

Neptune. Was the Roman God of the Sea—represented as an old man, with a long beard and a trident.

Nero. When the name is used to describe a cruel tyrant, the Nero meant is Claudius Nero (A.D. 54-68). He is said to have set fire to Rome because he wanted to see what Troy had looked like when it was ablaze. He is also said to have fiddled as he watched the flames. But a lot of nonsense has from time to time been written about Claudius Nero, who was a talented man and a scholar.

Nessus, The Shirt of. A fatal present. The legend is that Nessus (the centaur—half man, half horse) was ordered by Hercules to carry Dejanira, wife of Hercules, across a river. The centaur attempted to carry her away for his own uses, and Hercules shot him with a poisoned arrow. Nessus, in revenge, gave Dejanira his tunic, falsely telling her that it would preserve for her her husband's love. She gave it to Hercules, who was devoured by the poison still remaining in it from his own arrow. Dejanira, in remorse, committed suicide.

Nest egg. If a china egg is placed in a hen's nest, it is an inducement for the hen to put one of her own by the side of it! Thus, a nest egg is an inducement to add to it. The nest egg, incidentally, is of considerable antiquity, for in 1611 Cotgrave wrote of "a neaste egge." And its meaning of money in hand is illustrated in "Sponge's Spring Tour," where Surtees wrote, "The Mangeysterne hounds wanted that great ingredient of prosperity, a larger nest-egg subscriber."

Never is a Long Day. The proverb dates from round about 1386. Chaucer, in "Canob's Yeoman's Tale," gives it as, "Never to thryve were too long a date."

Never Trust a Little. Apperson, in his "English Proverbs and Proverbial Sayings," explains: "Although this saying is nearly universally used under another name in the Bishopric (Durham) and elsewhere in the North of England, I have reason to believe that the above is the correct form, and the other a mere adaptation. A family of this name (Little) were celebrated rievers, or thieves."

New, Brand. *See* "Brand new."

New England. Name given to Maine, New Hampshire, Vermont, Massachusetts, Rhode Island and Connecticut, the six Eastern States of the U.S.A., because the people there are all descended from the Puritans of England and Scotland.

Newfangled. The "d" has been added since the word came to its meaning. Newfangle is derived from the Mediæval English *fangel*, and the Anglo-Saxon *fang*, from *fon*, to take, and means ready to grasp, or take, to some new thing.

Newington Butts. A London district was so-called because it was the site of archery butts.

New Scotland Yard. The original Scotland Yard was a palace built about 970 by King Edgar as a residence for Kenneth II, of Scotland, when that monarch came to England once a year to pay homage to England's King. The palace fell into decay, and was demolished during the reign of Elizabeth. The present London police headquarters were built on the site of the yard of the old palace.

New Style Calendar. The reformed, or Gregorian Calendar, adopted in England in 1752. When it came into force, Wednesday, 2nd September, was followed by Thursday, 14th September, eleven days being wiped out.

New Year Gifts. Have been known from the days of the Greeks and the Romans. The latter called these gifts *strenae*. Earliest references to gifts in Britain are from the ancient Druids who, "with great ceremonies, used to scrape off from the outside of oaks the misleden (mistletoe) which they consecrated to their great Tutates, and then distributed it to the people through the Gauls, on account of the great virtues which they attributed to it."

English nobility used to send the King a purse of gold each New Year's Day. Henry III, according to Matt. Paris, used to *extort* gifts from his subjects. Probably the most splendid New Year's Gift ever made in these old days was the gold cup, richly chased and engraved, of the value of £117 17s. 6d.

It was formerly the custom to bribe magistrates with gifts on New Year's Day. It was, however, abolished in 1290.

The origin of the Roman *strenae* is said to be from the presenting of branches of trees cut from the forest sacred to the Goddess *Strenia* (strength), to Tatius, King of the Sabines, on New Year's Day. The French custom of giving *etrenne* is a survival of the Roman story.

News. Is not derived from the fact that it represents the points of the compass—i.e., N.E.W.S. Any doubts on the subject may be dispelled by the fact that the word was originally spelt *newes.* It is really derived from the French *nouvelles*, through the Latin *novum*, a new thing.

Newspaper. The first newspaper on record was the *Peking News*, which went out of existence only so recently as 1935, at the ripe old age of 1,572 years. Journalism in the Western world is thought to have originated with the *Acta Diurna* (from the Latin *diurnus* comes our word journal) which was published from Cæsar's time onwards.

Nib. Is not a pen. It is the *point* of the pen. The invention of writing was ascribed by the Ancient Egyptians to the God Thoth. He was the scribe of the Gods, and was typified on earth by the sacred bird, Ibis. And Ibis wrote mystic signs on the smooth mud of the river-banks *with his pointed beak.* The word for beak was *neb*, which came easily to nib.

Nice. Another strange corruption led to this word being descriptive of agreeable, or delightful. The derivation is the Latin *nescius*, ignorant; and the Old French *niche* meant simple, foolish, ignorant. A similar curious changed meaning has altered the application of fond, which originally denoted foolishness and weakly affectioned.

Niche. The usual origin given to this word is the Italian *nicchio*, a shell. It must, however, be looked upon with considerable suspicion. It seems clear that the first niches were shallow recesses or hollows in the walls of a church, for the purpose of containing a statue, or other decorative object. There seems nothing of the shell about this.

On the other hand, there is the Latin word *nidicare*, formed on *nid-us*, from which came the French *nicher*, meaning to nest or nestle, place as in a nest. This would seem to fit niche better than the Italian shell.

Nickname. Is derived from the Icelandic *aujanafn*, from which came the Anglo-Saxon *eke*, meaning "also." Nickname is, in fact, a corruption of eke-name, i.e., the "also"-name. There were nicknames as long ago as 1303. Robert Brunne records (Handlyng synne) "a vyle eke-name."

Nicotine. The poisonous extract of tobacco was named from *nicotiana*, Latin name of the tobacco plant. The name was given the plant in honour of the man who introduced tobacco into France in 1560—Jean Nicot, French Ambassador to Madrid at the time.

Night-cap. Colloquial name for a last drink before going to bed. Its origin lies in the custom of our great-grandfathers who wore a night-cap, and fancied that they could not sleep without it.

Nightmare. What the present generation calls a nigthmare is not, the writer fears, much like the nightmare of the days when the word was coined. The real nightmare was a female spirit (hence "mare") supposed to beset people and animals by night, settling upon them when they are asleep and producing a feeling of suffocation by its weight. It was at one time thought to be an incubus (q.v.). Chaucer refers to it in a sentence in which he wrote, "Blisse this house . . . fro the nightes-mare"; and Topsell, in "Serpents" (1658) wrote, "The spirits of the night, called Incubi and Succubi, or else Nightmares."

Nil Desperandum. Latin, Never Despair. Never give up hope. It comes from Horace: "Nil desperandum Teucro duce et auspice Teucro" (There is naught to be despaired of when we are under the leadership and auspices of Teucer).

Niminy-Pinimy. Imitation of a mincing utterance. It seems first to have appeared in 1786, or thereabouts, in "The Heiress," where one of the women characters is told that the way to acquire the paphian "mimp" is to stand before a glass and keep pronouncing *nimini - pimini.* "The lips cannot fail to take the right plie."

Nincompoop. A fool, blockhead, or a ninny. Dr. Johnson gave its origin as a corruption of the Latin *non compos mentis*, but the *Oxford English Dictionary*, contesting this, states that such an origin does not agree with the earliest forms. It defines the origin as obscure. There is, however, an old Dutch word, *poep*, meaning a fool, which may have had some bearing on it.

Nine. One of the mystical numbers, the other two being five and three—the *diapason, diapente* and *diatrion* of the Greeks. From the earliest times nine has been associated with superstition and with religion. The Pythagoreans regarded man as a full chord of eight notes, with the Deity next. Lars Porsena, it will be recalled, in "Horatius" swore b y t h e *n i n e* gods. Deucalion's ark was tossed about for *nine* days. There were *nine* Muses; there were *nine* rivers of Hell; Milton makes the gates of Hell thrice three-fold, which makes *nine*; the old hags in "Macbeth" sang in their witches' song, "Thrice to *nine* . . . . "; in early astronomy there were *nine* spheres; Odin's ring dropped *nine* other rings.

There are *nine* orders of Angels, and among ecclesiastic architects there are *nine* different crosses recognized. In older days all leases were granted for nine hundred and ninety-nine years.

Nine Days' Wonder. The religious festivals of the Church lasted nine days. During this time the image of the saint in whose honour the feast was celebrated was paraded with relics and votive offerings. The naturalist, Bates, recorded in one of his books: "The grandest of all these festivals is that in honour of Our Lady of Nazareth. It lasts, like the others, nine days." The Latin *novenus* means nine each. There is a curious and unfathomable phrase in the "Troilus" of Chaucer, however, in which it is stated, "Eke wonder last but nine daies never in towne."

Nine-pins. The game, now called skittles, was played as far back as 1580, when Holleyband records it. By 1647, it is stated by Peachum, "The most ordinary recreations of the countrey are football, *skales or nine-pins.*" And Urquhart, in 1657, observes: "They may likewise be said to use their king as the players at nine-pins do the middle kyle, which they call the king, at whose fall alone they aim, the sooner to obtain the gaining of their prize."

Nine Tailors make a Man. Tailors, in this connection, is a corruption of "tellers." A "teller" was the stroke of the passing bell of a church, rung for a death. In many rural churches to-day it is still rung. Three strokes (tellers) rung together denote that the death is of a child, six of a woman, and nine "tells" a man.

In connection with this proverb Carlyle tells an excellent story of the wit of Queen Elizabeth who, receiving a deputation one day of *eighteen* tailors, greeted them with, " Good morning, gentlemen both."

" Nine Worthies." Three Paynims, three Jews, and three Christians. They were: Hector, Alexander the Great, Julius Cæsar; Joshua, David, Judas Maccabæus; Arthur, Charlemagne, and Godfrey of Bouillon.

Nines, Up to the. The origin seems obscure. It is suggested that the " nines " to which reference is made are the Nine Muses, and that up to the nines means perfection. It seems a doubtful interpretation. Another " source " is that the phrase had reference to the old game of nine-pins—with going up to the nines, in the sense of going out for an evening's sport in the nine-pins alley, or getting up to the nines with the " cheese." " Poor Robin," in his almanac for 1695, records:

" Ladies for pleasure now resort
Unto Hide Park and Totnam Court;
People to Moorfields flock in sholes,
At nine-pins and at pigeon-holes."

The writer does not like this " origin," but it is a better one than the Nine Muses.

Ninety-nine. " Say ninety-nine " says the doctor, because of all the sounds formed by the speaking of words or figures, ninety-nine gives the purest bell-like ring through solid matter. Through a stethescope it sounds like a sixpence being tapped on an empty tumbler. Fluid on the lungs, as in pleurisy, gives back a muffled note; and a doctor can tell from the tone of ninety-nine whether a patient is suffering from pneumonia or not.

Ninny. It is difficult to understand the amateur philologist who will say, first, that nincompoop is a corruption of *non compos mentis*, and later on describe ninny as short for nincompoop, and " thought to be derived from pickaninny." In point of fact ninny is a pet form of " innocent."

Nip of Whisky. It will come as a shock to present-day people who drop in for a " nip " to learn that the measure known as nip was a very little under half a pint. Nip is short for nipperkin; and in those days nipperkin was about half a pint.

Nipper. This slang term for a boy originally meant a boy who assisted a costermonger, carter or workman. In " London Labour " Mayhew states: " Such lads are the smallest class of costermongering youths; and are sometimes called cas'alty boys or nippers."

There is no truth in the statement that nippers were boys trained to steal from the person " and then nip off."

Nisi. Latin for unless. A decree nisi in divorce is a decree " *unless* " some reason is found for it being otherwise, such as a successful intervention by the King's Proctor.

Nix. " Working for nix "—comes from the German *nichts*, nothing.

No Penny, no Paternoster. The proverb is stated to go back as far as 1528, and to have arisen from the practice in some Roman Catholic Church of buying indulgencies.

No Quarter. In Ancient Egyptian warfare, a soldier by way of earning money refrained from killing a vanquished opponent on condition that he received a quarter of the vanquished's pay. The order " no quarter " meant that all had to be killed.

No Rose without a Thorn. In the original, " Nulla est sincera voluptas." By Ovid, in his poem " Metamorphoses." (Ovid, 43 B.C.—A.D. 17). Lydgate, in " The Fall of Princes," wrote: " As there is no rose Spryngyng in gardeyns, but ther be sum thorn."

Noah's Ark. There is no truth whatever in a story, told in great detail by a Russian named Roskovitsky, who claimed to have been one of the crew of an aeroplane which, during the reign of the last of the Czars, " discovered " Noah's Ark intact on the top of Mount Ararat. The entire story, which has been published by a tract Society, is full of glaring errors, and is a pure invention.

Nob. " *One of the Nobs.*" Nob was in olden days, a pet form of Robert. It will be remembered that the Bastard of Faulconbridge (" King John " i, 1) describes his brother Robert as Sir Nob. But the " nob " of " one of the nobs " comes from the University reference books wherein in earlier days " nob," in brackets after a name, meant that the holder of the name was one of the nobility.

There is a possibility, however, that *nob* is also derived from knob, which in its turn came from *knop*, which meant top of anything, from the summit of a hill to a man's head.

Nobby Clarke. Nobby is the nickname given to every Clarke. The origin is possibly that Clarke was confounded with *clerk*. The clerks of early days were indigent, shabby-genteel, men who were expected to dress well on a starvation wage. (The clerk of this age is typified in Dickens's Bob Cratchit.) They, however, tried to raise their social prestige by putting on airs, to such an extent that they were regarded as nobs, i.e., " toffs."

Fraser and Gibbons, in suggesting that the nickname is of naval origin, fasten it on to Admiral Charles Ewart, who was known as " Nobby " Ewart. The Admiral was captain of H.M.S. *Melpomene* (1859-62), and was noted for his personal neatness and, when a captain, for his insistence on the spic and span appearance of everything on board his ship. According to one story, objecting to the appearance of a goose in its coop, he had the goose's bill and feet blackened and its body white-washed, so as to be in keeping with Navy regulation as to colouring! The story went round the Fleet, and on at least one occasion caused the gallant officer some embarrassment. At the Opera at Malta, one night, it is told, on Captain Ewart taking his seat in the stalls, a crowd of bluejackets in the gallery broke out in chorus with, " Who whitewashed the goose? " Those on the opposite side of the gallery responded with, " Why, Nobby Ewart," and they kept it up alternately till the harassed captain got up and walked out.

It will be noticed, however, that this origin does not explain why Nobby CLARKE.

Nobel Prizes. Under the will of Alfred Bernard Nobel, the Swedish chemist and inventor of dynamite, prizes were endowed to encourage work in the cause of humanity. They numbered five—for noteworthy work in physics, chemistry, medicine, idealistic literature, and the furtherance of universal peace. The last of the peace prizes was awarded in 1939 to Viscount Cecil of Chelwood, for his services to Disarmament!

Nocent. This is a word which has now fallen into disuse, although we have kept its opposite, in-nocent. Nocent, from the Latin *nocens* (pres. part. of noceo) meant guilty; and appears as such in the account of the trials of those concerned in the Gunpowder Treason plot.

Nod. " *On the Nod.*" The term is an allusion to the auction room, where most things are bought " on the nod " of a bidder.

Noise. Two suggestions have been put forward for the origin of this word. One is the Latin *nausea*, from which we get our word nauseous; and the other *noxia*, from which we get our English word noxious. However attractive both are to the senses' revolt against noise, the actual sense of the word is against either of them. There was a Mediæval English *noyse* and an Old French *noise*, both having the same meaning as our present word.

Non. The Latin negative *not.* Many words are made clear if this is kept in mind. Nonconformist, for instance, means one who will *not* conform to the established church; non-existent, something which does *not* exist; and so on.

Non compos mentis. Mad, unhinged in mind. From the Latin *non,* not; *compos,* having power; *mentis,* of the mind—not having the power of the mind.

Nonce. *For the Nonce.* The word was originally *ane* (one thing, occasion, etc.), *ane* being the Anglo-Saxon for one. Anes was the plural, and the phrase "for the ones" was written for them anes. The phrase by wrong division, says the *Oxford English Dictionary,* was altered (as in newt for ewt) for the nones, and thus has perpetuated the word nonce. It means for the (one) particular purpose.

Nonconformists. The oldest Dissenter church building in England is stated by the Congregational Union (most ancient community of Dissenters) to be Horningsham Congregational Church, near Warminster, Wiltshire. It dates back to 1566, and has a thatched roof.

None but the Brave deserve the Fair. The words were written by John Dryden in "Alexander's Feast," an ode composed in 1694, in honour of St. Cecilia's Day (22nd November).

Nonplussed. "*He was properly nonplussed*" means that the person had nothing more to say, was unable to continue the argument, being perplexed, puzzled. From the Latin *non plus,* no more.

Noon to Dewy Eve. Often misquoted as from morn to dewy eve. The phrase comes from Milton's "Paradise Lost":

"From morn
To noon he fell, from noon to dewy eve."

Norfolk Dumpling. Nickname for all people born in Norfolk. Day, in the "Blind Beggar" (Act I, Scene iii), uses it: "Make me your gull . . . you Norfolk dumpling." It arose from the fact that dumplings were what the Norfolk man of the date had as his major bill of fare.

Nose. *As clear as the nose on your face.* The origin of this phrase is Burton's "Anatomy of Melancholy," part iii, section 3, memb. 4, sub-sect. I. The correct sentence is: "As clear and as manifest as the nose in a man's face."

Nose. *To pay through the Nose.* The meaning is to pay an exorbitant price. The Greek word *rhinos* meant money, and the slang word for money is *rhino*; it is suggested in some circles that the two are related to paying through the nose. But a more likely derivation is that in mediæval times, when the Jews were being bled for money, any objection by them to paying was greeted with a slitting of their noses.

Nose bleeding. Bleeding at the nose was, in the sixteenth century, regarded as a bad portent. Burton, in his "Anatomy" (1621) says, "To bleed three drops at the nose is an ill omen." Melton observes, "When a man's nose bleeds but a drop or two, it is a sign of ill-luck; that when a man's nose bleeds one drop, and at the left nostril, it is a sign of good lucke, but on the right, ill."

Lancelot Gobbo, in "The Merchant of Venice," says: "I will not say you shall see a masque; but if you do, then it was not for nothing that my nose fell a'bleeding on Black Monday last at six o'clock i' the morning."

And in Webster's "Dutchess of Malfy" (1623) is:

"Ant. My nose bleeds.
One that were superstitious would account
This ominous, when it merely comes by chance."

Nosey Parker. The nickname given to everybody unfortunately suffering from the surname, Parker. There is no certain origin known for the cognomen. Harold Wheeler, in "How much do you Know?" suggests that the original "Nosey" was Matthew Parker (1504-1575), Chaplain to Anne Boleyn and Henry VIII, and afterwards Queen Elizabeth's Archbishop of Canterbury. He possessed a long nose and a reputation for prying into other peoples' business.

On the other hand, Stanley Rogers, in "From Ships and Sailors," asserts that the original was one, Richard Parker, who so pushed his nose into things that should not have concerned him, that he was hanged from the yardarm of H.M.S. *Sandwich* on 30th June, 1797, for leading the Sheerness Mutiny of that year.

The author doubts, however, whether either of them is the correct origin. A "nose" was a slang term for an informer in underground circles—a copper's nark, in fact. And Parker may be a corruption of *pauker,* from the dialect *pauk,* meaning to be inquisitive. Nosey inquisitive would seem to express the sentiment perfectly.

Nostradamus. Much has been heard of this alleged prophet since the outbreak of the Second World War, by reason of the many prophecies of the struggle and its duration ascribed to him. Michael Nostradamus was a French astronomer (1503-66). He published an "Almanac" each year, and in 1555 his "Centuries"—the book of his prophecies. It was condemned by the Pope in 1781. The trouble with the "prophecies" is that they cannot be seen as prophecies until after they have come true! His supporters worked out, soon after the outbreak of the 1939 war, that the war would come to an end in June, 1944.

Not worth a Rap. A "rap" was an Irish coin issued in the eighteenth century. Its value, less than a halfpenny, together with its base metal, explains the expression.

Not worth a Tinker's Dam. *See* "Tinker."

Not worth his Salt. To realize the significance of this phrase, we must hark back to the Latin, *Salarium,* from *sal,* salt. Salarium was the allowance made to the Roman soldier in order that he might buy salt. Salary, our present equivalent, also comes from the Latin *sal.* To be not worth one's salt, then, is not to be earning the salary paid one.

Nous. "*He's got no nous.*" The word is Greek for mind, intellect.

Novel. A work of fiction in book form. The ancestor of the modern novel was the Italian short, pithy story in prose. Boccaccio in the Decameron (1348-1358) was the first to write them, and called them by the Latin name *novella,* meaning little novelties. It is from the novella that the novel gets its name.

Nuff is as good as a Feast. The phrase is, of course, nonsense. Lamb, in his "Popular Fancies," makes short work of it: "Not a man, not a child in ten miles round Guildhall, really believes this saying. The inventor of it did not believe it himself. It was made in revenge by someone who was disappointed of a regale is a vile cold-scrag-of mutton sophism, a lie palmed upon the palate, which knows better things." And Lamb was undoubtedly right.

Nulli Secundis. Latin for second to none.

Nunky Pays for All. Is an American expression, meaning that Uncle (Sam) pays.

Nuremberg Eggs. An old colloquial name for watches. The original watches were egg-shaped; and they were invented and first made at Nuremburg about 1500.

Nutmeg State. Connecticut, in the U.S.A. The story goes that the inhabitants at one time manufactured wooden nutmegs for export—and got away with it.

Nuts in May. "*Here we go gathering Nuts in May.*" There are not, of course, any *nuts* in May to gather. August is the first month in which nuts could be picked. But there is May (hawthorn) in May and there are *knots* of May to be gathered. And that is what the nuts of the old rhyme really were.

O

O'. Usually used as an Irish patronymic, coming from the Gælic *ogha*, or the Irse *oa*, a descendant. O'Reilly a descendant of the Reilly. But where it is used in the sense of "To church o' Sunday" it belongs to the Mediæval English *on*.

Oaf. In early English *ouph* was an elf's child, a goblin's child. The notion was held in those days that idiot children, or those deformed in any way, were changelings left by the elfs, who had stolen, in exchange, the real child of the parents. Thus, the word oaf, or *ouph*, came to mean a half-wit, dolt or booby.

Oak-Apple Day. 29th May. The day of the restoration of Charles II, when oak apples or leaves are worn in memory of his hiding from his pursuers in an oak, on 6th September, 1651. The identical oak is claimed by, roughly, about a dozen places; but may be accepted as the "Royal Oak" at Boscobel, Worcestershire.

Oaks of Britain, Famous. The following are the principal named oaks of Britain, and the reason for their names:

Abbot's Oak which stands near the Woburn Abbey, because the Abbot in 1537 was hanged on one of its branches, by order of Henry VIII.

Cowthorpe Oak, over one thousand five hundred years old, according to tradition, will hold seventy people in its hollow. It is at Wetherby, Yorkshire.

The Ellerslie Oak, near Paisley, is said to have sheltered three hundred men of Sir William Wallace.

Owen Glendower's Oak. From the cover of this tree Glendower watched the battle between Henry IV and Henry Percy. It must, therefore, have been a fully grown tree in 1403.

Major Oak, at Edwinstowe, in the Sherwood Forest, was a full grown tree in the time of John.

Parliament Oak, in the Sherwood Forest (at Clipston) was the tree under which Edward I, in 1282, held his Parliament.

Reformation Oak is that under which Ket, the rebel, held his counsel of war, in 1549. Nine of the rebels were hanged from the tree.

Oaks, The. A race for three-year-old fillies founded in 1779, and run at Epsom on the Friday after the Derby. Its name is due to the founder, the twelfth Earl of Derby, whose estate near Epsom was named The Oaks.

Oar. "*To have (or put) an Oar in Somebody Else's Boat.*" The proverb dates from 1542, in Udall's translation of the "Apophthegmata" of Erasmus (1532): "Whatsoeuer came in his foolyshe brain, Out it should, wer it neuer so vain. In echemans bote would he haue an ore, But no woorde, to good purpose, lesse or more." And in 1551, R. Crowley, in "Works," wrote: "You had an owre in echmans barge."

Oat, Wild. *To Sow One's Wild Oats.* To commit youthful excesses, or follies. In conjunction with this must be taken two other proverbs, i.e., "Wild and Stout Never Wants a Staff," and "Wildest Colts make the Best Horses."

The allusion is held to be sowing bad (wild) grain instead of good grain. This has never been a satisfactory explanation, however, since nobody would go to the trouble of *sowing* bad grain, when he might just as well use the same time in sowing good grain. It might be as well to mention, therefore, that in Denmark there is a phenomenon at the break of Spring, in the form of thick vapours, or mists, which are called by the Danes *Lokkens havre* (Loki's wild oats). The comment of the Danes on its appearance is that Loki is sowing his wild oats. It is more than probable that the saying came to us by way of the Danes.

Obey. It is a curious feature of this word that its component parts are the Latin *obedire*, to give ear—*ob* being the preposition with *audire*, hear. Thus, the Eastern phrase is the nearer to the word; an Eastern servant, given an order, replies, "To Hear is to Obey."

Obiter Dictum. Latin for a thing said by the way. In law, an expression of opinion given by a judge in the course of either argument or judgment, but not forming an essential part of the reasons determining the decision.

Obliged. "*I am obliged to you.*" The word comes from the Latin *obligare*, to bind, or tie around. But there is a deeper meaning in its real sense than being "under an obligation."

The real meaning is I am *bound* to you. In olden days an hostage was *bound*, he was *obliged* to his captors. That meaning dated back to Biblical days, when Joseph took Simeon from his brethren and *bound* him before their eyes, meaning that the brothers were bound (obliged) to return if they wanted the release of Simeon.

Odd. It is a very ancient belief that there is luck in odd numbers. The chief of the odd numbers are one, three, five, seven, nine. *One* represents the Deity, *three* the Trinity, *five* the chief division, *seven* the sacred number, and *nine* is the three times three, the great climateric.

Virgil wrote, *Numero Deus impare gaudet* (the Gods delight in odd numbers). And in the Christian religion the Trinity, three in one, supports him. Three dominates most of the mythical emblems: Hecate had a *three*-fold power; there were *three* Graces; the Nine Muses were *three* times *three*; there were *three* Furies; the symbol of Jove was a *triple* thunderbolt; Neptune has a sea *trident*. The instances could be repeated at length.

Oddfellows. The beginning of this now great Friendly Society dates back to 1812, with five Manchester shoe-makers. Their wages were small, their job precarious. After talking things over they decided that each of them should subscribe a few pence weekly to a sick fund common to them all, to be used in case of need. They called themselves odd-fellows, because the idea was odd, and so were their numbers. Others quickly saw the advantages of the little society and joined it.

Odds, Long. The longest odds paid on a British race-course is said to be 3,410 to 1, paid on Coole in a race at Haydock Park in 1929. The biggest racing win is believed to be that of Mr. Merry, owner of Thormanby, winner of the Derby in 1860. He won, it is said, £500,000.

Odour of Sanctity. "*He Died in the Odour of Sanctity.*" The meaning is obvious; the origin not so clear. It arose from a belief, held in the Middle Ages, that a sweet odour was given off by the bodies of saintly persons on their death. The odour, however, was mostly that of the incense used at the Viaticum, or of the embalming medium. The phrase is used to-day, alas, mostly in sarcasm, for a person who's church benefaction was not in accord with his private life.

'Ods. The word is a minced form of God, which came into vogue about 1600 when, to avoid the profanation of sacred names many minced and disguised equivalents were prevalent.

Odd Rot It. Was a perversion of the Crusaders' curse, "God Rot Them"—the Saracens, against whom they were fighting.

Odd Zounds. Was a perversion of "God's Wounds."

Odds Bodikins. Was a perversion of "God's Body," a reference to the Eucharist.

'Ods (or Odds) Fish. A corruption of "God's Flesh," or the body of Christ. This was a favourite ejaculation of Charles II.

Odyssey. Frequently used to-day as an adjective for a long series of wanderings in all realms of art. For instance: "The odyssess of historical music scores might form the subject of an interesting volume." The "Odyssey" is the name given to one of the two great epic poems of ancient Greece, attributed to Homer, which describes the ten years' wanderings of Odysseus (Ulysses) on his way home to Ithaca after the fall of Troy. The word *Odyssey* is an adjective formed out of the hero's name, and means the things, or adventures, of Odysseus.

Off the Hooks. There is a double meaning to this phrase. To be off the hooks means, in one sense, to be finished, finally, and once and for all. The second use of the word is for a person out of his mind; he's gone right off the hooks. The latter is sheer slang. The former is said to have as its origin the Maypole stored away in Shaft Alley, Leadenhall Street, London. So long as it rested on the hooks, so long was there a hope that it might come once again into use; but once it was off the hooks, it was gone for ever.

The story of the stored Maypole is connected with the Church of St. Andrew, in Leadenhall Street. From the tall shaft, or Maypole, which stood in front of its doors, and which was lavishly decorated on Saints' and Festival days, it was referred to as St. Andrew Undershaft. After the Reformation, the Maypole was taken down and kept in an alley nearby. For thirty-four years it remained there, "on the hooks," until it was deemed to be a relic of Papish superstition, and was taken off the hooks, sawn up and publicly burned. The alley has ever since been called Shaft Alley.

It should be added that the first reference which Apperson makes to the phrase "Off the Hooks," in his "English Proverbs and Proverbial Phrases," is from Beaumont and Fletcher's "Pilgrim": "What fits this? The pilgrim's off the hooks, too," and Apperson comments, "Mad. Off his head."

Offa's Dyke. The name given to the entrenchment running from the mouth of the Wye at Beachley, to Flintshire. It is not clear whether Offa, who was King of Mercia (757-96) constructed the entrenchment, or whether he only repaired an earlier one, to mark for himself the border between Mercia and Wales. It seems a doubtful origin to the "dyke."

Ogre. There is a fine etymological story about this frightening word. It tells how it is of Eastern origin and is derived from a savage race called Agurs, inhabitants of Asia, who overran parts of Europe in the fifth century!

A second story is that it was derived from the Latin *Orcus*, the God of the Infernal Regions.

Well might the Ogre be a leading figure in the fairy-tales! The truth of the matter is that the word was first used, and invented, by Perrault, in his "Contes," 1697.

Oh, Dear. This mild and usually feminine expletive is a wolf in sheep's clothing. It is merely a corruption of the Italian "*O Dio mio* which, translated, is "Oh, my God."

Oil on Troubled Waters. The reference is, of course, to the fact, well-known, that the force of rough waves is lessened by pouring oil on the waters. The antiquity of the saying is, however, interesting. Apperson gives its earliest use in print as Kingsley's "Westward Ho!" (Ch. IV), where "Campion . . . the sweetest-natured of men, trying to pour oil on the troubled waters." That was in 1855, but the Venerable Bede, who died in 735, tells in his "Historia Ecclesiastics," that St. Aidan handed to a priest, who was to accompany a maiden destined for the bride of King Oswin, a cruse of oil to pour on the sea if the waves became threatening. The event happened, and the priest, poured the oil on the sea, and produced a veritable calm.

O.K. A laconic slang term, imported from the United States, and meaning "it's all right." Its "origins" are many. It is usually said to have been used originally by Andrew Jackson, seventh President of the U.S.A., as an abbreviation of All Correct which, the saying goes, he spelled Orl Kerrect. It is, the writer fears, a slander on the President.

Another version fathers the phrase, in the same terms, on an illiterate Irishman, name and place unspecified.

A third refers the use to "Old Keokuk," an Indian chief, who is said to have signed all treaties with the initials "O.K." It is a pity somebody has not produced one of the treaties from the archives.

It is also strange that nobody has hitherto advanced as an explanation the Choctaw Indian *Okeh*, "So be it."

Old as Pandon Gates (or Yatts), As. The saying was old in 1649. Halliwell in his dictionary says: "As old as Pandon Gate, a very common saying. . . ." There is a gate called Pandon Gate at Newcastle-on-Tyne. In "Denham Tracts" (Folk-lore Society) it is stated: "As old as Pandon Yatts. . . ." The latter is used in the southern portions of the Bishopric (Durham) and County of York. Nothing is more general than the above saying, when anyone would describe the great antiquity of anything. Pandon Gate is believed to have been of Roman workmanship.

Old Bags. The nickname of Lord Eldon, Lord Chancellor, from his habit of carrying home with him in different bags the cases requiring his judgment.

Old Bailey. Bailey comes from the Latin *ballium*, a rampart, through the French *baille.* The term *bailey* meant the open space or courtyard between the castle and its embattlements. Now, Ludgate stood in line with the Old Bailey at its southern extremity, so that there must have been a fortification behind the Roman wall when the Sessions House came to be built. It would seem that the name was retained after the wall was demolished.

Old Christmas Day. Under the old style calendar, Christmas Day fell on 6th January.

Old, Eld and Ald. The three components of place-names given above all mean our word "old." Examples are Ald-bourne, Elt-ham, Alt-on. They are not however, altogether reliable as to age, for a number of fairly recent mushroom towns have been given similar names. Similarly, places in which "new" plays a part are of considerable age.

Old Fogey. A disrespectful appellation for a man advanced in life, or with antiquated notions. It has been assumed that it is derived from the Danish *fjog*, a stupid old man, or one in his dotage. It may be so. But there is a perfectly good word in the English language, *foggie* and *fogram*, meaning in the first place a use of foggy, and in the latter case meaning antiquated, old-fashioned, or out of date.

Old Grog. *See* "Grog."

Old Harry. Said to be a corruption of Old Hairy—the Devil. Why, the writer fails to understand, since there is no suggestion in the various reproduction efforts of the Evil One of any hairy covering.

Old Hickory. Was the nickname given to General Andrew Jackson, President of the United States, by his own soldiers, in allusion to his tough, unyielding disposition. Parton, author of Jackson's life, describes the circumstances of the name as follows: "The name was not an instantaneous inspiration, but a growth. First of all the remark was made by some soldier who was struck with his commander's pedestrian powers, that the general was tough. Next, it was observed that he was as tough as hickory. Then he was called hickory. Lastly, the affectionate adjective *old* was prefixed, and the general thereafter rejoiced in the completed nickname."

Old King Cole was a Jolly Old Soul. It is said that the old King Cole of the rhyme was the father of St. Helena, which would make him grandfather of the Emperor Constantine. Robert of Gloucester refers to him as a British King (legendary, of course). Another source says that Colchester was named after him. This is exceedingly doubtful, for Colchester was the first self-contained Roman colony in England, and was almost certainly named from the Latin *Colonia*.

Old Lady of Threadneedle Street. The nickname of the Bank of England. There is no doubt that it sprang into common usage after the appearance of a cartoon by Gilray on 22nd May, 1797, with the caption, "The Old Lady of Threadneedle Street," in reference to the temporary stoppage of cash payments, 26th February, 1797, and the issue of one pound banknotes in the following month. But there is some dispute as to how Gilray came by the idea of an old lady for his caricature.

A popular version is that some time before, a demented old lady persisted in walking up and down Threadneedle Street, passing and re-passing the bank, in the entrance to which she looked long and earnestly each time. Day after day she appeared, exciting no little curiosity. Then one day, she failed to visit the street, and she was never seen again. It is suggested that Gilray, who must have known of the old lady, used her as his caricature.

Old Man Eloquent. Is what Milton called Isocrates, who, when he heard of the result of the Battle of Chæronea, knowing it to presage the fall of Greek liberty, died of grief.

Old Nick. This is, of course, one of the many names for the Devil. There are legions of names. The earliest of them on record is the Anglo-Saxon *se ealda*, which meant "the Old 'Un." Nick first appeared in the seventeenth century, and etymologists ever since have been endeavouring to discover why "Nick"? Samuel Butler, in "Hudibras," humorously identified him with Niccolo Machiavelli. Strange to relate, a century later it was taken seriously and put forward as an origin. Another theory, supported by Dr. Brewer, derives him from the obsolete *nicke*, water-sprite, which, seeing that the Old Gentleman deals in fire, puts him rather out of his element. Other derivations are St. Nicholas, on the grounds that the saint was, among others, the patron saint of highwaymen. The *Oxford Dictionary* gives up the problem, contenting itself with the remark, "obscure." The probability is that the word was merely a popular name taken at random.

Old Reeky. Or, as it really should be, "Auld Reekie"—the name given by Scotsmen to Edinburgh old town, because it is usually capped by a cloud of reek, which in England would be called smoke.

Old Scratch. Another name for the Devil. Grose connects this with claws, which is bad. Its derivation is from an earlier *scrat*, which came from the old Norse *skratte*, goblin.

Old Shoe, To Throw. The throwing of old shoes for luck at a wedding dates back before 1546, for Heywood, in his "Proverbs," records: "Nowe for good lucke, cast an olde shoe after mee." And Braithwait, in his "Natures Embassie," wrote: "One should haue throwne an old shoo after thee."

Old Sweat. The name given to an old soldier, chiefly one who fought in the war of 1914-18. Although the origin is somewhat obscure, the writer has little doubt that it was taken by a British soldier from a German during that war, and popularized in the strange way that words do become popularized in war-time. For it is a rehash of the German *alter Schwede*, literally, Old Swede, used during the Thirty Years' War, and brought back by Dalgetty and his companions.

Old Tom. A slang dictionary of 1823 describes Old Tom as a cask or a barrel containing strong gin and thence, by a natural transition, the liquor itself. Wagner, in "Names and their Meanings," states that Old Tom was named after Tom Chamberlain, senior partner in Messrs. Hodges' well-known distillery.

To complete the story: It is said to be the name first given to gin by Thomas Norris. Having been employed for many years by Messrs. Hodges, he left, opened a gin palace in Covent Garden, and perpetuated the name of Old Tom Chamberlain, his former master.

Oliver. Cant for the Moon. The first highwaymen were broken Cavaliers, so it seemed legitimate on their part to conjecture an allusion to the broad red face of the great Protector. The only Oliver recorded in the *Oxford English Dictionary* is the name of the primitive treadle hammer of the Staffordshire nail-makers.

Olympia. A small plain in the Valley of Elis, in the Peloponnese, Greece, so-called because the famous games in honour of Zeus were held there.

Olympiad. Among the ancient Greeks, the period of four years between the Olympic games.

Olympic Games. Originally the great athletic festivals held at Olympia. They lasted five days, and took place every four years at the first full moon after the Summer Solstice. There was a record of victors from 776 B.C., though it is known that the games were played much earlier than that. They were abolished in A.D. 394, but have been revived in our time, being held in a different country each year. It was from Olympia and the Olympic Games of ancient Greece, that a sports arena, inside or outside, became termed Olympia.

Olympus. The Olympus of the Mythology of ancient Greece was a mountain in the north of Thessaly, on the confines of Macedonia, some 9,700 feet high. There Zeus held his court with the Gods, "on high Olympus."

Omega. Usually used in the phrase, "Alpha and Omega, the first and the last." Omega is the last letter in the Greek alphabet, as Alpha is the first.

Omelettes are not made without Breaking Eggs. Cheales, in his "Proverbial Folk Lore," (875), fathers this saying on the French revolutionary leader, Robespierre.

Omen. The word is best described as some phenomenon or unusual event to be taken as a prognostication of either good or evil. The word is Latin, but it was not used until the sixteenth century, and its origin is not known. It is thought to have some connection with *audire*, to hear.

Superstitious men have consulted the omens from earliest times. Themistocles was assured of his victory over King Xerxes, says one scribe, by the crowing of a cock.

Edward IV, at the Battle of Mortimer's Cross, is reported to have seen three suns, which blended immediately afterwards into one, and to this vision is said to be due the addition of the sun to his coat of arms.

"Rats, gnawing at the hangings of a room," says Grose, "is reckoned the forerunner of a death in the family."

Clocks are a great source of "omen." The writer has, during the last few months, been given twenty-three instances of clocks which have suddenly struck as many as a hundred chimes after being silent for years, the striking being followed by a death in the family. Other clocks have stopped and defied all attempts to re-start them—until after, so it is said, a death has taken place.

Omnibus. From the Latin *omnis*, all. Now shortened to bus. It was first applied to a public vehicle in Paris in 1828. The following year George Shillibeer who had been in business as a coach-builder in Paris, returned to London and, with two vehicles which he called omnibuses, started a service for the public along the Paddington Road. Strangely enough to Londoners to-day, the business did not prosper, and he gave up the omnibuses and started out as an undertaker. These, the first omnibuses in London, began running on 4th July, 1829.

On Tenterhooks. After cloth has been woven and milled it is fastened by hooks to a frame and stretched in order that it may dry evenly and without shrinking. The hooks in the frame are called tenter-hooks. Thus, to be on tenter-hooks is to be stretched in anxiety, or to the height of expectancy.

On the Tapis. The same as "on the Carpet." Tapis is French for carpet. (Tapestry is from the same root.) The phrase came into use in Britain at the time when the language of the Court was French. Court officials who were rebuked were put on the tapis—from the carpet that covered the Council Chambers.

On Tick. To buy goods on tick is to have them on credit. The origin will now be obvious. Tick is a shortening of ticket—the bill of account to be paid at some date posterior to the delivery of the goods.

On Tip-toe of Expectation. Stand in a street queue which is awaiting the coming of a procession, or some person of distinction, and watch the feet of the spectators as the sounds of approach are heard. Each and every person will at once rise on tip-toe in order to peer over the person in front, and thus obtain a better view.

One Crowded Hour of Glorious Life. Usually attributed to Scott, is a quotation by him from a poem by T. O. Mordaunt.

One Dog, One Bull. A North Country saying, meaning fair play for all. It is derived from Shropshire and the days of bull-baiting there. Only one dog was allowed to be loosed on the bull at a time, hence the phrase, which is even now used extensively for fair play among miners in the North of England.

One Gate for Another, Good Fellow. The origin of this Midlands' proverb is said to be a passage between one of the Earls of Rutland and a country man. The Earl, riding alone, overtook the country-man, who civilly opened for him the first gate they came to, not knowing who the Earl was. When they came to the next gate the Earl waited, expecting the same courtesy. "Nay, soft," said the country-man, "One gate for another, good fellow."

One-Horse. *A One-Horse Town.* Once again this phrase comes from the soil. A ploughing team is, or was before motor tractors, *a pair* of horses. It was only an impecunious farmer who harnessed a *single* horse to his plough. Thus a "one-horse" thing is a pretty poor article, and a "one-horse" town one of small, or limited resources or capacity.

Once in Seven Years. The origin is the belief that once in seven years the worst farmers have the best crops.

Onus on Him. The word *onus* is Latin, meaning burden. Thus, to have the onus of anything on one's shoulders is to have the burden of it, the charge, or responsibility or the duty of it.

Oof. This term for money is relieved to some extent from slang by its believed origin—it is understood to be short for *oof-tish*, a Yiddish interpretation of the German *auf tische*, i.e., *auf dem tische*, money laid on the table, money down. (To table in German is *auftischen.*) The philologist who explained recently that oof comes from the Oof-bird, the source or supply of money, the "goose that lays the golden eggs," was not correct; the Oof-bird comes from the oof!

O.P. Riots. When Covent Garden Theatre was re-opened in 1809, after it had been destroyed by fire, the management announced very greatly increased prices of admission. Every night for three months crowds thronged the pit shouting "O.P." (old prices), and the voices of the players could hardly be heard. As a result, the management were, in the end, compelled to go back to the old prices.

Opal. To say that the name is derived from the Latin *opalus* is only half the truth. It goes back beyond that to the Greek *apallios*, through the earlier Sanscrit *upala*, precious stone. It was first brought from India, and the play of varied colours in the stone, together with its iridescence, has given us the adjective opalescent.

The opal has always been regarded as a stone of ill-luck, except to those born in October, whose birth-stone it is. Probably the remarkable exhibition of this superstition is that connected with Alphonso the Twelfth, of Spain. He had his magnificent opal set in a ring which he presented to his bride on their wedding day. Her death occurred shortly afterwards. After the funeral he gave the ring to his sister; she died within a few days. It was next given to his sister-in-law. Within three months she, too, was dead. Denying that the deaths could be in any way connected with the opal, Alphonso put it on his own finger, and died within a few weeks. His mother finally broke the curse by suspending the opal round the neck of the Virgin of Almudena of Madrid.

Open. The origin of the word may not seem of particular interest at first sight. The interest, however, lies in the root; the word in all languages is common to the Teutonic "UP." And in all languages, as the *Oxford English Dictionary* points out, it has the form of a strong passive participle as if meaning "set up." The word would seem to date back to those days when the door was not an affair on hinges which was pushed *open*, but was something hanging—a skin, we might suggest—which had to be "put up." To put up the door was to open the door. We might quote one German sentence, "macht die thue auf"—"the door is up, put it to," to express the meaning. The English language still refers to opening "up" a country by means of railways or other form of progress.

Opera. There are many musical people who will be surprised at the origin of the name for the music to which they are devoted. Opera means, in its original Latin, "labours," works. It is, in fact, the plural of *Opus*, a work.

Opportune. Portunus was the old God of Harbours, their protecting Deity. The harbour was called, in Latin, *portus*. Taking the prefix *ob* (Latin before), we get *ob-portunus*, before the harbour God. In other words, an opportune arrival was the arrival safely in harbour. The best example of the word in its true meaning is the old, and apt, phrase, "When my ship comes home," which is opportune in the literal and etymological sense of the word. The actual word is said to have been coined by Rochefort in reference to Gambetta and his followers, in 1876.

Optimism. Is the name given to the doctrine propounded by

Liebnitz in his "Theodicee" (1710), that the actual world is the "best of all possible worlds," being chosen by the Creator out of all the possible worlds which were present in his thoughts as that in which the most good could be obtained at the cost of the least evil—in other words, optimism is the omnipotence of God. The word is French—*optimisme*.

"Or I'm a Dutchman." A term of opprobrium current during the rivalry in the seventeenth cenutry between England and Holland. The word Dutch stood for all that was false and hateful. The strongest term of refusal to do anything was: "I'd rather be a Dutchman than do it."

Oracle, The. This was a priest whom, in ancient Greek temples, was consulted by the devout on all questions of import, and who spoke in the name of the God. Usually, the pronouncement respected some future event. The most famous of Oracles was that in the Temple of Delphi, who gave his answer in a whisper in the ear of the inquirer. In most of the temples, however, a woman sitting on a tripod made the reponses, in the name of the God. These were usually as obscure and ambiguous as our present-day "The Stars Foretell" newspaper writers. Whatever happened the Star gentlemen can retort, "We told you so"; and Oracles were pretty much the same.

Orange Blossom. The bridal head-dress is associated with the purity of the white flower, and the prolificness of the orange, than which few trees bear greater crops. It was introduced into England from France about 1820.

Orangemen. The name given to the Protestants in the northern provinces of Ireland. The exact origin of this use of the word "orange" is somewhat obscure. There was in Belfast at the time a celebrated Lodge of Freemasons styled The Orange Lodge. But whether this had anything to do with the ultimate name of Orangemen, or whether, as is generally suggested, it was on account of the adherence of the Protestants to William of Orange (William III) in opposition to the Jacobites, or adherents of the Stuart James II, is not clear.

Orange Peel. One of the many names given to Sir Robert Peel, because of his strong anti-Catholic views. His other nicknames were "Bobby" and "Peeler" for members of the police force.

Oratorio. Because the first sacred musical dramas were performed in the Church of the Oratorians, the religious Order founded by St. Philip Neri at Rome in 1540. They were virtually examples of the older mystery play, but improved and adapted to a religious service.

Orchard. When man ceased to be a cave-dweller, and built a hut, or some other habitation, in which to live, almost the first thing that he did to it was to surround it with a fence. It is to this that the word orchard really dates. In Anglo-Saxon *ortgeard*, parallel to the Gothic *aurti-gards*, garden. The first element of both is considered to be the Latin *hortus* (later *ortus*), a garden. Sandys wrote of it in this sense: "The ortyard entering, admires the fair and pleasant fruit." It should be remembered that gardens as we know them to-day, with crops of family vegetables, flowers, etc., did not exist as such in the times of the *ortgeards*.

Orchestra. The origin of this word will come as a shock to the music-lover at present unaware of it. It had, originally, nothing whatever to do with musical instruments. Derived from the Greek *orchesthai*, it was the space in the ancient Greek theatre *on which the chorus danced*. Later, in the Roman theatre, it was that part of the building reserved for the seats of senators and persons of distinction. In this connection the name is (unwittingly, the author fears!) still perpetuated in its correct sense in the reserved orchestra s t a l l s o f London theatres. There is no record of when the word came to mean a body of musicians banded together for the performance of works.

Ordeal. Was the ancient form of trial by *per Dei judicum* (Judgement of God) which held that Divine providence would intervene to protect the innocent from unjust condemnation. So a suspected person was put to, say, the boiling water test. If, after plunging his arm up to the elbow in boiling water, the skin was uninjured, he was pronounced innocent! Other ordeals were:

By Cold Water. The suspected person was thrown, bound, into a river. If he sank, he was acquitted; if he floated he was guilty.

Ordeal of the Bier. It was held that a corpse touched by the suspected murderer, would bleed at the touch. If it did not bleed, the accused was freed.

Ordeal by Fire. The accused had to hold a piece of red-hot iron in his hand, or walk bare-footed among nine red-hot plough-shares. If he escaped uninjured he was guiltless. A sufficient comment on this "justice" is the fact that he could, if he was a man of rank, undergo the test by deputy!

Orders, Holy. The official profession of a clergyman of the Church of England is "A clerk in Holy Orders." To deal first with the Holy Orders, these refer to the orders, or ranks, of the Church. In the days of the unreformed Western Church these numbered eight, i.e., bishop, priest, deacon, sub-deacon, acolyte, exorist, reader and *ostiarius*, or door-keeper; but in the Anglican Church only three Holy Orders are recognized, those of bishop, priest and deacon.

The "clerk" description is a little more involved. With it is bound up the days when only priests were able to read and write. Clerk is derived from Cleric, the late Latin *clericus*, a clergyman of, or belonging to, the *clerus*. Thus, the original sense of clerk was a man in a religious order. As the scholarship of the Middle Ages was practically limited to the clergy, and these performed all the writing, notorial and secretarial work of the time, the name clerk came to be equivalent to scholar, and especially applicable to a secretary, accountant and a penman. It is now almost exclusively restricted to the latter; but the clergyman retains, officially, his old description of a clerk.

Organ. In 1935 there was discovered, at Aquincum, an old settlement of the Romans, near Budapest, what is believed to have been the oldest organ in the world. Dating from A.D. 150, it had fifty-two pipes. There is, however, said to have been an organ built by the Greek scientist, Hero of Alexandria, in 100 B.C. According to report, this instrument had seven stops. No trace of its existence can, however, be proved.

Orgies. The name for drunken or riotous revels comes from the Greek *Orgia*. And the *orgia* were the secret festivals, held always at night, in honour of Bacchus, the mythical God of Wine.

Original Sin. This is the term applied to the corruption, the innate depravity, or evil tendency of man's nature held by the Church to be inherited from Adam in consequence of the Fall of Man.

Orkneys, The. The name Orc, or Ork, was that given by early writers to a fabulous monster of the sea which would devour men and women, and was of a ferocious nature. Sylvester wrote of it, in 1598, "Insatiate Orque, that even at one repast, Almost all Creatures in the World would waste." We know now that the monster thus fabled was a whale, and that is the whale's generic name in Zoology to-day. The remaining portion of the name Orkneys is either the Gælic *innis*, or the Norse *ey*, both meaning an island. Thus, we arrive at the meaning of the Orkneys—the Island of Whales.

Orphan. Contrary to general belief, need not mean the loss of *both* parents. The etymology of the English language accords to an orphan the description " bereft of *either* or both parents."

Orpheus and His Lute. Orpheus was the famous mythical musician and singer of Thrace, who was said to move rocks and trees by the strains of his lyre or lute. The legend of his lute is that his wife, Eurydice, died and was taken to the Infernal Regions. Orpheus visited the Infernal Regions, and so charmed Pluto with his lute that the Lord of the Dead released Eurydice to him, on condition that Orpheus would not look back until he had reached the earth. Eager for a sight of his beloved Orpheus, as he was about to put his foot on the earth looked over his shoulder, and Eurydice vanished from him. The legend adds that his prolonged grief at the death, finally, of Eurydice, so infuriated the Thracian women that in one of their Bacchanalian orgies they tore him in pieces.

Orrery. The name given to a piece of mechanism which, worked by clockwork, represented the motions of the planets round the sun. It was invented by George Graham, somewhere around 1700. Graham sent it to an instrument maker, named Rowley, for a model to be made to be presented to Prince Eugene. Rowley secretly made a second copy, which he gave to the third Earl of Orrery, and the mechanism was named in his honour. There is an orrery in a Glasgow museum.

Orthodoxy. The best explanation of orthodoxy the writer has ever come across is that given in " Priestley's Memoirs." Lord Sandwich, during the course of a friendly debate, remarked, " I have heard frequent use of the words ' orthodoxy ' and ' heterodoxy,' but I confess myself at a loss to know precisely what they mean."

Whereupon Bishop Warburton replied in a whisper, " Orthodoxy, my lord, is my doxy ; heterodoxy is another man's doxy."

Ostler. The name has come to a sad downfall. The present groom of the stables was once the *hostelier*, the keeper of the hostelry, the landlord.

Ostracize. The curious history of this action lies back in its Greek meaning—*Ostrakon*, an earthen vessel. Ostrazism, the banning of a person, was introduced into Athens by Cleisthenes, in 508 B.C. Once a year the Athenian citizen (or voter) had the privilege of writing on an *Ostrakon* (an earthenware slate) the name of any statesman whom he thought it would be desirable not to have in power. If there were six thousand votes adverse to the statesmen, the decree of banishment took effect. He was ostracized—and by the votes of the people. It may seem to many, nowadays, an admirable idea !

Out of Sight, Out of Mind. The earliest recorded use of this phrase, or proverb, is in the Proverbs of Aifred, in " Old English Miscellany," round about the year 1270 : " For he that is ute bi-loken (shut out meaning absent) he is inne sone for-geten."

Out of Sorts. One of the few phrases to be born in the printing world. Sorts are the different sizes and kinds of type used by the compositor, or type-setter. If he runs short in his " case " of the particular sorts he is using, the work has to be suspended for a time until the necessary sorts are obtained, either by sending for more type, or by dissing (re-distributing from type no longer needed to be kept in the forme). A compositor, with no particular desire to get on with the job, was said by his colleagues to be " out of sorts," and the phrase spread to common usage outside the profession.

Ovation. When a writer says of a statesman or speaker that he received an ovation, he is not particularly complimentary. For the Roman *Ovatio*, from which it comes, meant only a minor triumph, in which a general entered the city on horseback or on foot (instead of in a chariot) after a minor success. He was not considered worthy of a full triumph.

Owl (as a bird of evil). From the days of the Ancients, the owl has been regarded as a bird of ill-omen. Pliny called it, " Funeral owl and monster of the night." Ovid, Lucan and Claudian bestow on it similar epithets. Virgil claims it to have been an owl which foretold the death of Dido. Ross, referring to the death of Valentinian, says : " An owl which sate upon the top of the house where he used to bathe, and could not thence be driven away with stones."

The legend of the owl's evil omen is that a baker's daughter refuse to give bread to Christ, and was transformed into an owl.

Grose tells that a screech owl flapping its wings against the windows of a sick person's chamber, or screeching at them, portends that someone of the family will shortly die.

Oxford. Is called in Domesday Book Oxeneford—a ford for the passage of oxen across the River Isis.

Oyster Part. A theatrical slang term for a part in a production in which the actor has only one line to speak, such as " The carriage waits, my lord."

P

P's and Q's, Mind Your. *See* " Mind your P's and Q's."

Pacific Ocean. The Latin word for peaceful is *pacificus*, from *pax, pac-em*, peace. When, in 1520, Magellan discovered the ocean, he gave it the name of Pacific because he had found it relatively free from storms and bad weather, after his tempestuous sailing through the adjoining straits.

Pack-horse. This name on the sign of a public-house denotes that at some time the original house provided accommodation for " pack-men," and also had pack-horses for hire.

A pack-man was a pedlar, a man carrying goods for sale in a pack ; and a pack-horse was a horse used for carrying packs or bundles of goods, usually in panniers.

Pad the Hoof. To walk. The early Frisian word for tread, go along, was *padden*, and the Anglo-Saxon *paeddan*. It reappeared as a cant word for a walker (hiker we should say to-day) in the sixteenth century.

Paddington Fair. In the days when executions were public in England, large crowds generally gathered at the scene of the gibbet, and a rare trade was done in food and drink, and amusement. London's principal place of execution was Tyburn, which is in the parish of Paddington. Public executions, by the way, were abolished in 1868.

Paddle Your Own Canoe. The phrase originated in the West. An Indian canoe afforded room for only one person. If a man could not paddle it himself, then nobody could paddle it for him. Thus, the phrase came over here as meaning a man who was self-reliant.

Paddock. *As Cold as a Paddock.* The lament has nothing to do with the grass paddock. In 1608 a paddock was the name for a toad. And the clammy cold of a frog or toad is well-known. Topsell, in his " Serpents," wrote : " There be three kindes of frogs . . . the first is the little green frog ; the second is this padock, having a crook back."

Paddy. Every Irishman in England is dubbed " Paddy " as a matter of course. It is an Irish pet-form of Padraig, or Patrick ; and comes, of course, from the patron saint of the island, St. Patrick. To be in a paddy, or a paddywhack, means to be in a bad temper, an allusion to the Irishman's willingness at all times to take part in a fight.

Padre. The soldier's name for a chaplain, or a clergyman, of any denomination. It may come as a surprise to know that it has been used to describe a chaplain for more than two hundred years in the British army. It dates to the days of the East India Company. There were Portuguese settlements in the East Indies, and as they were Roman Catholics, their priests were called *Padre*, that being the Portuguese word for father, the church title of Roman Catholic clergy. British troops serving in India used the word to describe their own chaplains, and brought it back to England. And the name has been used ever since.

Incidentally, the German name for a padre is "Sundenabwehrkanone," which means Anti-sin-gun.

Padre's Flag, The. The historic Union flag used all over the Western Front in the war of 1914-18 at celebrations of Holy Communion, other religious services, and at the funerals of hundreds of soldiers, finally performing its last rites at the burial of the Unknown Soldier in Westminster Abbey. It now hangs permanently from a pillar at the side of the grave. The flag was given, originally, to the Rev. David Railton, afterwards Vicar of Margate, on his appointment as Chaplain in the 47th (London) London Division, in 1915. It did duty at his services at Vimy, Ypres, the Somme, Messines, and elsewhere. The Chaplain brought it back from the Front with him, and it hung in his own church until offered for the funeral of the Unknown Warrior. After the funeral the flag was dedicated in the Abbey, and was placed in its permanent position by representatives of the 47th Division.

Pæan of Praise. A shout of triumph. A general and sustained praise given to anyone or anything. Pæan was the Homeric name given to the physician of the Greek Gods, and the pæan of praise was a hymn or chant of thanksgiving for deliverance addressed to Apollo. It gained the name Pæan from the opening "*Io paean*," the *Io* being a Greek or Latin exclamation of joy or triumph.

Pagan. The word now used to describe a non-believer in Christianity has come to a curious corruption from the original. It is an adaptation of the Latin *paganus*, and the word then meant a villager, or a rustic. It was used of rustics chiefly by the Roman soldiery, and expressed their contempt of people who, being so far removed from the cities, had little knowledge of Roman mythology and the brave deeds of the Gods. When, accordingly, the early Christians called themselves *Miles Christi*, "Soldiers of Christ," they designated, as soldier slang, *paganus* for the non-soldiers of Christ, who knew nothing of their God.

Pageant. "*A Pageant of History*." Put into plain English, it is merely a *page* of history. From the Latin *pangere*, to fix or arrange in place, came the word *pagina*. Pagina was a slab on which figures or letters were arranged in a decided order. Our "page" comes from the word. When living characters, instead of written ones, were used to tell the story, the *pagina* was called in Old English *pagin*. It was changed to *pagent*, and then to pageant.

That, at any rate, is the considered opinion of the writer, though most authorities, including the *Oxford English Dictionary*, state that the origin and history is obscure, while at the same time accepting the English-Latin *pagina*, given above.

Pagoda. Strange to say pagoda, regarded as essentially Chinese, had nothing to do with China, but is apparently a corruption of a name found by the Portuguese in India. The statement of some etymologists that it is a corruption of the Persian *butkadah*, idol-temple, is disputed, and with good reason, since the word idol was not used in Persia. A better possible origin would be the Sanscrit *bhagavat*, holy, divine, or some corruption of the word.

Paint the Lion. A sailor's term meaning to strip a person and smear his body with tar.

Painter. The rope with which a jolly-boat is attached to the parent vessel, is said to derive its name from the Latin *panther*, through the French *pantier*, a *drag*-net. The writer can find nothing to justify the origin.

Pal. *To be a Pal.* Slang term for a friend, but not really such slang as it would seem. The gipsy word *pal*, means brother; the Turkish gipsy has a similar word, *pral* or *plal*, also meaning brother; and the Transylv. gipsy's brother is a *peral*.

Palace. The original palace was the name given to a dwelling on the Palatine Hill (the principal of Rome's seven hills), built by Augustus. It meant the house on the *Palatium*. Tiberius and Nero later built houses there, followed by other of the Roman nobles, until the entire hill was covered with magnificent buildings. Hence its name to spacious buildings everywhere. The word depreciated to describing a garish display, and in the early days of the films we had picture palaces and, to descend to the very depths, gin-palaces.

Palladium. How the name Palladium came to be applied to a music-hall, or other place of entertainment (there is the London Palladium) is a complete mystery. The original Palladium was an image of the Goddess Pallas, in the citadel of Troy, on which the safety of the city was supposed to depend. It was reputed to have been taken there from Rome. Later, the word came to mean anything on which the safety of a nation, institution, privilege, etc., is supposed to depend—a safeguard, in fact.

Pall Mall. The fine thoroughfare, and one of the best known of London's fashionable streets, developed from a wooden mallet used in a game. The word (French) means, literally, a "ball-mallet," from *palla*, any kind of ball, and *maglio*, a mallet or beetle. The ball and mallet gave the name to a game called, originally, *paille-maille*, which was popular in Italy and France in the sixteenth century, and in England in the seventeenth century. A boxwood ball was driven by the mallet through an iron ring, or hoop, suspended at some height above the ground at the end of an alley. The player who, starting from one end of the alley, could drive the ball through the ring with the fewest number of strokes, or within a given number, won the game. Our present Pall Mall was the alley in which Charles II played, he having brought the game back with him on his return from his exile in France.

Palm. "*That takes the Palm.*" The phrase, signifying an achievement in anything (even in lying!) dates back to the Roman Games, when the successful competitor in the games, or the victorious gladiator in the arena, was handed a branch of palm. It represented the same standard in combat or games as the bay leaf of the poet.

Palm It Off. This has nothing to do with the palms of victory, or of pilgrimage, but is an allusion to the art of the conjuror in "palming" (hiding in the palm of his hand) the article which he intends to produce from another place at a later stage in the trick.

Palmer. Those persons rejoicing in this not uncommon surname, can take it that an ancestor of the family had made a pilgrimage to the Holy Land. A pilgrim, on returning, carried with him a palm branch, or leaf, attached to the headgear, as proof that he had accomplished his self-imposed task. On arrival home, it was the custom to take the palm to the church and offer it to the priest, who thereupon placed it on the altar.

Palmy Days. *See* "Palm."

Pampas. A romantic word when read in stories of the West. In reality treeless plains, almost deserts, sometimes three thousand miles long and four hundred miles broad, in South America. There are 750,000 square miles of them.

Pamphlet. There are almost as many "origins" given for this word as there are numbers of pamphlets scattered broadcast on the public. One is that it is derived from the Old French *paume-fueillet* (*paume*, palm, the hand, and *fueillet*, a leaf), as a leaf of paper held in the hand. Another from the old Latin *pagina filata*, a threaded (sewn) leaf. A third to a supposed use of the French *par un filet*, by a thread. Still another, that it is so-called after Pamphilia, a Greek female historian of the first century, who wrote epitomes of history. These explanations are all untenable. A possible solution is found in the Latin *papyrus*, paper, on the assumption that the Middle Latin *pamphiletus* means, literally, "a little paper."

Pan Out. "*I hope it will pan out all right.*" A phrase from the gold diggings. The gold ore (auriferous earth) was placed in a shallow pan, and water was swirled through it. The earth was washed away, the gold, being the heavier part, sinking to the bottom of the pan and remaining there. Thus the search for gold panned out.

Panacea. The word comes from the Greek, meaning "all healing"—in our understanding a remedy, cure or medicine reputed to heal all diseases. The story is that Panacea was the daughter of Æsulapius, the God of Medicine. In the Middle Ages, the search for the panacea was one to which the great alchemists set their hands—unsuccessfully. Fable tells of many such panaceas, such as Promethean unguent supposed to render the human body invisible, Aladdin's Ring, favourite of the fairy stories, Achille's Spear, etc.

Panama Hat. The hat has nothing to do with Panama, but is a corruption of Palmata Hat, from the native head covering in equatorial South America, which is made out of the large leaf of the Cardulavia palmata tree.

Pancake Day. Pancakes were originally flat cakes made in a frying-pan, to be eaten to sustain the stomachs of those who would have, perforce, a long wait to be shriven after confession on Shrove Tuesday. (*See* "Shrove Tuesday and Ash Wednesday.")

When, some time ago, we wrote this "origin," we were assailed by correspondents who asserted that the pancakes were used as a convenient way of getting rid of all the fat which the housewife had stored in the larder, since fat was not permissible during the Lent season. This may have been the reason for a large number of pancakes (!) but it was not the "origin" of the pancake; it was, perhaps, an improvement on it!

Pandemonium. An unearthly row. It is self-explained when it is recorded that it is a Greek word meaning, "All the demons."

Pander. The sense in which the word is used is that of supplying someone with the means of gratifying desire. It is an Anglo-French form of the Latin *pandarus*. Properly, it is a proper name used by Boccaccio, and after him by Chaucer in "Troilus and Crisyde," as that of the man fabled to have procured for Troilus the love and good graces of Chryseis, the name and character being alike of mediæval invention.

Pandora's Box. Pandora, in mythology was the first woman, and Jupiter gave her a box which she was to present to the man she married. She married Epimetheus who, despite the advice of friends, accepted the Gods' gift. He opened the box, and at once all the ills and evils that man is heir to, flew out. Ever since they have afflicted man. All that remained in the box was Hope. Hence, "Pandora's Box" is used to describe a gift which, though it looks valuable, is in the end a snare.

Panic. The word comes from the God Pan, the idea being that sounds heard at night, and which spread fear for which there is no reason, were, and are, caused by him.

Panjandrum, The Great. The term applied to a country worthy who fills every public office available in a village. It was a word invented by Samuel Foote in a string of rigmarole as a test for the memory of Macklin, the actor. Macklin had boasted that he could remember anything he had read once. Foote wrote this:

"*So she went into the garden to cut a cabbage leaf to make an apple pie, and at the same time a great she-bear came running up the street and popped its head into the shop. 'What! No soup?' So he died, and she—very imprudently—married the barber. And there were present the Picninnies, the Joblilies, the Guryulies, and the Great Panyandrum himself with the little Red Button a'top and they all fell to playing the game of catch-catch-can till the gunpowder ran out of the heels of their boots.*"

Macklin, in a fury, refused to repeat a word of it.

Pansy. Ophelia, in *Hamlet* iv, 5, says, "There is pansies, that's for thoughts." There is a suggestion that the pansy, being heart-shaped in its eyes, was thus named after Pan—i.e., Pan's-Eye. But it is more likely that the name is a corruption of the French *pensee*, to think, which would seem to come into line with Ophelia.

Pantaloon. One of the characters in the old pantomime; a Venetian character in Italian comedy, dressed in loose trousers and slippers. The name is said to have come from San Pantaleone, patron saint of doctors. But the point is that the name "pants" for our under-garments and trousers came from pantaloon.

Pantechnicon. How the word came to be given as a name for the cumbersome van in which furniture is removed from house to house is a mystery, because the word, a Greek one, means "Belonging (or an assistant) to the Arts," and was used for the conveyance of pictures and art treasures to and from exhibitions. In this country it was first applied to a bazaar for the sale of artistic work in Belgrave Square, London. The bazaar failed, and was turned into a furniture store. Perhaps they kept the art vans!

Pantheon. The name is a combination of the Greek words *pan*, all, and *theos*, god, in other words, meaning the temple of all the gods; and as such was the Roman temple built by Agrippa, son-in-law of Augustus, about the year 27 B.C., in memory of the victory obtained by Augustus over Anthony and Cleopatra. It was presented to Pope Boniface by the Emperor Phocas in A.D. 609, when it was dedicated as a Christian Church, being known as Santa Maria Rotunda. It still stands to-day as the finest circular building without pillars, or columns. The external diameter is one hundred and eighty-eight feet, the height (exclusive of the flat dome) one hundred and two feet, and the porch is one hundred and three feet wide.

Pantomime. Was known in ancient Greece and Rome. The Greek name was *pantomimus*, an imitator of all or everything. The Roman *mimes* were: (1) Actors who confined themselves to gesticulations or dancing, the accompanying test being sung by a chorus; and (2) mutes at funerals who imitated the characteristic actions of the deceased, e.g., the virtue of generosity.

In Britain, the first pantomimes were also dumb show acting. The first panto-*mime* was John Rich, who opened the Lincoln's Inn Fields Theatre on 8th December, 1714. A man devoid of education, he was a dismal failure as an actor. There was, however, strong dramatic genius in the coarse illiterate man, and in 1717 he appeared in a pantomime called "Harlequin Executed"; and it was recorded of him that in his dumb action he could rival the power and pathos of the most accomplished tragedian. In rivalry to him, Drury Lane produced "Harlequin Doctor Faustus," which may be considered the first real English pantomime, and the forerunner of Drury Lane's famous pantomimes. The nearest approach to-day of real panto-*mime* is the ballet.

Papal Bull. Name given to an edict of the Pope. The bull is a contraction of *bulla*, a seal embellished with the symbol of St. Peter.

Paper. From "Papyrus," an Egyptian reed, the stalks of which, opened out and dried, furnished material for writing upon. Britain's oldest manuscript written on paper is in the Bodleian Collection in the British Museum. It is dated A.D. 1049.

Paper King. He was John Law, projector of the Mississippi Scheme, the prospectus of which promised fortunes to speculators. Instead, it ruined them. It was one of the greatest swindles in history, in which a vast fortune existed on paper.

Paper Money. Bank-notes. The first paper money in England was issued by the Bank of England in 1694. The circumstances are a little peculiar. Up till then banking, as we know it now, had not existed. But in that year the goldsmiths, who were the moneylenders of the country, in return for lending their capital, in gold, to the Government—the amount was £1,200,000—were granted, as a charter, the right to call themselves the Bank of England. The other terms are worth remembering, in view of what followed. They were that the Government should guarantee the loan of £1,200,000, and pay a high rate of interest on it; and that, because the moneylenders had parted with their working capital in gold, they should be entitled to issue £1,200,000 worth of moneylenders' promissory notes (paper promises to pay gold on demand) and use these notes for trade. These notes being, in effect, covered by the £1,200,000 in gold owing by the Government, were honoured throughout the land in exchange for goods, etc., and later became known as bank-notes. The smartness of the deal can now be seen. The moneylenders who had started that day in 1694 worth £1,200,000 in gold, went to bed worth £2,400,000, since not only did they own the gold lent to the Government, but they had created out of thin air a further £1,200,000 in paper money that became known as bank-notes, and were honoured in payment of anything, just as gold was.

It was this lending of the moneylenders' gold to the Government that laid the foundation of our present National Debt.

Parachute. The first living creature to come to earth safely by parachute from mid-air was a dog. In August, 1785, Blanchard, the balloonist, during a three hundred mile trip starting from Paris, threw out a parachute containing the dog in a basket beneath. The parachute descended "according to plan," and the dog reached the ground unhurt. The first human descent by parachute was made by Andre-Jacques Garnerin from a balloon on 22nd October, 1797.

Paradise. The original "paradise" was the tree-studded parks around the palaces of the Persian kings, being derived from the Old Persian *pairidaeza* (*pairi*, around, plus *diz*, to mould, or form). The Greeks seized the word and termed it *paradeisos*. It was first used in this sense by Xenophon; and then by the Septusgint for the Garden of Eden; and finally by the New Testament and Christian writers for the abode of the blessed, which is the earliest sense recorded in England.

Earthly Paradise. In very early times it was believed that there existed somewhere on earth a land, or island, where everything was beautiful, and where there was no death or decay, and that the place could be found for the seeking. Its believed location was somewhere east. Cosmas (seventh century) placed it beyond the coast of China. Ninth century maps put it in China itself. The letter of Prester John to the Emperor Emmanuel Comnenus stated that it was within three days' journey of his own territory. The Hereford Map (thirteenth century) shows it as a circular island near India. The search still proceeds!

Paraphernalia. From the Greek *para*, beside, and *pherne*, dowry. Paraphernalia is, in law, those common articles which common law has recognized the right of a married woman to own and keep, notwithstanding the marital right of her husband to her personal property in general. It applies, also, to all that a woman can claim at the death of her husband if he dies intestate. It is used, literally, to describe clothes, ornaments, trappings, etc., used on parades of ceremony.

Parasite. We still use the word in its original Greek meaning, which was *para sitos*, literally one who eats at the table of another, hence one who lives at another's expense, whether it be a human being, a tree, a plant, or anything else.

Parasol. An Italian word; but the Italians borrowed it from the Greek *para*, beyond, and *sol*, the sun—beyond (out of) the sun.

Parchment. After many years of argument over the origin, there seems no doubt now that the word is derived from the name Pergamus, a city in Mysis, Asia Minor, now called Bergamo. But there is still a doubt as to who was the actual inventor—Eumenes of Pergamus, founder of the celebrated library, about 190 B.C., or Crates of Pergamus. The latter, about 160 B.C., introduced it as a substitute for papyrus because Ptolemy Epiphanes had put a ban on papyrus, in an endeavour to prevent Eumenes collecting a library to equal, or better, the one at Alexandria.

Parchment is made from the skins of very young calves, sheep or goats. The better makes come from the skin of still-born lambs or kids.

Pardon Bell. The Angelus—because of the indulgences once given for reciting certain prayers forming the Angelus.

Pariah. Is the name we give to an outcast from society. In actual fact, a pariah is a member of the lowest caste of Hindu in Southern India. It is an adaptation of the Tamil *paraiyar*, a word meaning (hereditary) drummer, because it was pariahs who beat the big drums at certain Hindu festivals.

Parish. Britain is divided up into parishes, in a local government sense as well as in a church division. It is curious, therefore, that the origin of parishes is lost in antiquity. Camden states that England was thus divided as early as A.D. 630, yet it is pretty plain from the evidence of Seldon that long after this the clergy were living in common. Yet, a parish is a township, or a cluster of townships, having its own church, and ministered to by its own priest. Its Greek name, *paroikia*, suggests the ecclesiastical origin, the word being made up of *para*, beside and *oikos* a house. In other words, the procedure followed seems to be like the present missionary system, whereby a missionary goes and and gathers round him a band of natives, converts, and establishes his "house" (House of God) and becomes their priest, and the company his parish.

Parliament. The first National Parliament is now generally recognized as that summoned by Edward I on 27th November, 1295, at Westminster. It was composed of ninety-five bishops, abbots and priors; sixty-seven earls and barons; thirty-nine judges; and representatives of the lower clergy, and counties, cities and boroughs. There was for a considerable time reference in history books to the first Parliament as that held at Shrewsbury in 1283, and which later removed to Acton Burnell, seven miles away. This was not a complete Parliament because, for one reason, the clergy were not summoned. Similarly, the claim of the Simon de Montfort Parliament of 1265 cannot be accepted as the first NATIONAL assembly.

Parlour. From the French *parler*, to talk. It originally designated a room set apart in a monastery where conversation was allowed and visitors admitted.

Parlous Plight. Parlous is a corruption of perilous.

Parnassus. "*To climb Parnassus.*" To write epic poetry. Parnassus is a mountain near Delphi, Greece, having two summits. In mythology the one summit was consecrated to Apollo and the Muses, and the other to Bacchus. The name is said to be a corruption of *Har Nacas*, hill of divination.

Parr, Old Man Parr. Was Thomas Parr, a Salop man who was said to have lived through the reign of ten sovereigns, to have married a second wife when more than one hundred and twenty years of age, and to have had a child by her. He is said to have died in 1635 at the age of one hundred and fifty-two. There is no confirmation of either of the statements, though an exhaustive search of all possible documents has been made.

Parsley. There is nothing of an origin to record about this concomitant to mutton; but it is interesting to note that it was associated by the Greeks with death—the Greeks decorated tombs with it because it kept green a long time. They had a proverb for a man who was on his last legs, whether physically or in a financial sense: "He has need now of nothing but a little parsley." This is definitely in contradiction to Coles, who stated that "Parsley was bestowed upon those that overcame in the Grecian games in token of victory." It most certainly never was.

Parson. Is just an ordinary "person." In Latin he was *persona*, in Mediæval English *persone*. According to Blackstone the word was given to a clergyman because by his *person* the Church, an invisible body, is represented.

Part. "*Till Death us do Part.*" Most people will be familiar with the phrase through the marriage service, where the sentence quoted above comes in the vows exchanged at the altar. The real meaning was, however, better expressed in the old Prayer Book, in which the wording ran: "Till death us *depart*." Blunt, in his "Annotated Book of Common Prayer," remarks: "Depart is sound English for 'part asunder' and was altered to 'do part' in 1661, at the request of the Puritans, who knew as little of the history of their native language as they did that of their national church."

Parthenon. The great temple built at Athens to Athene (Parthenos, the Virgin), friezes and fragments from which are now in the British Museum in London. It was begun by the architect Ictinus about 450 B.C. The embellishments were mainly the work of Phidias, including the colossal statue of Athene herself. The Elgin Marbles came from the temple.

Parthian Shot. The war tactics of the Parthians were to spread their mail-clad warriors (horsemen) like a cloud round a hostile army, pour in a shower of arrows, and then evade any closer action by rapid flight, still firing arrows backwards upon their enemies. Probably the first "withdrawal according to plan"!

Partington, Dame. The taunt, "Dame Partington and her Mop," is used against those who oppose any progress in any walk of life, or Art or Science. The origin of it is that a Mrs. Partington had a house on the shore at Sidmouth, in Devon. In 1824 a November gale drove up a high tide, which flooded her house, and Mrs. Partington laboured with a heavy mop to sop up the water. The story was first put into a taunt by Sydney Smith, speaking on the House of Lords' rejection of the Reform Bill in October, 1831. He compared the Peers to Mrs. Partington, trying to push back the ocean, saying, "She was excellent at a slop or a puddle, but should never have meddled with a tempest."

Passe-partout. How this came to be the name of a form of framing pictures is a riddle which Philology has yet to solve, for in its original language (French) it means "pass everywhere," a master key.

Passing Bell. The bell rung from the church steeple announcing the death of a parishioner. *See* "Nine Tailors make a Man."

Grose stated: "The passing bell was antiently rung for two purposes: one to bespeak the prayers of all good Christians for a soul just departing; the other to drive away the evil spirits who stood at the bed's foot, and about the house, ready to seize their prey, or at least to molest and terrify the soul in its passage. But by the ringing of that bell (for Durandud tells us evil spirits are much afraid of bells) they were kept aloof and the soul, like a hunted hare, gained the start, or what is by sportsmen called law."

Passing the Buck. The original meaning of the phrase was "swagger talk," and it was first used by the military in India, having been taken by them from the Hindustani *Bak* or *Bukh*. The correct meaning of *Bukh* is, "I want none of your old buck," meaning, "I don't want any swagger talk."

There is, however, a more modern version of passing the buck, described by Hayle in reference to the game of Straight Poker. He says: "Each person puts into the pool an agreed sum. As a matter of convenience it is frequently arranged that each player, in turn, puts in for all. To avoid dispute as to whose turn it may be, a pocket-knife, known as the buck, is passed round, resting with the player whose turn it is to 'chip in' for the remainder. Having done his duty, he then passes the buck to his neighbour on the left."

There is nothing in this to negative the Hindustani *Bukh*, since the person with the knife is, in effect, doing the talking for all—in fact, talking big.

Passing the Port. It is the traditional custom in military or naval messes to pass the port clockwise. The real origin lies in the distant era of sun worship; and, incidentally, the sun ripens the grape which produces the wine. Therefore, the time-honoured custom is symbolical, representing, as it does, the earth revolving on its axis, and turning towards the beneficient sun.

In effect, however, the custom is again associated in more modern times with the possibility of attack. It was the practice, when the loving-cup was passed round at banquets, or in messes for two persons to stand up, the one to drink and the other to "defend" the drinker. On finishing, the drinker passed the cup to his defender, and the next person then rose to defend him, and so on. In defending, a swordsman could the more easily guard against a stab in the back if he stood on the left of the drinker rather than on the right. Hence the way the port passed.

Passion Flower. The legend that this plant of the genus *passiflora* resembles in its part the instruments of the Crucifixion, seems to have risen in mediæval Spain. The resemblances are said to be as follows: The leaf symbolizes the spear; the five anthers the five wounds of Christ; the tendrils the cords or whips; the column of the ovary the pillar of the Cross; the stamens the hammers, the three styles, the three nails; the fleshy threads inside the flowers the Crown of Thorns; the calyx, the glory; the white tint, purity; the blue tint, Heaven; it keeps open three days, signalizing the three years' ministry.

Passover. The name of the Jewish feast commemorative of the "passing over" of the houses of the Israelites whose doorposts were marked with the blood of a lamb when the Egyptians were smitten with the death of their first-born. The feast has been extended to cover the succeeding seven days, the whole making the days of unleavened bread. See *Exodus* xii, 8.

Patent. Letters patent is a document conferring the exclusive right to make or sell for a given number of years some new invention. The word patent is from the Latin *patentem*, lying open. Once the patent is granted for an invention, then its secrets can be "laid open" for all to see, since it is safeguarded against infringement.

Patient. The true meaning of the word may be gained from its Latin original—*patiens*, the present participle of *patior*, I suffer, I endure.

Patrick, Saint. Whatever nationality the patron saint of Ireland was, he was NOT Irish, any more than the present south of Ireland leader, Mr. de Valera is (his father was a Spaniard).

One account of the Saint says that he was born at what is now Dumbarton, about 373, his father being a Roman centurion, Calpurnius, and his mother un-named. As a boy, the account goes on, he was captured in a Pict raid and sold as a slave in Ireland. He escaped to Gaul about 395, where he studied under St. Martin at Tours before returning to Britain.

But there is another account (by Jones) which gives the Saint's birthplace as Carnarvonshire, and adding that his mother's name was Concha, and his own Welsh name Mænwyn. His ecclesiastical name, it is added, was Patricius, given to him by Pope Celestine when he consecrated him a bishop and sent him as a missioner into Ireland.

Jones goes on to say that when St. Patrick landed at Wicklow the inhabitants were about to stone him for attempting an innovation in their religion. Given an hearing, he did not gain much ground with them when he attempted to tell them that the Trinity was contained in the Unity. He therefore plucked a trefoil from the ground and expostulated with the Hibernians: "Is it not as possible for the Father, Son and Holy Ghost, as for these three leaves to grow upon a single stalk." Then the Irish were immediately convinced of their error, and were solemnly baptized by St. Patrick.

Well, there are the two stories. There is as much authority for the one as for the other.

Patronage. Was originally associated with the Church. Blackstone wrote: "Whoever under the Roman Empire built a temple to a God had the right of nominating the officiating priest; and in the reign of Constantine, to induce wealthy men to found Christian churches the same privileged patronage was transferred to them." It still applies in the Church of England to-day.

Patter. The conjuror uses patter to distract the attention of his audience from his sleight-of-hand. The comedian's material is called patter. It is a quick-running commentary of story and wise-cracking. It may, therefore, come as a surprise to learn that "patter" is derived from the Paternoster (Lord's Prayer). The colloquism arose from the rapid and mechanical way in which priests recited the Paternoster and other prayers during the Mass. Surtees in "St. Cuthbert," 1450, wrote: "He saw him wende into the water Nakyd and thar in stande and *pater* in his prayers."

Paul Pry. Was the name of a very inquisitive character in a comedy of the same name by John Poole, 1825. It gave the description to any person having a prying or inquisitive character.

Pax. *The Kiss of Peace.* It is given in the Roman Catholic Church at High Mass, except on the Thursday before Good Friday, when it is omitted from horror of Judas, who betrayed Christ to the High Priests by a kiss.

It is also the name given to a tablet or disc of wood, metal, ivory or glass used in the Church as a means of passing the Kiss of Peace from the priest (representing Christ) to the congregation. The pax occurs in the English ritual as far back as the thirteenth century.

In mythology, Pax is the Roman Goddess of Peace.

Pay. *Devil to Pay.* The origin may be one of two: The devil is the name given to the seam between the garboard strake and the keel of a ship, and to "pay" is to cover with pitch, from the Old French *payer*, to pitch.

On the other hand, The Devil was the name of a famous inn in Fleet Street, London, much frequented by barristers; and a common request to clients in search of a barrister who was absent from his chambers was, "Go to the Devil." A barrister accepting a poorly marked "brief" explained his action as being due to "there being The Devil to pay" for his drinks.

Pay the Piper. An allusion, of course, to the story of the Pied Piper of Hamelin, and what happened when the populace refused to pay him.

Peace at any Price. This was the sneer of Lord Palmerston at the Quaker statesman, John Bright, as a "peace at any price" man. In the war of 1914-18, the phrase was condensed into the one word pacifist. In 1939 Mr. Neville Chamberlain, then Tory Prime Minister, was called a "peace at any price" man both before and after his visit to Hitler at Munich, when he brought back a signed "understanding." Waving this to those assembled to greet him when he arrived back in England by aeroplane, he shouted out, "It's all right now. It is peace." A few months later the war broke out.

Peach. When it is not Americanese for a girl, it is used as a slang term for "telling." In other words, to peach is to inform against someone or something. In this sense it is a contraction and a corruption of the good old word *impeach*.

Peacock. Where this is exhibited as an inn sign, it stands as a remembrance of the Crusades. The flesh of the peacock, being regarded as incorruptible, the bird was adopted by many knights as a crest typical of the Resurrection. "By the Peacock" was a favourite oath of the day.

Peal of Bells. This is not the eight bells in the belfry. Those bells peal, but are not in themselves a peal. A peal of bells is the name given to 5,040 changes, that is, the varying of the order in which the bells each come down as they are being rung. "To ring the Changes" is another allusion to bell-ringing.

Pearls. Most people know the origin of pearls. A small foreign body—maybe a piece of sand—gets inside the shell of the oyster. The irritation thus caused is overcome by the oyster covering the article with a secretion, which in time reaches the size and substance of a pearl. Pliny had another version. He argued that pearls were caused by drops of rain falling into the oyster's shell while it was open, the raindrops being hardened into pearls by some secretion in the oyster. But Pliny omitted to say how the raindrops got into the shell when the oyster spends his time at the bottom of the river.

For some years now, what are called cultured pearls have been on the market. They are obtained by deliberately *putting* a small foreign body inside an oyster-shell, and leaving the oyster to it. By this means, the supply of pearls has been greatly increased. The pearls are of exactly the same quality as the real pearl; the only artificial part of them being the centre core.

Cleopatra's Pearl. You have probably heard of the story of Cleopatra's action to impress herself upon Antony; how, when he remarked on the lavishness of the entertainment provided, and the cost, Cleopatra took one of her great pearls, dissolved it in the goblet of wine and drank Antony's health with it. Antony marvelled at it. The writer has no doubt he WOULD have marvelled—at the fact that any liquid strong enough to dissolve a pearl did not, at the same time, dissolve Cleopatra's throat!

Similar stories are told of other people, the medium of the dissolving being, generally, vinegar. The stories are utter nonsense. Vinegar will not dissolve a pearl.

Peats. "*Turn the Peats*" is an old North Country expression meaning change the subject. The allusion is to the days of peat fires. When one side of the square block of peat became red-hot, it was turned over so as to allow the heat to escape from it into the room, while the other side was getting heat from the fire.

Peccavi. *To cry Peccavi* means to acknowledge oneself in the wrong. The word means, "I have sinned." It was, on one occasion, the subject of an excellent pun by Sir Charles Napier after he had won the Battle of Hyderabad. He said to his staff, "Peccavi" (I have *Sinde*!)

Peculiar People. A religious sect, founded in 1838. It takes its stand on the literal interpretation of texts in the Epistle of St. James and other parts of the New Testament, and on this ground objects to medical treatment of the sick. A more modern organization on much the same lines is Christian Science.

Pecuniary. From the Latin *pecunia*, money. The word, however, goes back further than that mere statement. The Latin word *pecunial* meant property, and the word *peculium* meant the property which a Roman father allowed his child, or a master allowed his servant to hold as his own. In both cases, the word was derived from *pecu*, cattle. Cattle were the ancient medium of barter, and even in Mediæval England a man's fortune was judged by the cattle which he possessed. Ancient coinage was frequently marked with the image of a sheep or an ox. Thus pecuniary, taken to its origin, means value in cattle.

Pedagogue. The word, to-day, means a school teacher, and particularly one with dogmatic views. This is one of the best examples of the changed meanings of words over the centuries. The original pedagogue was a slave, whose duty it was to attend his master's son to school and home again, from the Greek *pais*, boy, and *agein*, to lead.

Pedlar. The amateur philologists have been busy on this word for an itinerant trader. The pedlar walks round with his pack, so the amateurs tell you with gusto that the word is derived from the Latin *pedes*, the feet. On the contrary, if there is any likely derivation, it is the Old English *ped*, a hamper with a lid, in which is stored fish or other articles to hawk about the streets. Even this, however, is doubtful, and the philologists of the *Oxford English Dictionary* state, candidly, that the origin is obscure.

Peel. A Celtic word meaning a stronghold. Peel, Isle of Man, is an instance; and others are component parts of place-names on the Scottish border.

Peeler. Slang name for a policeman, after Sir Robert Peel. It was first given to members of the Irish Constabulary, founded when Sir Robert was Chief Secretary (1812), and was transferred to London policemen when Sir Robert brought in the Metropolitan Police Act, 1829. But long before that it was a slang term for a robber who pill-aged (robbed) pedestrians.

Peg Away at It. The peg in this case is probably connected with a ship's colours, which used to be raised or lowered by pegs. The higher the colours were raised the greater the honour. To peg away at it is to strive to raise the colours higher.

Peg down. In this case the peg was that inserted in tankards, in olden days, at equal distances down the vessel. The idea was that when two or more people drank from the same tankard, none might exceed his just portion.

Peg-out. *To peg out.* To die. The term comes from the military who, when they depart from a spot finally, take the pegs out of their tents, strike the tent . . . peg-out.

Pelf. Slang term for money. Usually referred to as "filthy pelf." A more often used phrase is, however, "filthy lucre." It comes from the Old French *pelfre*. Our pilfer is taken from the same root; and both mean the same thing, pilfered or stolen gains.

Pelican. The "origin" here is of that statement, widely expressed, that the pelican feeds its young with its own blood. It does nothing of the sort. The impression is gained by the fact that the pelican macerates small fish in the large bag attached to its beak and then, pressing the bag against its breast, transfers the macerated food to the mouths of the young birds. It is, of course, inevitable that some fragments of the mascerated food should foul the breast.

Pell Mell. With indiscriminate vigour, disorderly. It was coined to describe the rushing of players in Pall Mall (q.v.).

Pelorus Jack. A dolphin that for many years picked up and accompanied ships along Pelorus Sound. He swam close to the ship, and slightly ahead, and all sailors and travellers looked out eagerly for his appearance. By the Maories, Pelorus Jack was regarded as a minor Deity, and the New Zealand Legislature passed a resolution for his protection. It is unlikely from the many years Pelorus Jack undertook his duties that it was any particular fish. It was probably a succession of "jacks."

Pen, Pencil. A pen was in Latin *penna*, meaning a feather. This is not, however, so strange as it may seem, since the earliest pens were quills—feathers cut into the form of pens with a "pen-knife."

A pencil in Latin was *penicellum*, a paint-brush. This will come as no surprise to artists, since their brushes are still referred to in works on art as "pencils."

The first steel pen was made by a Mr. Wise, of London, in 1803. Joseph Gillott, and others, later improved on this.

Pence. *Take Care of the Pence and the Pounds will Take Care of Themselves.* The person who coined this universally-used phrase for thrift is, alas, unknown. It was in use, however, before 1724, and is quoted in the "Chesterfield Letters" in 1834.

Pendulum. It is likely that the pendulum was invented by Ebn Junis, of Cordova University, in A.D. 1100; and Gerbert, a friend of Junis, is said to have devised the escapement. It was not until five hundred years later, however, that pendulums were fitted in clocks.

Penny. In Britain was first coined by Offa, King of Mercia, A.D. 757-796, who used as a model the foreign coin known as *Novas Denarius.* The first copper penny was struck by the Paris Mine Company, Anglesey, in 1787 (the one dated 1784 is a forgery). The bronze penny dates only from 1860.

The *Denarius* mentioned above is the source of our "d" for pence. It was introduced by the Lombard merchants, who also used the Latin *Libra* (£) a pound, *solidus* (s.) a shilling.

Penny Dreadful. Description which elders gave of the "Blood-curdling" literature printed in penny booklets for the young generation some forty years ago. The books were mostly stories of "Palefaces" and "Indians." They were blamed for the bad habits of naughty boys, in much the same way as "The Cinema" shoulders the blame to-day.

Penny Gaff. This was the name given to a low type of theatre which existed in the early days of the theatre in London and the provinces. The name is said to have been derived from the cock-pit, in allusion to the iron hook, fork or spur with which the cocks were armed for their fighting. The fact that many of these low-down theatres were built on the sites of old cock-pits, and that a penny was charged for admission, earned for them the name *penny* gaff.

Penny in the Forehead. This is an allusion to the old game of making a child believe that a coin pressed on the forehead and surreptitiously removed is still there. There is a reference to it in the *Diary* of T. Burton, dated 9th March, 1658: "Sir A. Haslerigg turned from the chair, and they called him to speak to the chair. He said, 'I am not bound always to look you in the face like children, to see if you have a penny in your forehead'."

Penny Wedding. It was, and still is in certain parts of the rural areas, the custom for all the villagers to be invited to a wedding of a popular belle. In such a case each person contributed his or her quota towards the entertainment and wedding breakfast. This quota was usually limited to a small figure such as sixpence, children paying a penny.

Penny Wise and Pound Foolish. First appeared as a proverb in Camden's "Remains," in 1870.

Peppercorn Rent. A nominal rent. A peppercorn has no appreciable value. Occupation of the premises or estate for which a peppercorn rent is paid is virtually a gift; but the demand for the peppercorn rent is a symbol that the owner still holds his property. In modern times a penny rent is frequently charged in such circumstances. There is an entry in the "Boston Record," 1669, stating: "He payeinge a pepper corne to the said treasurer upon demand for ever on the said 29th of September."

Percy. This surname, according to tradition, should be Pierce-Eye. The story is as follows: Malcolm of Scotland, having invaded England, forced into surrender the Castle of Alnwick. Robert de Mowbray brought him the keys of the castle by which to enter, suspended on his lance. In handing them down from the castle wall, still on the lance, he thrust the lance into one of the king's eyes. "From which circumstance," says the writer, "Pierce-eye has been the name borne by the Dukes of Northumberland ever since."

Perfect Number. One of which the sum of the divisors exactly measures itself. The first example is six. Its divisors are one, two and three, making six. The next perfect number would be twenty-eight.

Perfume. Has a curious origin. Its derivation is the Latin *per fumun,* from smoke. The original perfume was obtained from the combustion of aromatic wood and gums to counteract the offensive smell of burning flesh of old-time sacrifices.

Periwinkle. The origin of the succulent dainty is obvious from its original Anglo-Saxon name of *pine-winkle,* from the Latin *pina,* a mussel, and *wincel,* a corner, from its much convuleted shell. The latter component part came easily to our "wrinkle."

"Perm." A woman's contraction for permanent wave, meaning a curl given to her hair which lasts about six months! It was invented by a Swiss named Karl Nessler, in 1906.

Petard. "*Hoist with his own Petard.*" The petard was an ancient small engine of war. It consisted of a metal, bell-shaped container, inside which was a large charge of gunpowder. The box was attached to the gate or wall of a city, generally on a kind of tripod, and was fused to go off within a very short time. The man charged with the task of putting it against the wall or door in the face of the enemy, was under the double risk of being shot by the enemy or being killed by the petard exploding before he could get safely away from the vicinity. Once exploded, the petard blew a gap in the wall, through which troops could breach the defences. It was because of the number of men killed by the charge as they were placing it that the phrase, "Hoist with his own Petard," came into being.

Peter Out. To peter out means to have reached the end of the profitable supply, either of money or commodity, from which one has been drawing. The *Oxford English Dictionary* gives the source as the U.S. gold-mining camps, but adds that the origin is obscure. The writer is indebted to an old gold-digger of British Columbia for the origin. He was among the earliest men to use the phrase. "The dictionary is correct," he says. "It did originate in gold-mining camps." The method of panning gold is known as "Placer mining," and is obviously surface work. But actually to mine gold, the rock is drilled and charges set to blast the rock. The explosive, in the old days, contained saltpetre, and was colloquially known as "peter." After a lead, or seam, had been exhausted, and there was no further object in blasting, we were wont to say that we had petered it out, or that it was "petered out." This is the correct origin of the word.

Peter's Pence. Was an annual tax or tribute of a penny, first from every house-owner and later from each householder having land or livestock beyond the value of thirty pence. (*Note.*—The penny in this case was the silver penny.) At first it was used for the support of an English College in Rome. Later, however, the Pope shared the gift, and eventually took the lot. The institution of Peter's Pence has been attributed to Ine, King of Wessex (688-728). It is mentioned as "due by an ancient law" in a (Latin) letter of Canute, in 1031. It was discontinued by statute in 1534.

Petrel, The Stormy. The real name of the birds which sailors call "Mother Carey's Chickens." Petrel is said to be a corruption of Peter; and the name given to the birds because during stormy weather they appear to fly patting the water with each foot alternately, as though attempting to walk on it, as did St. Peter when he walked on the water with Christ in the Lake of Gennesareth. The Italian name for the bird is *Petrello,* "Little Peter."

Petticoat. The now very abbreviated article of feminine attire was even more abbreviated when it first was given this description. Its origin is plainly told in the name—a petty coat, a little or small coat. The first petty-coats were worn by men under their coat of mail, or, in the case of civilians, under the doublet. It later was given to the garment worn by women, also a short coat. There is no reliable date at which the petticoat slipped down *below* the waist of women.

Petticoat Lane. The famous London market is not officially Petticoat Lane. The name is a nickname, its directory name being Middlesex Street. The nickname was bestowed on it because of its clothes market, in the days when a popular woman's *outer* garment was a short coat called a petty-coat (petty from the French *petite*, little).

Phaeton. Why this name was given to the open four-wheeled carriage drawn by two horses is not known, but it must obviously have been some play on the original Phæthon. In classical mythology, Phæthon was the son of Helios (the sun) and Clymene. He obtained permission to drive his father's sun chariot, but driving dangerously upset it, and thus caused Libya to be burnt and parched into barren sands, and all the inhabitants of the area to be blackened. The catastrophe, adds the myth, would have set the entire world on fire had not Zeus transfixed Phæthon with a thunderbolt.

The Eighth Army "desert rats" of the World War may be interested in the Libyan story!

Phalanx. In its Greek interpretation, phalanx was a line or array of battle, especially famous in the old Macedonian army, where a body of heavy artillery was drawn up in close order, with shields joined and long spears overlapping. From this it became applied to any determined body of people joined together in support of, or opposition to, some cause—a united front, for instance, is a phalanx in the present meaning of the word.

Pheasant. The game bird gets its name from the Greek *Phasianos*, meaning "pertaining to the Phasis." The Phasis is a stream which flows into the Black Sea from Colchis, and pheasants abounded in great numbers near the mouth of the stream. There is no doubt that they were brought to Europe from Colchis. Their generic name is *Phasianus colchicus*.

Philander. It is a queer change of meaning of a word that a philanderer is to-day a reproach of a man who makes love to all women, but never seriously. For the original Greek word was composed of *philos*, love, and *andros*, a male, or husband, meaning thereby a lover-of-a-man, a dutiful and loving wife!

Philip Sober. "*I shall Appeal to Philip Sober.*" The story of the proverb, if it may be called that, is that a woman appealing to King Philip of Macedon for justice for her husband, was curtly refused by the monarch. She retorted, "Philip, I shall appeal against this judgment." "Appeal," roared the supreme arbitrator, "to whom will you appeal?" "To Philip Sober," was the reply.

Philosophers' Stone. For countless ages the dream of great men. The Philosophers' Stone is the name given to a reputed solid substance, or preparation, supposed by the alchemists to possess the property of turning other metals into gold or silver. Its discovery was the supreme object of alchemy. Being identified with the Elixir it had also, according to some, the power of prolonging life indefinitely, and of curing all wounds and diseases.

The search for it was never successful, in so far as the "Stone" is concerned, but it succeeded beyond dreams when it is realized that in the search our chemistry was born, and has borne all the inventions in modern chemistry.

While looking for the Philosophers' Stone, Botticher found the formula for Dresden China, Roger Bacon the composition of gunpowder (which is rather a pity!), and Helmont discovered the properties of gas.

Philter. Incredible though it may seem, there are still people in Britain who believe in the efficacy of love philtres, or philters. Only a year or so ago a woman confessed to administering a concoction in order to secure the love of the man. The word comes from the Greek *philtron*, from *philein*, to love. The Thessalian love philters were famous; and in the Roman and Greek times philters were commonly used. The age was a dangerous one for those thus sought. Caligula, the Roman Emperor, is believed to have been poisoned by a philter given to him by his wife to preserve his love. Lucretius, undoubtedly, was stricken to madness by a similar draught.

Phlegmatic. We use the term of a person lacking in ardour, or spirit. The Greek word means strange to relate, *to burn*. It is *Phleg-ein*.

Phœnix. "*Rising from the Ashes.*" The name, and the pictured description, of a bird surrounded by mounting flames, is derived from the Greek mythical bird, the Phœnix. It was fabled to be of gorgeous plumage, the only bird of its kind in the world, and to live five or six hundred years in the Arabian desert. As her time for death approached, the Phœnix was fabled to build herself a funeral pyre of sweet-smelling wood. This was ignited by the sun, and the flames fanned by her own wings, and in the midst of the flames the Phœnix perished, only to rise from her own ashes a new and youthful bird.

Photography. Is derived from the Greek words *photos* light, and *graphein*, to write—to write with the light, which is what photography *does* do.

Pianoforte. Before the piano, as we know it, there was the old harpischord, and the clavichord. Before that there was the dulcimer, played as to-day (only it is now called a xylophone) by striking certain "plates" with a hammer. Now, in all these there was only one tone. It could only be softened or strengthened by a light or a hard blow or "pluck."

Somewhere about 1710, B. Cristofori, in Padua, Italy, devised an instrument, probably the harpsichord, *with keys and dampers*, whereby soft or loud gradation of tone could be obtained by the performer, as compared with the unvarying tone of the old harpsichord. He called it *piano e forte*, Italian for "soft and strong." And pianoforte it is to-day, meaning the tone can be either loud or soft at the will of the player. In music a soft passage is still marked *pianissimo* and a loud passage *forte*.

The record period for which a piano has been played without stopping is eleven days and nights, by a pianist named Hajek, in New York in 1939. In Britain the record is one hundred and twenty-two and a half hours by John Strickland of Bolton, at Blackpool, in 1934.

Picnic. The first mention of picnic in England was about 1800, but it was in use in Germany about 1748. It was, originally, a fashionable social entertainment in which each person present contributed a share of the provisions. There is no clear indication of when the change to an *al fresco* entertainment came about.

Pied Piper (of Hamelin). Everyone knows the story, of course; how the piper not having been paid for the rats he enticed, played all the children away. The story was for long regarded as historical, and the actual event was said to have occurred in 1284, with the name of the piper given as Bunting. But the legend, it was subsequently discovered, is told of other places as well as Hamelin. It probably arose, originally, from the "Children's Crusade," in 1212, when a boy, Nicholas of Cologne, put himself at the head of twenty thousand young Crusaders, many of whom perished.

Pig and Whistle. This public-house sign is a corruption of *Piggen Waissail*. Piggen was the Anglo-Saxon for a milking pail. When a large party adjourned to a beer-house the liquor was placed before them in a pail, from which they helped themselves by filling their "pigs"—a mug was called a pig, being the diminutive of piggen. That disposes of the "pig" component. Whistle, it has already been said, was a corruption of waissail, which was the Anglo-Saxon *Was hael*, "Be in health."

Pig in a Poke. The allusion is to the old device of showmen at country fairs selling a cat for a sucking pig. One pig was openly displayed; the others were supposed to be tied in a bag (then called a *poke*) ready for carrying away. Should a suspicious customer not buy the pig in a "poke" without examining it, and opened the bag, the cat leapt out. In other words, the "cat was out of the bag"!

Pigeon English. Should be *pidgin* English. "Pidgin" is the nearest Chinese pronunciation we can get to the word business. Thus Europeans who talk pidgin English are talking business English to their Chinese clients. A Chinese cannot pronounce the letter "r." Hence their "Solly" for sorry.

Pile. "*To make your pile.*" To have made enough money to retire on. Said to be a phrase from the Californian gold-diggers, and refers to either the pile of gold dust from the washings, or the pile of earth which marks the extent of his digging; the bigger the pile the more gold the miner must have washed out.

It should be stated, however, that a *piler* was an English word, now obsolete, for anyone who had accumulated wealth; while the Dutch *peye* was a certain mark, and *boven de peyl* meant "above a set mark." Thus, a man had made his pile (peyl) when he had reached his previously determined mark.

Pillar-boxes. Anthony Trollope, the novelist, was responsible for the placing of the first pillar-boxes in the streets.

Pillar to Post. "*To go from Pillar to Post.*" The phrase was, originally, post to pillar; and it is said to have been a figure drawn from the tennis court and used chiefly with toss. But, as Ernest Weekley states in his "Something About Words," what the association with tennis was is not apparent. The phrase is very old. Lydgate's "Assembly of Gods" (1420), contains the sentence, "Thus fro poost to pylour was he made to daunce." The date is right, for tennis, under the name Tenetz, was introduced into Florence by French knights early in the year 1325. It is said not to have been introduced into England until at least thirty years later, which makes it difficult to account for the date of the quotation given above by Lydgate.

Another version of from "Pillar to Post" is that it is a corruption of from pillory to (whipping) post, and relates to the whipping through the streets of an offender tied to the cart-tail.

Pin. *To Pin One's Heart on One's Sleeve.* A knight in the Brave Old Days went into combat with his lady's favour pinned to his sleeve.

There is another proverb on pins, which runs, "I do not pin my *faith* upon your sleeve." The origin of this is the custom in feudal days of wearing badges of the leader or faction to whom, or which, the wearer subscribed. A man not trusting the good faith of a person wearing the badge of his purported leader, was greeted with the phrase given above.

Pinchbeck. A word used as meaning spurious, counterfeit. Somewhere around 1732 a Christopher Pinchbeck began the manufacture of cheap watches and jewellery in Fleet Street, London. They looked like gold, but were actually an alloy of five parts of copper with one of zinc, and were the first imitation gold ever seen in this country. Anything spurious which looked like the genuine article was quickly nicknamed "Pinchbeck," as, for instance, Thackeray, in "Virgin": "Those golden locks were only Pinchbeck." And Trollope, in "Framley Parsonage": "Where, in these pinchbeck days, can we hope to find the old agricultural virtue in all its purity?"

Pink Snow. The phenomena is seen in several parts of the world, but principally in the snow on Grasshopper Glacier, Cooke, Montana, in the U.S.A., where footsteps in the snow turn pink. The reason is that a peculiar flora, consisting mainly of algæ, frequently occupies the surface of the perpetual snow-fields of the Alps, the Andes, and the polar regions. Over wide areas the snow when disturbed may, in consequence, exhibit a red colour due, in the main, to the resting cells of chlamydomonas nivales. With a different flora, yellow snow sometimes occurs in the Antarctic and also in the Alps.

Pinks. On no fewer than one hundred and twenty-five occasions the writer has been asked to explain why the pink is thus termed, when the flower is mostly white. The name has nothing whatever to do with the colour of the flower; the "pink" is said to be an allusion to the edges of the petals which are scalloped, or "pinked."

Pins. Were *not* introduced into England by Catherine Howard, the fifth wife of Henry VIII, as is so often stated. Nor were they invented by Francois I, at least, not unless the age of Francois when he died was somewhere about two hundred and thirty years. For, in 1345, twelve thousand pins were delivered from the Royal wardrobe for the use of Princess Joan.

Pin-up Girl. A photograph of any shapely girl in a state of undress, and therefore any girl who posed for such a picture. The term became general during the early days of the World War, 1939-45, when there was a demand by the men in the Forces for pictures of such girls, mostly film star "stills," to decorate their messes, recreation rooms or sleeping quarters. Newspapers and magazines, before the era of paper rationing, printed "pin-up" girls in large size to enable them to be cut out and posted up. The phrase for such pictures had existed in America before the war but it did not reach the state of an adjective until about 1940.

Piper calls the Tune. Another allusion to the Pied Piper of Hamelin.

Piping Times of Peace. From Shakespeare "Richard III" i, 1. When war was far off and the pastoral pipe for dancing was the only music heard on the village greens of England.

Pistol. Was so-called from Pistoia, in Tuscany, say three authorities. The writer cannot imagine why, for the town of Pistoia in Tuscany was famous for the *pistolet*, which had nothing whatever to do with firearms, but was a dagger. The *Oxford English Dictionary* gives the origin as Spanish *pistola*, from the French.

Pit of a Theatre. The place which is now immediately behind the stalls of a theatre was so-called from the pit at Drury Lane. The original Drury Lane Theatre was built by Killigrew on the site of the famous old cock-pit in Drury Lane. In its earliest days the folk who went into the pit sat on the earthern floor, as they did at various other theatres in London and elsewhere. They sat, in fact, on the actual pit of the cock-pit.

Pittsburg. The American city was thus named after William Pitt, Earl of Chatham, the British statesman. It means, of course, Pitt's town (burgh). It was given to the town by General Forbes, in 1758, after he had captured the place, then called Fort Duqesne, from the French and Indians.

Plague of London. Devastated the capital in 1665. In London alone sixty-eight thousand people (a third of the then population) died. The word plague is derived from the Latin *plaga*, a blow, a stroke.

Plain as a Pikestaff. The last word is a corruption of *pack* staff. The packman (q.v.) carried his goods in a pack. The pack was slung over a shoulder on a staff — a stout stick — which rendered it easy to carry. The staff was plain, because any embellishments on it would have been painful resting on the shoulder. The "plain" is also a description to distinguish it from the many embellished staffs of office.

Platonic Friendship. The name given to a supposed mutual esteem and love between persons of opposite sexes free from carnal desires, as advocated by Plato and his school of philosophers.

Plaudits of the Crowd. In the days of the Roman theatre, it was the custom of the actors to come to the front of the stage and call *plaudite*, "applaud ye." The variety actor still does it—silently. He WAITS for the applause. The phrase "he received the plaudits of the crowd," means that the recipient was cheered, or approved of, by his fellow men.

Play Fast and Loose, To. The origin of this is said to be an old cheating game called "Pricking the Belt." The "victim" was invited to stick a skewer through a folded belt so as to pin it to the table. The "banker," thereupon taking the two ends, proved that the belt had not been made fast at all. The "trick" was on the same lines as the device to-day to "pull a handkerchief tied round a leg through the leg, leaving the knot still tied." An effective, but childishly simple deceit.

Plebeian. From the Latin *plebeius*, belonging to the Plebs. Although the word is now used as synonymous with vulgar, or low, it is an incorrect interpretation. The Plebs of Rome were the Roman Commoners as opposed to the patricians, senators and knights. In other words, a Pleb was a person not of noble or privileged rank. But there was nothing vulgar about them.

Plebiscite. We use the term to-day for a direct vote of the whole of the electors of a state to decide on some question of national importance. The word comes from the same source as Plebeian (see above). In Latin the word was *plebiscitum*, and was a law enacted by the Plebs assembled in the *comita tributa*.

Plod. "The ploughman homewards *plods* his weary way," wrote Gray, in his "Elegy." Literary research has so far failed to decide, satisfactorily, the origin of the verb "to plod." The one thing that *can* be said of it is that it is not connected with the Mediæval English *plodder*. There is a consensus of opinion among philologists, however, that it may be connected with the Gælic, or Mediæval English, *plod*, a pool, and *plodan*, a little pool, the implied interpretation being a man tramping through mire and wet, and therefore walking laboriously. It would seem to have been used in this sense by Gray in the "Elegy," where the ploughman, who would work on the damp earth, is trudging wearily home on a dull and apparently wet evening. On the other hand, this is the only evidence that can be brought to bear on this translation of the word.

Plough Monday. Although now fallen into disuse, Plough Monday was a great day in the rural districts of the country. It was the first Monday after Epiphany when, the Christmas festivities having come to an end, farm labourers were supposed to return to the plough, that day being regarded as the commencement of the ploughing season, especially in the North and East of England. The day was celebrated by a procession of disguised ploughmen and boys (plough bullocks, plough-jags, plough-witchers, etc.), dragging a plough through the village streets, and begging from door to door for "plough-money" to spend on a last jollification at the village inn. It was in use in the East of England until quite recently.

Plus. +, —. Plus and minus symbols used in arithmetic and mathematics. It was in 1202 that an Italian merchant, Leonardo of Pisa, invented the minus sign to point out his debts. The plus (+) was, of course, the obvious opposite. Both symbols had come into general use all over the world by the fourteenth century.

P.O. Prune. The name coined by Mr. Anthony Armstrong, the novelist and playwright, for the pilot officer of the R.A.F. who lands with his undercarriage up, and always presses the wrong knobs. Mr. Armstrong, who is himself in the R.A.F., invented the character—and the pilot officer — for humorous books which bore the title, "P.O. Prune."

Poacher. Is only interesting by reason of the fact that poach in the sixteenth century was *poche*, and poche was a collateral form of the Old English poke, meaning a sack or bag. (*See* "Pig in a Poke.") A poacher, then, was a person who bagged or pocketed somebody else's property. We cannot see how, as some philologist has worked out, it comes from the Old French *pocher*, to thrust or dig out with the fingers.

Pocket Borough. An old name for a Parliamentary constituency where the influence of a family, or a local magnate, can generally command the votes for a candidate of their choice. Such a constituency is now usually referred to as a "safe seat!"

Poets' Corner. In Westminster Abbey, where are buried some of the greatest British poets of all ages. They include Chaucer, Spenser, Drayton, Ben Johnson, a statue of Shakespeare, Samuel Butler, Cowley, Gay, Addison, Goldsmith, Dryden, Sheridan, Burns, Southey, Coleridge, Macauley, Longfellow, Dickens, Thackeray, Tennyson and Browning, and many others.

The name Poets' Corner was given to it by Oliver Goldsmith because it contained the tomb of Chaucer. Addison, however, had earlier alluded to it as the "Poetical Corner."

Pogrom. This word for an organized massacre comes from Russia, where the word is, in Russian, *gromit*, to thunder, to destroy without mercy. It was first applied to the massacre of the Jews in Russia in 1905.

Point - to - Point Race. *See* "Steeplechase."

Poker to draw up a fire. The author has lost count of the number of times he has been asked to judicate between husband and wife in friendly argument as to whether or not a poker laid leaning across the front of the grate with its point towards the chimney makes the fire draw. The answer is that it all depends whether the wife believes that by so doing she drives away Lob, the house spirit, who loves to lie in front of the fire and play mischievous jokes. Apart from this, the poker has no effect whatever on the drawing up of the fire. The idea of the leaning of the poker across the bars is to form with them the Cross, against which all spirits are helpless.

Pole. *The Barber's Pole.* The familiar red and white striped insignia of the barber dates back to the days when barbers were surgeons as well as hairdressers, and were the blood-letters in times when nearly all illnesses were supposed to need a little less blood in the body to cure them. The white stripes represent the bandages on the arm, and the red ones the blood percolating through. The gilt knob at the end was, originally, a brass bowl with a curved gap in it to fit the throat, and was used for lathering the customer for his shave.

The barber-surgeons, as they were called, had a Royal Charter, and operated as such for nearly three hundred years. When, in 1745, it was decided that the businesses of barber and surgeon were really independent, the two were separated, but the barbers were allowed to hold still their old charter and their guild. According to Dr. Brewer, the last barber-surgeon in London was a Mr. Middleditch, of Great Suffolk Street, in The Borough.

Pole. *Up the Pole.* Crazy, foolhardy. Pole in this case is the sea term for that part of the mast above the rigging, up which no man in his right senses would climb.

Polony. The name for the red-skinned breakfast table delicacy is merely a corruption of "Bologna"; and Bologna was a type of sausage first made in that town.

Pommell. *To pommel someone.* Curiously enough, the word comes from *pomme,* apple, and that was the name given to the rounded knob on top of the hilt of the old sword, because of its apple-like shape. To pommel a person in those days meant to hit him with the pommel of the sword. It now means, of course, to belabour him with the fists.

Pontefract Cakes. Are so-called because they were first made, and are still made, in Pontefract. They are liquorice lozenges, impressed with the image of a castle. The name Pontefract comes from Pontefractus, given to the town by John of Hexham about 1165, the reference being to the broken Roman bridge over the River Aire—*pont,* bridge, and *fractus.*

Poor as a Church Mouse. Since there is no larder or any kind of provisions kept in a church, the mouse unwise enough to make its home there is hard put to it, indeed, to make both ends meet.

Pope. There is a curious circumstance about this name for the head of the Roman Catholic Church. There is in Latin a word *popa,* but this has nothing to do with Pope, being, on the contrary, the description of an inferior Pagan priest. The Pope is taken from the child's name for father, *papa,* and from *pappas,* the Greek infantile word for father.

Pope, English. In all the history of the Church of Rome there has been only one English Pope. He was Nicholas Breakspear (subsequently titled Adrian IV), born at Langley, Herts. He became first a monk, then an abbot in France, and subsequently a Cardinal. His election to Pope was in 1154, and he died in 1159. Incidentally, he was the Pope from whom Henry II of England asked permission to conquer Ireland.

Pope Joan. This story, which crops up at regular intervals with a mass of alleged detail, is a myth. There was never any such person. The story is that Joan, who was said to be of English birth, conceived a passion for a monk, whose name is given as Folda. In order to gain admission to him she assumed a monastic habit and entered the monastery. So pious and holy did she show herself that on the death of Leo IV (885) she was elected Pope. The story ends with the explanation that the deception was revealed when she gave birth to a child during her Papacy.

Popinjay, the name given to an empty-headed fellow, was an old name for a parrot. There was at one time, in certain parts of the country, an annual shooting match at a popinjay. In a letter to Henry VIII from Lord Mountjoy, Captain of Tournay, in 1514, it was stated that there was a shooting at the popinjay by the fraternity of St. George, and that for the current year the provost or mayor of Tournay had acted as his deputy. The provost hit the mark, "and soo," says his lordship, "is yor grace king of the popyngay for this yere." The popinjay in these shootings was, of course, an artificial parrot.

Pork and Beans. The nickname given to the Portuguese troops serving on the Western Front during the 1914-18 war. According to a well authenticated story, when the Portuguese first arrived the military authorities happened to have on hand a large surplus of tinned rations of pork and beans, of which our men had long been heartily sick. Opportunity was taken to pass it on to the newcomers. To the general surprise, the Portuguese took to the menu with avidity. Their fondness for it amused everybody, and at a Divisional concert party a song came out with the refrain, "Pork and Beans for the Portuguese." Someone in authority became anxious lest this should give offence to the Portuguese, and an order was issued which stated, "In future the Forces on our left will be referred to by all ranks as 'Our Oldest Allies,' and not, as hitherto, 'Pork and Beans'." The order, intended to be confidential, by mischance found its way to battalion orders, with the result that it became a general jest.

Portmanteau. The handy bag now in common use is from the French *porter,* to carry, and *manteau,* a cloak. In other words, the original portmanteau was a receptacle for carrying one's cloak.

Port Side (of a ship). The opposite side is, of course, starboard. And for many years the port side was known as the larboard. The disadvantage of this became apparent after many accidents and mishaps caused by the orders from the bridge being misheard, and the ship turned to larboard instead of starboard. The name was, accordingly, changed to "port." The reason for the port was undoubtedly by reason of the fact that when, as in those days, the steering of a ship was usually on the starboard, it was necessary to enter and tie up in harbour, or port, with the larboard side towards the port.

In passing it may be stated that a ship's port-holes are not from the same "port" but from the Latin *porta,* meaning a door. The port itself is from the Latin *portus,* a haven.

Poser. *To set someone a poser.* It was originally an opposer or an apposer, the name given to Fellows who set examination papers at colleges of a University. They "opposed" the efforts of the scholars to pass to their degrees. The term "posers" is still applied to two Fellows of New College, who examine at Winchester.

Post haste. In a hurry. The term arose from the old coaching days, when a person wishing to conclude a journey by coach in the quickest possible time arranged for a relay of horses at the posting stations along the route of his journey.

Post Mortem. Latin for "after death." A medical examination on a body to ascertain the cause of death. The phrase is also used, to-day, for an investigation into the causes of such things as a lost game of cards, or a defeat at the polls.

Posy. Is not, properly, a bunch of flowers. In its original form it was a verse, hence its real designation, *poesy.* The verse of poetry in the poesy was usually engraved in patterned language on the trinket given as a gift.

Pot Calls the Kettle Black. The first mention of this in print was in Shelton's "Quixote": "You are like what is said that the frying pan said to the kettle, 'Avaunt, Blackbrows'."

Pot, Gone to. Gone beyond recovery, like stolen golden or silver articles which have been slipped into the melting-pot, and are now beyond recovery or identification.

Pot-Luck. Is a reminder of the old days when a pot was kept waiting over the fire, being constantly fed with anything that came to hand—meat, vegetables, etc. Visitors were invited to join in a meal, and dipped into the pot, taking what came to the ladle or fork—pot-luck, in fact.

Potato. The statement that Sir Walter Raleigh introduced the potato into England is not true. There is not the least vestige of proof of it. On the other hand, there is every proof that it is inaccurate. Dr. Brewer perpetuates the error by saying that it was introduced into Ireland and thence to England by Raleigh. Other accounts state pacifically that Raleigh introduced it in 1693, after his return from Virginia. Firstly, Raleigh never visited Virginia; secondly, it was known in England long before 1693. In Europe, the potato was first introduced into Spain, it is said, from Quito, soon after 1580, and thence in 1585 into Italy. In 1587 it was being grown at Mons, in Hainault. It was not until 1596 that it is recorded as being grown in England by Gerarde. He himself, rather boastingly, proclaimed that he obtained it from Virginia. The plant is not a native of Virginia, and was not cultivated there until the sixteenth century.

Poverty comes in at the door, love flies out of the window, When. The earliest record of the proverb in print is by Braithwait, in the "English Gentlewoman," 1631, and it is prefaced with, "It hathe beene an old maxime, that . . . "

Poverty makes strange Bedfellows. Was first used by Lytton in his "Caxtons," in 1849: "I say that life, like poverty, has strange bedfellows."

Praise from Sir Hubert. The quintessence of recommendation. The phrase should be "Approbation from Sir Hubert Stanley is praise indeed." It is a line taken from the old play, "A Cure for the Heartache," a comedy by Thomas Morton, produced at Covent Garden on 10th January, 1797.

"Praise the Lord, and Pass the Ammunition." The title of the song which became a popular number during 1942, in the middle of the Second World War. The story told is that Captain W. H. Maquire, then a chaplain in the U.S.A. Fleet, was on the dock in Pearl Harbour when it was attacked by the treacherous Japanese on 7th December, 1942. Despite a fierce fire he got back to his ship. There he found the men hard pressed, and helped to carry ammunition up a ladder to the guns. He is said to have used the words: "Praise the Lord, boys—and pass the ammunition."

The words of the first verse of the song run:

"Down went the gunner, and then the gunner's mate.
Up jumped the sky-pilot, gave the boys a look,
And manned the gun himself, as he laid aside his book,
Shouting . . .
Praise the Lord, and pass the ammunition,
Praise the Lord, and pass the ammunition,
Praise the Lord, and pass the ammunition,
And we'll all be free."

Captain Maquire afterwards stated that he does not remember using the words, but a year later admitted that he might have done so!

Prang, To. A phrase used by the personnel of the R.A.F. to describe a heavy bombing raid on a target. When completely efficient it is a "wizard prang." It came into use after the Norwegian evacuation, and was then used to describe the effects of a few five hundred pound bombs dropped on the invasion ports and enemy naval bases.

The origin is doubtful, and contested. In Devonshire *pranging* is one of the oldest methods of fishing. *To prang* is to stab from above. The Scots had a word *pran* (or prann) meaning to hurt or wound. The Gælic *pronn* is to pound or mash. In Norway, *prange* is to make a parade or great show. The real origin probably lies between the Zulu *to prang*, which means to spear; or the Malay *perang*, war, and *perangi*, to attack. It is likely that officers of the R.A.F. who had seen service in one or both of those countries introduced the word over here.

Precarious. The un-Godly will see a certain aptness in the origin of this word, meaning untrustworthy, uncertain. It comes from the Latin *precarius*, obtained by prayer, or by entreaty; and means, held at the pleasure of another.

Prefabrication. A word which has just come into great prominence during the latter part of 1944, when the problem of houses to replace the blitzed homes of England was under discussion. Prefabricated houses, workshops, and indeed all kinds of things, were advocated; and pictures of prefabricated houses were, in fact, displayed in most newspapers in order that the people could get some idea of this "new-fangled idea."

The author places on record the fact that prefabricated buildings were not the originality of Government departments in 1944; they had then been known for a matter of five hundred years. William the Conqueror, when he invaded England in 1066, brought over with him from Normandy the timbers to make a fort. These were all framed and fitted together beforehand; and the pins to fix them were packed separately in barrels.

Prelate. Although the word means anyone in an ecclesiastical office which gives him jurisdiction over other of the clergy, it is used in this country only as in reference to bishops. It comes from the Latin *praelatus*, meaning carried before.

Prester John. Was the name given in the Middle Ages to an alleged Christian priest and king, originally supposed to reign in the extreme Orient beyond Persia and Armenia. Since the fifteenth century, however, he has been generally identified with the King of Ethiopia or Abyssinia. According to Sir John Mandeville he was a lineal descendant of Ogier, the Dane who penetrated into the north of India with fifteen of his barons, among whom he divided the land. He was said to have been made sovereign of Teneduc, and to have been called Prester because he converted the natives.

He has furnished material for a vast number of legends. According to one of these he had sixty kings for his vassals and was seen by his people only three times a year.

Prestige. The remarkable thing about this word is the honour with which "prestige" is connected. To be a man of good prestige is to be a man of good character and sterling worth, honest and above-board. Yet the word is the French *prestige*, meaning an illusion, a deception or imposture, as in a conjuring trick. The "magic" *Hey, presto,* comes from the same source.

Prima Donna. Is Italian for "first lady," and that is, of course, what a prima donna is in grand opera.

Primrose Day. 19th April, the anniversary of the death of Disraeli, Lord Beaconsfield. When the statesman was laid to rest the coffin was adorned with a wreath of primroses sent by Queen Victoria, and inscribed, "His favourite Flower." This gave rise to the formation of the Primrose League, and the annual decoration of the Beaconsfield statue in Westminster with a wreath of primroses on this day.

The Primrose Day tradition is, however, most likely founded on a mistake. It is stated that the "his" of the favourite flower in all probability represented not Beaconsfield, but the only "him" of whom Victoria ever thought—the Prince Consort.

Printer's Devil. A boy employed in a printing office. Aldus Manutius, the Venetian printer, had a negro boy, and in those days printing was supposed to be a Black Art. Hence the term printer's devil.

Printing in England was born in 1477, when Caxton set up our first printing press in Westminster, near the Abbey. His first printed work, and the first English printed book was, "The Dictes and Sayings of the Philosophers."

Profane. To treat sacred things with contempt. *Fanum* is Latin for temple, and *pro*, also Latin, meant before (or outside), thus to be profane was to be outside the temple, speaking in a literal sense; or, taken colloquially, those who stood outside because they refused to accept the teaching.

Proletariat. From the Latin *proletarii*, the lowest class of the community in ancient Rome, regarded as contributing nothing to the state except offspring. It is a striking commentary to-day that the less wealthy members and usually the lower class of our state are the greatest contributors of offspring.

Pronto. Quickly; at once. Brought into the Army by the U.S. troops during the 1914-18 war. They had taken the word from the Spaniards in one of the Mexican wars. The word is Spanish.

Propaganda. This word, of which so much is being heard at the time of writing (in the fifth year of the World War), comes from the modern Latin title, *Congregatio de propaganda fide*—congregation for propagating the Faith. Congregation in this sense means college; and the college was a committee of Cardinals of the Roman Catholic Church having the care and oversight of foreign missions It was established at Rome by Pope Gregory XV in 1622.

Public Father. In legend Junius Brutus, the first Consul of Rome. It is said that he held the office in 509 B.C. The term "Public Father" was given him by Thomson, in a poem describing his act of condemning his own two sons to death for their share in a conspiracy to restore the throne to the banished Tarquin. The poem runs:

"The public father who the private quelled,
And on the dread tribunal sternly sat."

Pudding. The present sweet was, originally, made from the stomach or one of the entrails of a pig, sheep or other animal stuffed with a mixture of minced meat, suet, oatmeal, seasoning, etc., and boiled and kept till needed—a kind of sausage. It was not exactly a delicacy.

See "Pudding Lane," below.

Pudding Bell. It was the custom in the North of England for the sexton of a church to toll the bell as the congregation left at the end of the morning service. The reason was to let the housewife at home know that the family would soon be with her, and to give her time to prepare to serve up the meal.

"Pudding" Bell because, in Yorkshire, it was the customary practice to serve the Yorkshire pudding, with gravy, before the joint, it being eaten separately. The idea, so 'tis said, was that after the children had filled up with the pudding they did not eat so much meat! But this may be a pleasant fiction.

Pudding Lane. This London street was thus described by Stow: "It was so-called because the butchers of Eastcheap have their scalding hose for Hogs there, and their puddings and other filth of beasts are voided down that way to their dung boats on the Thames."

Pukha, as Pukha sahib, etc. From the Hindu *Pakka*, meaning cooked, ripe, mature, hence thoroughly substantial.

Pulling your leg. Is an allusion to a type of footpad prevalent in London many years ago. These footpads were known to Scotland Yard as "trippers-up." They tripped people by the leg, and as the victims fell and lay on the ground, robbed them. The footpad pulled their leg, i.e., tripped them up.

Punch. Once a favourite drink of Britain, but now hardly heard of, its name came from the Hindu word *panch* (five), from the five ingredients required, or used, in those days. At least, that is the origin usually given. It does not, however, excite much enthusiasm in the author, who bears in mind that sailors who were engaged on the East Indian trade called the large casks in which their grog was stored, and mixed, *puncheons*. This seems a much more likely origin.

Punch and Judy. The Punch of the famous children's entertainment is an abbreviation for the Italian Punchinello. He himself, has two origins: (1) That he was an ugly comedian named Puccio d'Aniello; and (2) that he is supposed to represent Pontius Pilate. Anyway, he has been known in England since before 1700, when he was mentioned by Steele in *The Tatler*. It is believed that Punch and Judy first came to England a year before the accession of Queen Anne.

Purchase. If ever a word was brought back to its original meaning, this word *purchase* is that word in these days of rationing and "under the counter." For purchase comes from the old French *pour-chasser*, and that word meant to hunt for. It belongs to the days when there were no shop windows with goods on show, and goods required had to be hunted for. Usually, apprentices were stationed outside the shops or booths whose job it was to cry, "What do you lack?" or some such phrase; and on that, and a personal hunt, the purchaser had to rely.

Purple, Born in the. The phrase was coined from the custom of the Byzantines that the Empress should be brought to bed in a chamber the walls of which were lined with porphyry, or purple.

There is a story of the finding of the purple dye, which credits the discovery to a favourite dog of Hercules of Troy. He ate a species of fish known as a *purpura*, which it was seen had tinged his lips with colour. After experimenting, Hercules is said to have imitated the colour.

Purse Strings. "*To hold (or close) the purse-strings.*" A relic of the days, not so long ago, when purses were merely little leather bags secured round the mouth with a tied string. Anyone who held the purse strings could very effectually prevent anyone else opening it and spending the money.

Q

Q.E.D. Latin, *quod erat demonstrandum*, which was to be demonstrated. Appended to all Euclid theorems.

Q.E.F. Latin, *quod erat faciendum*, which was to be done.

Quack. Name given particularly to an itinerant dispenser of alleged cure-all drugs. It is a shortened or contracted form of quacksalver, an early Dutch word of the sixteenth century. Salve is the Dutch *zalf*, salve or ointment.

Quad. Short for quadrangle, and quadrangle comes from the Latin *quadr*, *quadri* (four) and *angulus*, angle. Thus, quadrangle means a piece of land having four angles, and therefore four sides. Quod, for prison is a corruption of the same word.

Quadrille. The dance still appears sometimes in programmes. It was of Spanish origin, and is said to have been introduced into England by the Duke of Devonshire in 1813. The word does not come from the Latin *quad* (see above), though it means the same; it is a corruption of the Spanish *cuadrillo*, meaning a small square. The dance, it will be realized, is executed by four sets of couples each forming the side of a square.

Quadrillion. In English numbering a million raised to the fourth power—a one followed by twenty-four noughts.

Quadroon. Like the other "quads," the word is derived from the Latin fourth. A quadroon is one-fourth negro and three-fourths white — the child of a mulatto woman by a white man. A mulatto is a half-blooded person, one parent being white and the other black.

Quagmire. Is merely a corruption of quake-mire, or boggy, soft ground that trembles, or quakes, under foot.

Quail. The bird of that name is derived from the Old Dutch *quackel*, a quacker. The origin of the word quail, as meaning to quail from a blow, is very different. Although a number of authorities state that the origin is obscure, it seems feasible that it comes from the Anglo-Saxon *cwelan*, to die, or the German *qual*, agony. The writer, however, would not be too dogmatic about it.

Quakers. This is the nickname given to the Society of Friends, the religious body founded by George Fox. The simplicity of their faith is well-known. They were first dubbed "Quakers" by Justice Bennet of Derby, in the following circumstances, told by Fox himself: Fox, summoned to appear before the Justice for the non-payment of tithes, admonished the Justice by bidding him "quake and tremble at the word of the Lord." Bennet at once applied the term Quaker to Fox's mission.

There were, however, former religious Quakers. For, from a letter of intelligence written in London on 14th October, 1647, it is recorded: "I hear of a secte of woemen (they are at Southworke) come from beyond sea, called Quakers, and these swell, shiver and shake . . . "

Quandary. The word describes extreme perplexity or dilemma, and it would seem to have justified its name, for of lexiconists no fewer than eight find a different origin for it. The *Oxford English Dictionary* throws in its hand in despair. Skeats's suggestion that it comes from the Middle English *wandreth* has nothing whatever to commend it. Johnson described it as a "low word," but still did not attempt to explain it. The writer can find very little against the suggested origin that it was derived from the French *Qu'en dirai-je*?—"What shall I say of it?"

Quarantine. Quarantine is, of course, the term given to the detention in port of a person arriving from abroad who might serve to spread a contagious disease, and also to the time which all animals must be retained in port on coming from abroad. The present term of quarantine is unlimited, but it was originally forty days—from the Latin *quarentena*, and the Italian *quarentina*, meaning forty.

There is another and little known quarantine—a law term meaning a period of forty days during which a widow, entitled to dower, has the right to remain in the chief mansion house of her deceased husband; hence the right of a widow to remain in the house for that period.

Quarrel. *To pick a quarrel.* Another Latin derivation. The Latin "to complain" was *queri*, and the Latin complaint was *querela*.

Quarry. It was the custom after a deer hunt to skin the killed animal and place on the hide certain parts of the offal. The hounds were then allowed to eat their fill from the offering. Similarly, in the case of the chase killed by hawks, the same custom prevailed. Now, the Old French word for skin was *cuiree*, and that is the source of our word quarry, meaning the hunted animal or bird. It was really not the huntsmen's quarry, but the quarry of the hounds and hawks.

Quarter. *To give quarter.* Despite Dr. Brewer's assertion, and that of the *Oxford English Dictionary*, the author puts forward the suggestion that "quarter" was, in fact, what those nearer to the date of the word stated—that it was the ransom demanded by a conqueror to spare the life of his vanquished foe. The two versions of the story are that the Spaniards and the Dutch, during their fighting agreed that the price of sparing an opponent's life, when he was at the mercy of the victor, was a quarter of his pay. When it was desired that no prisoners should be taken, the order went forth, "No Quarter."

The objection to the story is that quarters was well-known as a word meaning to provide lodgings, and to give quarter to an enemy meant that you gave him lodgings — had to provide him with quarters. The author feels entitled to ask that in such a case, since the word quarters was well-known in this connection, why the phrase was not "No Quarters." Also, the history of the earlier fighting before the Rules of Warfare, did not lean very much in the direction of providing quarters for vanquished opponents.

Quarter-deck. "*Behave as though he was on his own quarter-deck.*" There are two distinct derivations of quarter: (1) A fourth of anything, from the Latin *quartus*; (2) a place set apart, and this comes from the French *ecarter*. Quarters, such as soldiers' quarters, women's quarters, come from the French source—places set apart for special people or purposes; and quarter-deck means a deck set apart for officers or privileged people.

To behave as though on one's own quarter-deck is to behave as if the place belongs to one.

Quarter-master. There is no dispute in the origin of this word. The quarter-master is the man who looks after the quarters of the troops, quarters them, and supplies them with their stores, food, etc. Used in this sense, quarter does not derive from the Latin *quartus*, a fourth, but from the French *ecarter*, to set apart. Another spike in the denial that to give quarter (see above) meant to give the prisoner quarters.

Quasi. A word meaning to cast a doubt on the genuineness of the noun following. It comes from the Latin *quasi*, meaning "as if it were."

Quassia. Is almost the only botanical name which honours a negro. It is an American plant named after Quassi, a negro who, in 1730, was the first to make its medicinal properties known. Quassi was a Surinam negro. He communicated his discovery to C. G. Dahlberg, by whom it was made known to Linnæus. The latter gave the tree the name Quassia. And Mr. Quassia, says a "Treatise on Botany," ever afterwards enjoyed such a reputation among the natives as to be almost worshipped by some."

Queen. In Anglo-Saxon days a queen was just a woman, spelled *cwen*. In Old Norse a woman was *kvaen*; in Gothic it was *qens*; in Old German *kwaeni*. There seems no reason for the *Oxford English Dictionary* to apologize for the fact, and to add a footnote to the effect that "even in Old English *cwen* was app. not an ordinary term for a wife, but was applied only to the wife of a king or (in poetry) some famous person." It was nothing of the kind. The word is quite plainly given in the most elementary of Old English Grammars. We will take, for instance, Wyatt's. Mr. Wyatt is an M.A. of Cambridge, Scholar of Christ Church, and an Examiner in English of five Universities. And Mr. Wyatt's "Old English Grammar" gives quite plainly: "*cwen*, woman." And not a king or an important personage in sight.

Queen Anne's Bounty. A fund raised by tithes and first fruits, and originated at the instance of Queen Anne, for augmenting the incomes of poorly paid clergy.

Queen Anne's Dead. A caustic rejoinder to the retailer of old news. The first mention of the phrase was in a ballad in 1722, eight years after the queen had died. In Lady Pennymans' "Miscellanies," 1740, there appears: "He's as dead as Queen Anne the day after she dy'd."

Queen Dick. "*In the Reign of Queen Dick.*" The origin is unknown, but the phrase is the Old English version of the Latin *ad calendas Graecas* (at the Greek Calends), meaning never. The Greeks had no Calends; and we had no Queen Dick.

Queen Mab. Mab is a shortened Mabel. In Mediæval English it was applied, as Mably, to a witch (see Chaucer). In Tudor times she became Queen Mab, an attractive sprite, only to be reduced to map, mop, and to a disorderly dress as in the "Mobled Queen" of "Hamlet," and so to our mob-cap.

Queen of Hearts. The name given to Elizabeth, Queen of Bohemia, daughter of James I, who, by her amiable disposition and many gracious kindnesses, endeared herself to all hearts.

Queenhithe (London). "Hithe" meant a wharf. The "queen" came about because all the money taken in tolls at this wharf went to Queen Eleanor, wife of Henry II, for pin money, the port being part of her wedding dowry.

Queen's Messengers. The name given by the Queen to the Ministry of Food convoys which, during the great blitz of the Battle of Britain, carried food and comforts to badly bombed towns. The Units consisted of a water tanker holding three hundred gallons, two food lorries each containing six thousand meals, two kitchen lorries equipped with soup boilers, fuel and utensils, and three mobile canteens to distribute the food. The first of the Units was the gift of Her Majesty herself. They began their work in 1941. Each was staffed by a noble band of voluntary women workers, drawn from the Women's Voluntary Service (q.v.).

Queen's Tobacco Pipe. Was the name given to the furnace at London docks where contraband tobacco was formerly burnt. The burning was abolished a few years before the death of Queen Victoria.

Queen's Weather. It was noticed that whenever Queen Victoria appeared outside the Palace to attend a public function, fine and warm weather invariably favoured her, so that a fine and warm day was spoken of as "Queen's Weather." It is now referred to as King's Weather, but the *raison d'etre* no longer exists.

Queer Street. To be in queer street is to be in financial difficulty. The origin of the phrase is believed to have arisen through tradesmen putting a query (?) against the name of any customer whose solvency they had reason to doubt. Maybe it should be written "In query Street."

Queue. Housewives who have stood for long hours in food queues outside shops may like to know that *queue* is a French word meaning tail.

Qui s'excuse, s'accuse. A French proverb meaning that he who excuses or apologizes, condemns himself. A very popular cliche with literary gentlemen, who use it instead of the very good Shakespearean phrase, "Methinks the lady (gentleman) doth protest too much."

Qui Vive. "*To be on the qui vive.*" To be watchful, on tiptoes. *Qui Vive*, though generally interpreted as "Who goes there?" means, literally, "Who lives?"

Quibble. To dispute, to evade. It is derived from *quibus*, a word which appeared constantly in legal documents, and came into use because of the evasions and tricks which it afforded the law.

Quick. The real meaning of the original quick (*cwic*, Anglo-Saxon), is seen in the quick-set hedge—one of live wood, not dead palings; and in the Bible "quick" is also used as living—"the quick and the dead." Its present meaning is, of course, to move at a fast pace.

Quick as Lightning. The phrase was used by Lydgate in his "Fall of Princes," about 1440, where he wrote: "His conquest was swifft as wynd or leuene (lightning)."

Quid. Meaning a sovereign or a one pound note. Origin unknown, but probably related to *quid pro quo*.

Quid of Tobacco. Is a corruption of a *cud* of tobacco, because it is used for chewing. The allusion is, of course, to the chewing of the cud by a cow.

Quid pro quo. Latin, meaning something of equal value given for something received; or, in the other sense, tit for tat.

Quiet as a Lamb. From Langland, "Ploughman," 1362: "He is as louh (quiet) as a lomb."

Quintessence. Is generally used as a word meaning "the best" part of anything; perfect. Its Greek meaning is "fifth essence." The Ancients (of Greece) knew and acknowledged four elements only—earth, air, fire and water. To these the disciples of Pythagoras (the philosopher from 540 B.C.) added an element pure and subtle, naturally bright and incorruptible, and situated above the four terrestrial elements. It was named *ether*, the "Fifth Essence."

Quirk. A term applied to R.A.F. officers while under instructions qualifying for their "wings."

Quisling. Name for a traitor (coined in April, 1940), and means one who is content to accept the yoke of the conqueror for the sake of being given office, even against the feeling and expression of the conquered people, and prepared to use force against his own people to impose the conquerors' decrees.

The Times was the first to incorporate the name as a common noun in the language, by writing it with a small initial letter. The original Quisling was Major Vidkun Quisling, Norwegian officer and diplomat. For many months before the German invasion of Norway, Quisling, an ardent admirer of Nazism, had been preparing the way for the enemy. At the beginning of April, 1940, he went to Berlin for his final instructions. On 9th April, three days after his return, Norway was invaded, and Quisling was appointed Premier of the so-called National Government set up by the Germans. Public reaction, however, was so strong that after a week he resigned. On 28th September, 1940, he was nominated sole political leader in Norway.

Other political leaders in other countries who accepted a similar role under the Nazis, particularly Laval of France, were subsequently given the description "Quisling."

Quiz. The word which, since the outbreak of the Second World War, has come to the front in all manner of brain-testers, is a word which came out of nowhere. The manager of a Dublin theatre, a Mr. Daly, laid a wager in 1780 that he would introduce a new word into the language within twenty-four hours. The bet was taken; and a mystery word appeared chalked on every wall and bare space in the city. Within a few hours all Dublin was speculative on what the mysterious letters meant. The word was "Quiz." The bet was won, and the word was absorbed into the English language.

Quod. *See* "Quad."

Quota. From the Latin *quota*, how great a part. Housewives who were rationed by quota during the World War, 1939-45, will question the accuracy of the Latin interpretation; they will, probably, construe it into how SMALL a part! Anyway, its meaning is the share, or part of share, which is, or ought to be, paid or contributed to a total sum or amount, or from a sum or amount.

q.v. Latin *quod vide,* meaning which see.

R

Rabbi. A Hebrew word, of course, but it does not mean, or did not mean, originally, a Jewish preacher. *Rabbi* means "My Master," and is a title of respect (since the first century B.C.) given by Jews to Doctors of the Law. It should be properly applied only to one who is authorized by ordination to deal with questions of law and ritual, and to perform certain functions.

Rack and Ruin. To go to rack and ruin meant to go to *wreck* and ruin. Wreck was at one time written wrack (and frequently still is), hence the corruption of spelling to rack.

Rack, The. The ancient instrument of torture, upon which Guy Fawkes suffered until he had added inches to his height, was first introduced into England in the Tower of London by the Duke of Exeter, Constable of the Tower, in 1447; and it was then referred to as the Duke's Daughter. It was a frame in which a man was fastened, and his arms and legs stretched until the tension was sufficient to lift his body several inches off the ground.

Radicals. An exceedingly apt mind evolved this word as a description of that advanced part of the Liberal Party. For radical, from the Late Latin *radicalis,* means of, or appertaining to, a root. The Liberal Radicals were formed to *root out* the evils, in their view, of the hitherto constitutional system, which had been for generations maintained by Conservatives. The term first came to prominence when an effort was made to institute a *radical* change in the Parliamentary representation of the country, in 1818. It did, in fact, pave the way for the Reform Act of 1832.

Radiolocation. The art and science of detecting aircraft at a distance was invented in England some time in 1941, and had been successful in detecting enemy raiders approaching our shores in that year. It depends on the sending out of a wireless beam which is intercepted or reflected by aircraft in flight. By timing the interval between the emission of the beam and the arrival back of the same beam reflected, an estimate can be made of the distance of the aircraft sought. The bearing and altitude of the aircraft can be determined from the known direction of the beam which has intercepted the aeroplane.

The Germans discovered about 1944 a method of partially negativing the beam by dropping long strips of paper silver coloured on one side and black on the other.

Radium. There is an extraordinary authority extant which says: "The knowledge of radium is attributed to the discovery by Henri Becqueral, in 1896, of the Uranium rays, but there are prior claims to those of Niepce de St. Victor, and among those prominent among research on the subject are the names of M. and Mme. Curie." Was ever such nonsense talked by a philologist?

Radium was discovered, in pitchblende, by M. and Mme. Curie and M. Bemont, in 1898.

If all the radium in the world was gathered together and made into a ball at the time of writing (1944), that ball would equal in size the ball used by golfers in their game.

Rag. The first "rag," in the sense of which we mean raggy, or tattered, was the Old Icelandic *rogg,* and the Norwegian *ragg,* meaning in each case a rough tuft of hair. It became *ragge* in Middle English, when it came to mean a worthless fragment of woven material. Hence the word to-day, in whatever sense it is used. "Only a *rag* of evidence" means that the evidence is small and worthless.

Rag and Tag, to which "bobtail" is generally added, was a common expression in the sixteenth and seventeenth centuries for the common mob. Later they were referred to as the "Great Unwashed."

Rag on Every Bush, A. Meaning a young man who pays marked attention to more than one lady at a time. The phrase appears first to have been used about 1866.

Rag - time. Began to raise its head in America in 1901. On 6th April that year there is a passing reference to it by a writer in "The Sage Leaf": "The coon song with its rag-time accompaniment." It did not break into its full fury, however, until some years later; and it was about 1912 when it reached its way to England. The first big all rag-time performance was "Hello Rag-time" at the London Hippodrome in 1912, when Ethel Levey played the leading part. By 1920 there were little semi-amateur rag-time bands in every café and dance hall in the country. It pretty well died when Jazz came along, also from the U.S.A.

Ragamuffin. One in rags, and it can mean one whose moral or commercial reputation is also in rags.

Ragged Colt makes a Good Horse. For more than four hundred years this has been a country proverb. In Hill's "Common-place Book," published by the Early English Text Society, it is noted as well-known before 1500. The quotation in the "Common-place Book" reads: "Of a rwgged colte cwmeth a good hors."

Ragged Regiment. At one time in London dilapidated effigies of our monrachs and persons of note were carried through the streets at the obsequies of the subjects represented. The name The Ragged Regiment was given to the collection of images which were kept in Islip's Chapel in Westminster Abbey.

Ragman Roll. In 1296 Edward I of England went to Scotland, there to receive the homage of the Scottish King (Balliol) and of the Scottish nobles. The homage was not only of personal act, but also in the form of signed and sealed roll; and because of the quantity of seals pending from the document, it was nicknamed the Ragman Roll. The roll is preserved in the Records Office in London.

The word rigmarole, a long-winded harangue, is a corruption of ragman roll, the latter having gone out of use about 1600.

Ragout. This name for a seasoned meat stew, with vegetables cut small, comes from the French *ragouter,* meaning to bring back taste, and from the Latin *gustare,* taste, a reference to the spiced seasoning.

Rags, Glad. Men or women's evening dress. A term of sarcastic wit on the opposite to rags.

Railway. Was not, originally, the lines upon which trains run. The locomotive had not been invented when the first railways were laid. In 1602 British mining companies laid rail-ways along which to run their trucks of coal from the pit, and from the road to the harbour. These rails were, however, made of wood. Such rail-ways existed in Newcastle where they were, in fact, first used in 1602. It was not until 1820 that iron rails were used in this connection, and these were changed to steel in 1857.

Railway King. The nickname given to Mr. George Hudson, Chairman of the Midland Railway Company, who made a huge fortune by speculating in the early days of railways in England.

Railway Murder. The first murder on a British railway was in 1864, when Franz Muller murdered a Mr. Briggs on the North London Railway. He fled to New York, was traced, brought back and executed.

Rain before Seven, Fine before Eleven. This old country tag was being used as far back as 1853, and probably earlier.

Rain Cats and Dogs. There have been some extraordinary "origins" given to this old piece of description of heavy rain. Dr. Brewer goes to great and laborious efforts to explain it. "In Northern Mythology," he says, "the cat is supposed to have great influence on the weather and English sailors still say, 'The cat has a gale of wind in her tail.' Witches that rode upon the storm were said to assume the form of cats." Of dogs, Dr. Brewer continues: "The dog is a signal of wind and was an attendant of Odin, the storm God."

Quite so, but all this is mythology, so one might expect to find "raining cats and dogs" much earlier, say, than 1653, when the phrase was first used in print!

Now there was in the Greek language a word *catadupa*. And of it Pliny wrote (referring to the Nile): "The water he beareth hasteneth to a place of the Æthiopians, called *catadupa* where, in the last fall amongst the rockes that stand in his way, he rusheth downe with a mighty noise." So catadupe was a *waterfall*. Although now obsolete, catadoupe was also a French word for waterfall.

The obvious corruption, for a heavy fall of water, of *catadoupe* is, surely cat-and dog. And rain is a heavy fall of water, like a catadoupe, or waterfall.

Rainbow Chasers. Are those who hope for impossible things. The expression comes from the old-time belief that if one reaches the spot where the rainbow touches the earth, then one might dig and find a pot of gold.

Moon Rainbow. It is not generally known that the moon can form a rainbow. It does so in exactly the same way as the sun during or after rain, but the lunar colours are fainter.

Rainy Day, To Keep Something by for. The proverb first appeared in print in 1582 in Breton's "Works," where it was written: "Wise men say Keepe somewhat till a rayny day."

Raise your Screw. Employers in olden days handed over wages screwed up in paper of uniform size, says Johnson. The more money it contained, the less tightly the paper could be screwed, and the higher up was the screwing. Thus more wage represented a higher screw!

Rampage, On the. One of the few phrases of Scottish origin, connected with *ramp*, to storm and rage. It means, of course, to act in a violent manner.

Ranch. Was the name given (in Spanish, *rancho*) to huts occupied by herdsmen or labourers. A cattle ranch was where cattlemen lived and worked together. It is a Spanish-American term, and the original ranches were buildings in which labourers lodged at night. In effect, a ranch was a mess room.

Ransack. To ransack a house. The Danish *rann* represented a house; and *saekja* to seek, search. So that to ransack meant to search a house thoroughly.

Rap. "*Not worth a Rap.*" The phrase comes from Ireland where, in 1720, when small change was scarce, a counterfeit coin appeared. Nominally a halfpenny, its value was less than half-a-farthing. It was known as a "rap." Swift, in his "Drapier's Letters" (letter i), says: "It having been many years since copper halfpence . . . were coined in this Kingdom, they have been for some years very scarce, and many counterfeits passed about under the name of rap." Barham, in the "Ingoldsby Legends," writes: "His pockets were turned out, and the devil a '*rap's* left'."

Rara Avis. Though now used for anything very uncommon, its translation from the Latin is "A rare bird," and it was first used by Juvenal in writing of a black swan. Horace ("Sat." ii, 2, 26), also applied it to the peacock.

Rarest Flower. The *rara avis* of the flower world was undoubtedly the turquoise blue rose, which bloomed on a yellow rose tree at Kizablek, Bulgaria. It bloomed once, and never another rose of the colour appeared again.

Rascal. It is suggested that the word is from the French *racaille*, "the scum of the people." This is, however, by no means certain; and the *Oxford English Dictionary* decides that the origin is obscure. It can be said, though, that the term in the fourteenth century indicated the lean worthless deer of a herd, and was used by those in the Chase so to describe such a deer. Later, it came to be applied to people, and meant at one time the rabble of an army.

Rat, Cat and Dog. Some time in 1843 William Collingham wrote this rhyme:

"The Rat, the Cat and Lovel the Dog,
Rule all England under the Hog."

It cost Collingham his life, for the rat was Rat-cliffe, the cat was Cat-esby, Lovel was Francis, Viscount Lovel, called by the populace the King's "spaniel"; and the Hog was the Blue Boar, the crest of Richard III.

Rat-Catcher Churchill. A German newspaper abuse for Mr. Churchill during the 1914-18 war. It was an allusion to one of his speeches as First Lord of the Admiralty about the German Fleet in Wilhelmshaven and Kiel: "If they do not come out to fight, they will be dug out like rats from a hole."

Rattening. In 1861 the *Illustrated London News* reported: "Another rattening attempt was made in Sheffield." Rattening was a device of trade unions of that day to force workmen into the unions. It consisted of taking away the workman's tools, or of damaging machinery—it would be called sabotage to-day—in order that the men outside the union could not earn their living. It was prevalent chiefly in the North of England, and particularly in Sheffield.

Raven. The bird has always been regarded as one of ill omen, possibly because of its name and the belief that it followed armies in order to raven on dead bodies. (*Note.—Raven*, to devour voraciously.) It was held that where ravens were seen, there was death following after. Much the same is said to-day of the vulture in the desert. Ross informs us that "by ravens both publick and private calamities and death have been portended." Cicero is said to have been forewarned by the noise and fluttering of ravens around him that his end was near. Yet the only Biblical reference to ravens that we have was of their feeding the Prophet Elias during the drought, and as the first bird which Noah sent out from the Ark.

Razzle-Dazzle, On the. The phrase came from the United States to describe a jollification. Its first recorded mention in print was in Gunter's "Miss Nobody," in 1890, where he says: "I'm going to razzle-dazzle the boys with my great lightning-change act."

Read oneself in, To. This was, originally, a clerical term, and referred to the first duty of a new incumbent to a parish of reading the Thirty-nine Articles of the Church from the pulpit of the church to which he had been inducted. He made the Declaration of Assent to them at the same time.

Reading Between the Lines. *See* "Lines."

Really Not a Sailor. A chaffing expression coined in the days of the 1914-18 war for the Royal Naval Air Service, being a play on the initials R.N.A.S.

Reason. The Goddess of Reason was the leader of a blasphemous mockery of Christianity which was popular during the French Revolution. Women of questionable repute were enthroned and worshipped in the Cathedral of Notre Dame in Paris. Each in turn was titled the "Goddess of Reason."

Rechabites. It will be recalled that in Biblical days the Jewish family of Jonadab, the son of Rechab, refused to live in houses, or to drink wine. When, therefore, there arose a strong temperance or total abstention movement in the United States, it called its society the *Rechab*ites. About 1681 the English Rechabites were formed, and issued a publication with the title, "The English Rechabites, or a defiance to Bacchus and all His Works." From it sprang the present Independent Order of Rechabites, a well-known and popular Friendly Society.

Recluse. *He's a recluse.* A recluse is a solitary man, one who shuts himself away from his fellow-men ; and recluse is from the Latin *recludere*, to shut up.

Recreant. Is derived, somewhat curiously in view of the present meaning, from the Latin *re*, again, and *credo*, believe to believe again. In some way in Old French, the Latin came to be *recroire*, to yield in trial of combat. To-day, it typifies a craven ready to yield in fight.

Rector. The word means one who rules, from the Latin *rectus*, *regere*, to rule. In the Church of England the Rector is the clergyman of a parish where the tithes belong to him, as distinct from a vicar, where the tithes go elsewhere and he draws a fixed stipend.

Red Cross, for the care of wounded in battle, was a society formed voluntarily to carry out the views of the Geneva Convention of 1864. Its objects are to care for the wounded in war, and secure the neutrality of houses, hospitals, etc., and to relieve suffering from pestilence, earthquake, famine, floods, or any other calamity. It is supported by voluntary subscriptions.

Each country has its own Red Cross organization, such as the British Red Cross ; but there is also an International Red Cross, which acts as a protecting power in time of war to ensure that prisoners of war are being treated according to the Geneva Convention.

Red Flag. One thinks of Russia—Red Russia—but there were red flags long before the Russian emblem. In Rome the red flag signalized a call to arms and war. In the French Revolution the red flag was used as a symbol of insurrection. The reason for the choice of red by the Russian State is not far to seek. Red in Russia is regarded as the beautiful colour. The word for beauty is *kraca*. The Russian word for red is *kracnie*. Thus, the *red* army, the *red* flag, follow naturally.

Red Herring. "*To draw a red herring across the path.*" There was a sport somewhere about 1686 which consisted, according to Cox's "Gentle Recreations," in trailing or dragging a dead cat or fox (and in the case of necessity a red herring) three or four miles, and then laying the dogs on the scent.

This may have been the origin of the saying ; but a more likely origin is that the scent of a red herring, thus laid, would divert the dogs or hounds from the original scent. It is a fact that a red herring, drawn across the trail of a fox, destroys the scent, and thus faults the hounds. A red herring, incidentally, is one that has been dried, salted and smoked.

Red Lamp Corner. Was the name given to a notoriously perilous point near Festubert on the Western Front of the 1914-18 war. To warn our troops of its peril a red lamp was kept burning at the corner at night. Hence the name.

Red Letter Day. A joyful event. So-called because in olden times Saints' days were usually holidays, and they were printed in red in the Calendar of the Book of Common Prayer. Only the red letter days had special services provided for them in the Prayer Book.

Red Rag to a Bull, To Show a. The origin of this belief seems to have been the red cloaks flourished in the bull-ring by the matadors to attract the attention of the bull to themselves. The cloaks of red, embroidered with gold, made a splash of colour in the bull-ring, but the belief that red makes a bull angry, and that he will attack anyone wearing a garment of red, is fallacious. Red means nothing to a bull ; he will as soon attack a white-robed person as a red-robed one, if he has that desire.

Red Riding Hood. Riding-hood was the descriptive name given to a costume worn by women in bygone days for riding. Hats could not very well be worn on horseback—not the type of hats which the women of that day wore ; so the hood came in handy should the weather turn to rain. *Red* Riding Hood merely because the teller of the fairy story made the costume red in place of the usual black of the Riding-hood.

Red Sea. The description may seem a misnomer, since the water is the same colour as the other seas, but its bottom is composed of red sandstone, red rocks in parts border its stones, and there are red coral reefs, animaculæ and seaweed. The name Red Sea (*Mare rubrum*) has existed through the Romans in the days of the Ancient Greeks.

Red Tape. Charles Dickens is believed to have been the first to have used this expression to express the hide-bound and rigid application of rules and regulations, but he only gave a name to the officialdom upon which Carlyle had poured scorn for many years previously. It owes its origin, of course, to the fact that government officials—and lawyers—always tie their documents round with red tape.

Redcoats. This was the nickname of the British Army because, up to the last war (1914-18) their uniform properly consisted of red coats. The full dress uniform of the Guards still continues the red coat.

Red coats are also worn by members of the Hunt—although it is usually referred to as "the Pink." They are said to have been adopted for hunting kit from the fact that Henry II declared fox-hunting a royal sport—and red is the colour of the Royal livery.

Redheads. Judas Iscariot is stated to have had red hair. As a natural consequence, red-haired persons have the reputation—totally undeserved — of being deceitful and not to be trusted. Middleton, in "The Witch," relates how in the early centuries the fat from a red-haired person was in great demand for the preparing of poisons, and Chapman, speaking of flattery in "Bussy d'ambrois," states that it is "worse than the poison of a red-hair'd man."

Reduce. We use this word in the sense of to lessen, or to bring to a lower state, but its original meaning was to "bring back," from the Latin *re*, back, and *duco*, I lead. Bishop Jeremy Taylor, in his "Rule of Conscience" (II, iii, 19), uses it in its proper state : "A good man will go a little out of his road to reduce (lead back to his path) the wandering traveller."

Reekie, Auld. *See* "Auld."

Referendum. From the Latin *referre*, to refer. The referendum as a political expedient was introduced originally by the Swiss Government. It was first used against a vaccination law passed by the Federal Council, or Chamber, in 1882.

Refresher. This is a legal term, meaning the daily amount paid to Counsel for a case which lasts over one day.

Regatta. The first regatta was held at Venice, on the Grand Canal. It was a competition between the gondoliers of the city of canals. In the Italian language regatta means strife or contention, or, in the words of Florio, "a struggle for the maistris."

Regular Brick, A. "*He's a regular brick.*" For the origin of this phrase, meaning that a person is a "good sort," we have to go back some way into history. Plutarch, in his "Lives," tells this story of the visit of an ambassador from Epirus to Argesilaus, King of Sparta. The ambassador, failing to see the vast walls that in those days usually encircled a capital city, thus addressed the King: "Sire, I find no walls reared for defence. Why is this?"

"Indeed, Sir Ambassador," was the reply, "Thou canst not have looked closely. Come with me to-morrow, and I will show thee the walls of Sparta."

On the following morning the King conducted his guest to the plains outside the city where the Spartan army was drawn up in battle array. Pointing to them, he explained: "There, Sir Ambassador, thou beholdest the walls of Sparta—ten thousand men, AND EVERY MAN A BRICK."

As for the meaning of "a brick" as a good sort, a sport, or a man to be admitted to fellowship, the *Century Dictionary* says that the expression arose in English Universities as a humorous translation of Aristotle's perfect square—the inference being that a brick was a "square man."

"Remember." The cryptic word uttered by Charles I on the scaffold to Bishop Jaxon. What it was the Bishop had to remember was never revealed—if the Bishop knew! It has, however, been interpreted (says Dr. Brewer) as meaning that Charles, who was a Catholic at heart, feeling that his misfortunes were a divine visitation on him for retaining Church property confiscated by Henry VIII, had made a vow that if God would restore him to the throne he would restore the property to the Church. He was, Dr. Brewer adds, asking the Bishop to remember the vow and see that his son carried it out, but Charles II wanted money too badly to do that.

Rendezvous. From the French *rendez*, betake, and *vous*, yourself. Go to . . . the place appointed Originally, however, it applied only to a place appointed for the meeting of troops, and this true meaning is evidenced to-day in the signs which adorn many roads in military areas, such as "*Rendezvous No. 2.*"

Reply. We use the term as meaning answer back to a question. It is not quite the correct origin. Its meaning in Latin is *replicare,* to turn back. It may best be explained by "X" asking a question of "Y." The question is answered by "Y," who asks an additional question on the same topic. The answer to this additional question by "Y" is the REPLY—the turning back.

Resurrection Men. Were those ghouls who dug up bodies from their newly-dug graves in order to sell them to anatomists for dissection, in the early days of anatomical surgery. The Resurrection Men are commemorated in the story of Burke and Hare.

Reveille. An old Army Drill Book of 1701 says: "The Revally takes, as is most likely, its denomination from the French *Reveiller*, which signifies as much to arise up or awake from sleep; for this is beaten in the morning to give notice to the People that they may goe abroad, at which time the Out-centinels are taken off." So that Reveille is pretty nearly as old as the army itself.

Revolver. The rapid firing pistol, was first used in 1835. Its inventor was Samuel Colt, of Hartford, Connecticut, U.S.A.

Revue. A mixture of song, drama, comedy and farce, first appeared in this country in 1912. *The Tatler*, in October of that year, referred to "'Kill that Fly,' the new revue which is crowding the New Alhambra." Eight years later Gardiner was referring to "One of those dismal things called revues, that are neither comedies nor farces, nor anything but shambling, hugger-mugger contraptions into which you fling anything that comes handy." They ran, however, for many years, becoming full-length vaudeville shows.

Rhapsody. There sprang up in the days of Ancient Greece a class of wandering minstrels. From the "Iliad" and "Odyssey" these men picked out fragments and, combining them together, sang and recited them wheresoe'er they roamed, in much the same way as in French Provence centuries later, and in England later still, minstrels related the deeds of their masters. The fragments which the Greek minstrels strung together were called rhapsodies, from the Greek *rapto,* to sew, and *ode*, a song. Thus a rhapsody was, originally, verses "sewn" together and sung. A rhapsody to-day is, more often than not, fulsome praise of a very unworthy object.

Rhe. A component part of many place-names, with its allied word, Rhin. This means rapid, swift, and Rhin, that which runs. Of Gælic origin, it is generally used in connection with rivers. The River Rhea in Staffordshire, and the Rhee, in Cambridgeshire, are examples. The word as a suffix appears also in land place-names, and in this sense means a promontory, or a piece of land "running" out to sea.

Rhetoric. From the Greek *rhetor*, an orator. Originally the word was confined to the art of speaking eloquently in public. So much was thought of rhetoric in the days of Aristotle, that there was a science of rhetoric, for which Aristotle wrote a treatise.

Rhino. This, as a slang term for money, has been in use since the early days of the seventeenth century. Its origin is obscure, but is probably connected with nose, the Greek word for which is *rhinos*.

See "Nose, Pay through the."

Rhododendron. The name comes from the Greek *rhodon,* rose, and *dendron,* tree.

Rhubarb. Was known to the Greeks. Its name comes from the Greek *rheon barbaron* which, to give a free translation, means something which comes from the barbarous country of the Rha—the Greek name for the Volga. It was on the Volga banks that the rhubarb grew extensively, and whence it was first imported into England.

Rhyme. *It's neither Rhyme nor Reason.* A budding author took his first book to Sir Thomas More for his opinion. The Chancellor read it, and gave the verdict: "Turn it into rhyme." This the author did, and once more presented the book for judgment. "Ay, that will do," said Sir Thomas. "'Tis rhyme now, anyway, whereas before it was neither rhyme nor reason."

Ribstone Pippin. The name given to an apple, first grown at Ribstone, Yorkshire, from pips originally planted on his estate by Sir Henry Goodriche.

Rice at a Wedding. Rice among the Hindus is regarded as an emblem of fecundity. The custom of throwing rice at a bridal couple as they leave the church in this country is merely a practice designed in fun and friendship; but in India rice is thrown by the bride over her groom, and by the groom over his bride, as an offering to the Gods to gratify their desire for children.

Riddle. From the time of the early Greeks, and doubtless before, man has asked man riddles. The Greek name for a riddle was *ratsel,* from *raedan,* to read, and the meaning of the Anglo-Saxon *raedelse* was the same. Homer, according to Plutarch, died of chagrin because he was unable to solve a riddle set him.

Hiram, King of Tyre, lost a large sum of money to Solomon in a contest of riddles.

And Abdemon, one of Hiram's subjects, won it back from Solomon!

Riddle of the Sphinx. The most famous riddle in history. The Sphinx propounded it to the people of Thebes (Egypt). Those who could not decipher it, she devoured. The riddle was:

"What animal is it that has four feet, and two feet, and three feet, and only one voice; yet its feet vary, and when it has most it is weakest?"

After many ages, the riddle was correctly answered by Oedipus; and upon hearing the answer, the Sphinx slew herself. The correct answer was:

"MAN, for he crawls on all-fours as an infant, walks on two feet during his middle age, and in old age moves upon his feet and a staff."

Riding (of Yorkshire). The three administrative divisions of Yorkshire are called West *Riding*, North *Riding* and South *Riding*, because each forms a third part of the county, and the Scandinavian and Anglo-Saxon *thriding* meant a third part. The "th" was dropped by the amalgamation of North, East and West.

Riff-raff. Trash. Worthless people. *Raff* in Swedish meant sweepings. But *rit-et-raf*, an Old French term, stood for "one and all." A line on the present meaning may be got from the Old French *rifler*, ransack; and *raffler* snatch away. Anyone who stole and took away being **riff-raff.**

Rift in the Lute. Rift means a cleft or fissure in the earth, or a rock, or to break through something. The word is of comparatively recent origin, as philology goes, coming in the first place from the Scandinavian, about 1300. This fact makes its association with the lute, a musical instrument, impossible, since the lute was not then used.

We must, therefore, find another lute. In Latin we find the word *lutare*, which meant to fasten or fix with lute; and lute was a tenacious clay or cement used to stop a hole, or to render air-tight a joint between two pipes. Thus a rift in the lute can mean a split, or a fissure, or a cleft, in the covering (the lute) of any object, whereby its usefulness is impaired. A broken friendship would be covered by such a phrase.

"Right" and "Left." The Conservative Party is the party of the Right, because in Continental legislative chambers the Conservatives sit on the right hand of the Speaker, and the Liberals, Radicals and Labour sit on the "Left." The further to the Left one goes, the more Socialistic one is supposed to become.

Right as a Trivet. Tripet is from the Latin *triped*, or *tripes*; and a triped was a three-footed stand, from *tri*, three, plus *ped*, leg. If a tripet was not firmly on its three legs it could not stand. If it stood, then it was right. There could be nothing more right than a standing tripet. Trivet is a corruption of tripet.

Right Foot Foremost. To put the right foot foremost is a revival of the old Roman superstition that it was an ill omen for visitors to cross the threshold of a house with the left foot first. In noble Roman houses a boy was employed to see that guests were prevented from so doing. He was a "foot-man." The footman of our noble houses in this country is his descendant.

Right-hand Man. A man to be trusted, to undertake responsibility for one. Since the year 1000 the advantage of a right-hand man has been recorded in writing. The origin of the phrase is undoubtedly the fact that the right hand is the stronger of the hands; allied to this is the fact that it has always been the right hand which wielded weapons of defence. A man's guardian, or equerry, stood at his employer's right hand, in order to leave his own right hand free to draw his sword. Did he stand on the left hand of his employer, the employer's body would be an impediment to the free use of his right hand.

Right of Way. It is a fallacy that if a funeral cortege passes over certain property, hitherto not a public path, that it constitutes for the future a right of way.

Right of way for the public may be claimed by uninterruped usage over a period of years. It is to preserve the individual rights to a private road that, once a year, the road is barred to the public.

Rigmarole. "*It's all Rigmarole to me*," meaning a long-winded harangue of little meaning or importance. The word is a corruption of Ragman Roll, which it replaced about 1600. *See* "Ragman Roll."

Rile. To rile someone, or be riled. This is not, as is stated by one authority, a variation of "rail." It is a corruption of roil, an old word to describe, among other things, the stirring up of the sediment at the bottom of a container or stream, thereby clouding the water. To rile somebody is to stir them up.

Ring him up. Nine people out of ten will doubtless give the origin as the telephone. It is not. The telephone borrowed it from the stage. Ever since the stage has had curtains or very nearly that time, the curtain has been "rung up" on a scene. "Ring him up" is a direction to the stage manager when an actor is prepared behind the curtain to start his part. "Ring him down" is the call at the end of an act, or when something untoward has occurred on the stage.

Ring-leader. Name for the leader of a body of people, is derived from the old phrase, "To lead the Ring," the ring being a group of associated, and usually mutinous, people.

R.I.P. A frequent symbol on tombstones, is the Latin abbreviation for *Requiescat in pace.* May he (or she) rest in peace.

Rip. "*He's a Rip.*" The term is a corruption of reprobate.

Rip van Winkle. *See* "Winkle."

Ripon. *True as Ripon Steel.* It is stated that so hard was Ripon steel that spurs, for which the town was famous in manufacture, would strike through a silver coin without the point being "turned."

Rival. The original rivals were people who dwelt on opposite banks of a river, or other stream. The word has descended from the Latin *rivalis*, one living on the opposite bank from another, from *rivus*, Latin for a stream. The antagonism of such dwellers over their fishing rights quite possibly led to the word being used in connection with disputes of all kinds.

Rivers, The Longest. The longest river in the world is the Lower Mississippi and the Missouri, which join. The distance ascribed to it is four thousand five hundred and two miles. The longest river in Europe is the Volga, two thousand four hundred miles; in Africa the Nile, three thousand five hundred miles; in Britain the Thames, two hundred and twenty-eight miles. The Amazon, in South America, is four thousand miles.

Roam. To "roam" comes from the Eternal City—an allusion to the many pilgrimages undertaken. Skeats, while granting this possibility, and agreeing that the etymology is really doubtful attempts, also, to join the word with the Anglo-Saxon *ramian*, meaning to stretch after. It is an exceedingly remote connection.

Roast. "*To rule the Roast.*" The saying has been in common use since about 1530, but none of the earlier examples throw any real light on the precise origin of it. It is likely, however, that it came from the action of roasting meat, and that the ruler of the roast was the master of the house whose word when the meat was sufficiently roasted was law. It is in that same sense as master of the house that the word is still used.

Robbing Peter to pay Paul. By Royal Letters Patent dated 17th December, 1540, the Abbey Church of St. Peter, Westminster, was constituted a Cathedral, with a resident Bishop. Ten years later the Order was revoked and the diocese of Westminster was reunited to that of St. Paul's Cathedral. The result was that its revenues were given towards the repairs of the City's temple—what was taken from St. Peter's went to pay St. Paul's.

Robin Hood. To what extent, if at all, Robin Hood was an historical figure, has been the subject of much debate. One view holds that he was a twelfth century Anglo-Norman noble, Robert FitzOdo. Another insists that he was Robert, Earl of Huntingdon (and this is the "popular" view). It is exceedingly doubtful whether he ever did live; the truth probably is that many stories of derring-do of many times were gathered round an imaginary hero—Robin Hood. However, the story goes that he was born at Locksley (Notts.) in 1160, was bled to death by a nun; and the "authentic" bow and arrow (the last arrow he shot) are preserved at Kirklees Hall, Yorkshire, said to be the scene of his death. And the site of his grave is commemorated in the park of the Hall.

Robin Redbreast. The legend of this familiar and friendly little bird is that a robin picked a thorn from out of Christ's crown of thorns, and blood issuing from the wound made in His head by the thorn, dropping on the bird's breast, stained it red.

Robinson Crusoe. Alexander Selkirk, a buccaneer, was at his own request marooned on the island of Juan Fernandes, off the Chili coast, in 1704. He remained on the uninhabited island for four years; and Defoe's "Robinson Crusoe" is founded on Selkirk's adventures.

Rochester. From *Hrofoceaster*, after *Hrop*, a Saxon chieftain, who built a castle on the site of a Roman castra, encampment.

Rock of Ages. One of the most famous hymns of Christianity. It was written by the Rev. Augustus M. Toplady. While walking at Barrington Coombe, in the Mendips, he was overtaken by a violent storm, and found shelter in a gap cleft in a huge rock of limestone. It was as he sheltered there that the words of the hymn came into his mind—"Rock of Ages, cleft for me."

Rod. "*Spare the Rod and Spoil the Child.*" From *Proverbs*, xiii, 24.

Rod in Pickle, A. Birch-rods used to be kept in brine (pickle) to keep the twigs pliable. The salt in them had the additional advantage of getting into the cuts made by the twigs, thus adding to the pain.

Rogation Days. The three days preceding the Feast of the Ascension when, in the olden churches, the Litany was chanted in anticipation of the blessed event. The word comes from the Latin *rogare*, to beseech. The constant response in the Litany to "We beseech Thee, good Lord," is emphasized.

Roger de Coverley. It is rather remarkable that Dr. Brewer should assert, with others, that the name of this dance is really Cowley, near Oxford, and was always so intended. In 1719, in D'Urfey's "Pills," is given the refrain of a popular song, beginning, "O Brave Roger of Cauverly." Ralph Thoresby states quite definitely that the place-name is the same as Calverley in Yorkshire; and early references in print refer to the dance as having a North Country atmosphere.

Rogue. Is not, as is often stated, from the French *rogue*, arrogant. It appeared first in the English language, about the middle of the sixteenth century, to designate various kinds of beggars and vagabonds. From this it is surmized that the word came from the name Roger, which was frequently used to define such a person.

Rogue and Vagabond. Was a term which included all travelling actors, who were liable to be whipped on a complaint being made by a respectable member of the community. There is an instance recorded of a company of such actors, in which Madge Robertson was one, with her family, who owing to the business they were doing in their booth at Nottingham Goose Fair on one occasion, to the loss of the audience of the Theatre Royal in that city, were complained of by the manager of the theatre, one Charles, and were moved on by the police as "rogues and vagabonds." The old Act has never been repealed, and touring actors to-day are still, legally, rogues and vagabonds.

Rogue Money. A tax formerly levied on a parish or county to provide a fund for the expenses of the apprehension, prosecution and maintenance in prison of rogues. Act 25 and 26 Victoria states: "The proceeds of such sale shall be paid into the rogue money funds of the county."

Rogue's Yarn. The old name for the strands of coloured thread which was woven into ropes for the Navy, so that it could be traced if stolen.

Roland for His Oliver, A. Roland was the legendary nephew of Charlemagne, celebrated in the "Chanson de Roland," frequently together with his cousin Oliver. Their exploits are so similar that it is virtually impossible to keep them apart. What Roland did, Oliver did, and vice versa. Eventually the two met in single combat. They fought for five days on an island in the Rhine, and the contest ended in what we, to-day, would call a draw!

The phrase, "A Roland for his Oliver," means that whatever your rival (Oliver) may do, you will give him as much—supply a Roland to it.

Roll Call. A memory of those olden days when all writing was set out on one long roll of paper. To have a roll call was to read the names from the scroll, unrolling it as the names came. To be added to the rolls of a society meant, anciently, to have your name added, literally, to the rolled up sheet of membership.

Romany. From the gipsy *Romani*, feminine and plural of *Romano*, from the masculine *Rom*, a male gipsy, a Romany.

Romany Rye. Rye is gipsy for gentleman, and a Romany Rye is a non-gipsy who lives with the gipsies as one of themselves, learns their language, and enters into the gipsy spirit.

Romeo and Juliet. The "History of Verona," by Cortes, places the story of the two lovers of Verona in the year 1303. It was told in Masuccio's *Nouvel* in 1476; again in "*La Giulietta*" by da Porta, 1535; again in *Novella*, by Bandello, in 1554. It next became a poem by Arthur Brooke, "*The Tragicall historye of Romeus and Juliet,*" 1562; and a story in 1567 in Painter's "Palace of Pleasure." Then Shakespeare wrote it up!

Rookery, as the designation of a slum, has allusion to the rooks' nests in trees. The birds build closely together and are, in fact, overcrowded.

Root and Branch, To wipe out. Applied to people who want to go the whole hog. Its origin lies in the Puritans. When they wanted to extirpate the episcopacy they were called "root and branch" men.

Rope him in, To. Is a phrase from the wide open spaces of the cattle ranches of America. When cowboys "roped-in" a steer, they lassooed him.

Rosamund the Fair. The daughter of Lord Clifford, and the mistress of Henry II, is of interest in philology by reason of the fact that it was for her that the Labrynth was created. Henry had made for her a retreat through which "no man might come to her." The retreat was a house called "The Labrynth." It was set in the midst of a garden modelled into an astounding maze. Rosamund was eventually poisoned by Henry's queen, Elianor, who found the way to the Labrynth by a clue of thread.

Whether the story is true or not cannot be stated. The evidence given above was not available until two hundred years after the alleged event. It is added that Rosamund was the mother of Geoffrey, Archbishop of York.

Rose and Crown. This, as an inn sign, symbolized the end of the Wars of the Roses by the marriage of Henry VII to Elizabeth, daughter of Henry IV.

Rose, Under the. *See* "Sub Rosa."

Rosemary, That's for Remembrance. Ancient tradition held that the herb of rosemary strengthens the memory. And under the name Hungary Water it was used as a drug to quiet the nerves. The name means sea - dew, a reference to its supposed liking for soil near the sea.

Ross. Where it appears in place-names, means a headland, as Kin*ross*, Roslin and Montrose.

Rostrum. Still means a place from which a speaker addresses his audience. It is a Latin word meaning beak. Now the prow of a ship was called the beak of a ship. And in old Roman days the stand for public speakers in the Forum of ancient Rome was adorned with the "beaks" of ships taken from the Antiates in 338 B.C. That is the origin of the word rostrum.

Rota. This is not a Latin word, as at first sight seems obvious. It was the name given to a London club, founded in 1659 by J. Harrington. A political club, it had for its object the advocacy of rotation in Government offices. The club met at the Turk's Head, in Westminster. As may be imagined by its advocacy, its existence was short, but its name for an ordered rotation has lived after it. We still do things by rota, to-day. Rota, by the way, came from the Latin. It means a wheel.

Rotten Row. The famous horse-riding track in London's Hyde Park is a corruption of *route du roi* (Royal road)—*from the Palace of Westminster to the Forest*—a relic of the days when only French was spoken at the Court of St. James. There are several other "origins" which need not be considered.

Roue. This name for a dissipated man came about as follows: "*Roue*" is French for wheel, through the Latin *Rota*. The Duke of Orleans, Regent of France, gathered round him a body of companions as profligate as himself, "every one of whom," he himself said, "deserved to be broken on the wheel" (a punishment of the time, about 1720, for malefactors). The Duke therefore named his gang, "The Roues."

Rough and Ready. It is claimed that this description of something not elaborately or carefully ordered, comes from the nickname given to General Zachary Taylor, the twelfth President of the United States of America (1784-1850). If that is so, then Mr. Taylor must have been like it nearly from birth, for in 1810 F. J. Jackson, in "Sir G. Jackson's Diaries and Letters," speaks of "a rough and ready state of affairs."

Round Robin. Never had anything to do with a robin. It was originally *rond*, round, *ruban*, a ribbon, and was the invention of French Government officers to make known their grievances without any name heading the list. The ribbon at the end of the signature was cut and joined neatly together.

Rove, To. To wander about all over the place. Its origin goes back to the days of Britain's bowmen. To practice their shooting archers were wont to shoot their arrows at a mark selected at pleasure or random, and not of any previously known distance. Thus, they roved around with their arrows.

Rowdy. The first "rowdies" were backwoodsmen of America of a rough and lawless type. Hence a rowdy is a rough, disorderly person addicted to quarrelling, but how he came by the name rowdy is obscure.

Rubicon. "*To cross the Rubicon*," means to take a step from which there is no retracting. The Rubicon was a small river separating ancient Italy from Cæsar's province of Gaul. In 49 B.C. Cæsar crossed over the river with his armed forces, knowing that the effect was a declaration of war. It is said that as he crossed he uttered the words, "The die is cast."

Ruby. One of the most, if not the most, precious stones in the world. In the days of the Ancients, it was precious in more than a material way. It was believed to be an antidote against poison, a talisman that ensured that one would never contract the Plague, and would never turn one's mind to evil thoughts.

Rudge. In place-names means a back or a ridge, such as Rudge and Rugeley, which are on the ridge of the Downs of Surrey.

Rule Britannia. Was at its beginning merely words and music in a masque, "Alfred," by James Thompson and David Mallett. Thompson wrote the lyric and the music was by Dr. Arne.

Rum Chap, A. Not slang. Not even dialect. A "rum chap" is merely a gipsy lad.

Run Amok. One philologist explains the phrase thus: "The phrase is derived from the Malays who, while under the influence of opium, rush through the streets with drawn daggers, crying 'Amog, Amog' ('Kill, kill')." Well, he was very nearly right. The Malay *amoq* is an adjective meaning furiously to engage in battle with desperate resolution. The term Amuco was applied to Javanese who went into the streets and killed all the people who came into their path. In "Pinto's Travels" (1516) there appears: "That all those which were able to bear arms should make themselves Amoucos, that is to say, men who resolved either to die or vanquish." Thus, it is plain that the original Amok referred to the fighting men, and that the term for the frenzied Malays was a corruption of the original meaning.

Run the Hoop, To. An ancient sea custom. Four or more boys, having their left hand tied fast to an iron stake, and each of them a rope (called a nettle) in their right, being naked to the waist, waited the signal to begin. This was generally made by a stroke with the cat o' nine tails given by the boatswain to one of the boys. The boy struck with the nettle the boy in front of him, and every boy did the same, going round and round the circle. At first the strokes were gently administered, but each boy becoming irritated in turn by the strokes from the boy behind him instinctively strengthened his blows until, after some time, blows were being given in earnest. This "sport" was usually indulged in by the crew when the ship was becalmed at sea.

Rush. *Not worth a Rush.* From the days when even the most noble of homes in Britain had rushes for a floor covering. Honoured guests were given new, clean rushes for the floor. Less welcome guests had old rushes, and those who were of no consequence had no rushes at all, but walked on the stone floor. They were not worth a rush to their hosts.

Russians with the Snow on their Boots. Many thousands of people will remember the remarkable story that ran through the country during the Autumn of 1914, of mysterious Russian forces that travelled through Britain in locked and sealed railway carriages. They were described as still having snow on their boots, of singing wild songs in Russian. For months the Russians became almost a legend. The facts were these: A number of Russian officers, accompanied by their servants, arrived in this country to purchase munitions on behalf of their Government. At the time of their arrival the War Office was changing the location of various Territorial camps, and to secure secrecy all trains travelled at night with drawn blinds, not even the engine-drivers knowing what they were carrying. Meantime, a railway official had written to a friend mentioning that Russians were travelling on his trains—the officers and their servants. The friend talked, the talk grew with snowball proportions, and so the story of a vast Russian army travelling across England in the dead of night grew up.

S

Sabbatarians. Was the name given to the followers of Brabourne, a Baptist minister, who held that the real Sabbath was the seventh day of the week as set out in the *Book of Genesis*. The Sect, which arose in 1628, were also known as the Seventh Day Baptists.

Sabbath Day's Journey. A Sabbath Day's journey with the Jews in the time of Exodus had not to exceed the distance between the Ark of the Covenant and the extreme end of the camp. This was about two thousand cubits—just short of an English mile. In the time of Christ, the distance was two thousand *ammoth* (equals one thousand two hundred and twenty-five yards) as the utmost limit.

Sabines. *Rape of the Sabine Virgins.* The Sabines were a people of central Italy, who the Romans subjugated in 290 B.C. The rape story is that Romulus, founder of Rome, having difficulty in finding wives for his men, invited neighbouring tribes to send men as his guests to a series of games. While the men of the Sabines were thus absent Romans invaded the Sabine territory and carried off all the virgins they could find.

Sabotage. A sabot is the French name for a wooden shoe, made of a single piece of wood shaped and hollowed out to fit the foot, very much like our English clog. The "shoes" fixing the French railway lines to the sleepers were also made of wood, in a like manner to ours. The French name for them is the same as for their wooden shoes — sabots. During the great railway strike of 1910 French railway workers cut these *sabots* holding the lines thus preventing the lines from being used. It is from this that the word *sabot*-age has come to mean anything wilfully damaging or destroying vital goods or means.

Saccharine. The (in war-time) invaluable substitute for sugar was discovered by accident by an American, Mr. C. Fahlberg. After finishing (with a colleague) a day's experimenting in the John Hopkins' University in 1879, he washed his hands thoroughly and went home to dinner. During the meal he was surprised to find the bread extraordinarily sweet. Closer examination revealed that the sweetness came not from the bread, but from his hands. Returning immediately to the laboratory, Fahlberg tested the contents of each beaker and dish on the test bench until he came to the "sweet" substance. It is now known to most people as saccharine, but its scientific name is benzeyl sulphonicimide. It is a by-product of coal-tar, and at its strongest is five hundred and fifty times sweeter than sugar.

Sack. "*To get the Sack.*" The origin is somewhat obscure, but it is likely that it rose from the habit of a mechanic on getting a job, taking his own tools to the works. He carried them in a sack, or bag. At the job a locker was provided for him in which to leave his tools during the night. The bag was, it is stated, given to the employer to take care of. When the mechanic left, or was dismissed, he was given the sack in which to carry away his tools.

The author, on giving this suggestion, on one occasion received from a correspondent an account of the playful habit of the Sultan who, when one of his many wives became troublesome, had her put into a sack and thrown into the Bosphorus. This, however, had nothing to do with our phrase of getting the sack!

Sacrament. The etymology of this now sacred word is a curious one. It comes from the Latin *sacramentum*. In accordance with the functions of the suffix *mentum*, the etymological sense of the word *sacramentum* would be either a result of consecration or a means of dedicating or securing by a religious sanction. The second of these is the most likely; and it is probable, therefore, that the word was originally used in the form of a military oath taken by Roman soldiers not to desert their standards or their leaders. Later, the early Christians seem to have taken the oath in the same sense, as a sacrament not to desert their Christian standard and leader, hence its application to baptism, confirmation, etc.

Sacred Heart. This has been for centuries a favourite name for Convents and Convent Schools. The story of it is that St. Mary Margaret Alacoque, of Burgundy, a French nun, practised devotion to the Saviour's Heart after she had had a sacred vision. Her devotion was sanctioned by Pope Clement in 1732, and was extended to the whole of the Catholic Church in 1856.

Sad. A curious word in the English language because its meaning has completely changed. To-day, it describes mental heaviness; in its original meaning it represented firmness, settled steadiness, material heaviness, resoluteness. Thus, where in the present Bible, *Luke IV*, v, 48, reads: "It was founded upon a rock," Wyclif's Bible reads: "It was founded on a sad stoon!" In early English writings the Infant Christ is described as a *sade* child. Chaucer wrote:

"Yet, in the breast of her
virginitee,
Ther was enclosed ripe and
sad (strong) courage."

We still maintain part of the original meaning—heaviness—in "sad" bread.

Saddle. "*To be saddled with something.*" An encumbrance. A load. A saddle tells a horse that it is shortly to bear a load! Thus saddle, like yolk, comes to denote labour, burden, something to carry.

Saddle-bag Furniture. Was the name given to furniture upholstered in a cheap kind of carpet cloth, of a design based on that of saddle-bags carried by camels in the East.

Sadler's Wells Theatre. Digging in his garden one day, in 1683, a Mr. Sadler unearthed an ancient well. It proved to be the Holy Well of Clerkenwell Priory, for which marvellous cures had at one time been claimed. At the Reformation the well was stopped up, and apparently completely forgotten. Mr. Sadler turned his garden into a miniature spa; and in 1765 a Mr. Rosoman converted Mr. Sadler's garden into a theatre.

Safe. So long as you alone know you possess an article, and you alone know where you have hidden it, it is safe. Thus safe, meaning the steel strong-room, comes through the Old French *saub*, from the Latin *solus*, alone. You, alone, have the key to the safe.

Safety Match. An Austrian chemist, named Schrotter, in 1847 discovered that red phosphorus gave off no fumes, and is inert by itself. He already knew that mixed with chlorate of potash it exploded under slight pressure. Eight years later a Swedish chemist, Bottger, put the chlorate of potash on the box and the phosphorus on the match, thus producing a box of safety matches. It was a rather crude match. The present match is a mixture of chlorate of potash, sulphide of antimony, lichromate of potassium and red lead. On the box is a mixture of a morphous phosphorus and black oxide of manganese, which is the reason a safety match will not strike on any other surface; all the mixtures must be brought together.

Sail Close to the Wind. An allusion to the keeping of a vessel's head so close to the quarter from which the wind is coming (in order to keep the sails full) that she is in peril of heeling over and capsizing at any moment. In other words, the upright position is the safest, i.e., " honesty is the best policy."

Sailor's Collar Stripes. The three stripes on a sailor's " Blue Jean " (collar) do NOT represent the three great victories of Nelson. The belief, which is widely held, is a fallacy. They represent nothing but ornament. The same three stripes are worn by the American, French and German sailors on their collars—and they have no reason whatever to commemorate Admiral Nelson.

St. Bernard Dogs. Because they were originally bred at the famous hospice of St. Bernard in the St. Bernard pass, Switzerland, where the monks reared and trained them to track travellers lost in the snows of the wild mountain pass.

St. Elian's Well. It existed near Colwyn Bay, Denbighshire, and was used in its hey-day as a " cursing well." If, having an enemy, you wrote his name on a pebble and dropped it into the well without it touching the sides before it reached the water, then your enemy would be stricken with nearly all the ills that man is heir to, and in due course die. Well, that was the story, anyway!

St. Elmo's Fire. This name for the luminosity often seen on the masts and the rigging of ships at night is neither a corruption of St. Anselm, St. Erasmus, nor of Helena. Neither is there a Saint Elmo known, and why the lights are called St. Elmo Lights is a mystery.

St. John's Bread. The fruit of the Carob tree is so called. It is a long, flat, horn-like pod, containing hard seeds embedded in pulp. The fruit is generally held to be the husks on which the Prodigal Son of the Bible story lived; and it is believed, also, that they were the locusts eaten by John the Baptist during his forty days in the wilds—hence the name St. John's Bread.

St. Leger. The sweepstake for three-year-olds was originated in 1776 by Colonel St. Leger, of Park Hill, Doncaster. It was run at Doncaster in that year, but not as the St. Leger. That name was not given it until the third race.

St. Lubbock. The author doubts if one person out of a hundred could name the person thus " sanctified " in the popular mind of the people of his day. Yet it is to St. Lubbock that we owe our Bank Holidays. He was Sir John Lubbock, afterwards Lord Avebury, who introduced the legislation which legalized Bank Holidays. That was in 1871. Why " Saint "? Because holidays before this were Festival days—Saints' days, Holy days.

St. Luke's Summer. St. Luke's Day is 18th October; and it is round about that period that we get an Autumnal, or Indian, Summer. In North America the period is often the finest and mildest of the year.

St. Monday. The story goes like this: While Cromwell's army was encamped at Perth one of his partisans, a man named Monday, died. The Protector offered a prize for the best lines on his death. A Perth shoemaker (says the Folk Lore Society *Journal*), wrote the following:

" Blessed be the Sabbath Day
And cursed be worldly pelf;
Tuesday will begin the week,
Since Monday's hanged himself."

It so pleased Cromwell that he not only gave the reward, but ordained that Monday should be a perpetual holiday for all shoe-makers.

St. Swithin's Day. The correct legend about St. Swithin, Bishop of Winchester, is as follows: When he was dying, in 862, he expressed a wish to be buried not inside the church, but outside in the churchyard, " that the sweet rain of Heaven might fall upon my grave." This was done, but when he was canonized, the monks felt that a Saint should be buried in the Holy building. They, accordingly, made arrangements to remove the body on 15th July. It rained on that day, and continued to rain for forty days, " so that the monks saw that the Saint was averse to their plan, and abandoned it! " Then the rain stopped.

St. Valentine's Day. The old custom of sending " Valentines " on 14th February has nothing whatever to do with St. Valentine. The only connection between the day of the Saint is that, by chance, the Saint was clubbed to death in Rome on that day. Young people for generations before had followed the custom of selecting a lover, and exchanged gifts on 14th February, which from time immemorial had been regarded as the day on which birds began their mating. It is probable that the custom, too, had something to do with the Goddess Juno and her worship.

Salary. Salt - money was its original meaning, from Latin *Salarium*; and it was money paid to the Roman soldier to enable him to buy salt (*see* " Salt "). Salarium is the neuter gender for *salarius*, belonging to *sal*, salt.

Sally Lunn. The tea cake of that name was invented by a Bath pastry-cook named Sally Lunn, who hawked them round in a basket (eighteenth century). A baker named Dalmer bought her recipe—and the cakes became famous in a song.

Salt. From the Latin *sal*. The Norman word for the salt-stand was *saliere*, from which we get our salt-cellar. Salad, too, comes from salt; it was originally green vegetables seasoned with salt, the word salad meaning salted. Salt was a highly-prized commodity in the East, and was more so in Biblical days. It is referred to repeatedly in the Bible, one instance being: " If he be not worth his salt."
See " Salary."

Salt a Mine, To. To sprinkle real gold dust about in order to give the impression that there is gold to be obtained from the mine when, in fact, it is worthless. The first mention of the phrase to describe this trick appears to have been in 1864, when Hotten wrote, " At the gold diggings of Australia, miners sometimes salt an unproductive mine by sprinkling a few grains of gold dust over it."

Salt, in Superstition. The principal superstition existing about salt is that of spilling it at table. It is taken as an omen of bad luck, but can be averted, say the superstitious, if a pinch of the spilt salt is thrown with the right hand over the left shoulder.

The statement made that the superstition comes from the fact that Judas at the Last Supper upset a salt-cellar is not true. The only instance of this story is contained in a painting of the Last Supper by Leonardo da Vinci! There is no known authority for it; and, in fact, the spilling of salt as an omen for bad luck was feared by the Romans long before the time of Christ.

Salt was used in the early Biblical days by the Jews in their sacrifices. As an emblem of preservation it was ordered, by the Law of Moses, to be strewn over all flesh that was to be offered in sacrifice.

Grose, commenting on the spilt salt in his " Antiquities "

(1780) states, also, that it is unlucky to help epople to salt. The spilling of salt is also mentioned by Scot in his "Discoverie of Witchcraft," 1584, and by Gaule in "Mag-Astro-Mancers."

Both Greeks and Romans mixed salt with their sacrificial cakes, and in their lustrations made use of salt and water which, says Pennant, gave rise in after-times to the superstition of Holy Water. It was the custom in Northumberland to set a pewter-plate containing a little salt upon a corpse; and in the Black Country, at comparatively recent date, the author has known of this habit. It is still not uncommon to put salt into a coffin.

Salt, Not Worth His. Salt in the days of the Romans was a much valued commodity, and from it came salary (q.v.). A Roman soldier who was not worth his salt was not worth his salary, and was disposed of.

Salt, True to His. Exactly the opposite to "Not worth his Salt"—a Roman soldier who kept to his oath, his sacrament (q.v.) and earned his salary.

Salute. You salute a friend in the old meaning of the word when you enquire after his health. For salute is the Latin *Salus*, health, welfare.

Royal Salute. The firing of twenty-one guns.

Salvo. An artillery discharge in honour or welcome. A salute of artillery. The word comes from the Latin *salve*, "Hail."

Sam Browne. The belt which was compulsory for officers of the British Army until the World War (1939-45), when it was declared optional. It derived its name from its inventor, General Sir Sam Browne, V.C., of the Indian Mutiny.

Sambo. Came to be given to a North American negro from the Spanish *zambo*, but it should be used only in cases where the person is an offspring of various degrees of mixed negro and Indian or European blood. The Spanish *zambo* means bow-legged.

San fairy ann. Used by British soldiers in France as their interpretation of the French *sa faire rein*, it makes no matter, it doesn't matter.

Sands are running out, The. The allusion is to the days when time was told by sand running from one compartment of a glass to another—a similar glass, in miniature, exists to-day in the form of an egg-boiler measure glass. The sand-glass followed the water-clock. When the sands were running out, time was getting short. In "Tottel's Misc," 1557, there appears: "I saw mye tyme how it did runne, as sand out of the glasse."

Sandwich. The story about the sandwich centres round the notorious gambler, John Montague, Earl of Sandwich, who would gamble for forty hours at a stretch, ignoring meal times, but calling on his servants to bring him pieces of meat between bread, so that he might eat as he played. His servants named the meat and bread "sandwiches"; but it is only the name that belongs to the Earl. The Romans were partial to the same article—only they called it *offula*.

Sandy. Nickname for a Scotsman, is a contraction of Alexander.

Sang Froid. To show coolness, indifference; absence of excitement or agitation. The words are the French *sang*, blood, and *froid*, cold, meaning cold-blooded.

Santa Claus. Is a corruption of St. Nicholas, the patron saint of children. Although now associated with children, his day is really 6th December; and it was the custom of old for someone to dress up as a Bishop on the eve of 6th December and distribute toys among good children.

Saracen's Head. The name as a public-house sign was introduced here by returned Crusaders. As to the origin of the name Saracen, it is dubious. Ducange derives the word from Sarah, the wife of Abraham. Forster makes it come from the Sahara Desert, and Hottinger from *saraca*, to steal. A more likely origin, however, is the Arabic *Sharkeyn*, meaning the Eastern people, or those who dwelt in Palestine and Asia, as against the *Maghribe*, or the Western people who dwelt in Morocco.

Sarcophagus. This is the name given to a stone coffin, usually embellished with sculpture or bearing inscriptions. From the Greek *sarx*, flesh, and *phagein*, to eat, it is really the name of a stone which the Greeks believed to have the property of consuming the flesh of dead bodies deposited in it. They therefore used it for coffins.

Sardonic Laughter. Homer was the first to use the expression. In Sardinia there was said to be one, and only one, deadly herb. Anyone who ate of it died in laughter. Whether this is true or not, there does exist a herb called *Herba Sardonia* (from Sardis, in Asia Minor), which is so acrid to the taste that it causes an involuntary contortion of the nerves as to appear like a painful smile.

Sassenach. Is the Gælic for an Englishman, representing the Teutonic Saxon.

Satire. Is not derived from satyr, although this is a common belief due, probably, to the suggestion by old grammarians that the Latin *staira* was derived from the Greek satyr. It wasn't. The Latin word was originally *satura* and this meant a medley. *Lens satura* in the Latin meant, literally, a full dish, related to *satis*, enough (our satisfy is from the same root), and is said to have been a dish containing food composed of many ingredients.

Saturnalia. Its description to-day as a season of revelry dates back to ancient Rome, where Saturnalia was the great Winter festival in honour of the God of Agriculture, Saturn (after whom our Saturday is named). The Roman feast lasted seven days, from 17th December. It was this feast that the early Christians confiscated and turned into Christmas.

See "Christmas."

Satyr. One of a class of woodland gods or demons supposed to be a companion of Bacchus, the God of Wine. The satyr was usually represented with the legs and hind-part of a goat, and the forepart of a human.

Sauce. Is still another word from the Latin *sal*, salt. It means, merely, "salted," and in Roman days was boiled salted vegetables. These were served in a *Saucer*, and a saucer was a dish set on tne table, in which the "sauce" was served.

Saucer Oath. A Chinese in the witness-box says: "If I speak not the truth, may my soul be cracked and broken like this saucer," upon which he throws the saucer to the ground.

Save One's Bacon. *See* "Bacon." There is no truth in the extraordinary statement of one philologist that the phrase arose during the Civil War, "when housewives took extraordinary measures to save the bacon, stored up for Winter consumption, from the greedy appetites of soldiers on the march." The phrase was in existence a hundred years, and more, before the Civil War.

Say, To take the. Say is short for assay, and assay means a test. To take the as-*say* was the job of tasting all the dishes prepared for the meal of a person who feared death by poisoning.

Scales of Justice. The figure of Justice which surmounts the Old Bailey, London's Central Criminal Court, holds a pair of scales in one hand, symbolizing the just weighing of evidence; but the scales of justice go back to time immemorial. The ancient Egyptians held that the good deeds of a departed soul would be weighed against his evil deeds, and justice done between them. The Koran also teaches to-day that the merits and demerits of souls are weighed in the scales of the Archangel

Gabriel. "The good deeds," it states, "are put in the scale called Light, and the evil deeds in the scale called Darkness, after which they will have to cross the bridge Al Sirat, no wider than the edge of a scimitar. The Faithful will cross in safety, the rest will fall into the realms of Jehennam."

Scamp. Now more or less used as a friendly chiding of the perpetuator of some trick; but the word is steeped in ignominy. It comes from the French *escamper*, to flee, through the Latin *ex*, out of, and *campus*, the battlefield.

Scapegoat. In the Mosaic ritual of the Day of Atonement (*Lev.* xvi), one of two goats was chosen by lot to be sent alive into the wilderness, the sins of the people having been symbolically laid upon it, while the other was appointed to be sacrificed. The goat thus sent into the wilderness was the scape (escape) goat. It is rather a curious reflection that people of the heathen races have the same idea, despite the fact that they cannot read, and could not possibly have known of the Jewish traditions and customs. One such are the aborigines of Borneo who, once a year, launch a small boat piled with the sins of the peoples. The idea is that the sins will fall upon the crew of the first ship it encounters, and thus free themselves of their sins.

Scar. This word, when it forms a component part in a place-name, is Norse, meaning a cliff, or the face of a rock. There is an example in Scar-borough.

Scaramouch. Properly, in the Italian, *Scaramuccia*, a character, in old Italian farce, a braggart fool, aping the dress of the nobles. The character was introduced to the British stage by Tiberio Fiurelli, in 1673. The word, as a description of a type of person, has now practically died out of our language.

Scarborough Warning. There are two possible origins to this term, which really means without any warning at all. The first is that it is an allusion to Thomas Stafford who, in 1557, seized the castle at Scarborough before the people of the place knew that he was anywhere near. The second is that it refers to the very strong law which ruled there against robbers, who were gibbeted first and tried afterwards, very much like the Halifax Gibbet Law (q.v.).

Scavenger's Daughter, The. This was an instrument of torture invented by Leonard Skevington, or Skeffington, Lieutenant of the Tower of London, in the reign of Henry VIII. By bringing the head to the knees it so compressed the body as to force blood from the nose and ears. The name Scavenger's Daughter was a jocular perversion of the name Skevington.

Scenery. The queer thing about this word is that Nature has borrowed for her form a name from the stage, for scenery was originally the trappings of the scene being enacted on a stage. The derivation is the Greek *Skene*, a covered place. So the painted scene-ery of the stage was applied eventually. to the scenery of Nature.

Science. The Latin "to know" is *scire*. The present participle of *scire* is *scientia*, and from that, which means knowledge, is derived our science. Science, therefore, means to know instead of to guess or take on trust, which is what most of the Biblical stories of the Creation asks should be done.

Many great men have suffered for their devotion to Science, which has since proved of benefit to man.

Roger Bacon was imprisoned and excommunicated on account of his chemical researches.

Averroes, Arabian philosopher, was denounced as a heretic, because of his discoveries in medicine and philosophy.

Galileo was imprisoned for saying that the earth moved.

Boniface, Bishop of Salzburg, for asserting that the antipodes existed, was excommunicated.

Sceptic. The origin of the word is the Greek *skeptesthai*, the translation of which is "to examine." Pyrrho, in ancient Greece, founded the school of sceptical philosophy, which held that there was no adequate grounds for certainty as to the truth of anything, and doubted the possibility of any real knowledge of any kind. Thus, an unbeliever in anything brought forward as an acknowledged fact to-day is called, after Pyrrho, a sceptic.

School. The author gives the origin of this word for the delectation of any school-boy who may be spending a few moments with the book. School comes from the Greek *schole*; and the Greek *schole* meant *leisure*!

Scissors. It is a curious fact that during the last few months the author has been asked a score or more times to explain how scissors came so to be called. They derive the name from the Latin *cisorium*, from *cardere*, to cut. Until the sixteenth century, the word was spelt in this country without the "sc." It should not, etymologically speaking, be there now, for it was prefixed from a mistaken confusion with the Latin *scissor*, which did not mean to cut, but to rend or split.

Scorching. *To scorch along the roads.* To scorch a thing is to burn it. Scorching, as a term for fast driving, firstly of a cycle and later of a motor car, came in after a spell of what was described as "burning up the road." The French phrase is *bruler le pave*, burn the pavement.

Score. *To count the Score.* In early English days notches were cut on sticks to keep a reckoning. (*See* "Nick of Time.") Now the Anglo-Saxon word for the past participle of "to cut" was *scoren*, which was the term given to those notches cut in the stick. The *scoren* was the count. And score is a slight corruption of it.

Score, To Settle a. *See* "Settle a Bargain."

Scot Free, To get off. In Anglo-Saxon and Mediæval English days, *Scot* and *lot* was a municipal levy on all, according to their ability to pay. *Scot* was the tax, and *lot* the allotment or portion to be paid by a person. To "get off Scot free," therefore, was to be freed from payment of any of the tax. Scot-free now means free of any punishment or loss.

Scotland Yard. On the site of the present London police headquarters stood an ancient palace, appropriated to the use of the Scottish Kings who came to London once a year to pay homage to the English sovereign at Westminster Abbey. The short street which served the palace was known as Scotland Yard. It is recorded that the palace was first given as a home during homage by King Edgar to Kenneth II of Scotland, about the year 970.

Scoundrel. The description means one who should be shunned, from the Anglo-Saxon *scunner*, *scunean*, to loathe, to shun.

Scourge of God. Was the name given to Attila, King of the Huns, because of the havoc and disaster he left behind him in the towns through which he passed.

Scrap of Paper. The expression was made a by-word among the nations by Bethmann-Hollweg, German Chancellor, on the eve of the Great War of 1914-18. Sir Edward Goschen, British Ambassador to Germany, had called on the Chancellor to inform him that Britain was bound under her treaty to defend Belgium if she was invaded by Germany, and would do so. "Just for a scrap of paper Britain is going to make war on a kindred nation which desires nothing better than to be friends with her," was the reply of the German Chancellor.

Scratch. *To come up to Scratch.* The scratch is the line at the starting-point of a race, which all competitors are expected to toe. Thus, to come up to scratch is to be ready to take off in the struggle.

Screw. *See* "Raise one's screw."

Screw. *To put on the screw.* A reminder of the days of the thumb-screw torture, to induce confession. The two thumbs of the victim were compressed in a machine so as to inflict exquisite agony without endangering life.

Scrimmage. Is merely an altered form of scirmish. It passed to skirmish through scrimish.

Scrounge. This word, as meaning to appropriate without permission, was unknown, except in dialect, until the war of 1914-18. Who first introduced it into the soldiers' vocabulary to explain the visits out in search of food and drink, is not known. As early as 1909, Ware records the existence of the word "scrunging" in connection with country boys stealing unripe apples and pears, and explains that the term probably arose from the noise made in masticating.

Scruple. Hargrave once gave a remarkable definition of this. He described it as a small sharp stone (Scrupus) which, when a balance was made of wood, was used as a pivot to rest the balance bar. "The diminutive of this, quite a little stone of twenty grains, the *scrupulous*, was used as a weight," he adds, and concludes: "The Scrupus was anxiously watched by both buyer and seller, so the word meant not only a small stone, but anxiety."

The definition is more interesting than accurate. A *scruple* with the Greeks was one twenty-fourth of an ounce, twenty-fourth part of a uncia of land, the twenty-fourth part of an hour. It is now one twenty-fourth of an ounce in apothecaries' weight.

Scuttle. "*To scuttle off.*" A corruption of "scuddle off," from scud, which meant to hasten. The fleetness of "scud" is shown by the fact that its most likely of many doubtful origins is the *skut*, or tail of a hare, one of the fastest animals on four feet.

Scythian Defiance. The legend is that when Darius approached Scythia, he was met by an ambassador, who placed before him a bird, a frog, a mouse, and five arrows, leaving without uttering a word of explanation. Darius, seeking a solution to the strange gifts, was told that it meant either fly away like a bird, hide your head in a hole like a mouse, or swim across the river. Otherwise, in five days you will be laid prostrate by Scythian arrows. He did neither, and he was not laid low. The date was about 515 B.C.

Seagreen Incorruptible. Carlyle called Robespierre by this term in his "French Revolution."

Seamy Side (of Life). The wrong side, the worst side. Most carpets, tapestry and piled velvet show on the back (or wrong side) the seams or the ends of the pattern displayed on the "right" side.

Search. Perhaps you have noticed how, when you drop any article and look for it, you generally cover the likely area in a circle. That is the origin of search. The Latin word was *circare*, to go about in *circus*, a circle. The French abbreviated the two words to *chercher* (look for), which English translated into search.

Season, London. Is that part of the year when the Royal Court is in town—May, June and July.

Seasons of the Year. Spring starts, officially, on 21st March; Summer on 22nd June; Autumn on 23rd September; Winter on 22nd December.

Secular. In its original Latin, *sæcularis*, the word meant a generation or age, and it is in this sense that the Romans held once in one hundred and twenty years their Secular Games—games celebrated once in an age—which lasted three days and three nights. In a religious sense, secular means the world as distinguished from the Church and religion. The derivation is probably in reference to the Christian Age.

"See how it pans out." A miner's phrase from the gold-diggings. To separate gold from earth, the earth is put into a pan and washed away under running water, leaving the heavier gold in the bottom of the pan.

Sell the Pass. Meaning to betray one's own cause. It is said to have arisen from an Irish regiment sent by Crotha of Atha, to hold a pass against the invading army of Trathal. The pass was given up for a monetary reward, and Trathal assumed the title of King of Ireland.

Sent to Coventry. *See* "Coventry."

Seraglio. The word has several meanings, but the popular one is that connecting it with the Harem in the house of a Mohammedan sovereign, or great noble. It can, however, also be a place of confinement, an enclosure, or the palace of the Sultan at Constantinople. This palace is enclosed by a wall more than seven miles in circumference.

Serene. "*It's all serene.*" Merely a corruption of the Spanish reply to a sentry's challenge. "*Sere-no*" is Spanish for "All right."

Sergeant-Major's Tea. Tea with sugar and milk, or a dash of rum in it. An expression current among the rank and file in the last war, and before, suggested by the prevalent opinion that sergeant-majors had a way of securing such extras for themselves. Quite incorrect, of course!

Set. As a place-name component means either a seat, from the Anglo-Saxon, or a settlement or dwelling, through the Norse. Dor-set is an illustration of the former, and Ulster of the latter.

Setting the Thames on Fire. A man working on a sieve, would have to be working pretty fast if a friction set fire to the sieve, would not he? Now, when a man with a sieve was seen "slacking," his employer greeted him with, "You'll never set the *Temse* on fire." For the old name for a sieve was Temse; and the phrase has nothing whatever to do with setting the River Thames ablaze!

Settle a Bargain. In rural parts of Britain, the long seat (now padded) with the arms at each end is still called by old people, "the Settle"—as it was in Anglo-Saxon days, when neighbours discussing business settled themselves down on the Anglo-Saxon *Setl*, a seat, and *setl-d* a bargain! All other varieties of Settle—and there are many meanings to-day—sprung originally from this Anglo-Saxon seat.

Seven. *Seven Seas, Seven Wonders, Seven Sins, etc.* From earliest times Seven has figured as a mystic and sacred number. The number is interwoven with the whole religious life and history. The Pythagoreans regarded four and three (seven) as lucky numbers. There are seven days in Creation, Seven Graces, Seven divisions of the Lord's Prayer, Seven Churches of Asia in the Apocalypse. The Babylonians and Egyptians had seven Sacred Planets; and the Hebrew word "to swear" means, literally, to come under the influence of seven things.

Seven Gods of Luck. Are Japanese deities: Bishamon, God of War; Daikoku, God of Wealth; Benten, Love; Ebisu, Self-effacement; Fukurokujin and Jurojin, Longevity; and Hstei, Generosity. They preside over human happiness and welfare.

Seven Sages. They are generally agreed to be, with their mottoes:

Solon of Athens (638-559 B.C.), "Know thyself."

Chilo of Sparta (about 590 B.C.), "Consider the end."

Thales of Melitus (600-540 B.C.), "Who hateth suretyship is sure."

Bias of Priene (about 550 B.C.), "Most men are bad."

Cleobulus (about 580 B.C.), "Avoid extremes."

Pittacus of Mitylene (died 570 B.C.), "Seize time by the forelock."

Periander of Corinth (625-585 B.C.), "Nothing is impossible to industry."

Seven Sciences, The. They were Grammar, Logic, Rhetoric, Arithmetic, Music, Geometry and Astrology.

Seven Seas, The. This term, when first used, referred to the Arctic and Antarctic, the North and South Pacific, the North and South Atlantic, and the Indian Ocean.

Seven Senses, Scared out of His. The seven senses of ancient teaching were animation, feeling, speech, taste, sight, hearing and smelling. Each of these seven properties of the body, it was held by the Ancients, were under the influence of seven planets. A man scared out of all these senses would be scared indeed!

Seven Sleepers. These are, in the popular legend, Constantine, Dionysius, John, Maximian, Malchus, Martinian and Serapion. The story is that they were seven noble youths of Ephesus who fled in the Decian persecution (about 250) and hid in a cave at Mount Celion, where they fell asleep. They woke after two hundred and fifty years, but died almost at once. Their bodies, placed together in a stone coffin, were taken to Marseilles. The coffin is still preserved in Victor's Church in that city. It is probable that the fable owes its title to the Biblical phrase, "They fell *asleep* in the Lord," asleep here meaning they died.

Seven Stars of Destiny. Were the seven planets of the Ancients. The term is also used for the Pleiades and the Great Bear.

Seven Whistlers. These were, in 1855 or thereabouts, seven birds whose voices were said to warn Leicestershire miners of impending danger. In a publication ("Current Notes") about that time it was stated: "No one would descend the pit if he heard the seven whistlers, whose prophetic note no miner would disregard. Cases have been known in which men who had descended the pit after this admonition, lost their lives." The Whistlers seem to have been peculiar to Leicestershire, since there is no trace of the superstition in any other part of the coal-mining country.

Seven Wonders of the World, are the Pyramids of Egypt, the Hanging Gardens of Babylon, the Tomb of Mausolus, the Temple of Diana in Ephesus, the Colossus of Rhodes, the Statue of Jupiter by Phidias, and the Pharos (lighthouse) of Alexandria.

Of the Wonders of the Middle Ages, the seven would probably be: The Colosseum of Rome, the Catacombs of Alexandria, the Great Wall of China, the Leaning Tower of Pisa, the Porcelain Tower of Nanking, the Constantinople Mosque of St. Sophia and, possible, Stonehenge.

The present day Wonders might be classed as Radio, the Telephone, Electricity, the Aeroplane, Radium and the X-Ray, the Internal Combustion Engine, and Lister's Antiseptics.

It should be pointed out that the old Wonders of the World served no useful purpose in progress or for humanity, with the sole exception of the Pharos Lighthouse, whereas the Wonders of the present World are all placed in the realms of human progress.

Seventh Heaven. *To be in the Seventh Heaven of Delight.* To be supremely happy. The phrase is derived from the belief of the Mohammedans and the Cabbalists that there are seven heavens each rising in happiness above the other, the Seventh containing God himself and all his angels.

Sexton. Although the sexton of a church to-day is the man who does the cleaning and digs the graves, etc., he was at one time a high lay official of the Church. The word is a corruption of sacristan, into whose charge was trusted the *sacra*, the vestments, sacred vessels, relics, and the like. The present sexton's duties date from the sixteenth century.

Shadow Grow Less. "*May your Shadow never grow Less.*" An old Eastern phrase of the days of the Black Art. It was said that those who studied the Black Art, when they had reached a certain stage in their tuition, were chased by the Devil. If he caught up with them he took all or part of their shadow, which they never again got back, but they became great magicians, although bound for life to the Devil. Thus, a man whose shadow had grown less was in the hands of the Devil.

Shady Side of Forty, On the. The allusion is to the evening time of life. As the evening sun shines the shadows of everything on the shade side lengthen. Thus, to be on the shady side of forty means to have passed the hey-day and entered into the lengthening shadow.

Shaef. The initials of the Supreme Headquarters Allied Expeditionary Force, which came into active operation on "D-Day" (q.v.). Actually, it was the information section at General Eisenhower's headquarters. Three times a day newspaper correspondents from all parts of the world went to a map-lined conference room at Shaef to learn how the battle was going. Information was conveyed by them to the public in the formula, "It was learned at Shaef," a phrase coined by the Censor, which replaced the old formula, "says an official spokesman."

On a large-scale map which filled one end of the room the "front" was marked by a thick black line. Towns in the news went up in yellow if the Allies held them; in white if the Nazis were there.

Shakers. An American religious sect, first heard of in 1774 at Albany State of New York, so-called from the convulsive movements of the hands and arms as part of their peculiar form of worship. The founder was Ann Lee, self-styled "Mother Ann," who had seceded from the Quakers. She started the movement in her native city of Manchester, but, meeting with little response, emigrated with a few followers to America, where freak religions stood a great deal more chance of success—and profit.

Shakes. *No great Shakes.* Not up to much. It is probable that *shakes* here is identical with the provincial word shake, to brag, which must be of ancient usage, as *Schakare*, cracker, or boostemaker is to be found in the *Primptorium Parvulorum* about 1440. Dr. Brewer, however, suggests it refers to no great shake of dice—in other words, a low number of spots.

Shaking Hands. Our present habit of shaking hands on meeting and on parting is a friendly gesture, but its origin was far from being so. It was born of the fear of one and everyone, and as a measure of precaution. When two persons took the right hand of each on meeting, and particularly on parting, it was a very effective preventative of either of them getting to his sword! There is a survival, in part, to-day in the boxing ring, where opposing boxers, on walking to the centre of the ring to commence their bout, shake hands. Thus, no advantage can be gained by either by a surprise blow before the other is ready to counter it.

This custom of shaking hands in its original meaning is well illustrated in the Bible passage between Jehu and Jehonadab, where Jehu, seeing Jehonadab coming to meet him asked, "Is thy heart right as my heart is with thy heart?" and, receiving the answer, "It is," replied, "If it be, give me thine hand." And Jehonadab gave him his hand.

Shambles. A number of towns in Britain (Nottingham is one) still retain not only the name, Shambles, but its original Anglo-Saxon purpose. A

Shambles was a place where meat was displayed for sale, from *Scamel* (Anglo-Saxon stool) and Latin *Scamellam*, a little bench, on which meat was exhibited. The antiquity of Shambles is seen by Angrene's translation of Juvenal's " Satires," xi, where it says :

" Lurking in *Shambles* ;
where with borrowed coin
They buy choice meats."

Shamrock. The symbol of Ireland, because of the action of St. Patrick in using a leaf of it to illustrate the Holy Trinity. *See* " St. Patrick."

Shanks's Mare. *To go by Shanks's pony* means to get somewhere on one's own feet, to walk ; " shank " being the leg proper between the knee and the ankle. The origin is not known ; but it has been stated that it refers to King Edward I, nicknamed " Long Shanks," because whenever he rode a pony his long legs reached to the ground.

Shanties. Usually referred to as sea shanties, comes from the French *chanter*, to sing.

Shanty. This name for a rough and ill-built hut is derived from Canada, where early French settlers gave the name *chantier* to the headquarters' hut erected in the forests. In it the woodcutters assembled after their day's work. Chantier was also the name given to an establishment regularly organized in the forests in Winter-time for the felling of trees.

In this connection, *Chantier* was a Canadian-French term meaning a place where one slept, or put things to store. Thus shanty ; its corruption came to mean a Canadian log hut.

Shaver. A young, slang term for a boy. It is, however, not so slangy as it sounds, for it probably came from the gipsy *shavie*, *shavy*, or *chavo*, a son.

Shaving. When men first began to shave is unknown ; but even before the Bronze or Iron Ages a kind of razor was being used, a sharp edge being ground on flints, shells or bones. Razors are even mentioned in the Bible.

Alexander the Great, in the fourth century B.C., bade his Macedonians " shave off the handle," by which an enemy might seize them.

Sheathe the Sword, We Shall not. One of the famous phrases of the Great War of 1914-18. Speaking at the London Guildhall on 9th November, 1914, Mr. Asquith (afterwards Earl of Oxford and Asquith) said : " We shall never sheathe the sword, which we have not lightly drawn, until Belgium receives in full measure and more all she has sacrificed, until France is adequately secured against the menace of aggression, until the rights of smaller nationalities of Europe are placed upon an unassailable foundation, and until the military domination of Prussia is wholly and finally destroyed." Much the same thing is being said to-day in this present World War.

Sheet Anchor. One's last resort, or refuge. The sheet anchor is the largest anchor of a ship, used to hold her in violent weather. If that failed to hold the ship then, indeed, her last refuge was gone.

Sheets in the Wind, Three. The sheet, in nautical terms, was the rope attached to the lower end of a sail, and used for lengthening or shortening sail. Allowed to run free the sail would flop about in the wind, and this condition was called " in the wind." A sailing ship of the old days usually had three sails. If all the three sheets of the three sails were in the wind, the ship would lurch drunkenly on the ocean. Thus, a sailor seeing one of his mates rolling drunk in the streets, described him as being three sheets in the wind.

Shekel. *To count the shekels.* Meaning to count one's money. The shekel was the principal silver coin of the Hebrews, and was worth, at present English rates, about 1s. 4d. It was also an ancient unit of weight of the Phœnicians.

Shell-Shock. Was, originally, a neurasthenic condition caused by a shock to the nervous system due to the violent concussions, the result of explosion of heavy shells at close quarters. It was first notified during the War of 1914-18.

Sheraton Furniture. Was popularized by its inventor, Thomas Sheraton, towards the end of the eighteenth century.

Shillibeer. Was the name given to a combined hearse and mourning coach named after George Shillibeer, who introduced it. Shillibeer had returned to his native London from Paris in order to start an omnibus service in London. He introduced the omnibus to England, but his venture failed, and he went into the undertaking business instead. *See* " Omnious."

Shilling. The original root was the Latin *solidus* ; but Skeat, for some reason, endeavours to father the shilling on the Anglo-Saxon verb *scylan*, to divide. The basis of his assumption seems to be that the original Anglo shilling was marked with a deeply indented cross, dividing it into halves or quarters, which could be broken off to the amount desired. It seems bad etymology, for Skeat might as well have called the penny a shilling also, since this, too, was divided into four as were, also, the early farthings.

Shindy. Slang for a disturbance, comes from *Shinty*, an early and primitive game—probably the pre-runner of hockey—played with hooked sticks in the North of England. It was also called Bandy-ball. The U.S.A. were the first to connect in Shindy, the violent exertions of Shinty.

Ship-shape. *Let's have things ship-shape.* Although a ship is still one of the most tidy places, the phrase is not so applicable to the present vessels as it was when coined of the old sailing ship. A ship was ship-shape when she was fully rigged, or ship-rigged, as distinct from jury-rigged.

Shipton, Old Mother. Like so many other of these " prophets " and " prophetesses," there was never any such person. She was, however, supposed to have lived in the reign of Henry VIII, and to have foretold the death of Wolsey, Cromwell, and nearly every other person of note who died. In 1862, more than two hundred years after the first record of her, Hinsley brought out a new " Life and Death of Mother Shipton," in which she is credited with having prophesied steam engines, the telegraph, the telephone, and other modern conveniences.

Shire. The name we use for a county to-day means " sheared off," from the Anglo-Saxon *scir*, in conjunction with *Scirian*, to allot. When the Saxon Kings appointed an Earl, they gave him a " shire," or *scir*, of land to govern. Thus we get " shire " as an area. The Norman Conquest saw the title of Earl supplanted by that of " Count," when the " shire " became the " county."

Shivering Mountain. Derbyshire people will know this for the nickname bestowed upon Mam Tor, a hill of the Peak of Derbyshire. It is so-called from the shivers of shale and grit-stone which are continually breaking away from it—and have been doing so since beyond living memory.

Shoe-makers. Are called men of the " Gentle Craft," because St. Crispian and his brother, the patron saints of shoe-makers, supported themselves by making and repairing shoes during the time that they converted and preached to the people of Gaul and Britain.

Shoes (at Weddings). Where originated the belief that it is lucky to throw an old shoe after the bride, or tie it behind their bridal coach, the author is puzzled to decide. For the only connection of a shoe with marriage he can trace is the ancient Hebrew custom of the bridegroom lightly touching his bride's head with his shoe to signify his supremacy over her, and her obedience to it. The value of the shoe as a sign of supremacy is evidenced to the Psalmist's "Over Edon will I cast my shoe."

Shooting Stars. Are believed by the Arabs to be firebrands hurled by the angels against inquisitive genii who approach near to Heaven in order to peep in.

Stars shoot at regular periods. These periods, or swarms, are between 9th and 14th August, 12 and 14th November, and 6th and 11th December. Those shooting between 9th and 14th August were called by the Ancients, "Fiery tears of St. Lawrence," that being the time of St. Lawrence's festival.

The speed of the "shoot" of shooting stars is stated to be from thirty to forty-four miles per second.

Shopkeepers, Nation of. Napoleon said this of England; but the phrase had been used earlier by Adam Smith in "Wealth of Nations." Smith wrote: "To found a great nation for the sole reason of raising up a people of customers, may at first sight appear a project fit only for a nation of shopkeepers."

Short Counsel is Good Counsel. The proverb is generally associated with the death of Walcher, first Bishop of Durham appointed by the Conqueror. At Gateshead the Bishop had met the leaders of the people, and on retiring to the church the cry was raised, "Short rede, good rede, slay the bishop." The church was thereupon set on fire and the Bishop was slain. The date of the happening was 1080.

Short Shrift. Shrift dates back to the days of Roman Catholicism in England. To give a person shrift, was the action of a priest in hearing that person's confession and giving him absolution—in other words, shriving him.

Short shrift was the description of the shriving of a person about to be executed. He was allowed only a few minutes in which to make his confession to, and receive absolution from, the priest.

Shorthand. The record speed for writing shorthand is held by an American, Nathan Behrin, who, in the New York State Championship, in 1922, took down, and afterwards transcribed, a dictated document at the speed of three hundred and fifty words a minute.

Shot. *No Shot in the Locker.* Comes from the days when, on men-of-war, ammunition was kept in lockers.

Shot, Shott. A frequent ending to town names in England. Its origin is Anglo-Saxon, a "shot" meaning a glade in a wood through which game could dart, or shoot. It meant, also, a certain measure of land.

Shot his Bolt. *See* "Bolt."

Shovel Offertories. In several parts of the country, and particularly in the North, after a funeral, the sexton (who is responsible for digging the grave) stands by the church gate holding out his shovel for contributions for his services. This offertory is called in Wales *Offrwm-pen-rhaw.*

Show a leg there. The sea gave us this phrase; but it is not quite complete as shown. The original version, which was called by the bo'sun's mate when calling up hands in the morning was: "Show a leg; Show a leg, or a pusser's stocking."

It dates from the time when women were allowed to live on board ship, ostensibly as sailors' wives. A leg in a stocking put over the side of a hammock indicated that the occupant was a woman, who was allowed to remain until the men had cleared out.

Shrapnel. Was named after its inventor in 1784, Colonel Shrapnel, who lived at Punc-knowle, Dorset. At that time it meant a shell containing a large number of bullets which travelled forwards and outwards at high velocity when the shell was opened by bursting charge; but nowadays the term shrapnel is applied to fragments of the burst casing.

Shrew. It is a queer thing that while you insult a woman by calling her a shrew, you compliment a man by calling him shrewd. Yet both came from the same Mediæval English *Shrew,* a type of mouse with a long *sharp* nose. Its bite was believed in those days to be poisonous.

Shropshire. The Anglo-Saxon name for the place was *scrobbes byrg,* the burg (town) in the shrubs. Because the Normans could not pronounce "sc," the name was called by them Salopesbury. For the name of the county, the *bury* was naturally dropped, leaving Salop. And that is how Shropshire comes still to be described, for the county, as Salop.

Shrove Tuesday. The day when all good Catholics confessed their sins, and were shriven by the priests, in readiness for the first days of Lent, when they received on their heads the ashes. (*See* "Ash Wednesday," and also "Pancake Day.")

Siamese Twins. The original pair were Eng and Chang, born of Chinese parents 1814 (about), and found living at Mekong, Siam, in 1829. They were united by a band of flesh stretching from breast-bone to breast-bone. For a number of years they were a great attraction at exhibitions all over the world. They married two sisters, had families, and died within two hours of each other on 17th January, 1874. There have since been three other pairs of joined twins. They were the Orissas, born in that Bengal town, and joined by a piece of cartilage at the waist; Millie-Christine, negresses, billed as the two-headed nightingale; and Josepha and Roza Blazek, who were joined above the waist.

Sic. Usually written in brackets after a sentence or a word, "sic" means in Latin, "thus so." It should be used after a doubtful phrase or word, or a mis-spelling, to indicate that it is given exactly as it appeared in the original being quoted, and to draw attention to the fact that it is probably not correct.

Side of the Angels, On the. Addressing the Oxford Diocesan Conference in 1864 on Darwins' "Origin of Species," Disraeli said, "The qeustion is this: Is man an ape or an angel? I, my lord, am on the side of the angels."

Sidesman. Is the man who usually collects the offerings from the congregation in a church. The neme is a corruption of synod's-man. Synod, from the Latin *synodus,* means an assembly of the clergy of a particular church, diocese or nation, convened for discussing and deciding ecclesiastical affairs. A synod's-man was a person—he might be eihter a clergyman or one of the laiety—designated to attend the Synod.

Silence. "*More silent than Amyclae.*" The inhabitants of Amyclæ, a town in the south of Sparta, had been so often alarmed by stories of the approach of the Spartans, that a law was made forbidding anyone, on pain of death, to mention the Spartans. When, one day, the Spartans actually *did* come, no one dared to give warning and the town was captured. The English version of the proverb is, of course, "Crying Wolf."

Silhouette. Was so named after Etienne de Silhouette, Chancellor of the Exchequer to Louis XV. He was the first to have his "photograph" outlined, side view, on black paper. He was an "economical man," and legend says that the black paper was a cheaper way of getting his likeness than paying an artist to draw him!

Silly. The word originally had an entirely different meaning to that which it bears to-day. It is derived from the German *selig,* or Anglo-Saxon *soleig*, meaning blessed. An early quotation refers to Jesus as "the harmless *silly* babe," meaning "Blessed" babe. Later, the term was used for "innocent," and there is a reminder of this to-day in the explanation frequently given where a youth is charged with some offence. It was a silly prank—innocently done.

Silver spoon in one's mouth, To be born with. The allusion is to the silver Apostle spoon which used to be presented to an infant by its god-father at the christening. In the case of a child born to parents in a well-to-do position, it was a foregone conclusion that the child would get a silver spoon at the baptism. Such a child, by reason of its family prosperity was, as it were, born with a silver spoon in its mouth.

Simple Life, To Lead the. A phrase which came into vogue after the publication of a book entitled, "The Simple Life," by the Rev. Charles Wagner. It advocated the plainest living.

Sine die. (Latin, without a day.) When a case or inquiry is adjourned *sine die*, it means indefinitely, never, no day having been fixed for it to be resumed.

Sine qua non. An indispensable condition, without which something cannot be done. A Latin expression.

Sin-Eaters. The practice of sin-eating is probably one of the most curious of all England's queer customs. Sin-Eaters were people hired to sit beside the corpse of a departed member of a family, and take on themselves the sins of the dead, so that his soul might be delivered from Purgatory. There is an excellent account of the custom, as it was practiced in Shropshire, given by Bagford:

> "When a person dyed there was notice given to an old sire (for so they called him) who presently repaired to the place where the deceased lay, and stood before the door of the house, when some of the family came out and furnished him with a cricket (*Note*—Cricket: a low wooden stool, a footstool) on which he sat down facing the door. Then they gave him a groat, which he put in his pocket; a crust of bread, which he ate; and a full bowle of ale, which he drunk off at a draught. After this he got up from the cricket and pronounced with a composed gesture, the ease and rest of the soul departed, for which he would pawn his own soul."

Hazlitt records that in Hereford was a woman who for many years "kept a mazar bowle for the sinne-eater." The mazar bowl is also referred to in other localities. It is described as being made of maple wood and filled with beer.

Sinecure. The word is used of a job for which there is good pay but little work to do for it. It is a joining together of the Latin *Sine cura*, "without cure or care," care being in this interpretation "trouble." The term properly belongs to a Church benefice where the cure (priest) has a large stipend with few duties as a cure of souls.

Sinews of War. The phrase, meaning money to make and continue war, comes from Cicero's *Nervos belli pecumiam*, "money makes the sinews of war."

Sing Small. Is another phrase which carelessness in pronunciation has changed from the original. The phrase should be "Sink" small—to be lowered in the estimation of one's fellows.

Sinister. Foreboding, of ill omen. The word is he Latin *sinister*, left-handed. From the ancient days the left side has been regarded with superstitious fears. Nothing good could ever come from the left. An illegitimate child was said to have been born on the left side of the bed. A morganatic marriage was described as a left-handed marriage. To step over a doorway with the left foot first was an ill omen. Thus, left became the sinister side, and was thus looked upon all through the ages.

Siren. Until the air raid warning signal in the World War (1939-45) a siren was regarded as a woman. It was derived from the Greek *sirenes*, entanglers; and a siren was a mythical half-woman, half-bird, whom the Greek poets said sang and enticed seamen by the sweetness of her voice to forget everything, and stay with her until they died of hunger.

The genius who substituted for the siren of the bewitching voice the screaming warbling note of the air raid warning did not know, presumably, his Odyssey.

Sir-loin of Beef. The misspelling which has given us this name as a joint of beef, has led to a crop of stories of its "origin." Fullew states that Henry VIII, dining with the Abbot of Reading, ate so heartily off a loin of beef that the Abbot said he would give one thousand marks for such a stomach. "Done," said the King, and kept the Abbot a prisoner in the Tower of London, won his one thousand marks, and knighted the beef. A second story fathers the knighting on James I, and a third on Charles II.

In Taylor's "Great Eater of Kent" (published in 1860) occurs this: ". . . Should presently enter combat with a worthy knight, called Sir Loyne of Beefe, and overthrow him."

The plain truth of the matter is that the joint was always (and should be now) spelt "sur-loin"—French *sur* meaning above—the joint being that part of the ox above the loin.

Sixes and Sevens, All at. The phrase is now used as meaning all higgledy-piggledy; but the origin seems to have been the game of dicing. Earliest written records of it, such as, for instance, Chaucer, in "Troylus" (1374) refer to it as "on" sixes or sevens, and from this it is possible that the words meant something altogether different to being in a state of confusion, but rather to a dice player's decision to "set" on six or seven (to set on cinque and sice), these being the two highest numbers. A modern version might be the Pontoon player's decision to "stand on seventeen."

Sixteen String Jack. The nickname in which Highwayman Jack Rann (who was hanged in 1744) rejoiced, and encouraged. A man who was pleased to dress like a fop, he wore eight tags at each knee—sixteen in all.

Skedaddle, To. Meaning to leave hurriedly. It is said in some quarters to be of Danish or Swedish origin, and to have been in common use throughout the North-West in the vicinity of emigrants from those nations. There are not, however, any forms in Swedish or Danish to justify the supposition. There is slight evidence of the currency of the word in English and Scottish dialect before it became prominent in America, says the *Oxford English Dictionary*, but it is doubtful how far this is of imporance for its origin. It is more likely that it is a purely American slang term.

Skeleton at the Feast. There are one or two hypothetical stories in English records of the origin of this phrase, including one about a search for a lady who had not a care or trouble in the world; but who when found, as the searchers thought, opened a cupboard inside which was a skeleton which, she complained, her husband made her kiss each night, the skeleton being that of her husband's rival for her affections. But the real origin of the phrase lies in the custom of the Egyptians in always placing a skeleton in a prominent position at their banquets, to remind the diners that they were only mortal.

Skin of his teeth, To escape by. The origin of this very common phrase will surprise you. It appears in *Job*, xix, 20, and *Job* is probably the oldest of the books comprising the Bible.

Slave. This word, meaning an oppressed person, is a remarkable example of a complete change of meaning through the years. It comes from *Slavi*, a tribe which once lived on the banks of the Dnieper in Russia, and they were so-called from *Slav*, which meant noble. When conquered, they were sold into captivity and spread over Europe, and thus we came by the word slav-es. Miklosich's disputing of this etymology may be discounted.

Sleep. Scientists estimate that during an eight-hours' sleep the average human being changes position at least thirty-five times. The shortest period of undisturbed sleep is that which follows immediately after losing consciousness. It usually lasts about fourteen minutes.

Sleep Like a Top, To. A spinning-top is said to "sleep" when its gyrations are at their acme and the top is so steady that it seems hardly to be moving.

Sleep on a Clothes-line. "*I could sleep on a clothes-line, I am that tired.*" The phrase is a reference to an old custom by which down-and-outs who were not prepared to pay sixpence for a bed could lean over clothes-lines stretched across a room, for which a penny was charged. The method was for the men to lean their backs on the rope, with their arms over it and their hands in their pockets. They were thus supporting their bodies.

A correspondent sends us this account: There was a man in Newcastle-on-Tyne, who let his cellar at a penny a night to derelicts. A rope line was stretched at normal breast height from one side to the other. The gentlemen of the road used to hang over the line by their arms, taking the weight off their feet. At six o'clock in the morning the landlord entered the cellar, cut the rope—and all the sleepers were promptly awakened.

Sleeve, Laugh up one's. *See* "Laugh."

Sleuth-hound. Usually a bloodhound which follows by scent the sleuth (*sloth*, Norman, or *slot*) or track of another animal, whether beast or man.

Sling your hook. A naive explanation of this is that it is an admonition to a fellow angler to go away, and leave the angler already on the spot—to sling your hook further away. We should have thought that an invitation to an angler to "sling his hook," would mean that he could stay there and sling it. However, we do not know a better "origin," and we must say that the phrase is used to-day in the meaning described.

Slip. *There's many a Slip 'twixt Cup and Lip.* This phrase was used by a slave to Ancæos, helmsman of the ship *Argo*. The slave had told his master that he would never taste the wine of his own vineyard. Ancænos laughed, and had a bottle of wine (made from his own grapes) brought to the table. As he lifted the cup to his lips, servants told him that a wild boar was laying waste his vineyard. He put down the wine untasted, rushed out to kill the boar, and was himself killed.

Slogan. A war-cry from *Slaugh*, host, and *Ghairm*, outcry. The Gælic cry of the old Highland clans. It has sunk these days to a political or advertising catch phrase.

Slope Off, To. In Old English there was a word "Loup" (from Old Norse), meaning to leap. This was corrupted in the United States to lope, and slope is a further corruption. The sense of a hurried departure—a leap—is, however, still retained.

Small Hours. *In the Small Hours of the Morning.* Usually the early (small) morning hours from one a.m. to five or six a.m.

Snag. "*There's a snag in it.*" In the lumber camps of Canada a snag is a tree trunk which becomes fixed in the bed of the river by one end, the loose end coming up towards the surface and holding up the passage of tree trunks carried down by the stream.

Snake in the Grass. The sense of the phrase has for once never been changed since its original, in Latin (in "Virgil"), *Latet anguis in herba*.

Sneeze ("God Bless You"). The usual explanation of the use of the words "God Bless You" to a person who has sneezed, is that it was originated by St. Gregory during a pestilence in which sneezing was a mortal symptom. St. Gregory may have done so; if so, it showed that he knew his Aristotle and Thucydides, for the former mentions a similar custom among the Greeks, and the latter states that sneezing was a crisis symptom of the great Athenian plague. The Romans, too, followed the custom, their exclamation being, *Absit omen*.

Having exhausted these, we can turn to what is undoubtedly the real origin—the ancient Hebrew belief that when a person sneezed he was, at that moment, nearest to death in life. That opinion gave rise to a custom among the Hebrews of saying the equivalent in Hebrew to "God Bless You," which was answered by the grateful "Thank You."

Snob. The word is said to have been invented by Thackeray to describe George IV. He is said to have coined it from the entry against the names of "commoners" in the lists of colleges of "s. nob" (which stood for *sine nobilatate*, not of noble blood). In Cambridge, snob is still the college word for a townsman as distinct from a gownsman (a member of the University).

Snotty. There is a humorous, and probably libellous, origin to the term "snotty" for a midshipman. A "snot-rag," as every schoolboy knows, is a slang term for a pocket handkerchief. Now, the Lords Commissioners of the Admiralty ordained that the young gentlemen on board His Majesty's Ships should wear three buttons on the sleeves of their full-dress round jackets. At this the ribald lower deck asserted that the reason for the order of Their Lordships was to prevent the young gentlemen from putting the sleeves of their jackets to the use generally delegated to pocket handkerchiefs! So "snotty" they were called, and the author fears, snotty they will always be.

Soapy Sam. Was the nickname bestowed upon Bishop Wilberforce (1805-1873) of Oxford, because of his unctuous way of speaking. Dr. Brewer points out that, "it is somewhat remarkable that the floral decorations above the stall of the Bishop and of the Principal of Cuddesdon, were S.O.A.P., the initials of Sam Oxon and Alfred Post.

Soho. The cosmopolitan district in the West End of London has nothing to do, as has been stated, with the hunting cry when a quarry has been sighted. The district is named after the mansion of the Duke of Monmouth, which stood there in the time of Charles II.

Soldier. Was so-called from the Latin *Solidus*, "a piece of money." In other words, the Roman soldier was a hireling, or mercenary, engaged with money to fight.

Soloman's Ring, To have. Fable has it that King Solomon wore a ring containing a gem which told him all he desired to know. Which rather reflects on the "wisdom of Solomon," since he derived it, apparently, from his ring.

Song. The oldest written song in the English language is "Summer is i-comin' in," written by a monk about 1240. There were songs sung in the country before that; but they were never put into writing, being handed down by word of mouth.

Sop. *To be given a Sop.* The full quotation should be to "Give a Sop to Cerberus." Cerberus was Pluto's three-headed dog set at the gates of the Infernal Regions over which Pluto was King. The Greeks and Romans when burying their dead put into the hands of the corpse a cake. The idea was that the cake was a sop to Cerberus to allow the dead to pass unmolested.

S.O.S. The origin of the sea signal of distress was not a choosing of the initials of Save Our Souls. It was chosen because the letters in the Morse Code are the easiest to send and receive clearly—three dots, three dashes and three dots—and no matter how the signal may be interrupted, it can "pick up" its sequence at any time.

Sound. Name for a narrow sea, or strait, from the Anglo-Saxon word meaning swimming, or power to swim. A strait is believed to have meant, originally, a piece of water that could be swam.

South Sea Bubble. A financial scheme which ruined thousands of people in England, and almost smashed the Bank of England. It originated in 1711 and collapsed in 1720. It was proposed by the Earl of Oxford to fund a floating debt of £10,000,000 (in other words, to buy up the National Debt), the purchasers of which should become stockholders in the South Sea Company which was to have the monopoly of the trade with Spanish South America. A part of the Capital Stock was to constitute the fund. The refusal of the Spanish Government to enter into commercial relations with England made the privileges, and the Company, worthless. The money was used in other, and speculative, adventures with, amazing to relate, the backing of the Bank of England. By "rigging the market" £100 shares were run up to £1,050, so infatuated were people with the grandiose scheme put forward. The Bubble burst in 1720—the greatest financial crash England had ever known.

Spade-Guinea. A gold coin, worth twenty-one shillings, and minted 1787-1789. The coin was so-called because on the reverse side it bore a shield shaped like the "spade" on a playing-card suit of that name. The Sovereign's head on the coin was that of George III.

Spartan. A man of Sparta, one of the leading cities in Ancient Greece, whose people were renowned for their prowess, courage and discipline, but above all for their frugality. Spartan fare is frugal fare; Spartan courage, is the courage to bear pain with fortitude.

Spectacles. Were invented by the Chinese. The Latins knew of them. Nero wore an eyeglass of beryl. Alessandro de Spina, a Florentine monk, and Roger Bacon are both credited with their "invention" in Europe; and Benjamin Franklin invented the bi-focal lens.

Speculate. The Latin root, *speculari*, means to spy from a watch-tower. It is a little difficult to transfer it to "consider, or observe mentally," which is what the word means to-day.

As for the speculate of the financial speculator, it has no part or parcel with the original.

Spell of Work. *To do a Spell of Work.* A spell of work is, properly, a set of persons taking a turn of work in order to relieve others; a relay or relief gang; a shift. The word is derived from the Old English *gespelia*, substitute.

Spencer. The popular garment was introduced by the Earl of Spencer, who wagered that he could set a new fashion simply by appearing in the streets in any new kind of garment. He wore what is now called a spencer, and won his bet.

Sphinx. Represented in Greek mythology as having the head of a woman, the body of a lion, and winged; in Egypt as a wingless lion, with the head and breast of a man. The giant carving of the Sphinx on the edge of the desert, and below the great Pyramid outside Cairo, was old in the days of Cheops. It is hewn out of solid rock, one hundred and forty feet long and twenty-eight feet from crown to chin.

Sphinx, Riddle of the. *See* "Riddle."

Spick and Span. The phrase is really incomplete; it should be spic and span new. A spick is a spike or nail, and a span is a chip, and it is suggested that it first referred to a new ship, every spike or nail and chip being new. On the other hand, span-new may be from the Anglo-Saxon *spannan*, meaning span new; and the explanation of this is that *spannan* was used to describe cloth newly extended or dressed at the cloth-maker's, thus new cloth, or span new.

Spike his Guns. "*I'll spike his guns*"; I'll stop him. It comes, of course, from the old practice of rendering a gun useless to the enemy by driving a spike into the touch-hole.

Spinster. When the word was properly used, as in the Middle Dutch and Friesan language, a spinster was exactly what it spells—one who span. The women of the Anglo-Saxon household span, in Winter, the fleeces which had been taken from the sheep during the Summer. That was their expected task. It was a recognized axiom that no woman of that period was fitted to be a wife until she had spun for herself her body, table and bed linen. Thus, the task of spinning was generally delegated to the unmarried women of the house, who were the spinners or the spinsters.

It is an interesting sidelight on the custom that Alfred the Great referred to the women of his house as the *spindle* side; and Edward the Elder called the female the distaff.

Splice, To. In view of the fact that splice is a slang term meaning to marry, it is curious that its real meaning is to split, or divide, from the German *Spleissen*. The joining together version came from the seaman's method of repairing a damaged rope. He cut the rope in two, and then, by interweaving the strands of the two ends into each other by "splitting" the plaits, made the rope into one again.

Split an Infinitive. It seems an incredible thing in these days of education that the writer should have been asked on several hundreds of occasions to define what exactly is a split infinitive, and how to recognize, and avoid, it.

A split infinitive is a sentence with a word interposed between "to" and the verb. The most noteworthy example is seen in notices displayed in theatres or cinemas: "Ladies are requested *to kindly remove* their hats." This is a split infinitive. A lady cannot possibly be asked "to kindly"; she is asked to remove her hat. The way of avoiding it is to put the "to" somewhere else: "Ladies are requested *kindly to* remove their hats," or they are "kindly requested *to remove* their hats." Either way will do; but no lady can be requested "to kindly" because there is no such verb.

Sponge, To throw up. This comes, as may be guessed, from the boxing ring, where a man's seconds, seeing that he could fight no longer with any chance of success, threw in the sponge with which they stood by to wipe away blood.

Spoonerism. Laughable mistakes made by the fact that the brain, working too quickly for the tongue, results in such extempore phrases as: "The Lord is a shoving leopard," for The Lord is a loving shepherd, and "Kinkering Kongs their titles take." The name Spoonerism comes from the Rev. W. A. Spooner (1844-1920), Warden of New College, Oxford, who had an unfortunate (or fortunate!) penchant for making them.

Spooning. A term used of sweethearting couples. It is not, however, a slang phrase. In Wales, some forty or fifty years ago, a beau did, indeed "spoon" his belle. It was a Welsh sweet-hearting custom for a young man to make his girl a gift of a carved wooden spoon. Some of these were very elaborately done, with intricate stained patterns on the handles and bowls in the shape of flowers, and commonly with the initials of the lovers entwined. A few of these are still to be found in Welsh homes, and in one or two hostelries, where they are kept as mementoes of old local customs.

The pleasant little custom was killed by mass production, which has killed most art. Enterprising "business" men manufactured by machinery all types of spoons—and the local young men consequently had no further inducement to carve one for themselves.

Spouse. A man's spouse, in our translation, is his wife. It is a corruption of the real meaning. A spouse is a woman promised in marriage, if the word is used correctly. It is derived from the Latin *sponsus*, the past participle of *spondere*, to promise. Roman marriages were generally "arranged." The friends of the parties met at the house of the bride-to-be's father, and there the marriage contract and settlement were drawn up. This contract was called the *sponsalia*, and when it was signed the couple were *spouses*. We still use the word in its correct meaning when we say that a couple are espoused.

Spring-heel Jack. Was the name earned for himself by the eccentric Marquis of Waterford of a hundred years ago. His hobby was having springs fitted to his heels, and at night-time scaring people half out of their wits by springing over them.

Square the Circle, To. To attempt the impossible, since there is no known way exactly to determine the square contents of a circle. It is the one calculation that eluded Euclid.

Stalking Horse. A horse trained to allow a fowler (a hunter, or pursuer of game) to conceal himself behind it, or under its coverings, in order to get within easy reach of the game without alarming it. The word can also be applied to any object, such as a canvas screen, made in the form of any animal and used for the same object. It is derived from the Old English *stealcian*, to steal up.

Stalemate. To stalemate a person is to bring a project in which he is engaged to a standstill. The term comes from the Old French *estal*, stall; and was originally used in this form in Chess to denote that the king is the only movable piece on the board and, although not in check, cannot move without becoming so.

Stalin, Joe. The Russian leader. Prior to the World War the name Stalin was little known. His real name is Josef Vissarionovitsch Djugashvili. His mother called him Soso. Why Stalin? Because, persecuted by the late Czar for his political opinions, he was banished, and spent eight years behind prison bars. The privations and cruelties did not break his spirit—so he was given the name Stalin which, in Russian, means steel. Stalingrad, the city of steel, is named after him.

Stand Sam, To. A corruption of the old slang name, Sampsman, a highwayman. A victim unwillingly "stood Sam" when held up by a highwayman with the demand, "Stand and deliver." There existed, also, a very old English word, *Sam*, meaning to collect things together, and the German *Sommeln* and the Swedish *Samla* both implied money. Dr. Brewer suggests that the phrase is entirely American and arose from the "U.S." marked on the knapsacks of American soldiers, thus, in other words, that the government of Uncle Sam (q.v.) pays for everybody. The author fears, however, that the phrase existed over here many years before U.S. appeared on the knapsacks of American soldiers.

Staple. Where used as a component of place-names the word means a market. Thus Barnstaple was a market, and so was Dun-stable. The sense of the word still exists in our phrase *staple* industry, the established "market" of the inhabitants of the place to which reference is made.

Starboard and Larboard. Starboard was, and still is, the right-hand side of a ship as you face the bows, and larboard was for many years the left-hand side; but so many contretemps occurred through the simliarity of two names, that larboard was subsequently changed to "port side." Starboard was originally Anglo-Saxon *Steor* (steer, or rudder) side; and larboard Anglo-Saxon *leere*, empty.

Statue of Liberty. The great statue which first greets the visitor as his ship sails into New York harbour, was originally intended to decorate the Port Said entrance to the Suez Canal. The Canal authorities declined to accept the offering. Left with the statue on their hands, the owners organized a public lottery, and after they had recouped their expenses, presented the statue to America. That is the story. Anyway, the statue was presented to U.S.A. by the French. The lady was sculptured by Bartholdi, his mother being the model. Statue is three hundred and five feet six inches high.

Steamship. The first boat ever to be propelled under steam was built by John Fitch, born in Connecticut, U.S.A., 1743. His model was tried out on a mill pond in 1785, and in 1790 he was running a steamboat passenger and cargo service on the Delaware River.

Steeplechase. Has what is probably the queerest origin of any name in the language. It dates back only as far as the late eighteenth century, and the story is as follows: A number of fox-hunters were returning home from the hunt without a kill, when one of them saw in the distance the steeple of a village church. He proposed that they should run a race to the steeple *in a direct line*, regardless of all obstacles, the winner to be the one who first touched the stones of the steeple with his whip. This was done, and ever since cross-country races, over all obstacles, have been called steeplechases.

Stem the Tide. *To hold off disaster.* An ingenious "explanation" of this popular cliche is given by one authority who points out that though the stem of a vessel ploughs the wave, it can hardly be said to check the tide; "but," he goes on, "the Anglo-Saxon word *stemn* meant a staff, a stout cudgel, and we can imagine that one who found himself in danger of being swept down by the mob might resist the onslaught with his *stemn*." We *can*, but imagination is a pretty bad thing in philology; and the authority makes no attempt to get the "tide" in his mob!

He might have have had a look at the Old Icelandic *stemma*, in use long before his Anglo-Saxon, and the Dutch *stempen*, both of which mean "to stop the flow of." It might further be pointed out that though the stem of a ship ploughs through the waves, but does not check the tide, it is doing what it is made for, and is not supposed to check anything, whereas a wall or a breakwater, for instance, *will* check the tide, or stem it.

To stem the tide in the sense in which we use the phrase comes from the Icelandic *stemma*.

Step (father or mother, etc.). A prefix indicating that the person referred to is not a blood relation, but a relative only by marriage. Step, in this meaning, comes from the Anglo-Saxon *steop*, which is connected with *astieped* meaning bereaved.

Sterling. The name given to English money. There is little doubt that in this country the "sterling" owes its name to the Hause merchants in England, named Easterlings, who first coined money here in Mediæval English days; but whether it was by design or accident that the name fits Easterlings has never been satisfactorily answered. The Easterlings, it is said, derived their name from the fact that they came from the East parts of Germany. This complicates the position, because there was in Germany, also, a coin called the sterling (Middle High German word), and this could not have meant Easterling. "It seems probable," says the *Century Dictionary*, in an exhaustive research, "that Middle High German word is derived from the Mediæval English word, which must then be due, in spite of unexplained difficulties, to Easterling, or else is derived, as asserted in a statement from Linwood, from the figure of a starling (anciently called sterling) at one time engraved on one quarter of the coin so called." It should be added here that there is no historical evidence of any kind to support Linwood's assertion.

Steward. The name for a caretaker is derived from the Saxon *Stig-weard*, from *Stigo*, a sty, and *weard*, a ward. It dates back to the days when most of England was forest, and the chief wealth of the Saxon land-owner was his pigs. The pigs were driven home from the forest feeding grounds at night and penned in their sties, a man being employed to keep watch and ward over them. He was the *Stig-weard*—Steward.

Stickler. "*He's a stickler at it.*" The Anglo-Saxon language had the word *stightle*, which meant to set in order; and there was a second word *sticol*, meaning rough, difficult, sharp. From these the word stickler developed; and the earliest sticklers were umpires, or regulators, of a tournament, wrestling match or the like, to ensure that there should be fair play. A stickler over trifles, to-day, is a man who insists that the rule shall be carried out to the very letter.

Stilton Cheese. Is not, and never was, made in Stilton, but in the Vale of Belvoir, Leicestershire. The name Stilton Cheese came to it in this way: A man from Belvoir, who kept a coaching inn at Stilton, regularly imported his native cheese for his customers. The cheese—an excellent commodity, as most people know — became very popular in Stilton among those who had tried it, and visitors going to Stilton were advised to try "the Stilton Cheese."

Stock. To-day Stock is applied to shares in companies, to the contents of shops; in the home to the pot from which comes soup; on the land to cattle, and so on; but originally it was the Anglo-Saxon *Stocc*, a stick, wood, because wood had to be accumulated and stored for the Winter. Thus, anything stored came to be known as stock.

Stoic. One who practices indifference to emotion, pleasure or pain. The name was given to the school of Greek philosophers founded by Zeno about 300 B.C., because Zeno gave his lectures in the *stoapœcile*, the Painted Porch, in the Agora at Athens.

Zeno taught that men should be free from passion, unmoved by joy or grief, and submit without complaint to the unavoidable necessity by which all things were governed. The Stoics are famed for the sternness and austerity of their ethical doctrines, and for the influence which their tenets exercised over some of the noblest spirits of antiquity, especially among the Romans.

"Stoke." This suffix at the end of town names, such as Basing-*stoke*, Bishop-*stoke*, means that the original town was a stockaded place (i.e., defended by a barrier of stakes as well as pikes). It is of Anglo-Saxon origin.

Stoker. There aren't any stokers to-day! The man who stokes a railway engine, or a furnace, is a corruption of the old stoker of Anglo-Saxon and Dutch days, when fires were kept going by *Stocc* or Stoken—wood.

Stone Unturned, To leave no. After the Persian Mardonius had been defeated at Platæa (477 B.C.), it was reported to his victor, Polycrates the Theban, that he had left great treasures in his tent. Failing to find them, though he searched long, Polycrates consulted the Oracle of Delphi (q.v.). The Oracle told him, "Leave no stone unturned." Polycrates returned, turned every stone from its floor space, and the treasure was found.

Stool of Repentance. A low stool placed in front of the pulpit in Scottish churches, on which sat persons who had offended against the Church's strict rules. At the end of Divine Service, the offender was made to stand on the stool and hear the congregation's sentence.

Story. *Tell me a Story, or That's a Story.* Both mean that the "story" is a fable. Yet the word is but a corruption of the Greek *histor*, or perhaps an abbreviation is a better word, and *histor* meant history, which is fact.

Strafe. *To strafe someone.* German word, as most of us know. It is from the German *strafen*, to punish. It does not mean hate, as for so long has been quoted in the *Gott strafe England*, which is correctly interpreted God *punish* England.

Straw to Break with you. This phrase goes back to early feudal days in England, when tenancies (fief) were held at the will of the overlord. A fief was conveyed to a new tenant by giving him a straw, signifying his possession. To end the tenancy, because of some act of the tenant, the overlord went to the threshold of the door and broke a straw with the formula: "As I break this straw, so I break the contract between us."

To have a straw to break with someone, therefore, is to have a dispute with him.

Street *v.* Roads. "Street" comes from the Old English *straet*, from the Late Latin *Strata*, a paved road. On the other hand, "road" is from the Old English *rod*, derived from the verb *ridan*, to ride. Road meant, originally, a line of communication mainly for horse-riders.

Strike. This inalienable right of the workers to down tools was first given its name by sailors. They had refused to sail because of alleged grievances and, to make sure that the ship should *not* sail, they *struck* (lowered) the yards of the vessel.

Stump Up, To. An allusion to the orator who speaks from a soap-box, or from a platform for money given voluntarily by his audience. His speaking is called "stump oratory," from the original American early use of the stump of a felled tree as a platform. At the end of his address the audience was expected to subscribe stump money. If they were lacking in enthusiasm "stump up" was the appeal of the orator. Although the term stump-orator on this side of the Atlantic is used in a tone of contempt, it does not necessarily imply a derogatory meaning in America.

Submarines. Although submarines were talked of in theory for many years, the actual first under-the-sea boat was constructed in 1620 by Cornelius van Drebel, a Dutchman in the service of our King James I. It was tried out in the Thames, being navigated at a depth of twelve to fifteen feet for several hours—by twelve rowers.

In 1776, an under-sea attempt was made by American colonists to sink, with an under-sea boat, an English warship off New York. It failed; and not till nearly a hundred years later, during the American Civil War, was such an attempt successful. The first vessel to be sunk by a submarine was the warship *Housatonic*, torpedoed while blockading Charleston in 1864.

Subsidy. Nearly a household word in Britain in these days of war (1944), when subsidies are given to agriculture, bakers, and candle-stick makers, so to speak. The word comes from the Latin *subsidium*, help, aid, assistance. Almost the only people in Britain not subsidized during the Second World War were the men-in-the-street who paid the subsidies.

Suburb. From the Latin *sub*, under, and *urbs*, a city—in other words, a place under, or near, a city wall.

Suicide. From the Latin *sui*, of oneself, *cidium*, from *coedere*, to kill. To kill oneself. Suicides in the old days were buried on the high road with a stake driven through their heart, and without Christian rights. Even to-day a suicide, on whom has been returned a verdict of *felo de se*, cannot be buried in consecrated ground. It is because of this that coroners' juries invariably return a verdict of "suicide while the balance of the mind was disturbed," thereby stating, in effect, that the deceased was not responsible for his actions at the time. This allows burial in consecrated ground, and according to Christian rites.

Sun, The. Distance from the earth is 93,000,000 miles. Light travels at the rate of 186,000 miles a second, so it takes eight minutes and twenty seconds for the light from the sun to reach the earth.

Sun, heat of. If the heat radiation of the sun could be centred on a column of ice two and a half miles thick and stretching from the earth to the sun (93,000,000 miles), the heat of the sun would melt it in a second. The water resulting from the melting would be changed into steam in just about seven seconds!

Sun, weight of. Mathematicians have estimated that the sun's weight in British tons is two thousand quadrillion!

Sunday. So-called because the Ancients dedicated the day, the first of the week, to the sun, as Monday was dedicated to the moon.

"*A place in the sun.*" The phrase was used by Pascall in 1711, but was popularized by William II of Germany. In the crisis of 1911 at Hamburg, he said: "Germany would take steps 'that would make sure that no one can dispute with us the place in the sun that is our due'."

Sundae. The ice-cream and fruit concoction now so popular in this country during the warm months owes its name to the Sabbath Day; and in a curious manner. It appears that under the Blue Laws of Virginia, Va., U.S.A., soda drinks were not allowed to be sold on Sunday, so in Norfolk, Virginia, a drug store proprietor prepared a mixture of vanilla ice-cream and chocolate syrup to be sold on the seventh day. He named it Sundae after its birth-day. The drug store where it was born is still pointed out with pride in Norfolk.

Sunday School, The first. Usually ascribed to Robert Raikes, in 1780. This is not correct. A Sunday School was opened by Hannah Bell at High Wycombe, Bucks., long before this year. A window commemorating the fact is in the Town Hall at Wycombe. Raikes, learning of Hannah Bell's School, conceived the idea, and carried it out, of starting a NATIONAL Sunday School movement.

Supercilious. Literally, *super*, over, and *cilium*, eyebrow, over eyebrow; having an elevated eyebrow. The aptness of the term will be appreciated.

Surnames. From the Latin *super*, through the French *sur*, over, above, and *nomen*, name. Christian names were held first in Britain, and surnames did not develop until somewhere about the tenth century. Thus John, who earned his living by shoeing horses, became in time John Smith, and his son John became John-son. Surname means "the other," or "over" name to the Christian name.

Swallow the Anchor, To. The origin is, of course, the sea. To swallow the anchor is an old seaman's term for giving up the sea and retiring to dry land for the rest of his life.

Swan-Song. The fable is that the swan, which has no voice beyond a croak, sings beautifully just as it dies. It is quite untrue, though Plato, Aristotle, Europedes and Cicero all gave credence to it. Shakespeare apparently believed it, for he refers to it in "The Merchant of Venice" (iii, 2): "Rape of Lucrece" (1.1611). Dr. Brewer suggests that the philosophers argued thusly: "All birds sing. The swan is a bird, therefore it sings. As it has never been heard to sing it must therefore sing at its last moment."

Swindle. Came to us from the German *Schwindler*, a cheating company promoter. The word was introduced here by German Jews in 1760.

Symbol. *See* "Tally."

T

T. "*It fits to a T.*" The "T" is the artists' or mechanics' T-square, a rule with a cross-piece at one end forming exact right angles and, in conjunction with the square edge of a drawing board enabling correct and exactly parallel lines to be withdrawn.

Table d'hote. Most people appear to be under the impression that the description means a meal as served in a hotel. It is not so. Its literal meaning—it is in the French language—is "at the table of the host." A visitor to one's house takes *table d'hote*, and travellers who asked to be served with a meal in the old country inns invariably took it with the landlord at his own table.

Taboo. Applied strictly, the word taboo should be used only in connection with a religious ceremony, and it does not mean "forbidden" as we use it. The word comes from the Maori (New Zealand) *tapu*, or from the South Sea Island *Tabu*, both of which mean sacred. Tapu or Tabu was a religious ceremony which could be imposed only by a priest.

Taffy was a Welshman! Taffy was a Thief. The mention of this old saw raises fury in the hearts of all Welshmen, despite the fact that for generations they have been looked upon with mistrust. They deny, emphatically, that they were ever thieves; but add that if they were, the saw refers to the action in Welsh Border raids, when they stole back their own cattle from the Norman invaders who had first appropriated them.

A Devon reader, when I was commenting on this, wrote stating that the "Welshman" of the tag was really the Old English *welisc* and Middle English *Welish*, both meaning foreigners, and adding that from time immemorial foreigners in England were regarded as people not to be trusted.

Still a third "origin" put forward is that "Taffy" has nothing to do in the rhyme with Welsh, but is an ancient Dutch lampoon on greed and selfishness. The word "taffy," it is claimed, is a corruption of *tafyr*, which was the term for the high black caps worn by all Dutch priests at all outdoor functions; and these Dutch priests were notorious for their seizing of all the good things that were going.

Tailor. The name for a maker of suits comes from the Late Latin *taliatorem*, and *taliator*, a cutter. In France, by way of which it came to England, the word still retains much of its Roman meaning, for there remain *taileur de bois* (cutters of wood), *tailleur d'images* (sculptors), as there are *taileur d'habits* of clothes.

Take a Rise out of Him. A phrase from the fishing water. The angler fishing for trout with artificial fly "fishes for a rise." In other words, he casts his line and fly on a likely spot on the water, to tempt a fish. A trout, seeing the fly from below, comes up to take it; in fishing parlance he "rises to the fly," and the angler strikes as he does so. Thus he "takes the rise."

Take the Cake, To. *See* "Cake-walk."

Taken A'Back, To be. To be surprised. A seafaring term of sailing days, used when a ship's sails "back-filled" so that the ship lost "way."

Talent. To have talent is to possess a natural ability or aptitude, of capacity for success, but why this is called talent is one of the mysteries of philology, for the only root of the word talent is the Greek name for a weight, a balance, or a sum of money. The process of its change into a sense of mental aptitude is unexplained; unless it can be said to have taken such a sense from the Parable of the Ten Talents (*Matt.*, xxv, 14-30).

Talisman. Properly, a talisman is a stone ring or other object engraven with figures or characters, to which are attributed the occult powers of planetary influences. It has had that meaning since the seventeenth century; but the actual origin of the word was some considerable time before that. It is, however, of uncertain history, and was probably a mistaken or corrupted form of some Arabic or Persian or Turkish spoken word imperfectly caught by early travellers. Talisman was also a word formerly applied to a Turk learned in the Law.

Talk Turkey. To talk profitable business. The story goes that a white man and an Indian went hunting with the understanding that the game was to be divided piece by piece. The result of the sport was two wild turkeys and three crows. The white man, counting out, allotted a crow to the Indian, then a turkey to himself, and then another crow to the Indian, appropriating, of course, the second turkey to himself. To which the Indian complained: "You talk all turkey to you, and only crow *for Injun*."

Talkie-Films. The first talkie play film (made in the U.S.A.) was "The Jazz Singer," with Al Jolson. It was first shown in this country at the Piccadilly Theatre, London, on 27th September, 1928; but the first actual talking film was shown and heard in London, and was evolved by two London men. It was a sketch from a revue, and was called "The Gentlemen." Produced in 1925, it had a cast of three, and was not a success.

Tally. A tally was a piece of wood on which notches were cut to mark numbers, or amounts. Before writing became general in England, a tally was the method of keeping accounts. In purchasing or selling it was customary to make duplicate tallies of the transaction, or to split the tally through the middle. In the English Exchequer, tallies were used until the end of the eighteenth century. An Exchequer tally consisted of a squared rod of hazel wood, having on one side notches indicating the sum for which the tally was an acknowledgment. On two other sides opposite to each other the amount of the sum, the name of the payer and the date were written by an officer called the "Writer of the Tallies." This being done, the rod was then split lengthwise. One part was kept in the Exchequer, and the other given to the creditor. When the wood was returned to the Exchequer, usually in payment of taxes, it was compared with the one in the Exchequer to see if it *tallied*.

The size of the notch on the tallies varied with the amounts. The notch for £100 was the breadth of a thumb; for £1 the breadth of a barley corn; a penny was indicated by a slight slit. It is an amazing fact that the tally was not abolished until nearly the end of the eighteenth century, and not until the reign of William IV was the accumulation of tallies in the possession of the Government destroyed. They were burnt in a stove in the House of Lords, and overheated the stove which, setting fire to the panelling of the room, destroyed the Houses of Parliament!

Talley-man, or Tally-man, came from the same root, though his tally was a book, and a card. He retained the book, the customer had the card as a reckoning on his financial position.

Tally-Ho. Hunting-field cry on catching sight of the quarry. It is a corruption of the French cry *taiaut* (the aut is pronounced as "O"), similarly used on sighting a stag.

Tam. The word is a component part of many British river names. It means spreading, quiet, or still.

See "Thames."

Tam-o-Shanter. The soft, cloth cap is so-named after the hero of Burns's poem of the same name.

Tandem. Is a name for horses driven one in front of the other, or for a bicycle for two people, one being mounted behind the other. The name came from a University joke. There is a Latin adverb, *tandem*, meaning at length (after a space of time). A University wag, or punster, suited the word to the then popular custom of driving two horses, harnessed one ahead of the other . . . at length.

Tanks. The "battleships of the army," were first used in war by the British in an attack on the German lines at Flers, on 15th September, 1916. The reason for their name would seem obvious from their appearance; but there is a story that they were so-named (before their actual appearance) by the War Office to prevent any information as to their real nature leaking out. It is naively said that telegrams with inquiries about "tanks" would convey no suspicion if they fell into enemy hands.

Tanner. Slang for a sixpenny-piece. The origin of the name is obscure, but it is most likely to have descended from the Sanskrit *tanka*, a weight of silver equal to four moshas, a stamped coin. Hotten's suggestion that the term came from the gipsy *tani*, small or little, is untenable, since gipsies would hardly call sixpence "little" while threepenny pieces, twopenny pieces, and even pennies were in circulation.

Tantalise. In Greek mythology Tantalus was the son of Zeus and the daughter of Himantes. He was a Lydian king, high in honours. But in a misguided moment he divulged to mortals the secrets of the Gods and gave the mortals nectar and ambrosia, the food and drink of the Gods. In punishment, he was doomed to stand up to his chin in the waters of Hades, with a tree containing clusters of fruit just above his head. When he turned to drink the waters receded leaving only slime; when he put up his hand to take the fruit from the tree it withered at his touch. From this myth we get our *tantalise*, meaning to raise hopes and then take hopes away.

Tantalus, meaning a lock-up spirit chest in which the bottles are visible, but unobtainable unless one has the key to unlock the tantalus, comes from the same source.

Tantony Pig. Is the name given to the smallest pig of a litter. The name comes from St. Anthony, who was the patron saint of swineherds.

Tapis. "*On the tapis*." The word is French for tapestry. Since the table of a council chamber was covered with *tapis*, to be on the tapis meant to be on the table, in other words, being under consideration and discussion by those present.

Tar, Jack. The name for a sailor. Contrary to the usual "interpretation," Jack Tar has no reference whatever to the tarpaulin he is said to wear in rough weather. The phrase dates back to sailing days, when a ship, on reaching port, had to be tarred and caulked—a messy job which left "Jack's" clothes and hands and face so well tarred, that weeks were necessary entirely to remove it.

Tariff Reform. Older readers will remember the great political battle of the early 1900's between the Chamberlainites and the Campbell-Bannermanites over the imposition of a tariff on goods entering this country. Britain had enjoyed what was known as Free Trade. Mr. Joseph Chamberlain proposed an extension of such revenue duties as there were already, with the idea of preventing "dumping" of goods into this country at cheap prices, in many cases, it was said, at prices lower than the cost of manufacture over here. Opponents of the proposals stated that such a tariff would inevitably raise prices, particularly of food. "Free Food" and "Dear Food" were the rival election cries. As is well known, there have been for some years such duties on imports.

Tarred and Feathered. The origin of this is pretty well explained by a statute of King Richard I, of 1189: "A thiefe or felon that hath stolen, being lawfully convicted, shal have his head shorne and boyling pitch powred upon his head, and feathers or downe strawed upon the same, whereby he may be knowen, and so at the first landing place they shall come to, thereto be cast up." The time was, of course, the Crusades.

Tarred with the same brush. The reference is to the marking of sheep. An owner of a flock will have them all "marked" with the same device, in the same place. The marking is usually done on the wool with a brush dipped in some staining liquid, formerly tar, but now red ochre. Thus all sheep bearing that mark were tarred with the same brush, i.e., belonged to the same owner.

Tattoo. Used in recent years as a description of a night military display at Aldershot annually. Literally, however, it was a signal to "close the taps" or tabs. Phillips, in 1706, wrote "Tat-too, or Tap-too, the beat of drums at night for all soldiers to repair to their tents in the field, or to their quarters in a garrison." It is sometimes called "The Retreat." The Swedish, Russian, German and Danish languages all have approximately the same word.

Tawdry. The name given to cheap or gaudy finery is a corruption of St. Audrey (St. Etheldrida) lace, sold at St. Audrey's Fair, at the time held annually at the shrine of St. Audrey in the Isle of Ely, Cambs. It certainly did not bear the stigma applied to-day to tawdry. The change possible came about by worthless or showy reproductions of the real St. Awdry lace.

Te Deum. The Church's great hymn of praise. It is called the Te Deum from the opening words, "*Te Deum Laudamus*": Thee God, we Praise. It is said that St. Ambrose improvized the words while baptising St. Augustus, about 386. The probability is, however, that its date is much later.

Tea. This national beverage of England was first heard of between the years 300 and 400, when it was being drunk in China as a medicine. It was called *tscha*. It was not until the sixth century that the medicine *tscha* became a beverage. By the end of another three hundred years it had become the staple drink of China. From China it spread to Persia; and there, in 1579, Christopher Borough, an English traveller, partook of it and liked it. The same year, on his return, he introduced it into England.

Tea-Kettle Broth. According to Dr. Brewer "poor man's soup," consisting of hot water, bread, a small lump of butter, and pepper and salt to taste.

Teach your Grandmother to Suck Eggs. It is not uninteresting to trace this proverb from its earliest stages. Its story seems to start in print in 1542, when in Udall's translation of Erasmus' "Apophthegmata" appears: "A swine to teache Minerua was a prouerbe . . . for whiche we saie in Englishe, to teache our dame to spinne." Then, in 1611, we get Cotgrave writing: "Wee say to teach his grandame to grope ducks."

In 1659, the phrase had come to (according to Howell), "Go teach your grannam to grope a goose." In 1665 Howard, in "Committee IV" has it, "Pish, teach your grannam to spin." And so to Swift, in his "Polite Conversations" (1783), "Go teach your grannam to suck eggs."

Teeth are drawn, His. From the old fable of the lion who agreed to have his teeth drawn and his claws cut in order that he might marry a beautiful maid he coveted. When the deed was done, the father and the maid slew the helpless lion!

Teeth, False. The origin of substituting false teeth (dentures) for extracted natural teeth is lost in antiquity. The Egyptians were extracting teeth about the year 4700 B.C. Aristotle (fourth century B.C.) tells us of instruments for extracting and scaling teeth; and even as far back as 500 B.C. the Etruscans were restoring missing teeth—putting in false teeth—for specimens of bridge work have been discovered dating to that period, and are preserved in the Corneto Museum. The writer has in front of him illustrations of ancient Greek dental instruments, and it is a remarkable fact that they are not much different in design from those now being used.

Teetotal. Joseph Turner, an artisan of Preston, Lancashire, came to everlasting fame in this word. In September, 1833, so the story goes, he was addressing a meeting in advocacy of total abstinence. But Mr. Turner stuttered rather badly in moments of excitement, and the concluding lines of his address were as follows: "N-n-nothing but t-t-t-t-t-total abstinence will do—that or nowt."

The expression was at once seized upon by his opponents in the crowd, who christened the movement the t-t-t-totalism. And the supporters good-naturedly accepted it.

"Tell it to the Marines." The story of this presumed slur on the truthfulness of the Royal Marines is as follows: During a luncheon Charles II was told by a naval officer that he (the officer) had seen flying fish. Charles, incredulous, replied, "Go, tell that to the Marines." A Captain of Marines, who was present, protested vehemently at this slur, whereupon the King, somewhat surprised, explained that he had not meant a slur. What he intended, he said, was that if his Marines who had served in all parts of the world, and seen many strange things, believed the story, he himself would.

Ten. "*The Upper Ten.*" This phrase for *The Upper Ten Thousand* was first used by N. P. Phillips in speaking of the top strata of New York society which, at that time, numbered no more than ten thousand people.

Tenant. A tenant is a person who holds property, from the Latin *tenere*, to hold, and the French *tenant*, the present participle of *tenir*, to hold. It may interest those Socialists who hold that all land should be the property of the State, to know that all land in England belongs in theory to the Crown—since the days of William the Conqueror, who seized it.

Tenter-hooks, To be on. After cloth is woven, it is stretched on tenter-hooks, which are passed through the selvedge, to dry. Hence to be on tenter-hooks, is to be stretched—with anxiety or worry.

Terra Firma. Dry land, firm earth. Latin *terra*, earth.

Territorials. Britain's amateur (as distinct from the professional) soldiers came into being when, in 1908, the old-time Yeomanry and Militia, which were country-wide units for voluntary enlistment, were superseded for county regiments—in other words, on a territorial basis. (Territorial is a Latin word meaning territory.) The territorial regions under the scheme were counties. Earlier, in 1881, the Infantry of the Line, under an Army re-organization, had been made territorial regiments, by each one becoming associated in name and depot with a particular county.

Test "Ashes." These mythical ashes, which are contended for between English and Australian cricketers, originated in a humorist cricket writer. When, in 1882, Australia defeated England over here, a humorous "epitaph" on the game appeared in a sporting newspaper. It ended with the sentence: "The body (English cricket) will be cremated, and the ashes taken to Australia."

The "Ashes" tickled the fancies of both the English and Australian public, and "they" have been contended for ever since.

Test Match. In 1862 an eleven of English cricketers visited Australia on the exhibition system, and was followed by three others between that year and 1878. At first these elevens played against odds of eighteen and twenty-two members of the Australian team, but the Australians soon began to meet their visitors on level terms. In 1878 the Australians sent a team to England, and that began a series of visits either way.

Tete-a-tete. Tete is the French word for head. Tete-a-tete is a conversation "head-to-head," in other words, private.

Tether. *To come to the end of one's tether.* The simple origin is the rope or chain by which a horse, or other grass-feeding animal, was tethered to a stake. It could graze only in the confines allowed by the tether. There, its resources of food or exercise ended.

Thames, The River. Longest and most important river in England. To say that the name Thames has been derived from the alleged Latin *Thamesis* ("the broad Isis"), as is continually being put forward, is nonsense. It is nonsense, too, that it expresses the junction of the Thame and the Isis. If there ever was a clear-cut etymological descent from our early speech, Thames provides it. The Celtic word *tam* meant smooth, and the Celtic *esis*, was one of the variants of *usig*, meaning water. Thames means "smooth water." Why philologists must go wandering among bastard Latin for an origin, when there are perfectly plain words in a native language, is ever a source of wonder to the writer.

The Isis, it is true, runs past Oxford; but the name is scholastic only.

That's the Ticket. A corruption of the French *Etiguette* (*see* "Etiquette"), meaning "That is what you should do."

"The Best Years of my Life." A phrase used almost every day in anger, reminiscence, and in other circumstances. What *are* the best years of a person's life? Well, biologists agree that for a woman they are between twenty-five and forty; for a man between thirty and fifty-five.

The Glorious Twelfth. Name given by shooting men to the 12th of August, the first day of grouse shooting.

Thebes, Seven Against. The seven against were Adastrus Polynices, Tydeus, Amphiaraus, Hippomedpn, Capaneus and Parthenopæus, all Argive chiefs. They are said, in legend, to have undertaken an expedition against Thebes.

There, But for the Grace of God go I. Words uttered by John Bradford (1510-1555) on seeing criminals being taken to execution. The actual words he said were: "There, but for the grace of God, goes John Bradford."

Thespians. Name for actors, from Thespis, an Attic poet of the sixth century B.C., accepted as the Father of Greek Tragedy.

Thimble. The Old Norse *þumall* meant the thumb of a glove; and a leather thumb-stall was the earliest form of thimble. Metal thimbles were not introduced into England until the seventeenth century. Sailors still wear a thimble on the thumb. The Anglo-Saxon for thimble was *thymel*, and this, too, meant a thumb-stall.

Thin. "*It's a Bit too Thin.*" It's a bit too transparent is the real meaning. The origin is that one can see through a thing which is so thin as to be transparent. The phrase is very old. Shakespeare used it in 1613, in "Henry VIII."

Thirteen. The unlucky number. Perhaps the greatest superstition about unlucky thirteen is connected with thirteen at a table. It is likely that the superstition lies in fable, for the Greeks and the Romans each feared the number. The fable to which it is attributed was the banquet in Valhalla, at which twelve of the Gods were invited. Loki, the spirit of strife and evil, intruded, making thirteen, and Balder, the favourite of the Gods, was killed.

In Christian belief, it is pointed out that Christ and the Twelve Apostles, at the Last Supper, made thirteen.

Thistle. The thistle is said to have been adopted as the emblem of Scotland in commemoration of an unsuccessful attack by the Danes on Stirling Castle in the eighth century. The presence of the Danes was revealed through their advance section treading barefoot on thistles, and being compelled with the sudden pain involuntarily to cry out. The Scots routed them with great slaughter.

Thorn in the Flesh. A sect of Pharisees (the men who, the Bible records, thanked God that they were not as other men), used to set thorns in the hem of their cloaks to prick their legs in walking and make them bleed. And a thorn in the flesh to-day is something which is a source of constant irritation.

Thread of Destiny. According to Greek mythology the Three Fates (sisters) designed, arranged and ended the life of man. Clotho spun from her distaff the destiny of man, Lachesis worked out the pattern of the life, and Atropos cut the thread at the point where life was to end.

Threadneedle Street. The famous London street leading to the Bank of England was, in 1598, named Three Needles Street, and before that it was known as Broad Street. The origin of Three Needles Street is unknown, but it is a pointer that the arms of the Needlemakers' Company are three needles.

Old Lady of Threadneedle Street. A name for the Bank of England. The tradition is that towards the end of the eighteenth century a demented old lady wandered up and down Threadneedle Street day after day for a long period, until she suddenly disappeared. It was supposed that this old lady of Threadneedle Street must have been waiting for someone who went into the Bank, and according to her idea never came out again. When, therefore, in 1797, the Bank threatened a stoppage of payment, and one pound notes were issued, John Gilray, the artist, drew a caricature entitled, "The Old Lady of Threadneedle Street in Danger." Ever since the name has stuck to the Bank.

Three. *The Rule of Three.* Simple proportion by which, given the relationship of two entities, the proportional relationship of a third can easily and accurately be found.

Three Golden Balls. *See* "Balls."

Three Lights from One Match. Dates from the Boer War. Its "unlucky" reputation rose from the death of one of three men from a Boer bullet. The glow from the match shining across the veldt during the length of time it took to light the three cigarettes allowed time for the sniper to take careful aim.

Three Sheets in the Wind. Is a sailing metaphor for drunk. The "sheet" is the rope at the lower end of a sail, and is used for shortening or extending sail. If left free the sea term for the sail is "In the Wind." If all three sails of the ship were so left, the vessel would lurch and stagger all over the water—like a drunken man.

Three-legged Mare. Highwayman's slang name for the gallows, because it was composed of three parts. Ainsworth, in "Rookwood," wrote:

"For the mare with three legs, boys, I care not a rap,
T'will be over in less than a minute."

Three-ply Wood. The "wood" may be new; but three-ply is certainly not so. The ancient Egyptians used the idea in the preparation of papyrus, two layers being gummed together with the fibre at right angles. Cartonnage mummy cases were made of papyrus of three, four or even five-ply layers.

Threshold. Since this is a thing we cross a dozen or more times a day, it may be as well to know how we came by it. There seems to be general opinion on the fact that the "thresh" is connected with our present "threshing," in the sense of threshing corn. It will be remembered that in olden times this was done by trampling the corn underfoot, by treading out the corn by the feet of men or oxen. The Anglo-Saxon word for thresh was *therscan*. It is suggested, therefore, that the thresh part of threshold is symbolical of the treading by the feet of the step to our doors. The "hold" part presents more difficulty. It is probably a corruption of the Anglo-Saxon *wald*, or *weald* (more likely the former), meaning wood. It might not be out of place here to mention that when corn ceased to be beaten out by the feet of men, a flail took its place, and a flail was made of wood. It is, at the best, an unsatisfactory "origin," but it is the best available in philology.

Through Thick and Thin. Dates back to Livy, vi, 14: "Per onme fas ac nefas."

Throw Up the Sponge. Comes, of course, from the boxing ring where, when a boxer's seconds saw that their man had no chance of winning, and was in sore straits, threw up the sponge which dropped into the ring as a sign that they withdrew their principal from the fight.

Thug. In the West a cut-throat ruffian, but originally a class of professional robbers and assassins in India. The Indian Thugs had formerly been a religious sect worshipping Kali, the Hindu goddess who gave her name to Calcutta. Kali could only be propitiated by the sacrifice of humans who had been strangled. Thus, to obtain the sacrifice, the Thugs killed and murdered; and the possessions of the victims went to support the sect.

Thumbs Up! Is probably a survival of the ancient Roman custom in the Combat, in which the fate of vanquished gladiators in the arena was determined by the populace present. If the thumbs were turned *out*, the vanquished gladiator was slain by his victor. If the thumbs were turned *up* in the fist he was spared.

Thumb-screws. The instrument of torture invented by the Spanish Inquisition consisted of two bars of iron between which the thumbs of the victim were compressed over the thumb-nails by means of a screw. It was a popular form of torture of the Jewish money-lenders in this country when the King or the Barons wanted money which the Jews were not anxious to loan. The last person to be put to the torture of the thumb-screw in Britain was Carstares, who was sentenced to it by the Scottish Privy Council in order to extract a confession of his alleged share in the Rye House Plot. He was under the torture for nearly an hour.

Tiara. The jewelled head-dress ornament worn by women at evening social functions has an origin that goes back beyond discovery. Its source is unknown. The earliest use of it is as a raised head-dress, or high-peaked cap, worn by the Persians and other Eastern people, varying in shape according to the rank of the wearer.

As a proper name, the Tiara is the Triple Crown worn by the Pope. It is said that the Tiara was at first a simple mitre, like those of ordinary bishops. In 514, it is added, Hormisdas placed on his head the crown sent by Clovis. Boniface VIII is stated to have added the second crown about 1300; while the third was assumed by John XXII about 1415.

This is not, however, the only version of the Triple Crown. Another explanation is that the second crown was added by Benedict XII as a symbol of the spiritual and temporal power of the Papacy, and that the third is merely symbolical of the Holy Trinity. A third version is that the crowns represent, (1) High Priest, (2) Emperor, and (3) as Sovereign Father of all the Kings of the Earth.

Tick. "*To live on tick.*" To live on credit, not paying for goods supplied. The slang term has been used since, in the seventeenth century, acknowledgment of a debt or an account was called, not a bill, but a ticket.

Tiggy. *See* "Blind Man's Buff."

Time. *To take Time by the forlock.* Old Man Time is represented by a single lock of hair on his forehead, but elsewhere on the head completely bald. The saying, "To take Time by the forelock," is attributed to Pittacus, of Mitylene, who was one of the seven sages of Greece.

Time. Summer Time was first applied in the Spring of 1916, as an aid to war work, after it had been laughed out of the House of Commons ten years earlier, when suggested by Mr. William Willett. Double Summer Time was brought in during the 1939-45 war in order to avoid the delay in production caused by the continuous air raids when darkness fell during the great Battle of Britain.

Tin Hats (in the Army). This head protection against shrapnel was introduced by the French in the Spring of 1915. The British followed with them in October, 1915. The Germans first used them at Verdun in January, 1916.

Tinker's Damn, I Don't Care a. Strictly speaking, this should be a tinker's *dam*. In the old days the travelling tinker, given a job, would ask for a piece of bread. This he placed in his mouth until it was sufficiently moist to knead into a paste. The paste he pressed over the hole on the *inside* of the pot, the idea being to prevent waste of his solder running through the hole, and enabling him to build up the solder over the area. The job completed the dam—the piece of bread—was thrown away. There could be little worth less than this tinker's "dam."

To bandy words. *See* "Bandy."

Toast. "*To Drink a Toast.*" The *Tatler*, Number 24, gives the following account of the origin of the word "toast" in its present sense, stating that it had its rise from an incident in Bath during the reign of Charles II: "It happened that on a public day a celebrated beauty of those days was in the Cross Bath, and one of the crowd of her admirers took a glass of water in which the fair one stood, and drank her health to the company. There was in the place a gay fellow, half fuddled, who offered to jump in and swore, though he liked not the liquor, he would have the toast, meaning the lady herself. He was opposed in his resolution; yet this whim gave foundation to the present honour which is done to the lady we mention in our liquor, who has ever since been called a toast."

It was, however, the custom later, to put toast into the tankards of beer to (it was said) improve the flavour. Toast still floats in the loving-cups of the Universities, or it did at the University of the writer.

Tobacco. The name comes from the *Tobaco*, the name in the Carib of Hayti of the "Y" shaped tube, or **pipe**, through which the Indians inhale the smoke. That is the version of Oviedo, and is the usually accepted origin; but Las Casas, 1552, applied the word to a roll of dried leaves which was lighted at the end and used by the Indians as a rude cigar. Even before Oviedo's time *tobaco* had been taken by the Spaniards as that of the herb or its leaf, and it can be said for Oviedo that the island of Tobago, after which it has been said by some to be named, according to "Tobago, a Geographical Description" (1750), received its name from its resemblance in shape to the Indian pipe.

It may be as well to disperse the belief that it was Sir Walter Raleigh who introduced tobacco into England. It wasn't! Harrison's "Chronicles of England" relates: "In these daies (1573) the taking-in of the smoke of the Indian herbe called Tobaco, by an instrument formed like a little ladell, whereby it passeth from the mouth into the hed and stomach and is *gretlie taken up and vsed in England*." Raleigh, who was born in 1552, was only twenty-one years of age at this date, and could not have been more than thirteen when tobacco began to be used in England. His first journey to the Indies was about 1590.

On the other hand, Sir John Hawkins went to the Indies in 1564; and it was he who introduced the weed, and the potato, into this country.

James I wrote a book, "A Counterblaste to Tobacco," in 1604 for the sole purpose of calling the weed the "Invention of Satan."

Tobyman. Old name or a highwayman. Toby was a slang name for the road.

Toddy. Is the name given to a drink compounded of spirits, sugar and hot water; but, properly, Toddy is a sap obtained from the incised spathes of various species of palms, and used as a beverage in tropical countries. Its name is derived from the Hindu *tadi*, from *tar*, a palm.

Toff. "*He's a Toff.*" The appellation was first applied to a nobleman or Gentleman Commoner at Oxford University. In consideration of paying high fees, this species of undergraduate was at one time allowed to display a golden tuft, or tassel, on his cap (mortar-board). The wearers of this badge of rank were called "tufts," and the term became corrupted to "toff." Thus a toff, to-day, is a man who makes a display of his dress or manners.

Togs. *In one's best togs.* Tog as a word for clothes goes back nearly three hundred years. Tuft's "Glossary of Thieves Jargon" (1798) contains a reference to "Long Tog," as a coat. There is little doubt that the origin was the Roman toga, which was a single piece of undyed woollen cloth worn, flowing, round the shoulders and body.

Tom of Lincoln. Is a bell in the Cathedral. It weighs five tons eight hundredweights.

Tom of Oxford. Is the bell in the Tom Gate Tower tolled every night at ten minutes past nine. Its weight is over seven and a half tons.

Tomato. The strangest thing about the popular tomato is that when introduced into England from tropical America, it was cultivated in greenhouses here for its berries, not as something to eat, but as a floral ornament. It was many years before it became popular for its fruit.

Tommy Atkins. The name for the British soldier since August, 1815. In that year the War Office issued the first "Soldier's Account Book." Every soldier was provided with one; and when it was sent out a specimen form accompanied it to show how details asked for should be filled in. This form bore, at the place where the man's signature was required, the hypothetical name, "Tommy Atkins." That name continued to appear in later editions of the Soldier's Account Book until comparatively recent times. It has now, however, disappeared.

Tommy-rot. *It's all Tommy-rot.* Even to-day, in the North of England, and in the Black Country, the miner calls the food which he takes with him to the pit his "tommy." He carries it in a "Tommy-can." In the days before the Truck Act (1831) a part of the wages of workers was paid in kind—in food, etc. Employers of labour not infrequently owned shops to which the worker, in whatever trade he worked, had to go to draw his money; and there he was compelled to spend a portion of his wages on the purchase of the goods he must consume during the week in order to live. To the working man, these shops were known as "Tommy-shops"—the shops where he purchased his tommy, or food. The viciousness of this system will be realized when it is stated that the employer could charge pretty well what he liked in the way of high prices for the most inferior food, and the workman had no choice but to take it, or lose his job. Workers, inflamed at the poor stuff bundled on to them at high prices, referred to the goods of the Tommy-shop as Tommy-rot.

Tools. "*Give us the tools and we will finish the job.*" Said by the Prime Minister, Mr. Winston Churchill, in the House of Commons on 10th February, 1941. The words were addressed to America at a time before she had entered the World War.

Tooth and Nail. *To go for something tooth and nail.* To go all out. One of the oldest of our proverbs, which has come down unchanged from earlier than 1533, when Udall wrote: "He doeth all thynges . . . with tothe and nayle, as moche as in him lyeth."

Topsy-Turvy. In spite of the fact that the term topsy-turvy has been known in print since 1528, and was probably in popular use from an earlier period, no authenticated explanation of the component parts of it is known. Many suggestions have been offered. One of them takes topsy as being top-set or top-side, but the stumbling-block to all of them is the fact that the typical form, with mere spelling variations, has remained constant. It is, however, pretty certain that the first element contains "top," and probably the second element is related to terve, or *tirve*, which in Anglo-Saxon was *tearflian*, meaning to roll over and over, or to wallow. The suggestion that turvey might relate to the laying of cut turfs face *downwards* to keep them fresh has been discarded by philologists, as also the suggestion that it might be a corruption of t'other way.

Torch. The origin of torch is the Latin *torca*, from the stem of *torquere*, to twist; and the first torches were lengths of twisted cordage steeped in tow. A rope in Latin was *funis*, and from the extravagant use which the Romans made of torches at the burial of their dead is derived our word funeral.

The torch played a great part in all ceremonies of the early Greeks and Romans. At Roman weddings it was the custom for two children to lead the bride, and a third to bear before her a torch of white-thorn in honour of Ceres (the Roman name of Mother Earth). In Greek weddings, the torch was carried before the bride by her mother. In the Greek Church, too, the bride and groom enter the church with lighted tapers.

Torches at funerals were carried to show (according to Gregory's "Posthuma," 1649), "that the departed soules are not quite put out, but, having walked here as the Children of Light, are now gone to walk before God, in the Light of the Living."

Strutt tells that the burning of torches was very honourable. To have a great many was a special mark of esteem. By the will of William de Montacute, Earl of Salisbury, executed 29th April, 1397, "Twenty-four poor people clothed in blackgowns and red hoods are ordered to attend the funeral, each carrying a lighted torch of eight pounds weight."

From an account of Sir John Gresham's funeral in 1556, it appears that he had "four dozen of great staff torches, and a dozen of great long torches."

Torment. The word comes from the Latin *tortus*, past participle of *torquere*, to twist, from which we have also torture, extort. Thus, to torment or to torture, or extort, is to "twist" something out of the victim.

Tory. According to Macaulay's "History of England," Tory was originally applied, in the time of Charles II, to bog-trotting plunderers and to Popish outlaws, otherwise called Whiteboys, who found refuge in the bogs of Ireland. Hence, it was used to denote those who would not vote for excluding a Roman Catholic Prince from the throne. It thus came to designate, generally, the party which desires to uphold, as far as possible, without change, the existing order of things.

Tournament. Means "to turn," from the Latin *tornare*. The English word came from the Latin through the French *torneiement*, a meeting of knights to tilt The art of the tilting was to manœuvre or *turn* your horse, so as to avoid the lance thrusts of your opponent.

Town. From the Anglo-Saxon *tun*, an enclosure; and the German *zaun*, a hedge.

Town Planning. A subject much in the news at the moment (1944). Regulation in building and ground outlay, with a view to securing the greatest amenities for the general public, having regard to transport and health conveniences. The Town Planning Act (observed more in the breach than the keeping) was passed in 1909.

Town, The Oldest in England. The distinction of being the oldest original town in England would seem to lie between Thetford (Suffolk) and Wilton, the carpet town. Wilton was a Royal residence in 833, when King Egbert dated a Proclamation from his Palace there. Of course, it existed before that date, but how long before is not certain.

Thetford was the capital of East Anglia, and the seat of its Kings from 575 to 793. It claims that it was a Royal city of the Iceni even before the Roman invasion. This would make its antiquity one of some two thousand years.

Colchester's claim to be the oldest town can be disregarded. The city was *founded by the Romans* and peopled by them with discharged Roman soldiers, all of whom were massacred by Boadicea. This is made quite clear from the "Encyclopædia Britannica" and from the history of the Roman occupation of Britain.

Trade Unions. The earliest modern trade union was probably the combination of London cordwainers against their overseers in 1387. By the Trade Union Act of 1871 it was declared that a trade union, merely because its objects were in restraint of trade, should not be held to be unlawful, and its agreements were made binding, so that they would be recognized in law. The modern trade union, under that name, came into being about 1830.

Tram, Tramway. There is generally quoted as the "origin" of tram and tramway a certain Mr. Benjamin Outram, who in 1800 made certain improvements in connection with railways for common vehicles. This gave rise to the fiction that tram-road is short for Outram-road. As Skeats sensibly points out, accent alone is sufficient to show that Outram, if shortened to one syllable, must become "out" rather than ' ram " or "tram." The original meaning of the word was the German *traam*, a balk or beam, and was applied as early as the sixteenth century to trucks used in coal-mines, which ran on long wooden *beams* as rails. *Tram* was also the old Swedish word for a log of wood; and the first tram rails were wooden ones.

Traps. *I'll send a car for your traps.* In the colourful days of England the trappings of a horse—the covering spread over the harness or saddle—were the mark of a man's affluence. They were gaily and expensively embroidered, according to his means. From the trappings of his horse, the term came to mean personal adornment — dress, embellishments, etc., which he carried with him, or she with her, on a journey. The traps which a person carries with him to-day, confined in a suit-case, is merely a contraction of the "trappings" of the older days.

Tre. A component of place-names peculiar to Cornwall.

"By their Tre, their Pol and
Pen,
Ye shall know the Cornish
men."

Treasures, Mother's. In its true meaning treasure consists of wealth or riches accumulated, especially in the form of precious metals. "Mother's Treasures" goes back to the days of Cornelia, mother of the Gracchi (the great Roman family). A wealthy and distinguished lady from Campania called upon her one day and, after showing her jewels, asked that she might have the privilege of seeing the jewels of her famous hostess. Cornelia sent for her sons. "These are my jewels, in which alone I delight," she said.

Tree, Highest. The highest tree in the world is claimed by California, in the Hamboldt State Park, which is a giant sequoia (cross between fir and cypress) three hundred and sixty-four feet high, and estimated to weigh nearly two thousand tons.

Tried in the Balance, and found Wanting. The expression is found in the belief of the ancient Egyptians that the souls of men were weighed after death, and that their ultimate fate in the hereafter depended on the result.

Trounce. "*I'll give him a trouncing.*" There was in Middle English a word *traunce*, meaning fear of death, from the Latin *transire*, to pass over. Weekley suggests that *traunse* gave birth to a verb meaning to frighten, and that this verb subsequently became our present *trounce.*

Skeats derives the word from Old French *trons*, a truncheon, but he was apparently misled by the fact that *trons* was explained in old dictionaries as *troncon*, which he seems to have taken to mean truncheon. *Troncon* was, in fact, the diminutive of *tronc*, a trunk.

Trousers. The name for this unchanging male garment comes from the French *troussex*, to truss, to girt in. In their present form they were first introduced into England about the end of the eighteenth century, before which men wore breeches and silk stockings.

One of the earliest wearers of trousers was the Duke of Wellington, of whom it is recorded that he was refused admission to Almack's Club in

1814 because he was wearing them, in place of the customary breeches and silk stockings.

Trousseau. Is derived from the French *trousse*, a bundle.

Troy Weight. Was so-named because it was the weight system used at the great fair of Troyes, in France. It is now the weight used for precious metals. The pound is of twelve ounces, weighing 5,760 grains, as compared with the pound avoirdupois of sixteen ounces and 7,000 grains.

Truck Acts of 1831, 1887 and 1896 put an end to the vicious system of employers paying wages partly in goods which were sold by them in the way of business, or of making a condition that goods should be purchased from certain shops when wages were paid. One employer the author knew of paid his men in his grocer's shop, and unless the man spent a part of the money on groceries, for which the charge was above the price to the general public, he was dismissed.

See "Tommy-rot."

Trump Card, To Play a. Trump, used in this sense, is a corruption of triumph, from the Greek *thriambos*, a hymn to Bacchus, sung at festivals in his honour.

Tryst. *To have, or keep, a tryst.* The word means to have confidence, to have trust, from the old Norse *traust*. Thus, one makes a tryst with one in whom can be had confidence that it will be kept.

Tuft-Hunter. Was, originally, a man who toaded up to the wealthy or great. He hunted acquaintance with those who wore tufts, or golden tassels, at Oxford University.

See "Toff."

Tumble to it. Merely an American version of "Fall in with," meaning to agree to concur. The French say "Tomber d'accord."

Tumbledown Dick. A contemptuous name for a ne'er-do-well. The original Tumbledown Dick was Richard Cromwell, son of the Protector, a poor son of his father.

Tumbler. The name for a drinking glass, has existed from the glasses of the sixteenth century—the earliest glasses. They had a rounded or pointed base, and could stand only on being emptied and inverted. Any other way they "tumbled" over.

Tweed. This name for a soft woollen, twilled fabric came by accident. It should have been tweal, the Scottish word for twill. A consignment of the cloth sent to James Lock, of London, for sale in 1829, was accompanied by the name, Tweal, but it was so badly written that Lock though, it must be Tweed, since the cloth was made on the banks of the Tweed, and he called it that. Twill means two-threaded.

Twerp. An expression of good-humoured contempt (if such a term can be applied) which has gained great popularity. It sprang into being in Army circles during the 1914-18 war, being a term much applied by the front-line forces to the people at railheads and base depots. As to its meaning, we cannot better the description given by Vincent Trowbridge in "Notes and Queries" (Vol. 182, p. 335): "A 'twerp' is an unpleasant person of physical insignificance and basically weak character, with usually, but not necessarily, some minor office in which he can be obstructive and display self-importance;" but, in point of fact, the word existed a hundred years ago, when a twerp was the name given to a short-beaked racing pigeon flying from England to Antwerp. A suggested origin is that the word is a corruption of the Lancashire *twillip*, meaning daft-like.

Twig it? *"Do you see," (the point)*? A term popular throughout Lincolnshire. It comes from the Irish *tuigim*, I understand, discern. "They're a 'twiggin' of you, Sir," whispered Mr. Weller—Dickens, "The Pickwick Papers."

Two Evils Choose the Lesser, Of. Its first recorded appearance is in Cicero's "De Officiis": "Nam quod aiunt, minima de malis, id est, ut turpiter potius quam calamitose; an est ullum maius malam turpitudine."

Typing. The world's record speed at typewriting is one hundred and forty-nine words a minute for an hour, tapped out at Chicago in June, 1941, by Miss M. Hamma. The machine was an electrical model.

U

Uckeye. "All right." Soldiers' slang word in the 1914-18 war. It is a perversion of the Hindustani word *uchcha*.

Ugly as Sin. Scott introduced this phrase into literature in "Kenilworth," Chapter X, in 1821: "Though I am as ugly as sin."

Ulster. The original for this name of the northern provinces of Ireland is believed to have been *Ulladh* (pronunciation Ulla). The "ster" termination is due to the Norse settlers who went there, for "ster" or "stadr" means a settlement, or a dwelling. It will be realized that Leinster and Munster have the same termination.

Ulster (Coat). Was so-named because it was originally made of Ulster frieze cloth.

Ultra vires. Latin *Ultra*, beyond, *vires*, strength. Beyond strength, in excess of the power (in the law); in brief, unlawful.

Umble Pie. *See* "Eat Humble Pie."

Umbrage. "*To take Umbrage.*" The word means, of course, to take offence; but its literal meaning is to be in the shade, from the Latin root *umbra*, shadow or shade.

The author once saw the word used in anything but "shadow." During the 1914-18 war when the Russian campaign was in full swing, newspaper men had some curious name-places to seek on the map, many of which had never before been heard. A message arrived one night stating that the Russians had taken umbrage at something or other. Unfortunately for one small provincial daily paper, this came at a time when the only sub-editor on duty, left to watch for any item for the Late News space, was a youth of little experience. He did his best to find umbrage on the map of Russia, but failed. He, however, thought the news too good to miss and, accordingly, came out with a good-sized headline: "New Success—Russians Take Umbrage."

Umbrellas. The word comes to us from the Latin *umbra*, shade. The Chinese used umbrellas in the eleventh century B.C., so did the Babylonians. In the British Museum there is a bas relief from Nineveh representing a slave holding one over the head of a King; but they were more in use as parasols against the sun's heat.

It is generally accepted that the introduction of the umbrella in England as a protection against rain was due to Jonas Hanway, the Persian traveller. His use of it, about 1760, caused a disturbance among sedan chairmen and coachmen, whose vehicles had been up to then the only protection for the pedestrian from downpours. They rioted.

Umpire. Properly speaking, the word is *numpire*, derived from the Old French *nompair*, through the Latin *non*, not, and *par*, equal. Thus, the word means not equal, an odd or third person called in to decide an argument between disputants.

Umpteen Times. Many times. This word originated in signallers' slang, in much the same way as ack-emma and pip-emma.

Uncle. *Take it to Uncle* (the pawnbroker). Before pawnbrokers used the now common "spout" in which to place articles left in pledge, all pledges which consisted of clothing were attached to a large hook. When the hook could accommodate no more the rope from which it depended was unslung and the bundle carried by assistants to the storeroom. Now, the Lombards were the earliest pawnbrokers. They spoke Italian, which is very near Latin. And the Latin name for a hook is *Uncus.* It is supposed by some that "Uncle" is a corruption of Uncus, and that "take it to Uncle's" was really "take it to the Uncus."

The term was well-known as far back as 1756, for Tolderby uses it in that year.

Uncle Sam. Name for the U.S.A. Government. The story goes that the Inspectors of Elbert Anderson's store on the Hudson River were Ebenezer Wilson, and his uncle Samuel Wilson, who also went by the name of "Uncle Sam." The stores were marked on the cases "E.H.—U.S." (Elbert Anderson—United States). One of the employees being asked the meaning of U.S. replied that it stood for Uncle Sam. The joke stuck and, popularized by American soldiers, Uncle Sam came to mean the U.S.A.

It is a nice story, but Matthews in his "American Antiquities," states that there is no case for the origin being connected with various United States officials with the Christian name Samuel. Matthews, however, agrees that the suggestion that it arose as a facetious interpretation of the letters U.S. is as old as the first recorded instances, and it is probable that the name did, indeed, arise from the initials after the Government had caused U.S. to be painted or branded on all Government stores, in the way that the Broad Arrow is branded on British Government property. The nickname Uncle Sam was most probably conferred on the official whose job it was to see that the markings were carried out, and was passed on to the actual marking.

Unco. "*The Unco Guid.*" A Scottish word and phrase; but it has two meanings. Literally, it is the Scottish variant of our uncouth. In Scottish dialect, however, it means as an adjective, unknown, strange. As an adverb its meaning is the one usually ascribed to it by Sassenachs—very good, too good.

Under the Rose. Not to be mentioned; strictly between ourselves. It was the custom of the Germans at a feast to suspend a rose from the ceiling as a reminder that whatever might be said about people at the feast should not be repeated. The legend, giving rise to the custom, is that the rose was the flower of Venus, which Cupid consecrated to Harpocrates, the God of Silence; and it was, therefore, the emblem of silence, to conceal the mysteries of Venus.

Peacham, in "The Truth of Our Times" (1638) states: "In many places they have over their tables a rose painted, and what is spoken under the rose must not be revealed. The reason is this—the rose being sacred to Venus, whose amorous and stolen sports might never be revealed."

Under the Weather. The first record of the phrase in print is in Robert Louis Stevenson's "Wrecker": "You must not fancy I am sick, only over-driven, and under the weather."

Under Way. The "Manual of Seamanship" states that a ship is under way within the meaning of the rules when she is not at anchor or made fast to the shore, or aground.

Underwriter (Insurance). Rather a mystery name to people who know an underwriter only as some person behind insurance and stock deals. The simple explanation is this: "An underwriter is the man who *writes* his name *under* the policy, thereby announcing that he—and any other under-writer with him—accepts the risk." The practice of underwriting owed its origin to the excessively high rate of insurance charged by the only two companies which, previous to 1824, were allowed by charter to grant marine insurances. The underwriters who then took off much or most of their business, became known as Lloyds. At first underwriters undertook only marine insurance, but to-day they will insure against anything, even against rain falling at any given time on any given day.

Union is Strength. The wise saw was uttered some five hundred and fifty years before Christ, by Periander, the tyrant of Corinth; but it took a few centuries for the employed class to recognize the truth of it.

Union Jack. The national flag of Britain consists of three crosses on a blue background. The first is the cross of St. George, representing England; the second that of St. Andrew, for Scotland, which was added by James I; the third is the cross of St. Patrick, for Ireland, which was finally added after the union in 1801. That describes the flag part.

The suffix "jack" is concerned with the sea. A jack is a small-sized flag, used at sea as a signal, and usually flown at the bow or fore-part of the vessel. The staff from which it is flown is called the jack-staff. Thus, properly speaking, the Union Jack is only thus designated when flown in a size smaller than the Union, from the jack-staff of a ship. Elsewhere it should be called the Union Flag; but it never will be!

Unitarians. The Unitarians in Britain were founded by John Biddle (1615-62), the son of a Gloucestershire tailor. Unitarians are Christians who deny the doctrine of the Trinity, holding, instead, that God exists in one person only. Biddle, in 1645, published "Twelve Arguments" against the Deity of the Holy Spirit, and as a result, much of the remainder of his life was spent in prison.

University. The word comes from the Latin *universitatis,* the whole; but it does *not* mean, as nearly every philologist has said, the various colleges and halls incorporated as one great educational centre. When the word was first coined for our Universities, in the twelfth century, it was done so because of the entire, and whole, range of literature taught in the colleges—the *universitas literarum.*

Unknown Warrior. The presence of the Unknown Warrior in Westminster Abbey is due to the direct intervention of the late King George V. The proposal that the body of an unidentified, and unidentifiable, British soldier should be brought home and buried "among the Kings" had been made to the Cabinet in 1919, but the Cabinet, having no vision, refused to entertain the idea. A year later, the Dean and Chapter, with admirable foresight, laid the proposal before the King, personally, who requested the Cabinet to reconsider it, at the same time expressing his own approval. The Cabinet then gave its approval.

A number of buried bodies of unknown British soldiers were then disinterred at random in various cemeteries on the Western Front, and one was taken, again at random. On 11th November, 1920, the day the permanent Cenotaph was unveiled, the Unknown Warrior was taken to the Cenotaph, where the King laid a wreath on the coffin. It was then taken to the Abbey, and laid in its grave in the Nave. No living man, or woman, knows the name of the soldier.

Unlocking the Door for Death. The superstition prevailed at one time over many parts of the country, and particularly in Devon, that at the moment of a person's death, or as soon as before death as is possible, every door in the house should be unlocked and opened, so as not to cause uneasiness to, and hinder, the departure of the soul.

The superstition was founded on the idea that the ministers of Purgatorial pains took the soul as it escaped the body and, flattening it against some closed door, which alone would serve the purpose, crammed it into the hinges and hinge openings. Thus, the soul was in torment.

In Gloucestershire windows were wont to be thrown open at the moment of death in order that the soul should be free to escape.

Unlucky in Love, Lucky in Play. Is attributed to Swift who, in "Polite Conversations" (1738) says: "Well, Miss, you'll have a sad husband, you have such good luck at cards," but the term seems to have been well-known before that date.

Unpaid, The Great. A (contemptuous) reference to the Justices of the Peace, unpaid magistrates at Petty Sessions.

Unready, Ethelred the. The term does not mean that the unfortunate King was never ready as we understand the word. The original word was the Old English *un-rede*, from *redeless*, which meant wanting in counsel.

Unspeakable Turk. The name Turk was applied, in Crusading times, to all Mohammedans and unbelievers—"Jews, Turks, infidels and hereticks" in the Good Friday Collect, and was taken as a type of brutality and cruelty.

Unwashed, The Great. Burke was the first to use this term for the common mob; and Carlyle, in his "French Revolution," has: "Man against man, washed against unwashed."

Up Guards and at 'Em. Creasy is responsible for the statement that the Duke of Wellington issued this command for the last and victorious charge at the Battle of Waterloo. It appears in his "Fifteen Decisive Battles"—Creasy should have known better. The Guards were never in the final charge which broke the French lines and won the battle. The charge was, in fact, made by the 52nd Light Infantry; and Wellington did not say the words.
See "Waterloo won on Playing Fields of Eton."

Up the Pole. *See* "Pole."

Up the Spout. An allusion to the "spout" up which pawnbrokers send the articles pledged and ticketed. When redeemed, they return down the spout—from the storeroom to the shop.

Upper Crust (of Society). Because, in older days, it was considered a mark of honour to allow the most distinguished guest to cut off the top, or crust, of a loaf at the table.

Upper Ten Thousand. A name coined for the aristocratic or higher circles of Society. It is said to have been invented by Nathaniel Parker Willis, an American author (1806-67), and originally applied by him to the fashionable Society of New York, which he considered numbered at that time about ten thousand. It is frequently now shortened to "The Upper Ten," and sometimes referred to as the Upper Crust.

Ursula and the Ten Thousand Virgins. St. Ursula was a legendary Cornish princess. She was going to France with ten thousand virgins in twelve ships when adverse winds drove them ashore at Cologne, where all the virgins were murdered by the Huns. The story is, of course, nonsense, though visitors to Cologne before the war were shown piles of human bones behind a wall and cased with glass, which are said to be the remains of the ten thousand virgins.

Usher. Is the English spelling of the French *huissier*, which in turn was derived from the Latin *ostiarius*, a doorkeeper, from *ostium*, a door, and *os*, a mouth.

Usquebaugh. Irish, from *uisge-beatha*, "Water of Life," is the stuff you drink in "doubles." It is the original name of whisky.

Utilitarianism. John Stuart Mill coined the word for the doctrine that actions are right in proportion to their usefulness in the "scheme of things entire"—that the criterion of public legislation is the "greatest happiness for the greatest number."

Utopia. Sir Thomas More, in 1516, wrote a romance of that title. "Utopia" was an island enjoying the utmost perfection in life, society, politics and law. With a fine sense of humour he chose "Utopia" as the title. The word comes from the Greek *ou*, not, *topas*, a place. Thus, Utopia means no place!

V

Vade Mecum. A book or manual suitable for carrying about with one for ready reference. From the Latin *vadrer*, to go, and *mecum*, with me.

Vagabond. The Latin word for the verb "to wander" is *vagari*. A person who wandered without any settled abode is, in Latin, a *vagabundus*. The English word for a wanderer, therefore, is a vagabond. It is under this heading "to wander" that actors were first classified as rogues and vagabonds. The actors of that day were wandering players.

Our word vagrant, for a disreputable wanderer without means of subsistence, comes from the same source.

Valance. This article of adornment, which every housewife knows, has an origin veiled in obscurity. The *Oxford English Dictionary* suggests that it might be derived from the Anglo-French *valer*, through the Old French *avaler*, to descend; and, certainly, the valance descends from the point of contact.

The writer, however, suggests that the origin is more likely the Spanish town of Valencia, the staple industry of which was, at one time, the supply of bed drapery.

Vale. From the Latin *valere*, farewell.

Valentine. The saint of this name was a Roman priest who was gaoled for giving succour to early Christians. He became a Christian himself, and while in prison restored the sight of the daughter of his gaoler. He was, however, clubbed to death on 14th February, 269.

Valentine's Day. St. Valentine's Day has no connection with the saint other than it falls on his Saint's Day. The sending of Valentines on this day has reference to an old custom of England on 14th February—the traditional date of the mating of birds—of drawing lots for lovers, the person drawn by a man being his Valentine; but, as an instance of how far it is removed from St. Valentine, it may be stated that the custom of choosing lovers on this day, or round about it, was contained in an old Pagan superstition connected with the worship of Juno, Goddess of ancient Rome, and the special protectress of the female sex.

A possible explanation of the name Valentine is given in Butler's "Lives of the Saints." He says that it was the custom among the Romans on the Feast of Februata (13th February) for the boys to draw the names of girls to see who should be their mistress, and that this Pagan practice, giving offence to the Christian priesthood, the names of saints were substituted on the slips of paper for those of the girls.

Valet. This name for a man's personal man-servant is derived from the Old French *vaselet*, which was in itself an abbreviation of the still older *vassalet*, the meaning of which was vassal, and a vassal was an overlord's bound servant. Our varlet comes from the same root.

Valhalla. Is still used by literary men in connection with the dead, but it should be used only in connection with those killed in battle, for in Old Northern mythology, Valhalla (from Old English *wael*, slain in battle, and *holl*, hall) means the hall assigned to those who have died in battle, in which they feast with Odin, the hero of antiquity, who made himself an immortal God, and receives the souls of those killed in battle. The Anglo-Saxons called Odin by the name of Woden, and it is from him that our Wednesday of the week is named.

Valkyries, The. Immortalized in Wagner's opera. In Scandinavian mythology they were the twelve war-maidens supposed to hover round a battlefield, and in the fiercest of the fighting to ride with drawn swords into the melee, select those of the soldiers who were to die, and conduct them to Valhalla.

See "Valhalla."

Vallombrosa. The word is probably best known from the oft-quoted lines of Milton, in "Paradise Lost":

"Thick as Autumnal leaves
that strow the brooks
In Vallombrosa . . . ."

Which only goes to show that Milton wrote without checking his facts, for Vallombrosa, the Benedictine Convent in the Appennines, some sixteen miles from, and high above, Florence in Italy, stands amidst magnificent woodlands of *pine trees,* which do *not* strew the brooks with Autumnal leaves.

Vamoose. *To vamoose the ranch.* To go. The phrase came to us via America. It is not really slang, but merely an adaptation of the Spanish word *vamos,* meaning let us go. South America is essentially Spanish in language and customs.

Vamp. *To vamp a man.* Used in this connection, the word "vamp" is a slang contraction for vampire, the preying habits of which are well-known.

Vamp has more than this meaning. Vamping, in a musical sense, is to improvise.

The real meaning of vamp is probably little known. It concerns the mending or repairing by the use of patches, to put new uppers to old boots; it is also that part of a stocking which covers the foot or ankle. In general, to vamp is to make something by patching, or adding, out of old material.

Vampire. There is a real vampire bat, a native of South America, which sucks blood; but we can ignore that for the purposes of this "origin." The vampire of the fable is a person supposed to seek nourishment by sucking the blood of sleeping persons. In the original belief a vampire was a re-animated corpse. Although the vampire legend came to us from Slavonia and Hungary, the Greeks had a similar superstition.

The re-animated corpse must be that of a "wicked man," whose remains, though buried with the customary forms, did not suffer dissolution. Mr. Wright, in his "Essays" (1846) has given this account: "Instead of the body suffering dissolution, the skin became dry and distended like the parchment of a drum; and the man's spirit, or some demon, entered into it, and at night the dead man left his grave and walked about the streets, and knocked at people's doors, and always called by name some person in the house. If the person named answered, he was sure to die on the following day. Hence, from caution, it became a custom that nobody answered to his name at night until it had been called twice, for the vampire never called the same person a second time in one night."

That is the story. As for the origin, it is likely that the vampire tales are causes conceived in spiritual form to account for specific facts of wasting disease.

Van. The vehicle into which we load goods, as in a luggage-van or a delivery-van, is not, as is so often stated, related to, or abbreviated from, vanguard. It is a shortening of caravan, from the Arabic *qairawan.* These caravans were strings of laden camels, carrying merchandise across the deserts. *En passant:* The popular ballad, "Where my Caravan has Rested," also relates to this kind of caravan, and not the gipsy, or trailer, caravan.

Vandals. Is the name we give to any body of people who wilfully destroy anything venerable, beautiful, or worthy of preservation. For instance, anyone who defaced a famous statue would be committing vandalism.

The Vandals were a Teutonic (German) tribe, which in the fourth and fifth centuries invaded Western Europe, and established settlements in various parts of it, particularly in Gaul and Spain, finally, in 429, migrating to Northern Africa. In 435, their King, Genseric, led a marauding expedition against Rome, which he took and completely sacked.

It may be of interest to state for the benefit of the many thousands of British troops who have now seen the Colosseum of Rome, that the holes which disfigure every few feet of the remaining walls of that historic building were made by the Vandals in order to extract the iron bars which ran the height of the walls, and "bound" the stones of which it is erected. From that day to the present, the walls of the Colosseum have stood without any kind of binding, mortar or otherwise.

Vanguard. Was originally applied only to the leading, or advanced, guard of an army. It should properly be the French *avant-garde,* advance guard.

Vatican. The palace of the Pope is so-called because it stands on the *Vaticanus Mons* (Vatican Hill) of ancient Rome. Of more "origin"-al interest, perhaps, is the name Vaticanus for the hill. In Latin, *vaticinate* means to forbode, to fortell, to prophecy; and the Vaticanus Hill of Rome was where the soothsayers of ancient Rome gathered to conduct their soothsaying, and to pronounce their prophecies.

Vaudeville. Our modern form of theatrical light entertainment owes its existence to Olivier Basselin, a Norman poet, who wrote a number of light, convivial songs, usually of a satirical and topical nature. Basselin was born, and lived, in the Normandy village of Val (or Vau) de Vire; and he called his songs after his birthplace. (*Note.—Ville* is the French town.)

Vauxhall. The famous gardens, or pleasure resort, from 1661 till 1859, included the present London area of Auckland Street, Burnett Street, Prince Street, Brunel Street, Gye Street, Italian Walk, and Vauxhall Walk. Vauxhall derives its name from Fulke's Hall, from Fulke de Breante, a Norman knight, who owned the manor in the early part of the thirteenth century. The name is not derived from a certain Jane Vaux, occupant of the manor in 1615.

V.C., The First. The bronze cross "For Valour," premier award for heroism of Britain, was first won by a sailor, Lieutenant C. D. Lucas, of H.M.S. *Hecla.* He was eighteen years old at the time, and he won it by a deed in 1852, four years before the Cross was instituted. The Cross was first awarded in 1856, but Lieutenant Lucas was then recommended for his earlier deed, and was granted the Cross.

VE-Day. Victory in Europe Day: Tuesday, 8th May, 1945, which day the Allied Heads of State (Mr. Winston Churchill, Britain; President Truman, United States; and Marshal Stalin, Russia) announced as the official Victory Day over Germany. The Third Reich had, the previous day, signed an Instrument of Unconditional Surrender, at the headquarters (a school in Rheims, France) of General Eisenhower, Allied Commander-in-Chief. VE-Day, with VE plus One Day, were kept in Britain as public holidays. At the time of the surrender the Allies had in their hands more than four million Germans as prisoners of war. The war had lasted since 3rd September, 1939.

Vegetate (in the country). A sneer at rural people. Since the word comes from the Latin *vegetatus,* past participle of *vegetare,* meaning "lively," quicker, active, akin to flourish (*vigere*), it is difficult to discover how we came to apply it to idleness, and "vegetating" in the country.

Vendetta. The blood-feud in which the nearest of kin execute vengeance on the slayer of a relative, comes from the Latin *vindicta*, revenge. Its principal soil for flourishing was Corsica, but it was prevalent all through Italy and Sicily.

Veni, Vidi, Vici. According to some sources, these are the succinct words with which Cæsar announced his victory at Zela to his familiar friend Amintius. The phrase (Latin) interpreted is : " I came, I saw, I conquered." It is doubtful whether Cæsar ever did say it.

Venial Sin. Venial is the Latin *venia*, forgiveness, pardon, or indulgence ; and venial sin is one that may be pardoned, as contrasted with mortal sin, which the Church of Rome did not pardon.

Ventriloquism. Was known in the times of the Greeks and Romans. There is little doubt that some of the Oracles (q.v.) were ventriloquists ! Certainly, the art was practiced to some extent in the temples. But though they knew the art, they did not, apparently, realize the source of it, for they named it in Greek, and subsequently, the Romans named it the same in Latin, *ventri*, belly, and *loqui*, to speak, under the impression that the sounds were produced from the belly. In reality, the sounds are produced in the same manner as in ordinary speech.

Venus. The ancient Roman Goddess of Love, particularly sensual love. In Greece she was Aphrodite, and to the Phœnicians Astarte. Her " history " is varied. By some she is said to have come from the foam of the sea, by others to have been the daughter of Jupiter and Dione. She was the wife of Vulcan, but the lover of most of the Gods. Mythology claims her as the mother of Cupid, and of Ænæs, the former by Mercury and the latter by Anchises.

Venus de Milo. The half-undraped figure of the Goddess which was discovered by a farmer in the Island of Melos in 1820, and not by Admiral Dumont, as is often stated, although the Admiral was the means of it reaching the Louvre, in Paris. The arms were apparently broken off when the statue was buried. It dates from about 400 B.C., and is probably the finest single work of ancient art in existence.

Verb Sap. Latin, *Verbum sapienti*, meaning " a word to the wise," a veiled threat that if the hint is not heeded exposure will be made.

Verdict. From the Latin *vere dictum*, a true saying. It will be realized, therefore, the responsibility that lies on the shoulders of a jury.

Verger. The Latin for a twig or rod is *virga*, the French for a rod is *verge*, and a verger's duties, originally, were to carry a rod, or staff, before the bishop, or preacher, in a cathedral or minster. He was regarded by reason of his care and carrying of the staff, as the custodian of the building.

Vespers. Name given to evening services in a church. It is the Latin *vesperus*, evening, and the Greek *Hesperus*, evening, and also the name of the evening star.

Vespers, The Fatal. While Father Drury, a Jesuit, was preaching to some two hundred people on a balcony over the gateway of the residence of the French Ambassador to London, situated in Blackfriars, the balcony collapsed. Father Drury and another priest were killed, as were nearly a hundred of his congregation. The disaster occurred on the evening of 26th October ,1623.

Vesta. The Roman Goddess of the hearth and fireside has given the name to the wax match used by smokers in Britain. Vesta, in mythology, was the custodian of the sacred fire brought from Troy by Æneas and which, if allowed to go out, would be followed by calamity to the nation. The fire was kept burning within a sanctuary in the Forum at Rome.

Vestal Virgins. Were the spotless virgins, six in number, who tended the fire of Vesta in the Forum. They were required to be as pure as the flame of the Sacred Fire, and should they lose their virginity, the punishment was to be buried alive.

Vestry. This word, originally, meant a place where church vestments were kept, from the Latin *vestiarium*, a wardroom. In England the term came to mean a parish committee, to consider parish affairs, attended by qualified parishioners. The name was so applied, by reason of the fact that the meetings were invariably held in the robing room, where were kept, of course, the vestments.

Veto. Latin for " I forbid."

Via. To go to London *via* Bedford. It means " by way of." Thus, the Appian Way, named in Rome Via Appia.

Vials of Wrath. To pour vials of wrath on a person is to take vengeance. The allusion comes from *Revelations* xvi : " And the seven angels came out of the temple having the seven plagues . . . and gave unto the seven angels seven golden vials full of the wrath of God. . . . "

Vicar. The word means substitute, from the Latin *vicarius*. In the case of the title assumed by the Pope of Vicar of Christ, the meaning, " in the place of," is obvious ; but the Vicars to whom we are accustomed in the Church of England fall into a different category. Their origin lies in the fact that they were the substitute, or proxy, of another, who owned the tithes and finances of the church. (*See* " Rector.")

The title of Vicar arose when, following the Dissolution, many livings, or churches, which had belonged to the great monasteries, were given to nobles of the country. They thus became responsible for the services at the churches. Since they were not ordained, it was impossible for them to carry out the clerical duties, and they had, accordingly, to find a person in Holy Orders to do so on their behalf. These substitutes were called by the name Vicar—they performed their office vicar-iously. In return they received from the noble the use of all tithes except those coming from corn.

Vicar of Bray. *See* " Bray."

Vicar of Hell. Was the name given to John Skelton, the Poet Laureate. Skelton was the Rector of Diss in Norfolk, and it is from this that his nickname sprang, for Dis is the Roman name for Pluto, the Greek God of the Underworld, or Hades. It is said that King Henry VIII was the first to perpetrate the pun.

Vice Versa. Means " reversed," from the Latin *vicis*, change, and *versa*, turned.

Villa. The trim suburban, or provincial, little house was originally a land-owner's residence. Aptly enough, it frequently still is, in these days of building societies. *See* " Villain."

Villain. The only reason we call a thorough-paced scoundrel a " villain " is that arrogance which in earlier times persisted between the feudal lords and their servants. For a villain was, in feudal days, a serf attached to the ville of his lord (*see* " Villa," above). He was, as a rule, a hard-working man with little of what we call villainy in his character.

Vino Veritas, In. Latin for " In wine is truth," or, as we say, " When the wine is in the wits are out, and so truth generally comes out with them."

Violet. The story of the violet is linked with a story of the Trojan War. Ajax was a boaster, a braggart, who earned fame as a hero in the Trojan War. When, however, the armour of Hector was awarded to Ulysses instead of to himself, his mortification drove him mad, and he killed himself. The violet is said to have sprung from his blood. It is perhaps a little incongruous, therefore, that the violet should be regarded to-day as typifying, in the language of flowers, the virtue of modesty.

Virtues, The Seven. They are Faith, Hope, Charity, Prudence, Justice, Fortitude and Temperance.

Vitus, St. Vitus Dance. St. Vitus had no predilection for dancing and, far from giving his name to any such recreation, was a devout youth of Sicily who, during the Diocletian persecution, in the year 303, was martyred, together with his nurse and his tutor. It was more than twelve hundred years later that his name became associated with the "dance." Then, throughout Germany, the remarkable superstition took root that anyone who danced before the statue of St. Vitus on his feast day (15th June) would be assured of good health for a year. Thousands of people thronged round the figures of the saint on this day, and the dancing became almost a mania. So much so that it became confused with chorea (a nervous disease, characterized by convulsive movements), and chorea came to be called St. Vitus Dance. Eventually the aid of the Saint was invoked against the dance.

On St. Vitus, in older London days, the Skinners' Company, accompanied by girls strewing herbs in their path, and by Bluecoat Boys, marched in procession from Dowgate Hill, where their hall was, to St. Antholin's Church, in Watling Street, to hear service. The origin of the custom seems now to be unknown.

Viz. Is a contraction of the Latin *videlicet*, meaning namely, to wit.

Vocabulary. The question has often been asked of us: "How many words are there in the English language?" There is not, really, any authentic record. It is estimated that to read an ordinary copy of *The Times* with complete understanding of the words contained therein, a vocabulary of fifty thousand words is required. Most people get through the task, and obtain a working knowledge of the meaning of it, with a vocabulary of twenty-five thousand words.

Mr. Winston Churchill's working vocabulary is said to be thirty thousand, and his potential vocabulary fifty thousand to sixty thousand. Skilled lawyers, pleading in Court, have a vocabulary of fifty thousand; but the people possessing the greatest average number of words to their tongues are scientists. They cannot get through on fewer than eighty thousand. In 1937 a movement was started in literary circles for a Basic English Language of not more than eight hundred and fifty words, and in 1944 the Government appointed a committee to inquire and report into a suggested Basic English which would, as any philologist of repute will admit, make Shakespeare's works about a par with a fourth form schoolboy's writing of prose.

Volume. Although we now use the word to describe a book, its original was the Latin *volumen*, a wreath or a roll. Historically, a volume was a roll of parchment, papyrus, etc., containing written matter. Before the days of books, as we know them now, poems and the records of history were written on sheets of paper. These were fastened together lengthways and rolled up.

Voodoo. The name given to the magic charmers, of which the Witch Doctor is the leader. "Voodoo" probably came (the name we mean) from the French *Vaudois*, the name given by missionaries to the Waldensians who, as heretics, were accused of sorcery. The more likely origin, however, is that it comes from *vodun*, a dialect form of the Ashanti *obosum*, meaning a tutelary spirit.

Vox Populi Vox Dei. "The voice of the people is the voice of God." The phrase goes a little far, perhaps. Its real meaning is that the voice of the people is irresistible, as is the ruling of the Deity; but the voice is not necessarily beneficial to the people.

W

W.A.A.C., W.R.E.N., W.R.A.F. Meaning members of the Women's Auxiliary Army Corps and the Women's Royal Air Force of the of the 1914-18 War; and the Women's Royal Naval Division of the Second World War. There were also the A.T.S. in the Second War—a Women's Auxiliary Territorial Force.

Wager. To hazard on the issue of a contest, or on some question to be decided; a bet, or stake. It is connected with Old French *wageare*, and with *gage* and *wage*. The Latin *wadiare* meant a pledge.

Wager of Law. An old and little-known English mode of trial whereby, in an action of debt brought upon a simple contract between the parties, without any deed or record, the defendant might discharge himself by taking an oath that he did not owe the complainant anything. He was required, however, to bring with him eleven of his neighbours, called compurgators, who were to avow upon their oath that they believed in their conscience that he declared the truth.

Wait and See. One of the most famous political phrases of modern times is this nickname given to Mr. H. H. Asquith (afterwards the Earl of Oxford and Asquith). He first used it as an answer to a question in the House of Commons on 4th April, 1910. It did not arouse any comment at the time, but when to avoid awkward answers the Prime Minister reiterated it times without end, it became a by-word, and Members, when a question was put to the Right Hon. Gentleman broke into a chant of "Wait and See." Moreover, it was adopted by the general public as a catchword for any query put.

Waits. The name for the carol singers during the Christmas season traces back to the Anglo-Saxon *wacian*, which meant to watch, to wake. In early days the Waits were a body of people, attached to noble households, who paraded and watched during every night and sounded the hours. Many towns had licensed Waits, Exeter, for instance, having a regular company. The instruments they used were shawms—a kind of hautboy. The duty assigned to the Wait in the Black Book of Edward IV, 1748, was "to pipe the watch nightly, from Michaelmas to Maundy Thursday, four times within the Court, and in Summer three nights out, and to make good cheer. He was to eat in the hall with the minstrels, and was to receive for his supper half a loaf and half a gallon of ale . . . and, moreover, during actual attendance at Court, fourpence-halfpenny a day."

Wake. There are no fewer than ten columns of interpretations of the word "wake" in the *Oxford English Dictionary*. In the Black Country, in the author's young days, the word was applied to the fairs which periodically visited towns with their roundabouts and sideshows. In the North, this sense of the word is still retained in, for instance, the Blackpool *Wakes* week.

In Ireland the wake denotes the watching of a dead body, by the friends and neighbours of the deceased, throughout the night; and the watch usually ended in an orgy of feasting. The word would seem to have been derived principally from the Anglo-Saxon *nihtwaco*, nightwatch.

It may be that the true etymology of the word is connected with religion, and in this connection Dugdale (in a "Life of St. John") has written: "And ye shall onderstand and know how the Evyns were first found in old time. In the begynning of holy Churche, it was so that the pepul cam to the Chirche with candellys brennyng and wold *wake* and coome with light towards the Chirche in their devocions; and after fell to lecherie and songs, daunces, harping, piping and also to glottony and sinne, and so turnedd the holyness to cursydness, wherfor holy Faders ordenned the pepul to leve the *Waking* and to fast the Evyn."

Wales' Feathers, The Prince of. According to tradition the feathers were the crest of John of Luxemburg, King of Bohemia, and were found under his body by the Black Prince after he had slain John, at the Battle of Crecy. He at once assumed them, together with the motto "Ich dien" (I serve). The origin is very doubtful. It may be as well to point out that the hereditary title of Queen Philippa was Countess of Ostrevant (ostrich feather), and there already existed in Wales the motto *Eich dyn*, "Behold the Man."

Wales, Prince of. The "origin" of the title, Prince of Wales, usually given, is of the fairy story romance. According to it, when Edward I subdued Wales he promised, on their laying down their arms, that he would give them a Prince who could not speak a word of English. He then showed the new-born son of his Queen, Eleanor, and entitled him Prince of Wales. Since then the eldest son of the King has been Prince of Wales.

The entire story is nonsense, and ought long ago to have been espunged from the history books. Any reference to a reliable history of Wales will give the date of the submission of Wales to Edward as 1276. His son, born at Carnarvon, who later became Edward II, was not born until 1284, and was not created Prince of Wales until he was sixteen years of age—in 1301.

Neither is the eldest son of the King entitled Prince of Wales. He is born Duke of Cornwall, and is not Prince of Wales until that title is conferred on him by the King.

Walk. *To go for a walk.* To take a walk. To walk about. The word is probably one of the most remarkable in the language, because it originally had nothing whatever to do with going about on one's feet. Its derivation, according to the *Oxford English Dictionary*, was the Anglo-Saxon *wealcan*, and *wealcan* had two forms—(1) to roll or toss, and (2) to muffle up. From *wealcan* came wealcere, a fuller of cloth. It was not until the Middle English period that the word came to mean not "roll" but "move about, travel." And there is still no clue in philology as to how or why the change was made. The *Oxford English Dictionary* suggests that the Middle English sense had arisen in the Old English as a colloquial, perhaps jocular, use.

Walker, Hookey. "*That's all Hookey Walker.*" It's all nonsense. The story told of the phrase is that a London firm engaged a clerk named Walker, the possessor of a large and hooked nose. His task was to watch the workmen, and should they not fulfil their toll of work, to report them to his principals. His complaints, conveyed by the firm to the men, were received with so much incredulity that the firm, for the sake of peace, had to get red of Mr. Walker. Since when anything incredible reported is greeted with the shout of "Walker," or "Hookey Walker." And every Walker born of woman is fated to have the nickname "Hookey," just as each Clark will be called "Nobby."

Walking the Chalk. A stupid test for sobriety, or drunkenness, used by doctors called in to a man arrested for drunkenness. A chalk line is drawn across a yard, or a room, and the suspect is invited to walk along it. If he strays from the line, then he is usually accounted drunk. There are hundreds of men, teetotal, who may be highly strung, who could not walk along such a line without deviation.

Wall. *To go to the Wall.* To be pushed out of the way; to be supplanted. The best interpretation of this phrase that the author remembers is the quotation by Sir John Cheke, in "The Hurt of Sedicion, etc.": "When brethren agree not in a house, goeth not the weakest to the walls?" It seems to explain the position of the weakest perfectly.

Wall, To Give (or Take) the. The safest, or most advantageous, place in any roadway is the walled side. In England a gentleman would automatically pass to the outside of the lady, giving her the wall side. At one time, it was the custom of pedestrians to "give the wall" to any person higher in the social strata than themselves.

Wallflower. Another name for the gilly-flower, because it will grow and flourish in the nicks of old walls, and out of the walls of ruined buildings.

Wallflowers (at a dance). Because they decorate the walls of the dance hall, young ladies who have no partner for a dance are thus called.

Wallop. *To Wallop Somebody.* To give him a good hiding. A very good story of the "origin" of this word is given of an Admiral named Sir John Wallop. Here it is, in the philologist's own words: "In the year 1514 the French Fleet ravaged the coast of Sussex and burned Brighthelmstone (now Brighton), whereupon Sir John Wallop, one of the best Naval commanders of his time, was sent by Henry VIII to make reprisals. In this he succeeded only too well; he burned twenty-one French coast villages, demolished several harbours, and thrashed the enemy to his heart's content. His men, however, proud of the achievement, declared that they had Wallop-ed the French; and thus it came that a new synonym for 'thrash' came to be incorporated into the English language."

This is said to have happened in the year 1514, so it is curious, therefore, that wallop is not found so used before the *nineteenth* century—a matter of some three hundred years before Admiral Wallop's men thought out the pun!

It is curious, too, that our philologist did not look into Language, where he might have found the Middle English *walopen*, and the Old French *waloper*, each meaning to boil, or to gallop. Before the word gallop for a horse came into use, a horse's gallop was a wallop. If two horsemen rode a race the winner obviously *walloped* the other.

Walls Have Ears. For Catherine de Medici walls did, indeed, have ears. The Queen of France, who spent nearly all her later life balancing between the Catholics and the Protestants, had the Louvre so constructed that anything that was said in one room could be heard in one other. And that is how Catherine de Medici learned sufficient of both sides to retain her balance in her country's politics. The tubes of communication between the rooms and her room were called auriculaires.

Walnut. Has nothing to do with walls. The Anglo-Saxon word for foreign was *wealh*, and the Middle English word for walnut *walnote*, from *wealh* and *hnut*. The walnut was so-called by our ancestors in explanation of its foreign origin; it came from Persia.

Wandering Jew, The. A legendary personage who (according to a popular belief first mentioned in the thirteenth century), for having insulted Jesus on the day of the Crucifixion, was doomed to wander over the earth without rest until the Day of Judgment. In its earliest form, the Wandering Jew is called Cartaphilus, the door-keeper in the Hall of Pontius Pilate. He is said to have struck Jesus as He left the hall, saying: "Go on faster, Jesus." A second version gives the Jew as a cobbler, called Ahasuerus, who refused to let the Saviour rest on his doorstep, but pushed him off, saying: "Go away; away with you." But all accounts agree on the reply: "I go, but thou shall tarry till I come to thee again."

The interpretation of the legend formed a noteworthy play by E. Temple Thurston, staged by Mr. Matheson Lang, in which that actor gave a memorable performance.

Wangle. *To wangle something.* To manage or contrive something in an irregular manner. It has been suggested by the *English Dialect Dictionary* that "wangle" may be an old Oxfordshire folk-word; but the writer has been unable to find any justification for the statement. The earliest reference to wangle in print was in 1888, when in Jacobi's "Printers' Vocabulary" he gives the word as "a slang term used by printers to express faking, or for arranging matters to one's own satisfaction." In other words, to *wangle* the size of type to fit a given space. This is probably the true origin. The word came into general use during Great War of 1914-18.

War Paint, In Full. An allusion to the practice of the North American Indians (the Red Indians of our boyhood) of painting their bodies before going into battle.

War Path, On the. Comes from the same source as war paint.

Warming-pan. Not the long-handled pan of metal (brass or copper) to contain live coals formerly in use for warming beds, but the slang term for someone who is holding the place, temporarily, for another—keeping the job warm, as it were.

As a schoolboy, the author, a fag, was on numerous occasions in the cold of Winter ordered to lie in the bed of a monitor in order to warm it for him.

Because of the story that James II's son, afterwards the Old Pretender, was introduced into the Queen's bed in a warming-pan, her own child having been still-born, the "Jacobites" were nicknamed "The Warming-pans."

Warrior Queen. Boadicea (strictly Bondicca). She was a British Queen in the time of the Emperor Nero. Her husband Prasutagus ruled the Iceni (in what is now Norfolk) as an autonomous Prince under Roman suzerainty. On his death (A.D. 61), without male heir, his dominions were annexed brutally. In revenge, the Queen and her people (and with her half of Britain) arose. They burnt the Roman-founded towns of Verulam and Colchester, the mart of London, and massacred s e v e n t y thousand Romans and Britons friendly to Rome. Finally, however, Rome regained the captured country, and Boadicea took poison. Rome later adopted a kindlier policy. The decisive battle was in all probability fought at Watling Street.

Warwick. In Anglo-Saxon, *Woewic,* war town, because of the garrison maintained there permanently.

Washout. *It's a washout.* This is old naval slang, used to give instructions to clean the slate in the days when slates were used to take down the words of a signal or message. Later, in the Army, when iron targets were used, a rifle range order at the end of a squad's practice was to obliterate the bullet marks and prepare the target for the next squad, by blackening the bull's-eye and washing out the other marks by a coating of whitewash. This is also the probable origin of to whitewash.

Wassail. The usual story of the origin of the word is that told by Geoffrey of Monmouth in his "Historia Britonum" (about 1150). There he relates how the fair Rowena, daughter of Hengist, King of Kent, presented a cup of wine to her father's guest, Vortigern, with the remark, "*waes heil*" ("your health"). To which Vortigern replied, accepting, "*drinc heil.*" The snag about accepting this story is that there is no trace of these drinking salutations in early Teutonic literature. The practice seems to have arisen in England.

The Anglo-Saxon greeting was not *waes heil,* but *wes hal* (be hale), and the word *hal* was used in the sense of and to replace the Avel of the Vulgate. The earliest records of wassail show not the Anglo-Saxon *hal,* but the Old Norse *heil,* a greeting. As for the spelling "w," this course with words really beginning with "h" or "ho" is frequently recorded in the fifteenth century.

Watch (on board ship). The period of time called a watch on board ship, the reckoning beginning at noon or midnight. Between four and eight p.m. the time is divided into two short watches, or dog watches, in order to prevent the constant recurrences of duty to the same portion of the crew during the same hours. Thus, the period from twelve to four p.m. is called the afternoon watch, from four to six the first dog watch, from six to eight the second dog watch, from eight to eleven the first night watch, from midnight to four a.m. the middle watch, from four to eight the morning watch, and from eight to twelve the forenoon watch.

Watch and Ward, To keep. In the old feudal days watch was a guard by night, and ward was a guard by day.

Waterloo Cup. The greyhound coursing event, held at Altcar in February, derives its name from the fact that it was founded by the owner of the Waterloo Hotel, Liverpool, one Lynn, in 1836. Lynn was also the founder of the Grand National, run at Aintree.

"Waterloo was Won on the Playing Fields of Eton." Another saying of the Duke of Wellington in which there is not a vestige of truth. There were, in fact, only a very small number of officers from Eton concerned in the battle.

See "Up Guards and at 'Em!"

Wavy-Navy, The. Naval slang name for the R.N.V.R. To distinguish them from the Royal Navy, men of the Reserve have the three white lines on the collar wavy instead of straight, while the rings of gold lace on the officers' sleeves are also wavy.

Wayzgoose (or Waygoose). The *Oxford E n g l i s h Dictionary,* omitting the "z," states that the word is of obscure origin, but that there is no evidence that the second element is to be identified with goose. This seems rather a remarkable statement on the part of such an authority. Surely *wawz* was the now obsolete word for stubble, and the outings of printers invariably took place about September or later, after the well-known practice of farmers of turning their geese for final fattening into the stubble of the cleared fields. Old printers tell the author that it was a *sine qua non* that these outings should be provided with a goose for the mid-day meal. It should be noted here that the term wayzgoose was at one time restricted to a description of a printers' annual outing.

"We are not amused." This famous remark of Queen Victoria, first printed in "Notebooks of a Spinster Lady," 2nd January, 1900, and since in common usage as a jesting rebuke, is as yet an unsolved riddle. Where and why did she make the remark? She is said to have uttered the words: (1) To Albert Chevalier, after a Command performance; (2) to an officer who ventured to tell, in her presence, a funny story about his superior in rank; (3) to someone whom she discovered in the act of imitating her.

In regard to number three, the name of the late Admiral Maxse has been mentioned. There is no truth whatever in the suggestion, says his daughter, Viscountess Milner. She adds that he never spoke to Queen Victoria.

The most probable explanation is that given by the late J. A. Fuller-Maitland in "A Door-keeper of Music." He says: "I remember little about the concert (at Hawarden, in 1884) beyond the fact that Alick Yorke sang comic songs, one of them in a flannel petticoat bestowed upon him by the Queen after she had insisted on his giving his famous impersonation of herself in her own presence, as a *doucier* after the reproof she felt bound to utter in words that have often been quoted."

Weathercock. The author has been asked on many occasions why it should be that the figure placed on a weather-vane, to show the direction of the wind, is invariably a cock. The answer is, in all probability, the Papal enactment of the ninth century that the figure of a cock should be set up on every church steeple as the emblem of St. Peter, in allusion to his denial of Jesus. When, subsequently, the church steeple was used for the holding of a weather-vane, the cock was transferred to it, as it would then stand at the highest point, and the gaze of all who desired to note the direction of the wind would be turned to it, thereby reminding them of the reason for its position.

In "A Help to Discourse," first printed in 1619, the cock on the steeple is explained to signify that we "should thereby remember our sinnes, and with Peter seeke and obtaine mercy; as though without this dumbe cocke, which many will not hearken to, untille he crow, the Scriptures were not a sufficient larum."

However, Gramaye relates that the "manner of adorning the tops of steeples with a cross and a cock is derived from the Goths, who bore that as their warlike ensign. It is exceedingly doubtful that there is any truth in the suggestion.

Wedding Anniversaries. The names popularly given to wedding anniversaries are as follows:—

First year	Cotton wedding
Second	Paper wedding
Third	Leather wedding
Fifth	Wooden wedding
Seventh	Woollen wedding
Tenth	Tin wedding
Twelfth	Silk and fine linen wedding
Fifteenth	Crystal wedding
Twentieth	China wedding
Twenty-fifth	Silver wedding
Thirtieth	Pearl wedding
Fourtieth	Ruby wedding
Fiftieth	Golden wedding
Seventy-fifth	Diamond wedding

But the sixtieth anniversary is now regarded as a diamond wedding in place of the seventy-fifth, in honour of the Diamond Jubilee of Queen Victoria—sixty years a Queen.

Wedding Breakfast. Its purpose to-day is a jollification celebration at which the couple receive their friends, but in earlier Roman Catholic days, it had some significance. The entire wedding party fasted from midnight before they attended Mass next day. At the end of the marriage ceremony, and after Communion, the officiating priest regaled them with wine and cakes in the church porch, as a breakfast.

It is doubtful whether our wedding cake has any affinity with the Confarreation Roman marriages. Confarreation, the highest and most solemn form of marriage among the ancient Romans, was marked by the offering of a cake made of spelt. The cake was offered in the presence of the Pontifex Maximus or the Flamen Dialis, and ten witnesses.

It might, perhaps, be added that the Hebrews, long before the Romans, had a somewhat similar marriage rite.

Wedding Finger. The third finger of the left hand (or the *fourth digit* if the thumb be accounted a finger). The reason? Well, Appianus asserted that a very delicate n e r v e r u n s from that finger to the heart; and Swinburne, in his "Treatise of Spousals," wrote: "By the received opinions of the learned, in ripping up and anatomising men's bodies, there is a vein of blood, called *Vena amoris*, which passeth from that finger to the heart."

Wedding Ring. Although, to-day, the wedding ring of a woman is merely an ornamental badge, or symbol, of her claim to be a wife, it was in the earliest days of much more importance. It was, in fact, the seal which gave a wife the right to represent her husband in every way. In the days of the Old Testament, for instance, the ring was the seal with which all orders were signed. Pharoah told Joseph: "Thou shalt be over my house, and according unto thy word shall all my people be ruled. . . . And Pharoah took off his ring from his hand and put it on Joseph's hand." Again, in *Esther*, iii: "The king took off his ring and gave it unto Haman." Thirdly, in *Gen.*, xxxviii, Judah and the supposed harlot: "And he said what pledge shall I give thee, and she said thy signet . . ."

The delivery of the wedding ring was a sign that the giver endowed the person who received it with the power he himself received.

Wedding rings were not always of gold. In early Roman days only senators chief magistrates and, later, knights, had the right to wear a gold ring. The wedding ring of a wife of those days was of plain iron.

Wedlock. *Joined in Holy Wedlock.* This is a curious phrase for the church to use in relation to the marriage service. Its correct meaning is revealed in its Anglo-Saxon name *Wedlac*—"*Wev*" meant a pledge, and "*lac*" a gift. The pledge, however, was not a marriage-altar pledge, but a pledge on betrothal, and *lac* a gift on betrothal. The word in its original had never any reference to a lock, an indissolvable union.

Week, The. The present space of a week, seven days, is of very ancient origin. Strangely enough, when America was discovered it was not known among the natives there. Nor was it known among the Polynesians, the Japanese, or in ancient China; but it was universal in India. The early Greeks and Romans had no weeks. Cassius, in the second century A.D., wrote that "the week and planetary names for days have recently been introduced into Rome from Egypt." Another curious thing about the week is that although we owe the names of all the months to the Romans, the days of the week are all of Anglo-Saxon origin, as follows: Sunday (Anglo-Saxon *Sunnandoeg*), Monday (*Monandoeg*), Tuesday (*Tiwesdoeg*), Wednesday (*Wednesdoeg*), Thursday (*Thunresdoeg*), Friday (*Frigedoeg*), Saturday (*Saterdoeg*). Sunday is the day of the Sun; Monday, the Moon; Tuesday, day of Tiw, God of War; Wednesday, day of Oden, God of Storms; Thursday, day of Thor, God of Thunder; Friday, day of Freya, Goddess of Marriage; and Saturday, day of Saturn, God of Time.

Welsher. To welsh anyone means to swindle him. It was originally applied only to bets on the racecourse, and to a bookmaker who disappeared during the race and without paying out winnings. He was designated a Welsher. As to the origin, or rather origins, they are legion. It is, first and foremost, allied in public theory to the Welsh race, the authority being the old rhyme, "Taffy was a Welshman, Taffy was a thief." A second story is that the first "welsher" was on a ground in Wales.

Then we have the story written by a Welsh contributor to a Sunday newspaper. He is quite definite about the matter; no "alleged" or "theory" for him. He says:

"Welcher, as applied to the racecourse, has no reference to the Welsh, but was coined after an incident which happened many years ago on Epsom Downs, the subject of the term being one, Bob Welch. Mr. Welch had 'laid the odds,' found he could not pay up, and so cleared off. His emulators have ever since been dubbed Welchers. Unfortunately, the word is invariably mis-spelt."

The writer would like to know a little more of this Bob Welch, and a closer date given to his feat than "many years ago." Chronology is rather important to the philologist who endeavours to get the facts right.

The only facts that can be given about the term is that it was well-known, and in popular use as long ago as 1857, for in the London *Morning Chronicle* of 8th June that year, there is a comment: "He got his living by 'welching' and taking in the 'flats'."

West. *To Go West.* To die. Since the sun sinks in the West, there is little doubt that the sinking and disappearing of the sun in the West has had some influence on this phrase; but of the actual origin, there are various suggestions. Among the ancient Egyptians, the West was spoken of as the home of departed spirits. Mourners on the banks of the Nile uttered the cry "to the West."

From America, it s stated that the term arose from the Red Indians' phrase that a dying man had gone to meet the setting sun. A further suggestion is that it belongs to the days of the Palefaces and Indians, when prospectors did not return from the dangerous country West of the Mississippi. They were said to have "gone West."

But the phrase is as old in the English language as the early fourteenth century, for, in a poem of that time, with the refrain "This world is but a Vanity," there appear the lines:

"Women and mony wilsom wy,
As wynd and watter ar gane west."

In modern English: "Women and many a wilful man, As wind and water are gone west."

In the sixteenth century, the phrase was used of malefactors going from trial in London to the gibbet at Tyburn, Tyburn being west of London.

Wet. *To have a wet. To wet one's whistle.* Wet, as a slang term for a drink, or a state of intoxication, in the English language, is as old as the fourteenth century. In "Reeve's Tale," Chaucer has: "So was her joly whistle wel y-wet." And in the "Towneley Plays," (1388), is a reference to "Had she . . . wett hyr Whystyll."

Wheel of Fortune. Emblematical of her inconstancy, the Goddess Fortuna was always represented with a wheel in her hands.

Whig. A political nickname. Although the origin of the word is not certain, it is most likely from the word *whiggam*, an old Scottish expression on a par with our "gee-up." The fact that it was given to the party in opposition to the conservative policy of the Tories, would seem to lend some support to this origin. There is no historical foundation for the suggestion that it is connected with the word *whig*, current in the sixteenth century, for a beverage consisting of whey fermented and flavoured with herbs which, according to De Foe, "the poor, honest people were forced to drink."

Whisky. Not the drink, but the name given to a light one-horse gig, because of the quickness of transport compared with the heavier and two-horsed conveyances in general use. It whisked one from place to place.

A whisky-hearse was a single-horsed hearse, a device brought in to avoid the duty, per horse, of passing through toll gates.

The Whisky came into use in the late eighteenth century.

Whist. The card game for four people was given the name, according to Cotton's "Complete Gamester" (1680), "from the silence that is to be observed in the play." Whereas Dr. Brewer states that the game was formerly called "Triumph" (this is pure fancy thinking, because Trumps were originally so-called) and later "Ruff" or "Honours." Cotton observes, with greater likelihood of truth, that "Whist is a game not much differing from Ruff and Honours."

Whistle Down the Wind. Has no part or parcel with "Whistle for It." It was originally a term in falconry. The hawk was usually cast off against the wind in pursuit of prey, but with the wind when turned loose.

Whistle for It. Sailors in the old days of sail, when becalmed, held the superstition that the wind could be brought by whistling for it, an allusion to the sound of wind whistling through the rigging. The phrase, "You'll have to whistle for it," is the landsman's adoption of the sailor's whistling for the wind.

White Elephant. "*That's a White Elephant*," meaning a venture that has never shown a profit and is not likely to. The original White Elephant is said to have been that of Siam, where the beast was regarded as sacred, and was maintained accordingly. It was the custom of the King of Siam, when he wanted to dispose of the services of a courtier who had become obnoxious to him, to make the courtier a Royal present of a white elephant. The recipient was usually ruined by the cost of the animal's maintenance!

White Feather, To show the. The phrase came from cock-fighting days. True-bred game cocks possessed no white feathers. The presence of a white feather in such a bird indicated a cross-breed and, therefore, one who would not show gameness in the fight.

White Line. A ribbon of white paint, either in a continuous line or a series of short lines, to divide the roadway for "up" and "down" traffic, particularly round corners. The distinction of being the inventor of this road "safety-first" device has been hotly disputed. It has been claimed that Mr. J. H. Willacy, of Lancaster, first chalked a white line on the main road facing his business premises, "The Ever Open Door," an old toll-house in Lancaster Road, Hornby, between Bradford and Morecambe. Two farm lads had collided and were injured, and the white line, it is stated, was thereupon chalked in the roadway. This was in 1916. He was threatened by the County Council with action for tampering with the road, but in 1919 received a letter from King George V, who frequently passed that way, stating that the white line was a good precedent.

On the other hand, Mr. H. T. Chapman, in "Reminiscences of the Highway Surveyor," says that he marked out several dangerous turnings in Kent, on the suggestion of Alderman Amos of Kent, in 1914. Another account states that a white line was instituted in China in 1927. Mr. Robert Cooper, writing from Strood to a daily newspaper, quotes a Shrewsbury newspaper of 1823 mentioning white stones placed along the centre of the English bridge there.

There is no doubt, however, that the general use of the white line was imported here from America, and there is little doubt that it originated in America at Detroit. The start of the white line there is claimed by Mr. D. E. Jones, now living in Gloucester. He was an automobile road tester, and painted a white line for safety while road-testing at night. Mr Jones states that Mr. E. W. Hines, Highway Commissioner of Detroit, took an interest in the idea, and started white lines throughout Michigan.

Out of this mixture, one thing is clear—Hines was given a plaque in 1936 for having originated the white centre line for roadways about 1922.

Whitsun Ale. An old custom of the seventeenth and eighteenth centuries in the rural areas of England. Another name for it was "Church Ale." Carew explains it thusly: "Two men of the parish are yerely chosen by their last foregoers to be wardens, who, dividing the task, make collection among the parishioners of whatever provision it pleaseth them voluntarily to bestow. This they employ in brewing, baking and other actes against Whitsontide; upon which holy day the neighbours meet at the Church house, and there merrily feed on their owne victuals."

A Gloucestershire clergyman, in "A Serious Dissuasive against Whitsun Ales," 1736, wrote: "These sports are attended usually with ludicrous gestures, and acts of foolery and buffoonery—but children's play and what, therefore, grown-up persons should be ashamed of."

Aubrey, in his "Natural History of North Wilts," however, throws another sidelight on the celebrations: "There were no rates for the poor in my grandfather's days," he says; "but for Kingston St. Michael (no small parish), the church ale of Whitsun did the business. In every parish is (or was) a church house, to which belonged spits, crocks, utensils, etc., for dressing provisions. Here the housekeepers met and were merry, and gave their charity."

Whit-Sunday. A corruption of White Sunday, in allusion to the custom in the early Christian Church of newly-baptized converts wearing garments of white from Easter to Pentecost (or Whit-Sunday). These converts were called *Albati* (white-robed). The last Sunday, Pentecost Day, was called *Dominica in Albis*—Sunday in white. There is no vestige of support for the theory that it meant "wit" or "wisdom" Sunday, when the Apostles were filled with wisdom by the coming on them of the Holy Ghost.

Whittington—and His Cat. He was not a poor boy, and he was not chivvied about by a cook. Neither did he walk with a bundle over his shoulder accompanied by a cat. If he had a cat, it was probably the cat that carried Dick.

Having rid the story of its superfluous trappings, we can now give the facts. Richard Whittington, afterwards Lord Mayor of London, was a younger son of Sir William de Whyttington, Lord of the Manor of Pauntley, Glos. He was sent to London, and was there trained as a merchant by a relative of the family. He married the daughter of his employer, thus getting an excellent start in life, became a merchant himself, and prospered so well that he was able to help his King with a loan which would be, in itself, a fortune to-day.

As for the "cat"—there are two possible explanations. Being a merchant, Dick would have to import and export goods. To do that you want ships. A popular ship of the time was a Norwegian vessel used in the coal trade, and called a "cat." Sir Richard had some dealings in the coal trade; and the Moors of the fairy tale might well have been the coal-blacked gentlemen of his "cat."

Or the tale may be told of how, in the French language, which was extensively spoken in England in those days, trading for profit in merchandise was known as *achat*, which would quite easily come to the English tongue as a-cat.

Still, it is a nice little fairy story, and has done much to egg on youths to work hard for their masters in the hope of becoming another Dick Whittington! But it is not of much use to philologists, who require good, hard facts.

Wick. This suffix to town names meant a place where there was salt. It was Anglo-Saxon for a village, or a marsh. In Norse, it meant a bay or creek. In those days salt was obtained by evaporating sea water, hence the name "wick" was also given to any inland place where there was salt, such as Droitwich, Wicklow, and so on.

Wild Oats, To Sow One's. "In reference to the folly of sowing wild oats instead of good grain," says the *Oxford English Dictionary;* but since its first appearance was in 1542, when the soil gave Britain many proverbs, the explanation seems insufficient. No farmer would go sowing wild oats when, for the same labour, he could put in good grain. The writer searched round for a better explanation, if one existed. In this connection there is an old Danish saying, which the author has heard on several occasions, "*Lokkens havre,*" Loki's Wild Oats. The term refers to the thick mists which rise over the agricultural parts of Denmark in the early Spring. When the mists have finally dispersed, the Danes greet the better weather with the statement that Loki has "sown his wild oats"; and they may now rely upon being able to sow their own good ones.

Willow Pattern Plates. The willow pattern on crockery was introduced into England by Thomas Turner about 1780, when the craze for things Chinese was at its height. Funnily enough, the pattern does not illustrate any Chinese legend, and is not Chinese in origin. The house is popularly supposed to represent a Mandarin's residence, and the pattern is supposed to tell the love story of his daughter.

Window. This is a word which, although the object it describes has changed, remains itself unchanged. Window is a corruption of the Anglo-Saxon *vindauga—vindr*, wind and *auga*, eye-making window—Wind's Eye. It dates back to those days before the introduction of glass into this country, when windows were openings in a wall and were uncovered except with shutters or curtains. They also served the purpose of giving air to the room. Thus, they both acted as an eye for the folks within to peer outside, and as ventilation through which the wind could cleanse the atmosphere.

Wise Men of Gotham. The term is applied as a reproach to those who act in a foolish manner. There are many stories told of the "wisdom" (*sic*) of the men of Gotham, which is in Nottinghamshire. They could fill a book. Anyhow, one of them is that hoping to keep the Spring always with them they built a hedge round a cuckoo, since the cuckoo only stays in this country during the Spring. "The Cuckoo, as soone as she perceived herselfe incompassed within the hedge, flew away. A vengeance on her, said they. We made not our hedge high enough." The quotation is taken from a book, now in the Bodleian Library, entitled, "Tales of the Mad-men of Gottam."

Another of the stories is of a Gotham man "who did ride to the market with two bushells of wheate, and because his horse should not beare heavy, he carried his corne upon his owne necke, and did ride upon his horse, because his horse should not carry too heavy a burthen."

Wiseacre. Term applied in contempt to someone who claims to have knowledge beyond his fellows. Dr. Brewer tells a good story of a landed gentleman who boasted of his estates in front of Ben Jonson at the Devil Tavern in Fleet Street, London. "What care we for your dirt and clods?" said Jonson. "Where you have an acre of land I have ten acres of wit." The landed gentleman came back with the riposte, "Good, Mr. Wiseacre." This is not, however, the origin of the word—which came from the Middle Dutch *wijsseggher—wijs*, wise, and *seggher*, sayer, meaning wise-sayer, or soothsayer.

Wooden Horse (of Troy). Ulysses had a monster wooden horse made after the death of Hector, and announced that it was an offering to the Gods to secure a prosperous voyage back to Greece.

The Trojans dragged the horse into their city, but it was full of Grecian soldiers who, at night, opened a door in the horse, stole out, slew the Trojan guards, and opened the city gates for Troy to fall.

Woolsack, The. The seat of office in the House of Lords of the Lord Chancellor of England is so-named because it is a large bag of wool covered with red cloth. The story of it goes back to Queen Elizabeth's days, when a law was passed stopping the export of wool. To ensure that judges should keep in mind the importance of woollen manufacture in England (it was the source of our wealth in those days) seats filled with wool were placed for them in the House of Lords.

Wormwood. *Gall and Wormwood.* Something acutely vexing or mortifying to a person. It has nothing to do with worms or wood, but is a corruption of the Anglo-Saxon *wer*, defend, and *mod*, mind, the whole meaning keep-mind. It was believed that the herb, being a strong tonic, inspired man. It was very popular as a medicine among the ancients.

Worsted. The yarn was thus named because it was originally spun at Worsted, in Norfolk, now spelled Worstead. It was once a large and thriving market town.

Worth. Where this suffix appears in place-names, it denotes that it was once a place *warded* or protected, probably by an inclosure. It occurs in Tam - worth, Wands-worth and Wal-worth.

X

X. This mark on barrels of beer formerly meant that the cask had paid the excise duty and was, therefore, of a certain standard of strength. The appearance of two or three "X's" on a cask was intended by the brewer to make the customers think that they were getting better beer than that for which they were paying!

Xanthian Marbles, The. A collection of friezes and sculpture now in the British Museum. They were discovered by Sir Charles Fellows in 1838, at Xanthus, a Greek city in Asia Minor.

Xantippe. Is the name given to a scolding and bad-tempered wife, because that was the Christian name of the termagent whom Socrates married.

Xenocratic. The doctrine of Xenocrates (396-314 B.C.), who was noted for combining Pythagoreanism with Platonism. A disciple of Plato he had, perhaps, a leaning in the direction of his master.

Xeres. An alternative name for sherry, because sherry, once called sherris. was brought from Xeres, a town near Cadiz, in Spain.

X-Rays. In 1895, Mr. W. C. Rontgen was passing an electric current through a vacuum tube in his laboratory, and studying the effect of the rays thus produced. In the laboratory he had an unused photographic plate in the usual protective covering of a black-lined box. Some time later, he had occasion to develop this plate, and found strange markings on it. Prolonged thought led him to believe that the only thing that could possibly have caused the markings was the ray with which he had been experimenting that day. He tried an experiment with a new box of photographic plates, with the same effect. The discovery meant that Rontgen had found a ray that was able to pass through substances opaque to ordinary light. He did not, at that time, know just how penetrating the ray was, or would become; and because he did not at the time understand why the rays should be able to "see" through opaque substances, he named it the "X" ray—the "x" being, of course, the Unknown Quantity.

X-Ships. The name given to certain specially designed ships in the 1914-18 war, built for landing troops in Northern Germany at the suggestion of the late Admiral Lord Fisher ("Sack-the-Lot" Fisher). They were of shallow draught, with twin motors, burning shale-oil, and having a speed of six knots.

XXX. *The Three Exes.* Nickname of the old 30th Regiment of Foot, because of the Roman numerals for thirty. In the same way the 40th Regiment (XL) bore the nickname, "The Excellers."

Xylonite. Is the correct name for celluloid. *Xylo* is a Greek prefix meaning wood. Celluloid is made by a process of immersing paper in sulphuric and nitric acids.

Xylophone. As already stated, *xylo* is a Greek prefix appertaining to wood, while *phone* is voice. The Xylophone is, or rather was originally, a musical instrument consisting of a number of flat wooden bars, in graduated series, played by striking with a small hammer. The earliest mention of them in Britain was in 1868, when the "Athenæum" spoke of "a prodigy . who does wonderful things on a machine of wooden keys called a Xylophone, almost five octaves in compass."

Y

Yacht. The word is derived from the old Dutch *jachtin* and Danish *jugt*, to speed, and a chase.

Yale Lock. Is named after its inventor, a Mr. Yale, an American, during the nineteenth century.

Yama. Is said in Hindu mythology to have been the first man, and his sister, Yami, the first woman. Yama, too, was the first human to die. "He explored the hidden regions and discovered the road which became known as the Path of the Fathers." Because of this, he is regarded in Hindu mythology as King of the Dead. In Sir Monier Williams's translation of "Indian Wisdom" are the lines:

"To Yama, mighty king, be
gifts and homage paid.
He was the first of men that
died, the first to brave
Death's rapid rushing stream,
the first to point the road
To Heaven, and welcome
others to that bright abode."

Yama is described in his godhead as four-armed, sitting on a buffalo, and green in colour.

Yankee. Of all the "origins" of this term for Americans, the most probable is that of J. F. Cooper, in "Oak Opening," page 28: "For ourselves we do not entertain a doubt that the subsequent of *Yankees*, which is in every man's mouth, and of which the derivation appears to puzzle all our philologists, is nothing but a slight corruption of the word *Yengeeze*, the term applied to the English by the tribes to whom they first became known."

The theory is that Yengeeze was the nearest the Indians' tongue could get to English.

Yankee Doodle. There are several accounts of the origin of this National Air of the U.S.A. Groves, in his "Dictionary of Music," states that "the air, as a melody, has little beyond simplicity in its favour, but there is a quaint, direct and incisive character about which redeems it from vulgarity."

The tune is said to have been composed in 1755 by Dr. Schuckburgh, a surgeon in Lord Amhurst's arm in the French and Indian War, in derision of the provincial troops. The original name of the song (not the air) was "The Yankee's Return from Camp."

Yankee Jonathan. This was the nickname given to Jonathan Hastings, a farmer of Massachusetts, because of his patriotic addiction to using the word "Yankee" of everything which he thought good—a "Yankee good horse," or a "Yankee fine crop."

Yarborough is taken now as interpreting a hand at cards without a trump. The original Yarborough, however, had to contain no card over the value of nine. The second Lord Yarborough gave such a hand the name by his practice of laying 1,000 to 1 against such a hand in any game in which he took part, or at which he was present. "*Mathematician*" tells the author that the actual odds are 1,827 to 1—against.

Ye. The interest in this word is not that it is the archaic method of writing "the," but that it is universally pronounced by presumably educated people in the form of the second person plural, in other words, as *yee.* This is quite incorrect. It should be pronounced "*the.*" In Anglo-Saxon, or Middle English, there was a symbol, the letter thom, which is now written "th," but which used to be represented by "y." Consequently, "y" represents our present "the," which is the ancient, as well as the present, correct pronunciation of "ye."

Year. The period of the earth's revolution round the sun, or, more accurately, the interval between one vernal equinox and the next. The word comes from the Greek *horos,* a season, and the Latin *hora,* or hirer. The solar year contains three hundred and sixty-five days, five hours, forty-eight minutes and forty-six seconds, which, once in four years, produces an extra day. This, given to February, adds a twenty-ninth day to that month every Leap Year. The year 1752 in Britain contained only three hundred and fifty-four days, following our adoption of the Gregorian Calendar, which had been introduced by Pope Gregory XIII in 1582, to correct the old Julian Calendar, which by miscalculation had got eleven days too long.

See "Calendar."

Year and a Day. This is a legal space of time after which certain claims or accusations cannot be made. For instance, an appeal in law cannot be prosecuted at the expiry of a year and a day. If a person wounded does not die within a year and a day, no charge of murder can subsequently lie.

Yellow. Is the colour of jealousy, treason and betrayal. Thus, in some countries the law ordained that Jews should wear yellow robes because they betrayed Christ. In France, the doors of traitors were at one time daubed with yellow. In Spain the executioner wore red robes for the execution of a man who had shed blood, but yellow robes for carrying out the sentence on a person convicted of treason.

Yellow Jack. Is the flag flown by ships is quarantine, or which have yellow fever on board.

Yellow Press. The name given to papers which pander to sensationalism. It was first used to describe those papers, particularly in America, which in 1898 printed scare articles of the "Yellow Peril"—that is, the growing populations of China and Japan which, it was urged, meant that in order to contain their people, those nations would be compelled to make incursions into the land of white men by force of arms.

Yellow Sea. From the colour imparted to its waters by the huge quantities of alluvial soil carried into it by the Yang-tse-Kiang River.

Yeoman. There is a literary hull-a-balloo over the origin of this term of the land. Skeat believes it to have come from the Anglo-Saxon *ga,* a district, or village, with the suffix, *man.* Johnson avers the origin to be the German *gemein,* meaning common. Dr. Brewer says: "Anciently a forty-shilling free-holder qualified to serve and vote on juries, but not qualified to rank as gentry." The word is, however, much older than juries!

Others attach it to (1) the Anglo-Saxon *iu* (of yore) *man*; and (2) the Anglo-Saxon *iung* (young) man! In point of fact, the *eo* has no place in the word by any etymological research. The word should be *yo-man,* Mediæval English for a retainer, or guard. William of Palerne, of whom the above etymologists seem not to have heard, wrote:

"Yoman then dede the gates shette,
And Wizttili than went the walles for to fende."

It is possible, however, that the yeoman retainer was of a higher standing than the ordinary retainer. There are some grounds for supposing that there was little difference in rank between the Norman *escuier* (esquire) and the British yeoman, except that the former may have belonged to the ruling caste.

Yiddish. Dr. Brewer describes it as a Middle German dialect developed under Hebrew and Slavic influence, written in Hebrew characters, and used as a language by German and other Jews. The German word for Jewish is judisch.

Yogi. The explanation of this much publicized Indian devotee is that he is one who, by meditation and concentration. tries to attain to *Yoga,* meaning union—with the Supreme Being. *Yoga* is allied in formation with our yoke.

Yoke. *To bear the Yoke.* The yoke in this sense was an appliance similar to the yoke with which two animals are coupled together. This appliance was placed on the neck of a captured or conquered enemy.

The Romans carried out the same practice by symbol; they stuck two spears upright in the ground and placed a third across the top. Under this "yoke" all vanquished enemies, or captured prisoners, had to march, in sign that they accepted the Yoke of Rome.

Yokel. The origin is obscure and uncertain. Skeat suggests that it represents an unrecorded Anglo-Saxon word, *geacol,* meaning foolish, cuckoo-like, from *geac,* a cuckoo.

Yorker. Most cricketers know that a yorker is a ball which pitches almost directly underneath the bat. It is called a yorker because it was a Yorkshireman who first made a practice of putting such a ball, now and then, in his "over."

Yorkshire Stingo. A type of old ale, peculiar to the county of York, in allusion to its "stinging" qualities.

Yorkshire Toast. "Here's tiv us, all on us. May we never want nowt, noan on us."

And the Yorkshire motto is, of course: "Hear all, see all, say nowt. And if tha does owt for nowt, do it for thy'sen."

A gross libel on the people of Yorkshire; but they invented it themselves.

Young Cub, The. A nickname given to Charles James Fox, the English statesman and orator (1749-1806). He was also called Carlo Khan from the supposition that from the Bill which he introduced into Parliament, in 1783, respecting the East Indies, he intended to establish a dictatorship in his own person.

Ypres League, The. Founded in 1920 by Field-Marshal the Earl of Ypres (Lord French), and open to all relatives of men who fought or died in the Salient, "In order that they may have a record of that service for themselves and their descendants, and belong to the comradeship of those who understand and remember all that Ypres means in suffering and endurance."

Yule, Yuletide. There is some uncertainty among etymologists as to the derivation of this word for Christmas. Skeats harnesses it to noise or outcry. Dr. Brewer thinks it came from the Anglo-Saxon *geola,* from the Icelandic *jol,* with which possibly our "jolly" is connected. Johnson says it comes from the Norse *juul,* Christmas. And the latter is the present author's opinion.

Z

Zantippe. A variation of Xantippe (q.v.).

Zenana. The Persian *zan* means woman; and the zenana is that part of an Indian or Persian dwelling-house in which the women are secluded. In other words the Persian equivalent of the harem.

Zenith. "*From the zenith of prosperity to the Nadir.*" The zenith is the point of the sky directly over the head of the observer. The Nadir is the point immediately beneath the feet of the same observer. Thus the phrase means from the heights of fortune to the depths of misfortune.

Zephyr Breezes. We call any soft and warm breeze a zephyr breeze, but, properly, the name should belong only to a wind from the west. Zephyr is derived from the Greek *zophos*, which means the west. The explanation of the calling of any light breeze a zephyr breeze lies in the gentleness of the Deity Zephyrus, who was said to produce flowers and fruits by the sweetness of his breath. He had a temple at Athens, where he was represented as a young man of delicate form with two wings on his shoulders, and with his head covered with all kinds of flowers.

Zero. The word is Arabic for nothing; it is a cipher. Zero point in time is twelve o'clock midday, the time at which the twenty-four hour clock begins the day.

Zero Hour in War. Is the term for the time officially appointed for the opening of an attack. It can be any time previously agreed upon, the actual time being made known to the troops to be engaged only at the latest possible moment before the attack.

Zest. Of a person who plays or works with keen enjoyment, we say that he has a zest for the game, or for his work. It is a curious word to use, because the literal meaning of zest, from the Greek, is a cut piece of orange or lemon peel! Another meaning (through the Latin) is "divided," and Cotgrave describes it as explaining "the thicke skin or filme whereby the kernelle of a wall-nut is diuided."

Our zest would seem to have been derived from the flavour which a cut piece of lemon peel would give to any commodity with which it was mixed.

Zeus. In Greek "the Living One." Zeus is the Grecian Jupiter.

Zingari. The Italian name for a gipsy. Of I. Zingari, probably the most famous of England's cricket elevens, the name apparently refers to their practice (like the gipsies) of roaming anywhere to play their cricket.

Zodiac. From the Greek *Zodiakos*, "of animals." It is applied to that zone in the heavens through which the sun passes in the course of a year, because this zone contains the twelve constellations, which from the Ancient times have borne the names of the Ram, the Bull, the Twins, the Crab, the Lion, the Virgin, the Balance, the Scorpion, the Archer, the Goat, the Waterbearer, and the Fishes.

Zoo. From the Greek *zoon*, a living creature. The London Zoological Gardens were opened in 1828, but the Zoological Society had been founded two years previously.

Zoom. Before this word became airman's slang for the movement of his aeroplane in a certain exercise, zoom meant a continuous low-pitched humming or buzzing sound.

Zounds. An oath, or exclamation of Elizabethan days, much used by the Virgin Queen. It is a corruption of "God's wounds."